# LIFE AFTER ROE

David Closson

# LIFE AFTER ROE

## EQUIPPING CHRISTIANS IN THE FIGHT FOR LIFE TODAY

B&H ACADEMIC®
BRENTWOOD, TENNESSEE

*Life after Roe: Equipping Christians in the Fight for Life Today*


Published by B&H Academic®
Brentwood, Tennessee



ISBN: 978-1-4300-8800-4

Dewey Decimal Classification: 363.4
Subject Heading: PRO-LIFE MOVEMENT \
ABORTION--ETHICAL ASPECTS \ LIFE



Cover design by Gearbox. Cover images by Shutterstock.

Printed in the United States of America

30 29 28 27 26 25 VP 1 2 3 4 5 6 7 8 9 10

"David Closson brilliantly tackles the topic of abortion and shows how the overturning of *Roe v. Wade* has ushered in the next chapter in the ongoing fight for life. In addition to applying scriptural truth to the painful subject of abortion, the book explains the long-standing pro-life ethic of the Christian church and helpfully sets the historical context for the current debate about abortion. This book will equip readers to take an informed and convictional stand for the unborn in their churches, communities, and state capitals. I highly recommend it!"

—**Becky Currie**, state representative of Mississippi and author of pro-life law that led to the overturning of *Roe v. Wade*

"The end of *Roe v. Wade* and the ushering in of the *Dobbs* era was a landmark victory, one in which countless Christian believers played a role over more than five decades. Yet it's clear that the work of the pro-life movement is not over but has only received a new beginning. There remain hundreds of thousands of children to be saved and mothers served, and that beautiful project requires a fuller engagement by the church than ever before, all while combating a powerfully entrenched lobby dedicated to abortion on demand without any limits. David Closson's *Life after Roe* is thoroughly researched, articulates a comprehensive pro-life ethic, and speaks to a long history by which we should rightly be inspired and emboldened. I anticipate that it will become an indispensable tool in the library of every pro-life advocate concerned about the challenges we face, and who wants to be properly armed for the greatest human rights battle of our time."

—**Marjorie Dannenfelser**, president, Susan B. Anthony Pro-Life America

"Thankfully, *Roe v. Wade* is on the ash heap of history. But the fight for the sanctity of life is just beginning. David Closson has written an indispensable guide for Christians that not only articulates the moral imperative of opposing abortion but offers a road map for creating a culture of life in America after *Dobbs*. Every serious Christian should have this book in their library."

—**Daniel Darling**, director, The Land Center for Cultural Engagement, Southwestern Baptist Theological Seminary

"David Closson has researched and written a timely and compelling account of the abortion issue in America after the landmark *Dobbs* decision. He documents the urgency of thoughtful Christian engagement in the cultural and legislative debates over the sanctity of human life and the needs of women and families. *Life after Roe* makes the short list of must-reads as our nation grapples with issues that will steer its fate for centuries to come."

—**Chuck Donovan**, founder, Charlotte Lozier Institute

"David is a rising voice applying a biblical worldview for today's most pressing cultural issues. In his work, *Life after Roe*, David provides a compelling and compassionate defense for the pro-life issue with biblical, historical, and practical perspectives. In a post-Roe environment, Christians must be equipped to be a testament to the beauty of our biblical convictions applied to the care and defense of every human life. David provides the road map for believers to be theologically rooted and lovingly engaged in this calling to stand for life."

—**Lauren Green McAfee**, founder and visionary, Stand for Life and ministry director, Hobby Lobby Corporate

"Defending the dignity of every preborn person is in the DNA of our faith. In this comprehensive work, Closson proves that the pro-life posture is a consistent Christian conviction from the earliest days of the church. Combining extensive biblical support with concise philosophical reasoning, he arms believers with legislative knowledge and cultural discernment as we navigate a pro-life witness in a post-*Roe* world."

—**Katie McCoy**, author, *To Be a Woman: The Confusion over Female Identity and How Christians Can Respond*

"*Life after Roe* is a timely and important book. David Closson presents sound biblical, theological, historical, and legal arguments that make a compelling case for the protection of the life of unborn children. He highlights the poorly reasoned cases of *Roe* and *Casey*, as well as the long-awaited correction to those rulings in the *Dobbs* case, and he addresses the critical question at the heart of the book: What now? The victory for life in the *Dobbs* decision was only the beginning, as demonstrated by a number of political and legal defeats following that victory. In *Life after Roe*, Closson examines significant victories and defeats for the pro-life movement and surveys the challenges and opportunities that lie ahead."

—**Ken Magnuson**, executive director, Evangelical Theological Society and professor, Southwestern Baptist Theological Seminary

"David Closson is one of the bright young thinkers in the Christian world today, and *Life after Roe* is a very important argument for Christian involvement in the defense of unborn life. Clearly, what is needed at this hour is a reinvigorated, pro-life argument that is undergirded by Christian commitment and the quality of argument readers will find in this book."

—**R. Albert Mohler**, Jr., president and centennial professor of Christian theology, The Southern Baptist Theological Seminary

"Shakespeare said, 'What's past is prologue.' We need to understand where we've been to know where we need to go. With extraordinary documentation, David Closson reveals the biblical and historical church teachings about abortion, details the history of abortion in America, sifts fact from fiction about the political aspects of abortion policy, and shows how to boldly stand for life in a post-Roe America. This book has been needed for a long time. It will be a treasure to those who long for America to live up to its founding principles and protect every life."

—**Jeff Myers**, PhD, president, Summit Ministries

"Despite the overturning of *Roe v. Wade*, abortion remains a divisive political and cultural issue. The reason? Because abortion is a spiritual and moral issue first and foremost, it cannot be resolved by politics or policies alone. In *Life after Roe*, David Closson demonstrates that God's Word is profoundly pro-life and that Christians have affirmed this truth for millennia. Additionally, David's book provides a succinct yet engaging history of abortion in America, helpfully recounts how states responded to the overturning of *Roe*, and astutely examines the pressing issues still facing those of us engaged in the fight for life. I recommend this book to anyone with pro-life convictions and especially those with teaching and discipleship responsibilities."

—**Tony Perkins**, president, Family Research Council

"Since the overturning of *Roe v. Wade*, pro-abortion forces have tragically, yet effectively, weaponized abortion for their political benefit. *Life after Roe* makes a compelling biblical case for why Christians must continue standing for life. David Closson's book is exactly what the pro-life movement needs today: a theologically grounded, historically informed, and politically astute analysis of where the fight for life stands today. I highly recommend this book for Christian laypeople and pastors, as well as Christian legislators like me who want to make a difference in our state."

—**Jena Powell**, state representative of Ohio and
co-sponsor of Ohio's heartbeat law

"The fundamental right articulated in America's founding documents is the right to life, an unalienable right endowed by our Creator, who made us in his image, which imbues each of us with immeasurable worth—the born and unborn. Without the right to life secured, other fights for liberty necessarily pale in comparison. Life is not only the fundamental right but a fundamental fight of our time. David Closson gives Christians a road map forward in the fight of our lives, literally."

—**Colin Smothers,** executive director,
Council on Biblical Manhood and Womanhood

"Alliance Defending Freedom was privileged to serve on Mississippi's legal team in the case that overturned *Roe v. Wade*. For fifty years, *Roe* formed and discipled Americans to accept abortion as necessary for women to live full lives. The fall of *Roe* opened the possibility of changing that narrative and enacting public policy that makes abortion a thing of the past. But the fall of *Roe* also revealed the reality that any narrative and policy change will require deep work at the legal and cultural levels. Closson highlights the importance of that work and underscores the biblical underpinnings of the pro-life position. He encourages readers to build a consistent pro-life ethic in our homes, churches, and communities. While staking out challenges the pro-life movement faces, he also provides hope as we move forward together."

—**Kristen K. Waggoner**, CEO, president, and general counsel, Alliance Defending Freedom

"David Closson's *Life after Roe* is a vital book for understanding where the pro-life movement is and where it needs to be. Grounded in biblical truth, witnessing to church history, and conversant with philosophy, this volume is a wonderful one-stop volume for grappling with the sanctity of life in both Christian and civic domains. David is one of the most articulate and thoughtful evangelicals on the scene right now, and his faithful insight is coupled with key instincts that can help reliably guide the pro-life movement in a very difficult moment."

— **Andrew T. Walker**, associate professor of Christian ethics and public theology, The Southern Baptist Theological Seminary

"Many social commentators of our day are guilty of dealing with abortion in one of two ways: trivializing the significance of the intentional taking of human life in the womb or demonizing all who differ with one's own position through misrepresentation and false accusation. Where does one go to find levelheaded, fair, honest, and careful discussion on this issue? David Closson has done all interested parties an enormous service by writing one of the most thorough, carefully crafted, fair, informative, and inspiring treatments one could hope to read. Closson is pro-life, of course. But he does not allow his own position to lead to cheap shots and misrepresentations of his opponents' views. Instead, he writes with a clear objective to be fair toward others while impassioned with his own position, given the weight he understands to be carried by this issue. I highly recommend this masterly work, knowing many will benefit much from its capable discussion and insight."

—**Bruce A. Ware,** professor of Christian theology, The Southern Seminary Baptist Theological Seminary

To my wife, Abby: Thank you for your unwavering love and support.

And

to the justices of the U.S. Supreme Court who overturned *Roe v. Wade*:

Samuel A. Alito Jr., Amy Coney Barrett,

Neil M. Gorsuch, Brett M. Kavanaugh, and Clarence Thomas:

Your courage has made our nation more humane and just.

# CONTENTS

# PREFACE

The sights and sounds of the evening of May 2, 2022, are seared in my memory forever. At 8:55 p.m., I received a text message with a link to a *Politico* article. "What do you think about this?" my friend asked.

The headline of the article required a double take: "Supreme Court has voted to overturn abortion rights, draft opinion shows." Incredulously, I opened the article published just twenty-three minutes earlier. The first line read: "The Supreme Court has voted to strike down the landmark *Roe v. Wade* decision, according to an initial draft majority opinion written by Justice Samuel Alito circulated inside the court and obtained by POLITICO."[1]

My heart pounding, I skimmed the piece. Before I could finish the article, messages from friends across the country began flashing on my phone screen. "Is it true?" a friend from Arizona asked. "Pray pray pray!!!" a colleague in Washington, DC, texted me.

With social media abuzz, and unsure of how to respond, I drove to the Supreme Court, which was only a few miles away. Arriving around 9:40 p.m., I walked to the front of the building. Barricades were already in place to keep people off the west façade plaza and away from the front stairs. Approximately 100 people had gathered, a few holding lit candles though most were sitting quietly on the ground.

---

[1] Josh Gerstein and Alexander Ward, Politico, updated May 3, 2022, https://www.politico.com/news/2022/05/02/supreme-court-abortion-draft-opinion-00029473.

The uneasy silence was periodically broken by the soft sobbing of a few college-aged women who appeared to be consoling one another. Few people were talking, and there was no discernible media presence. But as word spread throughout the city and others began to arrive, the mood shifted.

Initially, a lone woman began yelling. Gesturing toward the Court, the woman launched into a tirade, hurling invectives at Justice Alito about the draft opinion. Soon, she was joined by others. By 10:30 p.m., the crowd had grown exponentially as thousands of people gathered outside the Supreme Court.

Since arriving at the Court an hour earlier, I had been praying. Walking amongst the protestors, I silently asked the Lord to protect the justices, their families, and their clerks. Anticipating the public campaign against the justices would be fierce, I prayed for courage for those who had signed Alito's opinion. As I prayed, I unexpectedly found friends from church who also worked in the pro-life movement. Amid the shouting and screaming, we huddled in a circle and prayed together.

At some point, two reporters asked if they could interview me. Recognizing that I was one of the few pro-life supporters among those gathered at the Court, I agreed to both interviews and sought to explain how, although not presently represented outside the Court, tens of millions of Americans were receiving the night's news with cautious optimism. I noted that if the leaked opinion proved to be legitimate, unborn children in many states would receive long-overdue protection from the abortion industry.

As the initial shock began to subside, I considered the implications of the leak. If the leaked opinion was legitimate, the Supreme Court was poised to overturn the infamous *Roe v. Wade* decision. After forty-nine years of abortion on demand, the power to protect unborn children would be returned to the American people, and previously unenforceable pro-life laws could go into effect across the states.

A myriad of questions went through my mind, including how the Court would respond to the unprecedented breach in protocol, the political ramifications of overturning *Roe*, and the best way to explain the leak to pastors and churchgoers. As I left the Court shortly before midnight, I couldn't help but feel a rising sense of hope.

Just a few months earlier, I had helped coordinate a prayer event hosted by Alliance Defending Freedom, Family Research Council, and the United States Council of Catholic Bishops. The virtual prayer meeting focused primarily on the *Dobbs* case and featured leaders from ministries around the country. Thousands of people united in prayer, pleading with God to intervene and for the Court to overturn *Roe*.

Was God really answering our prayers? Proverbs 21:1 teaches that "A king's heart is like channeled water in the Lord's hand: He directs it wherever he chooses." From an intellectual perspective, I understood and believed the truth of these words. But having lived under *Roe* my entire lifetime, it was hard to comprehend that the days of America's most notorious abortion case might be numbered.

Seven weeks later, the Supreme Court issued its opinion in *Dobbs v. Jackson Women's Health Organization* and officially overturned *Roe v. Wade*. The decision, released on June 24, 2022, comprehensively repudiated *Roe* and returned the question of abortion to the American people and their elected representatives. A high-water mark of the social conservative movement, *Dobbs*, in a single opinion, represented the culmination of decades of pro-life lobbying, campaigning, and political activity, not to mention the answer to countless prayers.

In the years since the historic *Dobbs* decision, abortion has remained a mainstay in American political and cultural discourse. The debate over abortion is raging in state legislatures and courtrooms across the country with no sign of abating. National surveys conducted before and after *Dobbs* show that a surprising number of professing Christians are unsure about the morality of abortion, and many are divided over whether the Bible offers any guidance on the topic. Evidently, after nearly fifty years of abortion on demand, the pedagogical effect of permissive abortion laws has been the searing of the nation's conscience to the point where even many Christians are confused about the topic.

Because the conversation about abortion continues in legislatures, courts, churches, classrooms, and homes around America, this book exists to help Christians engage thoughtfully in these discussions. By looking at the biblical, theological, historical, legal, and political dimensions of the debate, I hope that readers will be equipped to fight for life in post-*Roe* America.

Chapter 1 will consider American public opinion on abortion by reviewing several recent studies. In 2023, I commissioned and oversaw a research project for the Center for Biblical Worldview at Family Research Council that included several questions designed to assess what churchgoers believed about abortion. Many of the findings were startling and revealed the long road ahead for the pro-life movement after fifty years of Court-imposed abortion on demand. Additionally, the chapter will examine recent arguments put forward by pro-abortion pastors and politicians.

Chapter 2 summarizes the principles and passages that compose the Bible's pro-life ethic. I will argue that key themes and texts in the Bible make a compelling case that unborn children are persons who should be protected from the moment of conception. Well-known passages such as Psalm 139:13–16 and Luke 1:39–45 will be placed in their context and explained, in addition to lesser-known passages that also contribute to the Bible's pro-life message. The chapter will also address pro-abortion counter-arguments raised by progressive theologians.

It is not uncommon for abortion activists to claim that Christian commitment to the pro-life cause is secondary to political ends. However, a brief survey of history reveals that the church has been clear on abortion since the first century. Chapter 3 will provide evidence showing that for 2,000 years Christians have interpreted the Bible consistently when it comes to the value of unborn human life. Further study reveals that the most prominent leaders and authorities in the history of Christianity have publicly opposed abortion.

Chapter 4 will shift focus to the United States and explain the history of abortion in this country. The chapter will examine the Supreme Court's ruling in *Roe v. Wade* as well as the decision to uphold *Roe* in *Planned*

*Parenthood v. Casey* (1992). In addition, we will review subsequent decisions that chipped away at *Roe* and *Casey* and conclude with an overview of the *Dobbs* case and the historic leak on May 2, 2022.

In chapter 5, we will consider the effects of the *Dobbs* decision on abortion policy by briefly analyzing the decision itself and then reviewing how states reacted to their newfound ability to legislate abortion. Awareness of the political, legislative, and judicial responses within the first year of *Dobbs* provides insight into what is likely ahead for the pro-life movement. Through conversations with state legislators, lobbyists, and policymakers, this chapter will acquaint readers with the most relevant abortion history following the overturning of *Roe*.

The closing chapter will look at the road ahead for the pro-life movement in the United States. With abortion policy in the hands of the American people and their elected representatives, there is now a realistic opportunity to protect life in many states. However, there are still significant cultural, legal, and political challenges facing the pro-life movement, including chemical abortion, lack of consensus among pro-lifers on legislative strategy, messaging concerns, low thresholds for amending state constitutions, complacency and confusion within the church, and a secularizing culture. This final chapter will offer a realistic assessment of the pro-life movement following *Dobbs*, consider obstacles to establishing a culture of life, and present insights gleaned from interviews with national pro-life leaders.

The overturning of *Roe v. Wade* was something that many pro-life Americans never thought they would see in their lifetimes. Pro-life leaders, including Jerry Falwell, Nellie Gray, Henry Hyde, D. James Kennedy, Phyllis Schlafly, and an untold army of prayer warriors, sidewalk counselors, and pregnancy resource center workers, did not live to see the Court's reversal of *Roe*. However, for those of us who did, our obligation is to continue the work.

Until abortion—the intentional taking of an unborn child's life in the termination of a pregnancy—is both illegal and unthinkable, there is much work left to do.[2] May this book equip you to be part of the God-glorifying task of rescuing "those who are being taken off to death" (Prov. 24:11) and changing the hearts and minds of our friends and neighbors.

[2] In this book, the term "abortion" refers to what is medically known as an "induced abortion" or the intentional taking of an unborn child's life in the termination of a pregnancy. I am not referring to miscarriage. Although the medical term for miscarriage is "spontaneous abortion," a miscarriage is not the intentional taking of an unborn child's life. Additionally, in this book "abortion" does not refer to ectopic pregnancy treatment; even though an unborn child's chances of surviving an ectopic pregnancy are considered nonexistent under current medical technology, the treatment is not intended to end the unborn child's life. For a glossary of terms, see appendix 1.

# 1

# After *Roe*: The State of the Church and the Culture

Following the national election in November 2020, the balance of power in the United States Senate remained undecided. Because Georgia law requires candidates to win a majority of the vote in the general election, both U.S. Senate races went to an automatic runoff scheduled for January 2021.[1] In the contests, Republican incumbents David Perdue and Kelly Loeffler faced off against Democrat challengers Jon Ossoff and Raphael Warnock, respectively.

Although both races dealt with many of the same issues, abortion was especially prominent in the Loeffler-Warnock race because of the latter's

[1] In 2020, only Georgia's Class 2 Senate seat was scheduled to be on the ballot (held in 2020 by incumbent David Perdue). However, the state's other Senate seat was on the ballot as well because of the retirement of Sen. Johnny Isakson in 2019. Gov. Brian Kemp appointed Kelly Loeffler to continue Isakson's term, but Georgia law required a special election to finish Isakson's term. Thus, Loeffler faced off against Rev. Raphael Warnock in a special election.

role as pastor of the historic Ebenezer Baptist Church (previously pastored by Martin Luther King Jr.). A graduate of Union Theological Seminary, Warnock's positions on social issues were decidedly progressive.[2] With the balance of power in the United States Senate dependent on this race, the pastor's views on abortion were heavily scrutinized and a frequent topic of discussion on the campaign trail.

At the time of the election, Georgia had a pro-life governor and two pro-life senators. Thus, Warnock's decision to openly discuss his pro-abortion views was considered politically risky. But Warnock campaigned aggressively in support of abortion. In one interview in August 2020, the candidate stated, "I believe unequivocally in a woman's right to choose . . . [and] I will fight for that in the United States Senate." When pressed on whether his pro-abortion views were "consistent with God's view," Warnock responded, "I think that human agency and freedom is consistent with my view as a minister."[3]

Following his victory in the runoff election, Senator Warnock kept his word and vigorously advocated for abortion in the Senate. In 2022, Warnock co-sponsored the Women's Health Protection Act, legislation that would eliminate hundreds of state-level pro-life laws and even go beyond *Roe* in legalizing abortion in all fifty states until the moment of birth.[4] When the

---

[2] For those familiar with the landscape of Christian higher education, Warnock's theologically liberal views were predictable. Union Seminary's liberal theology is well-known. In recent years, student groups on campus have included "Seminarians for Reproductive Justice" and a caucus for "queer people of color."

[3] Ryan Foley, "Pastor Running for Senate: Abortion Rights Are 'Consistent' with My Beliefs as a Minister," *Christian Post*, August 26, 2020, https://www.christianpost.com/news/pastor-running-for-senate-abortion-rights-are-consistent-with-my-beliefs-as-a-minister.html. Throughout the campaign, Warnock referred to himself as a "pro-choice pastor." For example, see Raphael Warnock (@ReverendWarnock), December 8, 2020, 8:00 p.m., https://twitter.com/ReverendWarnock/status/1336490801413632002.

[4] See David Closson, "Unconscionable: New Bill Proves Democrats Are Okay with Abortion up until Birth," Family Research Council, September 28, 2021, https://www.frc.org/blog/2021/09/unconscionable-democrats-are-okay-killing

Senate voted on the bill, Warnock tweeted, "I've always been a pro-choice pastor, and I believe a doctor's office is too small for a patient, their doctors, and the U.S. government."[5]

When Raphael Warnock ran for a full term in 2022, he again campaigned on his support for abortion. Once again, Warnock eked out a victory in a closely contested runoff election.

Although a confluence of events (including unpopular Republican opponents in both elections) helped push Warnock over the top, his electoral success in 2021 and 2022 still surprised many election observers in part because the Peach State has historically been culturally conservative. Moreover, Georgia has consistently ranked in the top ten of the nation's most religious states. Using the metrics of church attendance, frequency of prayer, belief in God, and self-assessment of the importance of religion, Georgia was the eighth most religious state in the nation in 2024, with 66% of the adult population considered "religious."[6] Georgia's ranking among the states has not changed much over the last decade. It was also the eighth most religious state ten years ago, according to Pew Research Center, with

-babies-day-birth. As I've explained elsewhere, the Women's Health Protection Act would "eliminate almost every state-level restriction on abortion and codify *Roe v. Wade* into law. Additionally, the bill would weaken conscience protections for medical professionals, jeopardize prohibitions on taxpayer funding for abortion, enshrine late-term abortion into law, strike down commonsense pro-life laws, and equate the death of unborn children with routine medical procedures."

[5] Raphael Warnock (@ReverendWarnock), Twitter, February 28, 2022, 1:02 p.m., https://twitter.com/SenatorWarnock/status/1498373142829576196. Following the overturning of *Roe v. Wade*, Warnock stated, "This misguided decision is devastating for women and families in Georgia and nationwide. . . . I'll never back down from this fight because women should be able to make their own health care decisions." See Raphael Warnock, "Senator Reverend Warnock Statement on the Supreme Court's Decision to Overturn Roe v. Wade," Reverend Raphael Warnock U.S. Senator for Georgia, June 24, 2022, https://www.warnock.senate.gov/newsroom/press-releases/senator-reverend-warnock-statement-on-the-supreme-courts-decision-to-overturn-roe-v-wade/.

[6] World Population Review, "Most Religious States 2024," accessed May 20, 2024, https://worldpopulationreview.com/state-rankings/most-religious-states.

64% of residents at the time saying religion was "very important" in their lives. Of those who claimed a religious identity in that study, 79% identified as Christian, of which 38% self-described as evangelical.[7]

Given the religious composition of the state and Christianity's historic teaching on the sanctity of the unborn, it seemed doubtful at the onset of the 2020 election that a self-proclaimed "pro-choice pastor" could win a statewide race in Georgia. But Warnock prevailed and even earned the support of 11% of those identified as evangelical Christians in his 2022 election.[8]

Although Senator Warnock's success in a religious and culturally conservative state may initially seem counterintuitive, new research into what professing churchgoers actually believe on an array of cultural, political, and theological matters reveals that Christians are far from monolithic in how they view a variety of topics, including abortion.

This research provides, among other insights, a partial explanation for how a pro-abortion candidate like Senator Warnock could wage a successful campaign in a state with higher-than-average church attendance. In short, the research shows that Christians are not as pro-life as many pundits believe and that even those who claim a pro-life identity do not always vote for pro-life candidates. Furthermore, many Christians are unsure of whether the Bible even offers guidance on abortion.

With the overturning of *Roe v. Wade*, what Christians believe about abortion has never been more consequential. Because of *Dobbs*, lobbying and voting can directly affect the passage of pro-life laws in all fifty states. Unfortunately, at a time when the church's historic teaching and convictions about abortion matter more than ever, many American Christians have found themselves ill-equipped to engage in the national conversation regarding abortion.

---

[7] See "Adults in Georgia," in Religious Landscape Study, Pew Research Center, May 30, 2014, https://www.pewresearch.org/religion/religious-landscape-study/state/georgia/.

[8] "2022 Exit Polls," CNN Politics, January 10, 2022, https://www.cnn.com/election/2022/exit-polls/georgia/senate/0.

In one sense, this development was to be expected. After fifty years of Court-imposed abortion on demand, many Americans, including Christians, are still reckoning with the post-*Roe* legal and political landscape. For pro-life Christians, overturning *Roe* was an improbable dream for almost fifty years. As a practical and political matter, when the Court's abortion precedents were in effect, passing meaningful pro-life protections was virtually impossible, and for that reason, many Christians were resigned to the status quo. But when the Court finally overturned *Roe* in 2022, many pro-life Christians were caught flat-footed, unsure about how to proceed with messaging and strategy.

Conversely, pro-abortion groups capitalized quickly on the initial outrage sparked by *Dobbs* and successfully parlayed anger and confusion into electoral success. Aided by a largely sympathetic media,[9] abortion advocates have controlled much of the post-*Roe* narrative, resulting in further confusion among Christians. Thus, before turning to the Bible to clarify historic Christian teaching on abortion, we will review the lay of the land concerning what American Christians believe about abortion in the years immediately following the overturning of *Roe v. Wade.*

The goal of this first chapter is to examine recent polling on American public opinion on abortion following the Supreme Court's *Dobbs* decision. In addition to reviewing mainstream polling, we will look at a groundbreaking study commissioned by the Center for Biblical Worldview at Family Research Council (FRC). Led by researcher George Barna and published in August 2023, this was the first study after *Dobbs* that looked exclusively at the theological beliefs and worldview of those who regularly attend

---

[9] For examples of pro-abortion sympathy in the mainstream media, see Caroline Kitchener, "This Texas Teen Wanted an Abortion. She Now Has Twins," *Washington Post*, June 20, 2022, https://www.washingtonpost.com/politics/2022/06/20/texas-abortion-law-teen-mom/; also see a follow-up piece by the same author a year later: Caroline Kitchener, "An Abortion Ban Made Them Teen Parents. This Is Life Two Years Later," *Washington Post*, August 1, 2023, https://www.washingtonpost.com/politics/interactive/2023/texas-abortion-law-teen-parents/?itid=hp-top-table-main_p002_f001.

church. The survey shows that American Christians, including evangelicals, Catholics, mainline Protestants, and Pentecostals, do not hold monolithic views on abortion. In fact, the study revealed that many committed believers are confused and unsure of what the Bible teaches on the topic.[10]

## Polling Immediately after *Dobbs*

A national survey conducted by Pew Research Center a week after the Supreme Court released its opinion in *Dobbs* revealed that 57% of Americans disapproved of the Court's decision, compared to 41% who approved.[11] Among religious groups, 71% of white evangelical Protestants approved of *Dobbs*. In terms of political affiliation, 82% of Democrats and 29% of Republicans disapproved of the decision.[12]

[10] See George Barna, "Survey on Adult Churchgoers on Social Issues and Worldview: A National Survey from the Center for Biblical Worldview," June 2023, https://downloads.frc.org/EF/EF23H29.pdf. The 2023 study followed groundbreaking research published by Family Research Council in May 2021. Conducted by George Barna, the nationwide survey provided research-based insights about how many people believe they possess a biblical worldview, if and to what extent they seek to integrate that worldview into every dimension of life, what influences have helped them to do so, and whether they believe that such integration matters to God. According to the research, although 51% of adults claim to have a biblical worldview, only 6% do. Additionally, 81% of those who regularly attend an evangelical church claim to have a biblical worldview compared to 21% who do. (The percentage of those who have a biblical worldview is based on the findings of the American Worldview Inventory, an annual survey conducted by George Barna and the Cultural Research Center at Arizona Christian University. The survey includes 54 worldview-related questions divided into eight categories concerning belief and behavior. Respondents must score 80% or higher on the survey to qualify as having a "biblical worldview.")

[11] "Majority of Public Disapproves of Supreme Court's Decision to Overturn Roe v. Wade," Pew Research Center, July 6, 2022, https://www.pewresearch.org/politics/2022/07/06/majority-of-public-disapproves-of-supreme-courts-decision-to-overturn-roe-v-wade/.

[12] "Majority of Public Disapproves of Supreme Court's Decision to Overturn Roe v. Wade."

Because *Dobbs* was decided in the summer preceding the 2022 midterm election, abortion became an important election issue. On August 23, 2022, Pew Research Center published a report showing that a majority of registered voters (56%) reported that abortion "will be very important" for their midterm vote, up from 43% in March.[13] The increase came almost exclusively from Democrats: 71% of Democratic voters rated abortion as very important; fewer than half (46%) had said this in March. For Republican voters, there was almost no change (41% in August, 40% in March).

In April 2023, Pew published another report about Americans' views on abortion.[14] The survey, which was conducted after many states had enacted pro-life laws in 2022, found that views on abortion had remained largely unchanged since the previous year.

According to Pew, around six in ten Americans said that abortion should be legal in all (27%) or most (35%) cases, while 36% said it should be illegal in all (9%) or most (27%) cases. Predictably, there were wide partisan and demographic differences. The report found that 72% of those who identified as politically conservative opposed abortion whereas 94% of those who identified as politically liberal supported abortion.

When it came to religion, important differences surfaced as well. Protestants, defined generally, were split on the legality of abortion with 53% saying abortion should be illegal in all (14%) or most (39%) cases and 45% saying abortion should be legal in all (16%) or most (29%) cases.

Across sex, race, age, education, political ideology, and religion, the group that most strongly believed abortion should be illegal was composed

[13] "Abortion Rises in Importance as a Voting Issue, Driven by Democrats," Pew Research Center, August 23, 2022, https://www.pewresearch.org/politics/2022/08/23/abortion-rises-in-importance-as-a-voting-issue-driven-by-democrats/.

[14] "Nearly a Year after Roe's Demise, Americans' Views of Abortion Access Increasingly Vary by Where They Live," Pew Research Center, April 26, 2023, https://www.pewresearch.org/politics/2023/04/26/nearly-a-year-after-roes-demise-americans-views-of-abortion-access-increasingly-vary-by-where-they-live/.

of those who identified as white evangelical Christians. According to the survey, 75% of white evangelicals believed abortion should be illegal in all (23%) or most (52%) cases whereas only 23% believed it should be legal in most (17%) or all (6%) situations. Black Protestants (69%) and Roman Catholics (61%) were much more likely to indicate that abortion should be legal. Only 28% of black Protestants and 38% of Catholics said abortion should be illegal.

## *Gallup Polling*

Since 1995, Gallup has tracked Americans' self-identification on abortion. On June 2, 2022, Gallup released their annual abortion report.[15] Although the report was published before the *Dobbs* decision, the survey was conducted in the aftermath of the *Dobbs* leak, which ensured that abortion was top-of-mind for most respondents.

According to Gallup, in 2022, 55% of Americans identified as "pro-choice" and 39% identified as "pro-life" (the lowest number since 1996). Furthermore, 52% of Americans indicated they believe abortion is morally acceptable compared to 38% who believe abortion is not morally acceptable. Additionally, 20% of Americans indicated that abortion should be generally legal in the final three months of pregnancy (the highest incidence since Gallup began asking the question in 1996).

In May 2023, Gallup released another report on what Americans believed about abortion.[16] According to the survey, attitudes remained relatively stable, with 52% of the public identifying as "pro-choice" and 44% as "pro-life." Although "pro-choice" dipped slightly from its all-time high

---

[15] Lydia Saad, "'Pro-Choice' Identification Rises to Near Record High in U.S.," Gallup, June 2, 2022, https://news.gallup.com/poll/393104/pro-choice-identification-rises-near-record-high.aspx.

[16] "Where Do Americans Stand on Abortion?," Gallup, July 7, 2023, https://news.gallup.com/poll/321143/americans-stand-abortion.aspx.

in 2022, it remained above 50%.[17] When asked if they agreed with the Supreme Court's decision to overturn *Roe*, 61% of Americans said overturning *Roe* was a "bad thing," while 38% called it a "good thing."

When it comes to religious identity, the Gallup poll provides a few interesting insights that corroborate the findings of a 2023 FRC survey (discussed in the next section). First, church attendance was one of the most important indicators on whether someone identified as "pro-choice" or "pro-life." Among weekly churchgoers, 66% identified as "pro-life" compared to 28% who said they were "pro-choice." Among "nearly weekly/monthly" churchgoers, 56% said they were "pro-life" while 41% said they were "pro-choice." Among those who said they seldom or never attended services, 31% identified as "pro-life" while 64% claimed to be "pro-choice."[18]

Second, on a related topic, Gallup asked people to consider the morality of abortion. Participants were asked to put aside their thoughts on the legality of abortion and indicate whether abortion was morally acceptable or morally wrong. Once again, a correlation emerged between church attendance and a person's view on the morality of abortion. Among weekly churchgoers, 30% indicated they believed abortion was morally acceptable; 65% said abortion was morally wrong. An additional 4% said it depended on the situation, and 1% said they had no opinion. Among those who attended church nearly weekly/monthly, 42% said abortion was morally acceptable while 54% said it was morally wrong. The percentage of those who believed abortion is morally acceptable rose remarkably among

---

[17] From 2007 to 2021, no more than 50% of Americans identified as "pro-choice." See https://news.gallup.com/poll/321143/americans-stand-abortion.aspx.

[18] "'Pro-Choice' or 'Pro-Life' Demographic Table," Gallup, May 1–24, 2023, https://news.gallup.com/poll/244709/pro-choice-pro-life-2018-demographic-tables.aspx. The sample size for Gallup's 2023 poll was 1,011 U.S. adults: 230 indicated they attended weekly religious services; 234 said they attended nearly weekly/monthly; 544 said they seldom or never attended. Although the sample size for weekly church attenders was not large, these findings reflect some of the same findings of the 2023 FRC poll that surveyed those who attended church weekly (72% of respondents) or at least monthly (28%).

respondents who said they seldom or never attend church: 64% said abortion was morally acceptable; 26% said it was morally wrong; and 8% said it depended on the situation.[19]

The results of the Gallup poll reveal an obvious connection between those who regularly attend worship services and those who believe abortion is morally wrong. These results confirm, in part, the more substantial FRC study published in August 2023.

### *Center for Biblical Worldview*

In June 2023, the Center for Biblical Worldview at Family Research Council commissioned a nationwide survey on the theological beliefs and worldviews of Americans who regularly attend church. The survey yielded insights into what churchgoers believe about fundamental tenets of the faith and issues of social concern. Conducted by George Barna and published in August 2023, the survey included several questions about abortion.[20]

What follows are ten of the most significant findings pertaining to what churchgoers believe about abortion. Conducted exactly one year after the Supreme Court overturned *Roe*, the study highlights the guiding theological convictions of America's most devout believers (as measured by regular church attendance). The results—a mixture of encouraging and disconcerting findings—underscore the ongoing need for discipleship and instruction.

---

[19] "Morality of Abortion Demographic Table," Gallup, May, 2023, https://news.gallup.com/poll/244625/morality-abortion-2018-demographic-tables.aspx.

[20] Barna, "Survey on Adult Churchgoers on Social Issues and Worldview." The survey incorporated responses from 1,009 adults, age 18 or older, who attend a worship service at a Christian church at least once a month, either in-person or online. That segment of the population constitutes 44% of all U.S. adults. Of the 1,009 survey participants, 72% reported weekly church attendance, while 28% said they go to church at least monthly. It is also worth noting that survey participants came from Catholic, evangelical, nondenominational, mainline Protestant, Pentecostal/charismatic, and traditionally black/African American churches.

- About one out of every six churched adults (16%) admitted they had paid for, encouraged, or chosen to have an abortion. Among these, 56% indicated they read the Bible weekly, and 62% attend church weekly. Additionally, 50% of those who have participated in an abortion said the Bible was "clear and decisive" on the topic of abortion (only 26% said the Bible was "unclear or ambiguous"). Intriguingly, of those who have actively participated in an abortion, 20% admitted the Bible teaches that abortion is "always wrong."[21]
- Most respondents (63%) identified as pro-life, 22% identified as pro-choice, 10% said they lean one way or the other, and 5% said they do not know where they stand. When churchgoers were asked to provide further specificity on their position, 36% claimed to be "pro-life, with some exceptions or limitations," 27% identified as "pro-life without exceptions or limitations," and 5% claimed they "lean pro-life but could be convinced otherwise." An additional 14% of churchgoers identified as "pro-choice, with some exceptions

[21] Many Christians are surprised to learn that approximately 17% of female churchgoers have had an abortion, and 15% of male churchgoers have paid for or actively encouraged someone to get an abortion. However, Family Research Council's findings track with similar studies, including one by Lifeway Research in 2015 that showed 16% of women who have had an abortion identified as evangelical Christian. See Aaron Earls, "7 in 10 Women Who Have Had an Abortion Identify as a Christian," Lifeway Research, December 3, 2021, https://research.lifeway.com/2021/12/03/7-in-10-women-who-have-had-an-abortion-identify-as-a-christian/. To put these percentages into perspective, consider the Southern Baptist Convention (SBC), the nation's largest Protestant denomination. In 2023, the total membership across 47,198 SBC churches was 13.2 million. If we were to apply the 16% figure from the FRC and Lifeway surveys, approximately 2.1 million Southern Baptists have, at some point, actively participated in an abortion. In other words, statistics show that millions of theologically conservative Christians have a personal history with abortion, even if they do not talk about it. For SBC membership numbers, see Aaron Earls, "Southern Baptists grow in attendance and baptisms, decline in membership," Baptist Press, May 9, 2023, https://www.baptistpress.com/resource-library/news/southern-baptists-grow-in-attendance-and-baptisms-decline-in-membership/.

or limitations," 8% claimed to be "pro-choice without exceptions or limitations," and 5% said they "lean pro-choice but could be convinced otherwise."

- Two-thirds of respondents (65%) claimed the Bible identifies when human life begins, one-fifth (21%) said it does not, and 13% admitted they did not know.
- Among the 65% who said the Bible indicates when human life begins, 52% said it teaches that life begins "upon fertilization of the female egg." Other responses included "once the child has been delivered and begins breathing" (8%), "once the embryo/fetus reaches viability" (7%), "six weeks after the fertilization of the female egg" (6%), "sometime during the first three months after fertilization" (3%), and "sometime after three months but before six months after fertilization" (3%). An additional 12% who had initially indicated that the Bible identifies when life begins backed off this view when pressed for a particular moment, saying instead that the Bible is not actually specific. The final 8% conceded they did not know the moment in development when Scripture teaches life begins.
- Little consensus exists among churchgoers concerning what the Bible teaches about abortion. Some 35 percent of respondents said that according to the Bible abortion is not acceptable under any circumstances, while 19% said abortion is acceptable only when the mother's life is endangered. Other views include "the decision belongs to the couple involved" (10%); "it is acceptable if the child will be born with significant physical or mental challenges" (7%); and "it is acceptable under any circumstance" (6%). Approximately one-quarter (24%) of respondents ducked the question, with 14% saying the Bible teaches none of those perspectives and 9% saying they do not know what the Bible teaches on abortion.
- When churchgoers were asked to indicate "whether you believe the Bible is clear and decisive; unclear or ambiguous; or does not address" the morality of killing an unborn child, 65% of respondents

said they believed the Bible was "clear and decisive," 15% said the Bible was "unclear or ambiguous," and 13% said the Bible did not address the question.

- Less than half of respondents (44%) indicated that their church had provided a sermon or teaching on abortion during a weekend service in the past twelve months. However, the type of church attended factored heavily into the responses. A majority of Catholics (54%) credited their church with teaching on abortion, but none of the Protestant churches (evangelical, mainline Protestant, independent/nondenominational, or Pentecostal) hit 50%. Among Protestants, 45% of Pentecostal churchgoers reported hearing a sermon on abortion, followed by evangelical (41%), mainline (36%), and independent churches (32%). Overall, only 38% of respondents attending a Protestant church said they had heard a sermon or teaching on abortion within the past year.
- About one-third of respondents (31%) said they would prefer that their church teach about abortion in the weekend worship service "more often," 13% said they would prefer such teaching "less often," and 40% said they were satisfied with how much their church addresses abortion. An additional 8% said they did not care, and another 8% did not know if they wanted a change in how frequently their church taught about abortion. Additionally, an overwhelming percentage of churchgoers (70%) indicated that they would like their church to provide additional biblical worldview education related to abortion and the value of human life (44% said it would be "very desirable"; 27% indicated it would be "somewhat desirable"). Only three out of ten said it would not be desirable (15% said additional biblical worldview education was "not too desirable"; another 15% said such training was "not desirable at all").
- Most respondents (71%) said their moral and religious beliefs had the greatest influence on their views about abortion and the value

of human life. Political and policy considerations (11%) and public preferences and opinions (11%) tied for second. Another 8% did not know what influenced their position on abortion.

- Most respondents (58%) said they want their church to do more to help or support women facing an unplanned pregnancy. Only 6% said they wanted their church to do less, while 29% said their church should continue its current level of outreach to pregnant women. Almost two out of three respondents (62%) said their church provides specific and meaningful assistance or support to women facing an unplanned pregnancy, 20% said their church does not provide specific or valuable help, and 18% did not know whether their church provides such help to pregnant women.

## Summary of Results

The 2023 FRC report is a helpful diagnostic concerning the beliefs of churchgoing Americans. The results dispel the commonly held notion that churchgoers are monolithic when it comes to their views on abortion. Although a majority of those who regularly attend church identify as "pro-life" (63%), 37% do not hold firm pro-life commitments. Furthermore, among the 63% of churchgoers who identify as pro-life, there are key differences.

For example, among churchgoers who identify as pro-life, 79% claim the Bible is "clear and decisive" regarding abortion while 9% maintain the Bible is unclear. An additional 8% do not believe the Bible addresses the topic.[22] Thus, even among churchgoers who identify as pro-life, there are different views about whether the Bible addresses abortion.

---

[22] Breaking down the numbers by denomination, a high percentage of adults who attend evangelical churches (77%), independent/nondenominational churches (73%), and Pentecostal churches (75%) indicated that the Bible is "clear and decisive" on the morality of killing an unborn child. However, the number dipped to 68% of those who identified as Protestant, 66% of Catholics, and 56% among

Additionally, some of the results are surprising, such as the revelation that 16% of churchgoers have actively participated in an abortion.[23] Although previous studies told a similar story, it can be shocking to consider how many church members have a personal history with abortion.

There were also insights from the study that provide varying degrees of encouragement. For example, the fact that 63% of churchgoers identify as "pro-life" while 22% identify as "pro-choice" reveals that most churchgoers embrace the Bible's pro-life ethic. This finding corroborates the 2023 Gallup study that shows a direct correlation between regular church attendance and higher incidences of pro-life identification.

From a pro-life perspective, it is encouraging that only a small minority of churchgoers (6%) believe abortion is acceptable under any circumstance. Nevertheless, the diversity of opinion regarding what the Bible teaches about abortion demonstrates confusion among the faithful. For example, despite no biblical support for the idea that the Bible permits couples to determine whether or not to have an abortion, 10% of respondents believe the Bible endorses this perspective. This finding suggests a fundamental confusion among churchgoers about biblical teaching despite 65% of survey respondents indicating they read the Bible at least weekly.

In the hyper-politicized context of the 2020s, it is also promising that nearly a third of churchgoers expressed a desire for their church to preach or teach "more often" about abortion. Only 13% said they would prefer such teaching "less often." Likewise, it is encouraging that 70% of respondents want their church to provide biblical worldview training about abortion. In a post-*Roe* environment where abortion is routinely in the news, the

---

attendees of mainline Protestant churches. Additionally, across all denominations, there was a positive correlation between regular church attendance and Bible reading and those who said the Bible is "clear and decisive" on the question. Some 70 percent of those who attended church weekly and 72% of those who read the Bible weekly indicated that Scripture is clear on the morality of killing an unborn child.

[23] The FRC survey did not specify whether respondents who participated in an abortion did so before or after conversion.

high number of churchgoers who desire teaching about abortion from their church presents a discipleship opportunity.

It is also heartening that 71% of churchgoers claim their thinking on abortion is influenced primarily by their moral and religious beliefs. Only a minority of churchgoers claim that political considerations or public opinion served as the most important influence on their thinking. At the very least, this finding shows that most Christians view their moral and religious beliefs as a source of guidance for how to think about abortion.[24]

Finally, it is encouraging that 58% of churchgoers want their churches to do more to help women facing unplanned pregnancies. Pregnancy resource centers, many of them funded and supported by churches, already outnumber abortion clinics in America by a factor of three to one. According to one report, from 2016 to 2020, pregnancy resource centers saved an estimated 828,131 lives.[25] In 2019 alone, the approximately 2,700 resource centers offered support and tangible help valued at $270 million.[26] The fact that a majority of churchgoers (62%) said their church already supports

[24] For pastors and church leaders, this insight is particularly noteworthy. Most churchgoers credit their religious and moral beliefs for having the most influence on their views about abortion and the value of human life. Among them, 75% said they desired to learn more about abortion at church (only 26% said they did not want additional teaching on abortion at church). Among those who indicated that their moral and religious beliefs were the most important for their views on abortion (712 respondents), 50% said it was "very desirable," for them to hear more about abortion at church while an additional 25% said it was "somewhat desirable."

[25] Moira Gaul and Jeanneane Maxon, "Lives Saved Impact at U.S. Pregnancy Help Centers," Charlotte Lozier Institute, June 23, 2022, https://lozierinstitute.org/lives-saved-impact-at-us-pregnancy-help-centers/.

[26] "Pro-Life Pregnancy Centers Served 2 Million People with Essential Medical Education and Support Services in 2019," Charlotte Lozier Institute, October 21, 2020, https://lozierinstitute.org/pro-life-pregnancy-centers-served-2-million-people-with-essential-medical-education-and-support-services-in-2019/. This help included almost 732,000 pregnancy tests, more than 486,000 ultrasounds, 160,200 STI/STD tests, more than 219,000 clients attending parenting and prenatal education programs, more than 21,000 clients receiving after-abortion support, nearly 1.3 million packs of diapers, and more than 2 million baby outfits.

women in unplanned pregnancies and that 58% want their church to do even more speaks to an underlying pro-life ethic in many churches.

In addition to the encouraging insights from the FRC survey, there were indications of significant confusion among churchgoers regarding the Bible's teaching on abortion and the value of life. For example, only two-thirds (65%) of churchgoers claimed the Bible identifies when human life begins. Among this group, 52% of respondents said life begins at conception while 8% said the Bible teaches that life begins once the child has been delivered and begins breathing. An additional 7% believe the Bible teaches life begins when an unborn child reaches viability. Thus, even though many churchgoers maintain that the Bible identifies when human life begins, there is little agreement when it comes to specifics.

Likewise, it was discouraging to learn that a mere 35% of churchgoers believed abortion was unacceptable under any circumstance. Shockingly, 10% believed abortion was acceptable if the expecting couple desired an abortion. It was also surprising that 7% of churchgoers believed abortion was permissible if the child would be born with physical or mental challenges and 6% indicated abortion was acceptable "under any circumstance."

These findings, among others, indicate that many Christians are not studying the Bible carefully when it comes to abortion and suggest that in a post-*Roe* world, applying the Bible's teaching on human life to the issue of abortion ought to be a discipleship priority for churches.

## Recent Pro-Abortion Preaching and Scholarship

Before turning to the Bible's teaching on abortion, it will be instructive to review some of the recent arguments made by theologians, pastors, and activists who support abortion and offer theological arguments in its defense. Recently, there has been a renewed effort in theologically progressive circles to argue that the Bible does not oppose abortion. These arguments, often asserted with passion and energy, require Christians who affirm a pro-life ethic to think seriously about the biblical text.

Challenges to the church's long-standing teaching on abortion have come from a variety of sources. In academic circles, a handful of books have been published over the past decades that provide a defense of abortion from a Christian perspective. These include Margaret D. Kamitsuka's *Abortion and the Christian Tradition: A Pro-Choice Theological Ethic* (2019), Rebecca Todd Peters's *Trust Women: A Progressive Christian Argument for Reproductive Justice* (2018), and Beverly Harrison's *Our Right to Choose: Toward a New Ethic of Abortion* (1983).[27]

Significantly, these books advance a theological and moral case for abortion. Although Kamitsuka concedes that "a fetus is genetically human" and has value "no matter at what stage of development," she nevertheless argues that the overriding ethical consideration in abortion is "a pregnant woman's maternal authority to determine her reproductive life and the fate of her fetus."[28] Notably, she marshals a variety of biblical argu-

---

[27] Margaret D. Kamitsuka, *Abortion and the Christian Tradition: A Pro-Choice Theological Ethic* (Louisville: Westminster John Knox, 2019); Rebecca Todd Peters, *Trust Women: A Progressive Christian Argument for Reproductive Justice* (Boston: Beacon, 2018); Beverly W. Harrison, *Our Right to Choose: Toward a New Ethic of Abortion* (Boston: Beacon, 1983). Another book, geared toward a more general Christian readership, is Kira Schlesinger, *Pro-Choice and Christian: Reconciling Faith, Politics, and Justice* (Louisville: Westminster John Knox, 2017).

[28] Kamitsuka, *Abortion and the Christian Tradition*, 151, 117. Elsewhere, Kamitsuka states that "no one disputes that a fetus is human" (53) and that "the truism that fetuses are human has never been in question, even by pro-choice proponents" (54). Surprisingly, Kamitsuka repeatedly draws attention to and ascribes moral value to the unborn child throughout her book. For example, on page 153, she writes, "A fetus, at any stage, carries moral weight because it is a living and genetically human being that is developing intimately connected to its mother until birth." However, in Kamitsuka's scheme, the baby's moral value is subservient to its mother's choice: "To claim that a fetus has value means that the only person authorized to make the momentous decision to abortion is its gestating mother" (153). Notably, Kamitsuka never suggests a point in pregnancy when the unborn child attains personhood: "Until or close to that point of natal appearance, we are impelled to say that the fetus is not a person and that the fetus is not a nonperson" (153). In everything, maternal authority, which includes authority

ments to defend her thesis. For example, Kamitsuka contends that the traditional pro-life appeal to the concept of the *imago Dei* for establishing fetal personhood is based on a "dubious exegetical approach" that misreads the creation account.[29] Because image language in Genesis is limited, the New Testament's use of image language (e.g., 1 Cor. 15:49 and Phil. 3:21) should determine the concept's meaning. According to Kamitsuka, image language in the New Testament indisputably refers to discipleship, not ontology. In other words, because the participatory aspects of imaging Christ are emphasized in the New Testament—consider Paul's statement in Romans 8:29 that God has called believers to be "conformed to the image of his Son"—it is hermeneutically implausible to defend fetal personhood by appealing to the notion of creation in God's image. As Kamitsuka explains, "This call for the believer to be conformed to the image of Christ properly applies to agents capable of some response to this call."[30] Elsewhere, she dismisses attempts to extrapolate universal claims about God's care for unborn life from passages such as Psalm 139:13–16 as a "thinly disguised eisegetical attempt to claim biblical evidence for the idea one brought to one's reading of the text."[31]

Among nonacademic abortion activists, theological arguments have also been employed with increased frequency. For example, in 2019, a handful of Christian leaders made news when they blessed an abortion clinic in Texas.

---

to terminate a pregnancy, is determinative: "I am not asserting fetal value to serve as a restraint for maternal authority, which is how pro-life claims for fetal personhood function" (153). Consistent with her belief in unlimited maternal authority, Kamitsuka does not oppose late-term abortions, admitting, "I do not see viability either as a marker of where fetal value begins or as something to be invoked in any way to badger the statistically few pregnant women who actually face late-term abortions" (153–54).

[29] Kamitsuka, 50.

[30] Kamitsuka, 61. For Kamitsuka's full argument in favor of interpreting the *imago Dei* in terms of discipleship, not ontology, see 59–63.

[31] Kamitsuka, 64–65.

"We're gathered together today to affirm this as a sacred space," declared Cari Jackson, a member of the Religious Coalition for Reproductive Choice. Amelia Fulbright, another minister who participated in the clinic blessing, stated her view on the Bible and abortion bluntly, explaining, "Let's be clear, there is nothing in the Christian scripture that condemns abortion—it just ain't in there."[32]

During the 2020 Democratic presidential primary, then-candidate Pete Buttigieg offered a theological rationale for his pro-abortion position. Although conceding that it is a "tough issue for a lot of people to think through morally," Buttigieg argued that abortion is morally permissible, in part, because there are "a lot of parts of the Bible that talk about how life begins with breath."[33] For Buttigieg, the Bible's teaching on life and abortion is "something we can interpret differently."

Finally, Professor Rebecca Todd Peters has offered forceful arguments in sermons and a recent book for why Christians should support abortion. Since the Supreme Court's decision in *Dobbs*, Peters has given dozens of sermons and lectures on abortion. For Peters, who is a professor and an ordained minister in the Presbyterian Church (U.S.A.), the widely held assumption in many churches that abortion is morally wrong is rooted in Christianity's patriarchal vision of womanhood, not a faithful exegesis of biblical texts.[34]

Professor Peters laid out her pro-abortion ethic in a July 2023 sermon titled "Reproductive Justice: Beyond the Abortion Imaginary." Wearing a

---

[32] Sophie Novack, "'My Congregation Trusts Women': Progressive Faith Groups Counter Anti-Abortion Narratives," *Texas Observer*, August 28, 2019, https://www.texasobserver.org/my-congregation-trusts-women-progressive-faith-groups-counter-anti-abortion-narratives/.

[33] Will Maule, "Buttigieg Justifies Late-Term Abortion Stance by Saying Life Starts 'with First Breath,'" CBN, September 10, 2019, https://www2.cbn.com/news/politics/buttigieg-justifies-late-term-abortion-stance-saying-life-starts-first-breath.

[34] Yonat Shimron, "Rebecca Todd Peters Is on a Mission to Get Churches to Talk about Abortion," Religion News, July 13, 2023, https://religionnews.com/2023/07/13/rebecca-todd-peters-is-on-a-mission-to-get-churches-to-talk-about-abortion/.

stole embroidered with Planned Parenthood's logo, she lamented the fact that Catholics and evangelicals have "effectively shaped" the debate around abortion for the broader church community. For Peters, one of the most "disturbing" developments in American religious life is the widespread belief that abortion is sinful. Although "the Bible doesn't say anything about abortion," pro-abortion advocates within the church have allowed themselves to be bullied into silence by a "toxic theology" that condemns abortion.[35]

Although more could be said about Peters's views, the thesis of her argument is that proper interpretation of the biblical text leads to seeing abortion as a moral good that ought to be accepted and even celebrated in the church. Among those attending theologically liberal churches, this argument is gaining wide acceptance.[36] As we have seen from the FRC study, even some in conservative churches are questioning the Bible's teaching on abortion and the value of life.

How should we evaluate these arguments? Does the Bible teach that life begins with breath? Since the word "abortion" does not appear in the Bible, can Christians adopt a pro-abortion ethic? Is abortion a moral issue

---

[35] The Community Church of Chapel Hill, "'Reproductive Justice: Beyond the Abortion Imaginary' Rev. Dr. Rebecca Todd Peters," YouTube video, July 9, 2023, https://www.youtube.com/watch?v=CRgo8S9y-JQ&t. At one point, Peters rightly explains that everyone reads Scripture through a hermeneutic. In her view, "the lens through which anti-choice Christians read the Bible is the theological belief that from the moment of fertilization a zygote is biologically, morally, ontologically, and in every other way indistinguishable from a baby." Peters then claims, "When they [Catholics and evangelicals] read the Scripture through this lens, they arrogate all manner of text to support that position." In other words, pro-life readers of Scripture are not deriving pro-life themes and messages from the actual biblical text. Rather, according to Peters, theologically conservative readers are importing their biases and political beliefs into passages that, if read correctly, would render a pro-abortion ethic.

[36] In academic circles, two other books that defend abortion from a Christian perspective include Kathy Rudy, *Beyond Pro-Life and Pro-Choice: Moral Diversity in the Abortion Debate* (Boston: Beacon, 1996) and Daniel A. Dombrowski and Robert J. Deltete, *A Brief, Liberal, Catholic Defense of Abortion* (Urbana: University of Illinois Press, 2000).

that faithful Christians can agree to disagree on? Is the church's historic pro-life position grounded in sound exegesis? Whether advanced by Rebecca Todd Peters, Pete Buttigieg, or Raphael Warnock, pro-abortion arguments claiming to be grounded in Scripture and the Christian tradition are sowing confusion in the church.

Thus, to answer fundamental questions about the Bible's teaching on abortion, we need to turn to the biblical text. In my view, the evidence for a pro-life reading of Scripture is indisputable. However, this claim has been contested in recent years and therefore merits a vigorous theological and exegetical defense.

To this defense we now turn.

# 2

# The Bible's Teaching on Abortion and Life

On September 1, 2021, the United States Supreme Court declined to stay a recently enacted Texas pro-life law.[1] As a result, the law was allowed to remain in place and surgical abortion was effectively ended in the state.[2] Although many celebrated the law, which protected life at the point a fetal heartbeat could be detected, abortion supporters were furious. Those

[1] Supreme Court of the United States, Whole Woman's Health et al. v. Austin Reeve Jackson, Judge, et al. 594 U.S. 2021, https://www.supremecourt.gov/opinions/20pdf/21a24_8759.pdf?bcs-agent-scanner=8e5466e6-b002-964b-a176-65da618f4a28.

[2] Legislature of the state of Texas, Texas Heartbeat Act, S.B. No. 8, September 1, 2021, https://capitol.texas.gov/tlodocs/87R/billtext/pdf/SB00008F.pdf?bcs-agent-scanner=c0035305-fcc0-e148-a3a3-b264c8ac2fe9. The law, known as Texas Bill 8, restricts abortion after a heartbeat has been detected in the unborn child. This usually occurs around six weeks. For further information, see Katherine Johnson, "Explainer: What Is Happening with Texas' New Pro-Life Law?," Family Research Council, September 2, 2021, https://www.frc.org/blog/2021/09/explainer-what-happening-texas-new-pro-life-law.

in the media lamented the "human costs" of the law, and high-ranking politicians including Nancy Pelosi blasted it, describing the law as a "catastrophe to women in Texas."[3] Even the White House weighed in with President Joe Biden claiming the heartbeat law "blatantly violates" the Supreme Court's precedent in *Roe v. Wade*.[4]

In contrast to those upset by the new law, many Christians praised Texas legislators for their courage, seeing the law's enactment and the Supreme Court's decision to allow it to take effect as positive steps for the pro-life movement.

As debate continued over the heartbeat law, Family Research Council (FRC) posted a tweet on September 3, 2021, noting, "The Bible is ardently and unequivocally pro-life."[5] For an organization whose stated mission is to "advance faith, family, and freedom in public policy and the culture from a biblical worldview," tweeting support for the Bible's pro-life ethic was hardly controversial—or at least we didn't think it would be.[6]

But the tweet provoked instant outrage and went viral. In just three days, FRC's tweet generated 18 million impressions, 200,000 engagements,

---

[3] Jeevan Ravindran, "Explainer: What Is the Texas Abortion Ban and Why Does It Matter?," CNN, September 3, 2021, https://www.cnn.com/2021/09/03/us/what-is-texas-abortion-law-as-equals-intl-cmd/index.html; Congresswoman Nancy Pelosi, "Pelosi Statement on Supreme Court Shadow Ruling on Texas Reproductive Rights Case," September 2, 2021, https://pelosi.house.gov/news/press-releases/pelosi-statement-on-supreme-court-shadow-ruling-on-texas-reproductive-rights.

[4] President Joe Biden, "Statement by President Joe Biden on Texas Law SB8," The White House, September 1, 2021, https://www.whitehouse.gov/briefing-room/statements-releases/2021/09/01/statement-by-president-joe-biden-on-texas-law-sb8/.

[5] Family Research Council (@FRCdc), Twitter, September 3, 2021, 12:15 p.m., https://twitter.com/FRCdc/status/1433840977916141570.

[6] In 2023, FRC updated its mission statement. The new mission statement reads: "Family Research Council's mission is to serve in the kingdom of God by championing faith, family, and freedom in public policy and the culture from a biblical worldview." Vision and Mission Statements, Family Research Council, accessed September 13, 2023, https://www.frc.org/mission-statement.

7,000 re-tweets, and 17,000 replies (nearly all of which were negative).[7] Notably, many of the replies, some of which came from well-known pastors in theologically progressive churches, claimed that FRC was misinterpreting the Bible. Clearly, claiming the Bible is pro-life struck a nerve, including among a surprising number of self-professing Christians.

In a post-Christian culture, appeals to God's Word carry little weight with most people. As we've already considered, few people, including many churchgoers, have a consistent biblical worldview. But even if many Christians do not believe in the authority of Scripture, a biblical ethic concerning abortion—if it is to be truly biblical—must begin with God's Word.

A survey of the Bible reveals a remarkably strong and consistent pro-life message. To establish the Bible's affirmation of unborn personhood and opposition to abortion, this chapter will first define *personhood*, argue against the developmental view of personhood at the heart of the pro-abortion argument, and then consider the Bible's most prominent pro-life themes, which include the *imago Dei*, God's sovereignty over conception and birth, the prohibition against shedding innocent blood, and Jesus's ethic of love and embrace of children.

In addition to these pro-life themes, the Bible contains specific passages that detail how God is personally involved in the development of every child. We will review these passages and consider how God's calling, naming, and appointing of future leaders in utero is further evidence that unborn children are entitled to the right to life. Finally, the chapter will conclude by examining and responding to the counterarguments that claim the Bible does not present a pro-life ethic or is at least neutral on abortion. These pro-abortion claims have gained traction and merit a response.

In short, the goal of this chapter is to summarize the principles and passages that comprise the Bible's pro-life ethic. Taken together, they make a

---

[7] As of May 2023, the FRC tweet had generated a total of 20 million impressions and 218,000 engagements and prompted 32,469 people to visit FRC's Twitter page.

compelling case that unborn children are morally significant and should be protected from the moment of conception.

## What Is Personhood?

In 2008, Joe Biden, the then-Democratic nominee for vice president, conceded, "I'm prepared as a matter of faith to accept that life begins at conception."[8] Because of the candidate's public support for abortion, the admission surprised political observers and voters alike. If human life begins at conception, how could the future president support abortion? Quite easily, it turns out, because of his acceptance of personhood theory, the dominant philosophical assumption behind nearly every pro-abortion argument.

Although the words "human being" and "person" are used interchangeably in common parlance, personhood theory establishes what Nancy Pearcey calls a "two-tiered view of the human being" that ascribes different meanings to the terms.[9] According to personhood theory, "human being"

---

[8] Kate Phillips, "As a Matter of Faith, Biden Says Life Begins at Conception," *New York Times*, September 7, 2008, https://www.nytimes.com/2008/09/08/us/politics/08campaign.html. Biden made a similar comment in his 2012 vice presidential debate with Paul Ryan, noting, "Life begins at conception in the church's judgment. I accept it in my personal life." See Political Staff, "VP debate transcript," *Politico*, October 11, 2012, https://www.politico.com/story/2012/10/vice-presidential-debate-questions-transcript-oct-11-2012-082310. In 2015, Biden once again stated, "I'm prepared to accept that at the moment of conception is a human life and being." See YouTube video, "Joe Biden Talks His Catholic Faith, Pope Francis, and Politics," September 21, 2015, https://www.youtube.com/watch?v=xson7Rg5p3A&t=868s. However, in 2021, the then president Joe Biden changed his view, stating, "I respect them—they—those who believe life begins at the moment of conception and all. I respect that. Don't agree, but I respect that. I'm not going to impose that on people." See "Remarks by President Biden on the August Jobs Report," The White House, September 3, 2021, https://www.whitehouse.gov/briefing-room/speeches-remarks/2021/09/03/remarks-by-president-biden-on-the-august-jobs-report/.

[9] As Nancy Pearcey explains, personhood theory takes a two-tiered view of the human being: "To be biologically human is a scientific *fact*. But to be a person is

denotes a biological reality whereas "person" refers to an ethical reality determined by functionality. In this functionalist understanding of personhood, merely being alive in a biological sense does not confer moral standing. Rather, the achievement or emergence of various capacities bestows moral standing that warrants legal protection (i.e., personhood). Over the last few decades, many of the elite legal, philosophical, and scientific authorities have adopted this understanding of personhood.

Although a full critique of personhood theory is outside the scope of this chapter, its ad hoc, subjective nature presents a host of moral and practical challenges. For starters, personhood theory provides no consensus on what criteria should be used to determine personhood.[10] In fact, bioethicists

---

an ethical concept, defined by what we *value*." See Nancy Pearcey, *Love Thy Body: Answering Hard Questions about Life and Sexuality* (Grand Rapids: Baker Books, 2018), 20. The logic of personhood theory is evident in Margaret Kamitsuka, who argues, "Again, the truism that fetuses are human has never been in question, even by pro-choice proponents." Although she acknowledges that unborn babies are "human," she nevertheless does not see them as persons, noting later in her book, "The fetus is an unavoidably developmental uterine being who evolves incrementally toward born personhood." See Margaret D. Kamitsuka, *Abortion and the Christian Tradition: A Pro-Choice Theological Ethic* (Louisville: Westminster John Knox, 2019), 54, 152. Although Kamitsuka claims that "pro-choice proponents" have "never" questioned that fetuses are human, a book she cites in her introduction, *Our Right to Choose* by Beverly Harrison, makes that claim. For example, Harrison argues, "Analogies to us, I believe, are inappropriate if they attribute to a fetus autonomous and existent human life functions that its structural development could not support. Hence, to call a conceptus or an early differentiated fetus 'a human,' or even 'a person' is, in my view, genuinely absurd, because the actualized biological structure existent in early fetal development cannot conceivably manifest the qualities we impute to 'a human being,' much less to 'a person.'" Beverly Wildung Harrison, *Our Right to Choose: Toward a New Ethic of Abortion* (Boston: Beacon, 1983), 214.

[10] For a thorough critique of personhood theory, see Bruce Ware, "Human Personhood: An Analysis and Definition," *Southern Baptist Journal of Theology* 13, no. 2 (Summer 2009): 18–31. Ware argues for an essentialist model for discerning the personhood of individuals. Specifically, he suggests two senses of personhood, namely "essential personhood" and "expressive personhood." In Ware's formulation, the former refers to the primary, fundamental, and first-order status of personhood,

have proposed widely divergent criteria. For example, Joseph Fletcher has suggested fifteen qualities for determining personhood, including minimal intelligence, concern for others, self-control, a sense of time, the capability to relate to others, and curiosity.[11] Significantly, most of these qualities emerge gradually; fully developed adults possess traits like self-control and curiosity in varying degrees. Does a deficiency in self-awareness mean someone is not a person? Does someone with Alzheimer's disease who no longer remembers the past cease being a person? What about accident victims in a permanent vegetative state? These questions point to just a few of the problems with adopting a view of personhood based on functionality.

Due to personhood theory's dubious reliance on arbitrary capacities for determining personhood, a standard with objective criteria is needed. For Christians, a consistent view of personhood begins by denying the "two-tiered view of the human being" and acknowledging that the presence of human life—which, biologically speaking, takes place at conception—is the only objective criteria for establishing personhood. This essentialist view of personhood is supported by science, which demonstrates that the youngest human embryo possesses a unique genetic composition and fulfills the four criteria needed to establish biological life: growth, metabolism, reaction to stimuli, and reproduction.[12] Put simply, if personhood is not coextensive with being biologically human, it becomes hopelessly subjective. Thus,

---

which is attributed to every living member of the species *Homo sapiens* "who, as such, possesses an inherent rational nature," while the latter refers to the secondary, second-order status of personhood, which "is rightly attributable to any living member of the species *Homo sapiens* whose inherent rational nature gives rise to given expressions or functions appropriate to that nature and expressive of its natural kind." See Ware, 29–30.

[11] Joseph Fletcher, "Indicators of Humanhood: A Tentative Profile of Man," *Hastings Center Report* 2, no. 5 (November 1972): 1–4.

[12] Nancy Pearcey draws attention to this point when she notes, "Everything intrinsic to a human being is present from fertilization . . . the entire human being develops in a seamless continuum from conception." See Nancy Pearcey, *Love Thy Body*, 48.

although people are more than biological organisms, biology provides a baseline for identifying who is human. Moreover, as we will see, a Christian view of personhood must be grounded in the inherent nature or essence of a human being, which, according to Scripture, is humanity's creation in God's image.

The debate about personhood is important because separating "human being" from "person" typifies the chicanery abortion advocates have employed for decades. Infamously, Justice Harry Blackmun, in his *Roe v. Wade* majority opinion, invoked the logic of personhood theory when he ruled that unborn babies were not persons, stating, "The appellee and certain *amici* argue that the fetus is a 'person' within the language and meaning of the Fourteenth Amendment. . . . If this suggestion of personhood is established, the appellant's case, of course, collapses, for the fetus' right to life would then be guaranteed specifically by the Amendment."[13] Although chilling, Blackmun's explanation is consistent with a functionalist, developmental view of humanity, a perspective that has undergirded pro-abortion arguments ever since.

## Image of God

The Bible teaches that everyone is made in the image and likeness of God (Gen. 1:26–27; 5:3; 9:6).[14] This teaching grounds the Bible's approach to the doctrine of humanity and provides a starting point for understanding its pro-life ethic.

Although scholars debate the exact meaning of what it means to be made in God's image, the Bible is content with simply asserting that human

---

[13] *Roe v. Wade*, 410 U.S. 113 (1973), 156–57.

[14] According to Anthony Hoekema, "The most distinctive feature of the biblical understanding of man is the teaching that man has been created in the image of God." See Anthony A. Hoekema, *Created in God's Image* (Grand Rapids: Eerdmans, 1986), 11.

beings are somehow more like God than anything else in creation.[15] As theologian Bruce Ware has noted, technical terminology in the Bible is typically introduced but not explained in contexts where the audience is already familiar with specialized language.[16] In other words, the language of "image" and "likeness" must have had clear meanings to the original readers.[17]

Although the Bible does not provide a comprehensive definition, most commentators agree that the image of God refers to aspects of who people

---

[15] In terms of defining what it means to be made in God's image, three main views have been proposed throughout church history: (1) the substantive or structural view, which identifies some definite characteristic or quality (such as reason or spirituality) as being the image of God (this position was held by John Calvin and Martin Luther and is the view Millard Erickson defends in Millard J. Erickson, *Christian Theology*, 3rd ed. (Grand Rapids: Baker Academic, 2013), 470); (2) the relational view, which locates the image of God in the human capacity for relationship (Emil Brunner and Karl Barth held versions of this position); and (3) the functional view, which identifies the image of God in a function man carries out, usually seen in the exercise of dominion over the creation. For his part, Wayne Grudem believes the terms "image" and "likeness" had clear meanings to the original readers and that "much of the controversy over the meaning of 'image of God' is seen to be a search for too narrow and too specific a meaning." See Wayne Grudem, *Systematic Theology: An Introduction to Biblical Doctrine* (Leicester, UK: Inter-Varsity, 1994), 443.

[16] Lecture notes from Systematic Theology I with Dr. Bruce Ware. Ware serves as the T. Rupert and Lucille Coleman Professor of Christian Theology at The Southern Baptist Theological Seminary.

[17] Although the Bible does not define "image of God," the use of image language in the ancient Near Eastern (ANE) may shed light onto its meaning in Genesis. According to David J. A. Clines's seminal study on ANE image language, three features of image language are found in ancient literature. First, image language appears when a deity imputes a substance to an earthly king, enabling him to represent the divine. Second, "image" is used when the empowered king represents the deity by ruling as vice-regent. Third, only the king is given the privilege of "imaging" the deity. In the Genesis account, God breathed into Adam the breath of life (Gen. 2:7). Second, man is tasked with exercising dominion over creation (Gen. 1:28). Clines's third characteristic, however, does not apply. The Bible surprises us at this point by affirming that everyone, not just the king, bears God's image. See David J. A. Clines, "The Image of God in Man," *Tyndale Bulletin* 19, no. 1 (1968): 53–103.

are and what they do.[18] However, as Millard Erickson rightly notes, the image should primarily be thought of in terms of who a person is: "It refers to something a human *is* rather than something a human *has* or does. By virtue of being human, one is in the image of God; being so is not dependent upon the presence of anything else."[19] Likewise, as Ware explains, "We sense that there is something highly significant about the functional capabilities pointed to by theologians discussing what it means to be made in the image of God. . . . And yet, we realize that we are more than our functions, and that there are many cases when an individual's functioning falters or fails that there is still reason to consider the individual a person deserving of treatment and respect."[20] Put simply, who we are is more basic to imaging God than what we do.

Significantly, people continue to bear God's image after the fall, though in an imperfect way. This is seen in Genesis 9:6, where murder is prohibited on the grounds of the *imago Dei*: "Whoever sheds human blood, by humans his blood will be shed, for God made humans in his image." The logic of the text is that though fallen, man is still an image-bearer, and to murder another person is to attack the part of God's creation that most resembles God. Similarly, in James 3:9, the author condemns cursing others on the ground that people are made "in God's likeness." To

---

[18] For example, Anthony Hoekema argues, "It is my conviction that we need to maintain both aspects [the structural and functional]. Since the image of God includes the whole person, it must include both man's structure and man's functioning." See Hoekema, *Created in God's Image*, 69. Elsewhere, Hoekema writes, "These two aspects of the image of God . . . can never be separated. Whenever we look at the human person, both aspects must always be taken into account." See Hoekema, 72.

[19] In his discussion, Erickson argues that the image "should be thought of as primarily substantive or structural," though he adds, "we may and should think of the image involving all three of these foci [substantive, relational, and functional]." See Erickson, *Christian Theology*, 470, emphasis original.

[20] Ware, "Human Personhood: An Analysis and Definition," 28.

curse a fellow image-bearer is in effect to curse God, in whose likeness they have been made.

In summary, the Bible's teaching on the image of God bestows tremendous dignity on every single person. Everyone, by virtue of being created in the *imago Dei*, is indescribably valuable to God. Like a statue erected by an ancient king, mankind bears God's image in the cosmic temple of the world, representing his authority and dominion. Clearly, the Bible's teaching on the image of God has implications for debates surrounding personhood and abortion. In fact, the most powerful argument against abortion is that the unborn child is a unique person. As we will see, several passages in the Bible teach this truth and make a powerful case that unborn children should be considered as persons from the moment of conception.[21]

## Conception: An Act of God

The Bible's teaching about conception, birth, and children illustrates a high view for unborn human life. In particular, the Old Testament teaches that God is sovereign over conception; he alone has the power to open and close the womb.

For example, in Genesis 10, God appears to a man named Abram and promises to make him into a great nation (Gen. 12:2). Years go by, and Abram and his wife, Sarai, remain childless. By Genesis 15, Abram, who is advancing in age, becomes anxious. "Look, you have given me no offspring," he laments to God in Genesis 15:3. In response, God makes a covenant with Abram, promising that his descendants will be as numerous as the stars (v. 5). However, after more time passes, Abram and Sarai decide to

---

[21] This point is made by Wayne Grudem in his chapter on abortion in *Christian Ethics: An Introduction to Biblical Moral Reasoning*. Grudem uses Luke 1:41–44, Psalm 51:5, Psalm 139:13, Genesis 25:22–23, Exodus 21:22–25, and Luke 1:34 to argue for the personhood of the unborn and the immorality of abortion. For Grudem's exegesis on these passages, see Wayne Grudem, *Christian Ethics: An Introduction to Biblical Moral Reasoning* (Wheaton, IL: Crossway, 2018), 566–71.

take matters into their own hands, and Sarai offers her servant, Hagar, to Abram as another wife. For our purposes, Sarai's comment at the beginning of Genesis 16 is instructive: "Since the Lord has prevented me from bearing children, go to my slave; perhaps through her I can build a family" (16:2a). Although Hagar is ultimately not the means God uses to fulfill his promise to Abram—Sarai herself will eventually give birth to Isaac in Genesis 21—Sarai's insight reflects an accurate understanding of God's sovereign control over conception and birth. She rightly perceives that God is behind her inability to conceive.

The theme of God's sovereignty over conception is seen again in Genesis 17:16. In this passage, God reaffirms his promise to Abram (now Abraham). Speaking of Sarai (now Sarah), God says, "I will bless her; indeed, I will give you a son by her." Initially, Abraham struggles to believe God, laughing to himself as he considers his advanced age and the age of his wife. But God insists, "No. Your wife Sarah will bear you a son" (17:19). In Genesis 18, angels appear to Abraham and reaffirm the same promise: "The Lord said, 'I will certainly come back to you in about a year's time, and your wife Sarah will have a son!'" (18:10). Sarah's response is the same as her husband's; she laughs and questions how conception and birth are possible at her advanced age. After all, as the writer notes, "Sarah had passed the age of childbearing" (18:11). Thus, although Abraham and Sarah would not have understood modern medicine or biology, they knew that humanly speaking, God's promise of a son was impossible. Yet, God fulfills his promise and blesses them with a son, ironically named Isaac, the Hebrew word for "he laughs" (21:3, 6).[22]

---

[22] Reflecting on this episode nearly two thousand years later, the author of Hebrews, whose purpose was to highlight the faith of Old Testament saints, noted the impossibility, in human terms, that Abraham and Sarah were able to conceive and give birth. In Hebrews 11:11–12, the writer explained, "By faith even Sarah herself, when she was unable to have children, received power to conceive offspring, even though she was past the age, since she considered that the one who had promised was faithful. Therefore, from one man—in fact, from one as good as

The motif of God closing and opening the womb is seen again in Genesis 20:18. In this account, Abraham lies about his wife's identity, and Abimelech, a foreign king, takes Sarah for himself. However, before Abimelech can harm Sarah, God intervenes. Eventually, Abraham confesses his sin, and God blesses Abimelech and his household in response to Abraham's prayer. This prayer was necessary because, as the author notes at the conclusion of this episode, "The LORD had completely closed all the wombs in Abimelech's household on account of Sarah, Abraham's wife" (Gen. 20:18). Although the biblical author does not linger on this detail, it is yet another example of God demonstrating his power in the opening and closing of the womb.

There are other examples in Scripture that picture God as sovereign over conception. These include Rebekah (Gen. 25:21), Leah and Rachel (Gen. 29:31; 30:2, 22), Manoah's wife (Judg. 13:2), Hannah (1 Sam. 1:5), the Shunammite woman (2 Kgs. 4:14), and Elizabeth (Luke 1:7). Each of these women experienced a prolonged season of infertility before God opened her womb.[23] Another passage, Ruth 4:13, summarizes the theme of God's authority over conception when it narrates the birth of Obed, noting that "the LORD granted conception to her, and she gave birth to a son."

---

dead—came offspring as numerous as the stars of the sky and as innumerable as the grains of sand along the seashore." By noting that Sarah was "past the age" and that Abraham was "as good as dead," the author marveled at God's ability to fulfill his promise to the previously infertile couple.

[23] It is worth noting how prayer played a role in the experience of many of the previously barren women. In Rebekah's case, conception and birth were a direct answer to Isaac's prayer: "The LORD was receptive to his prayer, and his wife Rebekah conceived" (Gen. 25:21b). Likewise, God granted Rachel's prayer in Genesis 30: "Then God remembered Rachel. He listened to her and opened her womb. She conceived and bore a son, and she said, 'God has taken away my disgrace'" (vv. 22–23). Finally, in direct answer to Hannah's prayer, the Lord "remembered her" and "after some time Hannah conceived and gave birth to a son" (1 Sam. 1:19–20). This passage is significant because in verse 5 the text explicitly states, "the LORD had kept her from conceiving."

It is worth observing that every conception discussed in this section was received as a blessing from God. In fact, the Bible captures the joy associated with children in Psalm 127:3–5, where Solomon wrote:

> Sons are indeed a heritage from the Lord,
> offspring, a reward.
> Like arrows in the hand of a warrior
> are the sons born in one's youth.
> Happy is the man who has filled his quiver with them.
> They will never be put to shame
> when they speak with their enemies at the city gate.

For Solomon, children were a "heritage from the Lord" and a "reward." The man whom God provided with many children was "happy" and considered blessed.

Solomon's celebration of children in Psalm 127 epitomizes the Bible's attitude toward children. Children are a good gift from a kind God; the proper response to children is joy and gratitude. The reality that some children are not received as gifts reflects the tragic effects of a fallen world.[24]

## Prohibition against Shedding Innocent Blood

The Bible's prohibition of murder (i.e., the unauthorized taking of innocent human life) provides additional support for a theologically based pro-life ethic. In fact, two incidents in the early chapters of Genesis reflect God's high regard for human life. The first instance is God's punishment and protection of Cain in Genesis 4. Following Cain's murder of Abel, Adam's

[24] Unfortunately, it seems that an increasing number of people, especially in developed countries, have embraced a contraceptive mindset that sees children as a burden. As we will see in chapter 6, the only way the Food and Drug Administration (FDA) could approve the chemical abortion pill in 2000 was to mislabel pregnancy as an "illness." Describing a healthy pregnancy as an "illness" is diametrically opposed to how the Bible sees the conception and birth of children.

first son was banished: the ground would no longer yield to him, and he was consigned to live as "a restless wanderer on the earth" (Gen. 4:14). Perhaps worried that life as a vagrant would expose him to retribution by a blood avenger, Cain protested his punishment: "Whoever finds me will kill me" (v. 14). In response, God mercifully placed "a mark on Cain so that whoever found him would not kill him" (v. 15). In addition to giving Cain a sign that indicated divine protection, God said, "Whoever kills Cain will suffer vengeance seven times over" (v. 15).[25] In short, God's judgment against the world's first murderer appears tempered, in part, to mitigate the spread of further bloodshed. Even in judgment, God's concern for human life is evident.

Second, the Noahic covenant's prohibition of murder demonstrates a high regard for human life. Following the flood, God said, "From his fellow man I will require a reckoning for the life of man. Whoever sheds the blood of man, by man shall his blood be shed, for God made man in his own image" (Gen. 9:5–6 ESV). Notably, the prohibition against shedding blood is grounded in the *imago Dei*. Although fallen, man still bears God's image, and an attack on a fellow image-bearer is essentially an attack on God himself. Additionally, many theologians believe this passage contains the authorization for civil government.[26] As Jonathan Leeman observes, God "authorizes the use of coercive force in order to prosecute the taking of life. By implication it also authorizes a government to prevent the unjust

[25] In his commentary, Kenneth Mathews asks, "Why does God preserve the life of a murderer?" Mathews suggests an answer, noting, "Perhaps the answer is that by the 'sign' God prevents the spread of bloodshed that otherwise would escalate. Moreover, God is declaring that life and death are his prerogative, which he does not share with anyone except by divine sanction (cp. 9:5–6)." See Kenneth A. Mathews, *Genesis 1–11:26*, The New American Commentary (Nashville: B&H, 1996), 278.

[26] For a succinct discussion on how the Noahic covenant authorizes civil government, see David VanDrunen, "The Noahic Covenant's Importance for Government," *Church Matters* vol. 1 (April 2023): 104–9.

taking of life."[27] In other words, the theological rationale for civil government is protecting image-bearers from harm. As Gentry and Wellum put it, "Humans cannot be killed because they are owned by God—stamped with his seal of ownership."[28]

Notably, both passages (Genesis 4 and 9) describe events before the giving of the Mosaic law. This timing implies that God's concern for human life predates the constituting of Israel as a nation and suggests that the law's teaching as it relates to preserving life is a continuation and application of God's eternal, moral law.

The sanctity of human life is further underscored in the Decalogue's prohibition against murder (Exod. 20:13; Deut. 5:17). At first glance, the commandment is a straightforward injunction on the outward act of murder. But living out the commandment requires more than resisting the urge to give full vent to one's violent emotions. Obedience to the sixth commandment requires a commitment to affirm and protect life. Circumstances and abilities permitting, the spirit of the command includes the corollary to love and care for the well-being of other people.[29]

The ethical implications of some of the Ten Commandments are expanded in Jesus's Sermon on the Mount. For example, the seventh commandment, which prohibits adultery, also forbids the lustful intentions of the heart (Matt. 5:28). Likewise, the prohibition against murder encompasses much more than not killing. As Jesus explained, an unforgiving, angry heart also violates the commandment (5:21–22). Hateful attitudes and the inevitable destructive behaviors that issue from them violate Jesus's

[27] Jonathan Leeman, "What Authority Has God Given to Governments?," *Church Matters* 1 (April 2023): 50.

[28] Peter J. Gentry and Stephen J. Wellum, *Kingdom through Covenant: A Biblical-Theological Understanding of the Covenants* (Wheaton, IL: Crossway, 2012), 167.

[29] In the words of John Frame, the Decalogue promotes a "doctrine of carefulness," which entails taking precautions against the loss of life. See John Frame, *The Doctrine of the Christian Life* (Phillipsburg, NJ: P&R, 2008), 687–88.

ethic of love and are forbidden. As we will continue to see, Jesus's expansion of the sixth commandment has significant implications for the Bible's pro-life ethic.

The Old Testament manslayer laws also underscore the Bible's high view of human life. In the case of unintentional killing, the manslayer could flee to one of the cities designated as a city of refuge, where he was safe from the avenger of blood (Exod. 21:12–14). Even though the crime was accidental and there was no prior hostility toward the victim, the manslayer was culpable for not taking the necessary precautions to protect life. Thus, he was guilty of a crime of carelessness and had to wait until the death of the incumbent high priest. Only then could he return home in assured safety.

Finally, the Bible repeatedly underscores God's hatred for the shedding of innocent blood. As Proverbs 6:16–17 explains, "hands that shed innocent blood" are "detestable" to the Lord. God sees murder as a great sin and promises to judge those who kill with impunity.[30]

In summary, these passages teach that intentionally killing a fellow image bearer violates the Bible's prohibition against murder, and a comprehensive theological critique of abortion must take these prohibitions seriously.

## Jesus's Ethic of Love and Embrace of Children

Throughout his earthly ministry, a central theme of Jesus's teaching was love. In the final week of his life, Jesus responded to a question regarding the Old Testament's most important commandment by quoting Deuteronomy 6:5 and Leviticus 19:18: "The most important is Listen, Israel! The Lord our God, the Lord is one. Love the Lord your God with all your heart, with all your soul, with all your mind, and with all your strength. The second is,

---

[30] See Deuteronomy 19:10, 1 Samuel 19:5, 1 Kings 2:31, 2 Kings 21:16, and Isaiah 59:7.

Love your neighbor as yourself. There is no other command greater than these" (Mark 12:29–31).

According to Jesus, loving God and loving one's neighbor summarizes obedience to God's law. As Jesus explained to his disciples on the night of his betrayal, "By this everyone will know that you are my disciples, if you love one another" (John 13:35). Significantly, Jesus's teaching on love went further than most of his hearers expected (Matt. 5:43–48). In one instance, Jesus affirmed a man who acknowledged his duty to love God and neighbor. But when the man tried to narrow the scope of his obligations, Jesus responded by telling the parable of the good Samaritan, shocking his listeners by redefining neighborly love to include those beyond ethnic boundaries (Luke 10:25–37). It is not enough to love those in your family or ethnic group; our love must extend to everyone, especially the vulnerable.

Jesus's expansion of the concept of neighborly love is particularly seen in his attitude toward children. In fact, Jesus's interaction with young children and his teachings about them undermine the rationale of an abortion culture that labels some children as unwanted or undesirable.

Consider two examples. First, in Matthew 19, Jesus is on his final journey to Jerusalem. In verses 3–12, a group of Pharisees approach Jesus and attempt to trap him by asking a difficult question about divorce (v. 3). The stakes are high, but Jesus nimbly answers the question. Relieved, his disciples assume the journey can continue. But to their evident dismay, the crowd begins bringing young children to Jesus for a blessing. The disciples rebuke the people but are interrupted by Jesus, who says, "Leave the little children alone, and don't try to keep them from coming to me, because the kingdom of heaven belongs to such as these" (Matt. 19:14). Jesus then takes the children in his arms and blesses them (Matt. 19:15; cf. Mark 10:16).

Second, Jesus answers his disciples' question about greatness in the kingdom of heaven with a memorable object lesson. Placing a child before them, Jesus says, "Unless you turn and become like little children, you will never enter the kingdom of heaven" (Matt. 18:3). Jesus's point is that humble, childlike dependence on God is a prerequisite for entering heaven. In the same teaching, Jesus explains that causing a child who believes in him to stumble is an almost unimaginable sin. In fact, it would be better to drown in the sea with a millstone fastened around your neck than to cause a child to sin (v. 6).

In summary, Jesus's teaching on neighborly love challenges us to see everyone as worthy of compassion and care. This is especially applicable for vulnerable populations (e.g., orphans, widows, and unborn children). Alongside teachings on the *imago Dei*, God's sovereignty over conception, the prohibition against shedding innocent blood, and Jesus's love for children, an expanded notion of neighborly love contributes to the Bible's pro-life ethic, which becomes even more compelling when considered with key texts such as Psalm 139 and Luke 1.

## Key Pro-Life Passages

The most powerful argument against abortion is that the unborn child is a unique person. Several passages in the Bible teach this truth. Taken together, they make a powerful case that unborn children have moral standing and should be treated with dignity from the moment of conception. After examining two of the most celebrated pro-life passages—Psalm 139:13–16 and Luke 1:39–45—we will review additional passages that present the Bible's pro-life ethic.

### *Psalm 139:13–16*[31]

The most well-known passage in the Bible that establishes the personhood of the unborn is Psalm 139:13–16, where King David describes God's dealings with him in utero:

[31] All Scripture quotations in this section on Psalm 139:13–16 and its subsections are from the ESV.

For you formed my inward parts;
you knitted me together in my mother's womb.
I praise you, for I am fearfully and wonderfully made.
Wonderful are your works;
my soul knows it very well.
My frame was not hidden from you,
when I was being made in secret,
intricately woven in the depths of the earth.
Your eyes saw my unformed substance;
in your book were written, every one of them,
the days that were formed for me,
when as yet there was none of them.

Most Christians with pro-life convictions are familiar with these verses and can recite them from memory. But these well-known verses, if properly understood in their context, provide an even more convincing case for the personhood of the unborn than many Christians may initially realize.

## Setting Psalm 139 in Context: Verses 1–12

In Psalm 139, God's presence is the main theme of David's reflections. In four movements, David considers God's omniscience (vv. 1–6), God's omnipresence (vv. 7–12), God's presence from the beginning of his life (vv. 13–18), and the threat of enemies (vv. 19–24). For our purposes, it is important to see how verses 1–12 set up David's profound reflections on his prenatal development.

In verses 1–6, David meditates on God's omniscience: "You know when I sit down and when I rise up; you discern my thoughts from afar," the king writes in verse 2. God is "acquainted with all my ways" (v. 3b). God's knowledge of David is so comprehensive that "even before a word is on my tongue . . . you know it altogether" (v. 4). Although God's omniscience of everything is certainly in view, David appears particularly aware of and overwhelmed by God's knowledge of *him*: "Such knowledge is too wonderful for me; it is high, I cannot attain it" (v. 6). God's knowledge is a personal knowledge; reflecting on it prompts the king to praise.

But not only does God know everything about David; he is also with him wherever he goes. Thus, meditation on God's omniscience leads to reflection on his omnipresence (vv. 7–12).

In verse 7, David asks, "Where shall I go from your Spirit? Or where shall I flee from your presence?" Verses 8–10 directly answer the hypothetical questions: nowhere. There is nowhere that David can go where God will not also be.

Although David cannot physically do what he mentions—ascend to heaven or go to Sheol—the use of this merism enables him, as theologian Daniel Estes notes, to use "impossible conditions to make his point."[32] If David were to ascend to heaven, God is there. If David were to descend to Sheol—the shadowy holding place for the dead—God is there as well.

If verse 8 examined the vertical dimension (heaven and Sheol), verses 9–10 consider the horizontal. Even if David were to use the sun's first light that appears in the east and travel to the extreme west to "dwell in the uttermost parts of the sea," he would still be unable to outrun God (v. 9). Additionally, on the darkest night, God is still with him (vv. 11–12).

In a variety of ways, verses 7–12 communicate David's overarching point: God's presence is everywhere. God's reach extends to the uttermost ends of his creation, and no one, not even Israel's king, can escape or hide from him (v. 10).

To summarize what we've seen so far, David has considered and celebrated God's omniscience and omnipresence. David's meditations are personal; he is not merely considering God's knowledge and presence in a theoretical sense. He acknowledges that God knows *him* and has been with

---

[32] Daniel J. Estes, *Psalms 73–150,* The New American Commentary (Nashville: B&H, 2019), 554.

*him* at every turn. These recognitions lead to the third stanza, the most recognizable pro-life text in Scripture.

### Verses 13–16

In Psalm 139:13–16, David continues to reflect on God's presence. As he reflects on God's knowledge and personal care for him, David recognizes that God has been with him from the very beginning of his life. These considerations lead David to pen some of the most remarkable words in the Bible on the personhood of the unborn. From these verses, two themes emerge—unborn life is fully personal, and God is personally involved in the development of every unborn child.

First, David sees his unborn life as fully personal. The person in his mother's womb was not an impersonal fetus; it was David, whom God was forming and knitting together. From David's perspective, there is a clear continuity from the prenatal person in the womb to the adult person writing the psalm. As John Jefferson Davis explains, "David's praise, spoken from a postnatal perspective (v. 14), assumes his identity with the prenatal individual described in verses 13, 15, and 16."[33]

The personal identity of the unborn child is underscored by the repeated use of the personal and possessive pronouns "I" and "my." The application of first-person pronouns to the unborn child drives home the point that God

---

[33] John Jefferson Davis, *Abortion and the Christian: What Every Believer Should Know* (Phillipsburg, NJ: P&R, 1984), 42. In his reflection on Psalm 139, Davis also writes, "His [David's] language suggests that his personal identity is not restricted to his conscious memory, but extends back beyond conscious recollections, to the earliest time of God's creative control of his prenatal development. These verses strongly imply that personal identity is a continuum, beginning in the womb and extending naturally into postnatal life." Wayne Grudem, in his brief discussion of Psalm 139:13, also notes that David clearly thinks of himself as having been a person while he was growing in his mother's womb. See Wayne Grudem, *Christian Ethics: An Introduction to Biblical Moral Reasoning* (Wheaton, IL: Crossway, 2018), 568.

was forming David in utero. David praises God for forming "*my* inward parts" (v. 13). According to Israel's king, "*My* frame" was not hidden as God saw "*my* unformed substance" (vv. 15–16). God knew the "days that were formed for *me*, when as yet there was none of them" (v. 16, emphasis added).[34]

Second, David understands that his prenatal development is not a blind, haphazard process. Rather, his gestation and birth took place under God's active and watchful superintendence. In fact, God was involved with the smallest details, working like a master craftsman, "forming" and "knitting" David together in his mother's womb. The language of "knitting" in verse 13 is the language of needlework and alludes to the detailed, focused work required in embroidery.[35] God's work of knitting the unborn child together is a careful, deliberate, and skillful work.

The reality of God's personal involvement in the development of every child has implications for understanding the Bible's perspective on the worth and dignity of unborn children. In this passage, the unborn child is not perceived as an inconsequential clump of cells. Instead, the psalmist sees the developing baby as a miracle worth celebrating. For David, pondering the truths in verse 13—God's forming and knitting him in his mother's womb—leads to worshipping the Creator: "I praise you, for I am fearfully and wonderfully made" (v. 14). As W. S. Plumer notes in his 1867 commentary, "The very thought of his creation stirs his soul, and awakens praise."[36] The king cannot help but marvel at God's "wonderful" work in the creation of new human life.

---

[34] In his discussion of this passage, John Frame notes that other passages, including Job 31:15–18, Psalm 22:9, and Hosea 12:3, speak of unborn children as persons. Frame also notes that there are no texts in Scripture that speak of unborn children as anything other than persons. See Frame, *The Doctrine of the Christian Life*, 722.

[35] W. Dennis Tucker Jr. and Jamie A. Grant, *Psalms*, vol. 2, The NIV Application Commentary (Grand Rapids: Zondervan, 2018), 922.

[36] W. S. Plumer, *Psalms*, A Geneva Series Commentary (1867; repr., Edinburgh, UK: Banner of Truth, 2016), 1163.

Commenting on these verses, John Calvin writes, "It is sufficiently clear and obvious that David means that he had been fashioned in a manner wonderful, and calculated to excite both fear and admiration."[37] David perceives that his creation, and by implication the creation of every human being, is a miracle that should elicit awe, reverence, and praise.

Another aspect of the passage that deserves attention is David's description of the womb in verse 15. Recall that David is emphasizing how God has been with him since the very beginning of his life. To this end he explains that his "frame" (ESV) or "bones" (CSB) were not hidden from God when he was made "in secret, intricately woven in the depths of the earth" (v. 15). Most commentators agree that the reference to "depths of the earth" is a metaphor for the place of deepest concealment, i.e., the hiddenness of the womb.[38] Once again, David borrows a term used in embroidery or needlework to describe God's creative work in this concealed place (cf. v. 13b). In fact, the verb translated as "woven together" appears elsewhere in the Old Testament in reference to the embroidery work carried out for the tabernacle (Exod. 26:36; 27:16; 28:39; 35:35). As Tucker and Grant observe, "The intricate work of embroidery, the weaving of varied strands, is meant to parallel the intricate work of human creation as each person is woven into a tapestry."[39]

Finally, David concludes verse 16 by observing that God's eyes saw his "unformed substance." Additionally, he perceives his days were "written . . . when as yet there was none of them." David understands that God's presence with him extends to the earliest moments of his existence and that God had planned the contours of his life before his first breath. The king can rest secure, knowing his days are written in God's book. Reflecting on this aspect

---

[37] John Calvin, *Commentary on the Book of Psalms*, vol. IV (1843; repr., Grand Rapids: Baker, 2005), 214.

[38] For example, see Derek Kidner, *Psalms 73–150*, Tyndale Old Testament Commentaries (Downers Grove, IL: Inter-Varsity, 1975), 502.

[39] Tucker and Grant, *Psalms*, 922.

of God's care for him is overwhelming and leads David to praise God again (vv. 17–18).[40]

## *Luke 1:39–45*

The clearest affirmation of the personhood of the unborn in the New Testament is the narrative of Luke 1. In short, this text is perhaps the most compelling pro-life passage in the entire Bible.

In context, the angel Gabriel tells the virgin Mary she will bear a son through the power of the Holy Spirit: "The angel replied to her, 'The Holy Spirit will come upon you, and the power of the Most High will overshadow you. Therefore, the holy one to be born will be called the Son of God'" (v. 35).

---

[40] Regarding the relevance of Psalm 139 for determining personhood, some scholars, like Richard B. Hays, call for caution, arguing the passage must be interpreted within the poetic genre. This critique is made in a more pointed way by feminist theologian Margaret Kamitsuka, who cautions against extrapolating "a universal claim from a few, mostly poetic, verses in the Hebrew Bible or Luke's nativity stories." See Kamitsuka, *Abortion and the Christian Tradition*, 63. Although Hays is right to remind readers to pay attention to hermeneutics (the discipline of properly interpreting texts), it is unfair to say the passage's "bearing on the abortion issue is very indirect indeed." See Richard B. Hays, *The Moral Vision of the New Testament: A Contemporary Introduction to New Testament Ethics* (New York: Harper Collins, 1996), 148. In contrast to Hays, theologian John Frame argues that Psalm 139 is representative of how the Bible refers to the unborn as persons possessing moral value. Frame cites Job 31:15–18, Psalm 22:9, and Hosea 12:3 as other examples where the Bible speaks of unborn children as persons. See Frame, *The Doctrine of the Christian Life*, 722. Frame makes the obvious point that the Bible never speaks of unborn children as anything other than persons. Along these lines, Derek Kidner, who believes that the "main emphasis" of Psalm 139:13–16 is "our pre-natal fashioning by God," says these verses provide "a powerful reminder of the value he sets on us, even as embryos, and of his planning our end from the beginning." Kidner, *Psalms 73–150*, 503. Kidner goes on to note that "This appears to raise important ethical questions concerning the resort to abortion in the interests of, e.g., social convenience or an 'acceptable' level of health."

After the angel's announcement, Mary immediately goes to visit her relative Elizabeth, who was herself six months pregnant.[41] Luke relates their meeting in verses 39–45:

> In those days Mary set out and hurried to a town in the hill country of Judah where she entered Zechariah's house and greeted Elizabeth. When Elizabeth heard Mary's greeting, the baby leaped inside her, and Elizabeth was filled with the Holy Spirit. Then she exclaimed with a loud cry, "Blessed are you among women, and your child will be blessed! How could this happen to me, that the mother of my Lord should come to me? For you see, when the sound of your greeting reached my ears, the baby leaped for joy inside me. Blessed is she who has believed that the Lord would fulfill what he has spoken to her!"

A natural reading of the biblical text shows that after her encounter with the angel Gabriel, Mary journeyed as quickly as possible to Elizabeth. As Leon Morris explains, "Mary lost no time paying a visit to her kinswoman. . . . She must therefore have set out almost immediately after the angel's visit."[42] Mary's hasty departure suggests she is very early in her pregnancy in Luke 1:39–45. In fact, some scholars believe Mary had been pregnant for less than a month and perhaps for only a week or two when she

---

[41] The cause for Mary's hasty journey has been debated by scholars. Darrell Bock summarizes the common views as (1) Mary left to prevent her neighbors from discovering her pregnancy, (2) the Greek phrase μετὰ σπουδῆς, usually translated "with haste" (ESV), should be rendered "with serious intent," or (3) Mary's prompt departure reflects an instant response to God's leading. See Darrell L. Bock, *Luke 1:1–9:50*, Baker Exegetical Commentary on the New Testament (Grand Rapids: Baker Academic, 1994), 134. Bock himself argues for the third option, which agrees with Robert Stein's contention that "Luke here described Mary as a model believer eagerly responding in obedience to the heavenly message of Luke 1:36." See Robert Stein, *Luke*, The New American Commentary (Nashville: Broadman, 1992), 89.

[42] Leon Morris, *Luke: An Introduction and Commentary*, Tyndale New Testament Commentaries, vol. 3 (1974; repr., Downers Grove, IL: IVP Academic, 2008), 91.

visited Elizabeth.[43] As we will see, this detail takes on additional significance considering the conversation between the two women.

In verse 41, the text says that when Elizabeth heard the greeting of Mary, "the baby leaped inside [Elizabeth]." Elizabeth then exclaims, "Blessed are you among women, and your child will be blessed! How could this happen to me, that the mother of my Lord should come to me?" (vv. 42–43).

Three details of this exchange underscore the profoundly pro-life nature of this passage. First, John the Baptist "leaped" upon hearing Mary's voice. Through Elizabeth's explanation, we learn that the motive for John's leaping response was joy. Evidently, the unborn John felt joy in the presence of his unborn relative. Additionally, John's leaping appears to be the initial fulfillment of Old Testament prophecy.[44] According to Isaiah 40:3–5, the forerunner of the Messiah would herald the arrival of Israel's long-awaited Savior. Recall that this was John's purpose in life—"to make ready for the Lord a prepared people" (Luke 1:17; cf. John 1:6–8, 18–23).[45] Thus, the significance of Luke 1 is that John the Baptist's ministry of preparing the way

---

[43] Davis, *Abortion and the Christian*, 55–56.

[44] In his study of Luke's Gospel, John Calvin comments on the significance of John's leaping, noting, "It is natural that sudden joy, on the part of a pregnant woman, should cause a motion of the child in her womb; but Luke intended to express an extraordinary occurrence." See John Calvin, *Commentary on a Harmony of the Evangelists, Matthew, Mark and Luke* (1843; repr., Grand Rapids: Baker, 2005), 48. A careful reading of verse 41 within the broader context of Luke 1 indicates that the "extraordinary occurrence" is likely that John's ministry as the forerunner of the Messiah has begun.

[45] Some wonder how John's in-utero acknowledgment of Jesus in Luke 1 fits with John 1:31, where John the Baptist says he does not initially know Jesus. On this point, Bock offers a few explanations, including the suggestion that John not knowing Jesus in John 1 may relate only to knowing Jesus's exact position in God's plan. For his full discussion, see Darrell L. Bock, *Luke 1:1–9:50*, Baker Exegetical Commentary on the New Testament (Grand Rapids: Baker Academic, 1994), 135. Of course, the context of John 1 makes it clear that John the Baptist knew Jesus. Two verses before verse 31, John sees Jesus and declares, "Look, the Lamb of God, who takes away the sin of the world!" (John 1:29).

for the Messiah—signaled by a leap of joy—commenced while John was still in utero.

Second, Elizabeth referred to Mary as a mother at a time when most women do not even know they are pregnant.[46] Incredibly, she acknowledged that Mary was the "mother of my Lord." Jesus, in his embryonic state—perhaps even before the time of implantation in the uterus at approximately two weeks—was Elizabeth's "Lord."[47] The use of *kyrios*, the word translated "Lord," seems to function here as a christological title.[48] As biblical scholar John Nolland notes, "Elizabeth here expresses her overwhelmed realization that she is being visited by the one who is pregnant with the messianic child."[49]

In terms of a pro-life ethic, Elizabeth's affirmation of the unborn Jesus as "Lord" shows her understanding that Jesus was not an impersonal, nonhuman entity; rather, he was honored rightly as Lord by both Elizabeth and her unborn baby. As Robert Stein perceptively notes, "It is above all by the resurrection that Mary's child is recognized as Lord (Acts 2:36),

---

[46] Scott Rae makes this point while highlighting the significance of Christ's incarnation for the question of personhood and the unborn. See Scott Rae, *Moral Choices: An Introduction to Ethics*, 3rd ed. (Grand Rapids: Zondervan Academic, 2009), 130.

[47] Davis believes Jesus's prenatal personhood, which is taught in this passage, carries significant implications for understanding the personhood of the unborn. See Davis, *Abortion and the Christian*, 55–57.

[48] Robert Stein, *Luke: An Exegetical and Theological Exposition of Holy Scripture*, The New American Commentary, vol. 24 (Nashville: Broadman, 1992, 90. In his discussion of this passage, Darrell Bock notes that most scholars opt for a "messianic perception" for κύριος, the term used in Luke 1:43. See Bock, *Luke 1:1–9:50*, 137. As David Garland observes, this is the first time "Lord" has been applied to Jesus in Luke's Gospel and is the same term that will be used twenty-three times in the birth narrative to refer to the God of Israel. See David Garland, *Luke*, Zondervan Exegetical Commentary on the New Testament (Grand Rapids: Zondervan, 2011), 93.

[49] John Nolland, *Luke 1:1–9:20*, World Bible Commentary (Dallas: Word, 1989), 67.

although this verse [v. 43] indicates that from his conception he was already Lord."[50]

Third, Elizabeth's choice of words reveals a fundamentally pro-life perspective. In verse 44, she explains that "the baby leaped for joy inside me." The Greek word *brephos* is used to refer to her unborn child. This is the same Greek word used for children after they are born. In fact, the word is also used when Jesus is called a "baby lying in a manger" in Luke 2:16.[51]

A final observation about this passage is that both Elizabeth (v. 41) and the unborn John (v. 15) are filled with the Holy Spirit. By noting this detail, Luke wants his readers to perceive that the reactions of Elizabeth and John are appropriate; they are fitting responses to being in the presence of Jesus, who, although in utero, was the Son of God. Theologically, the implication of Luke 1 is that Jesus's incarnation—the point when the Second Person of the Trinity took on a fully human nature—did not begin at birth. Rather, the incarnation began at conception.

The fact that Jesus's incarnation began in utero can be deduced from what we've already considered in Luke's narrative. John's joyful leaping and Elizabeth's confession of Jesus's lordship are evidence that these witnesses, under the inspiration of the Holy Spirit, understood they were in God's presence by being in the presence of his unborn Son.

In short, the doctrine of the incarnation has profound pro-life implications. As theologian John Frame notes, "Jesus, then, was the incarnate Son of God, the second person of the Trinity, from the moment of his conception by the Holy Spirit. Was he, then, anything less than a person at any point in his conception? Certainly not. From conception onward, he was a

---

[50] Stein, *Luke*, 90.

[51] Other passages include Luke 2:12; 18:15; Acts 7:19; and 2 Timothy 3:15. See Frederick W. Danker, Walter Bauer, and William F. Arndt, *A Greek-English Lexicon of the New Testament and Other Early Christian Literature*, 3rd ed. (Chicago: University of Chicago Press, 2000), 183–84.

divine-human person."[52] In other words, the very means by which God fulfilled Isaiah 7:14—the promise to send Immanuel (God with us)—confirms the Bible's pro-life ethic.

## Additional Pro-Life Passages

Alongside Psalm 139 and Luke 1, additional texts present the Bible's teaching on the personhood of the unborn. This section will examine these passages in canonical order, noting details that contribute to the Bible's overall pro-life ethic.

### *Genesis 25:22–23*

According to Genesis 25, Isaac and Rebekah struggled through a season of infertility. However, God answered Isaac's prayer, and Rebekah conceived. Before the birth of twin boys, the passage says:

---

[52] John Frame, *The Doctrine of the Christian Life*, 724. Likewise, John Jefferson Davis explains, "In the New Testament, the incarnation of Jesus Christ is a profound testimony to God's affirmation of the sanctity of prenatal life. . . . His human history, like ours, began at *conception*. . . . The significant point is that God chose to begin the process of incarnation there, rather than at some other point, thus affirming the significance of that starting point for human life." See John Jefferson Davis, *Evangelical Ethics: Issues Facing the Church Today*, 4th ed. (Phillipsburg, NJ: P&R, 2015), 152, emphasis original. Both Wayne Grudem and Scott Rae make similar points in their discussion of Luke 1. According to Grudem, "These verses are significant because they mean that the incarnation of Christ did not begin when he was a newborn baby, a small child, a teenager, or an adult man. Rather, the divine nature of God the Son was joined to the human nature of Jesus from the moment of his conception in Mary's womb." See Grudem, *Christian Ethics*, 570. Likewise, Scott Rae writes, "The significance of the incarnation though likely not grasped in its fullness, is nonetheless recognized, not at Jesus' birth, but far earlier. . . . That is, the incarnation is recognized as having begun months prior to Jesus' actual birth." See Scott Rae, *Moral Choices: An Introduction to Ethics*, 3rd ed. (Grand Rapids: Zondervan Academic, 2009), 130.

> But the children inside her struggled with each other, and she said, "Why is this happening to me?" So she went to inquire of the LORD. And the LORD said to her:
>
> Two nations are in your womb;
> two peoples will come from you and be separated.
> One people will be stronger than the other,
> and the older will serve the younger.

In terms of its contribution to the Bible's pro-life ethic, this passage demonstrates that unborn children can be the subjects of God's election and calling. Although they were still in utero, God had plans for the twin boys and could speak of them already as ancestors of "two nations."[53] By God's sovereign choice, Jacob, while still in utero, was chosen over his brother to receive God's special covenant promises. Jacob's pre-birth election, which was before conscious faith, repentance, or any works by the future patriarch, reinforces the truth that God's choice in election is not contingent on human action but wholly a result of his sovereign grace.

Reflecting on this passage centuries later, the apostle Paul marveled at God's election of Jacob, writing, "For though her sons had not been born yet or done anything good or bad, so that God's purpose according to election might stand—not from works but from the one who calls—she was told, **The older will serve the younger.** As it is written: **I have loved Jacob, but I have hated Esau**" (Rom. 9:11–13). As Paul's writing makes clear, the marks typically associated with personhood—intelligence, self-control, capacity to relate to others, etc.—are absent in Genesis 25. Jacob and Esau are in utero and have not had an opportunity to do anything good or bad. Yet to demonstrate that election is God's prerogative, God sovereignly elected Jacob before his birth.[54]

In summary, this passage provides a remarkable glimpse into how God himself views the unborn; Jacob was not an impersonal amalgamation of

---

[53] Victor Hamilton discusses this point in his Genesis commentary. See Victor P. Hamilton, *The Book of Genesis* (Grand Rapids: Eerdmans, 1995), 176–79.

[54] Davis develops this point carefully in Davis, *Abortion and the Christian*, 47.

human tissue. He was a moral being capable of being chosen by God for a personal relationship.

## *Judges 13*

Judges 13 narrates the birth narrative of Samson. In verses 3–5, the angel of the Lord informs Manoah's wife that she will conceive and have a son. The angel instructs the previously barren woman to "be careful and drink no wine or strong drink, and eat nothing unclean, for behold you shall conceive and bear a son. . . . for the child shall be a Nazirite to God from the womb" (vv. 4–5 ESV). Because Samson will be a "Nazirite to God from the womb," his mother must keep the Nazirite restrictions herself throughout the pregnancy. These stipulations, outlined in Numbers 6:1–21, traditionally were undertaken voluntarily and applied for a limited time.[55] In Samson's case, these rules applied from conception; evidently, he would be defiled if his mother disobeyed the angel's order.

Thus, Judges 13 contributes to the Bible's pro-life ethic by providing another example of God relating to one of Israel's future leaders before his birth. Samson was to be set apart as a "Nazirite to God from the womb." The angel's careful instructions show that God was concerned about the child's holiness in utero. This is further evidence that God relates to unborn children as persons. As Daniel Block observes, "Reflective of the biblical conviction that a child is a special creation of God from the moment of conception, the same standards that will govern his postnatal life will apply to his prenatal condition as well."[56] Likewise, John Frame draws pro-life applications from Judges 13, noting, "Thus, Samson, like David, is a person from conception. As there is no reason to think that Samson and David are

---

[55] Arthur E. Cundall and Leon Morris discuss the Nazirite vow and the uniqueness of Samson's calling as a "Nazirite to God from the womb." See their discussion in Arthur E. Cundall and Leon Morris, *Judges and Ruth: An Introduction and Commentary* (Downers Grove, IL: IVP Academic, 2008), 151–52.

[56] Daniel Block, *Judges, Ruth* (Nashville: B&H, 1999), 402.

exceptions to the general rule, we should conclude that all unborn children are persons from conception."[57]

## *Job 3, 10, and 31*

Verses in Job presume a continuity between an unborn child and the adult person experiencing suffering. In Job 3:3, Job laments: "May the day I was born perish, and the night that said, 'A boy is conceived.'" In the throes of his anguish, Job uses poetic language to lament both the day of his birth and the night of his conception. For Job, birth and conception constitute his origin and are thus inseparable. In other words, the child who was born and the child who was conceived are the same person.[58]

---

[57] Frame, *The Doctrine of the Christian Life*, 723.

[58] In terms of invoking Job 3 and poetic texts as evidence of the Bible's pro-life ethic, Scott Rae notes, "Although it is true that these passages use poetic devices to make their point, one cannot dismiss such texts simply because they are using figurative language. Poetry is difficult to interpret in many places, but its figurative language is no reason to minimize its contribution. Figurative language always makes a literal point, and though it is not appropriate to take figures of speech in a woodenly literal way, they do have an underlying literal point that is being made, which . . . is the parallel between conception and birth." See Rae, *Moral Choice*, 136. Rae's comment about figurative language conveying a literal point is a helpful reminder; feminist theologians routinely dismiss the relevance of texts such as Psalm 139:13–16 to the abortion debate due to their poetic nature. For example, Kira Schlesinger argues, "It is highly unlikely that the author of Psalm 139 wrote verses 13–16 to address when life begins or the moral status of a fertilized egg, zygote, or fetus. The language and imagery that surround these verses makes a point about God as almighty and loving Creator. . . . Verses 13–16 are poetry that tell us that God is the all-knowing Creator of everything that is, not a literal, objective statement about the personhood of an embryo or fetus." See Kira Schlesinger, *Pro-Choice and Christian: Reconciling Faith, Politics, and Justice* (Louisville: Westminster John Knox, 2017), 57–58. Likewise, in her discussion of Psalm 139:13–16, Beverly Harrison writes, "Such powerful poetic metaphor beautifully conjures up the depth and all-inclusiveness of divine love, and, as a result, this passage has achieved a well-deserved place in both Jewish ritual and Christian liturgy. But biblicists, invoking it as evidence for the full personhood of fetuses, confuse poetry with science and fail to

Another similar passage is Job 10:8, where Job cries, "Your hands shaped me and formed me. Will you now turn and destroy me?" Amid intense suffering, Job recognizes that it was God who "shaped" and "formed" him. From Job's perspective, the same person who was fashioned in his mother's womb is the man who is now undergoing difficult trials. In other words, there is continuity between the preborn baby and the adult sufferer.

Finally, in Job 31:15, Job defends the way he has treated his servants by noting: "Did not the one who made me in the womb also make them? Did not the same God form us both in the womb?" Job understands that unborn life—his own and his servants'—has great value to God.

### *Psalm 22:10*

Returning to the book of Psalms, David confessed that his dependency on God began at the very beginning of his life, noting, "On you was I cast from my birth, and from my mother's womb you have been my God" (22:10 ESV). Significantly, David traced his relationship with God to before his birth; God was "my God" while David was in utero. Psalm 71, which contains several references and allusions to other psalms, conveys the same thought: "Upon you I have leaned from before my birth; you are he who took me from my mother's womb" (v. 6 ESV). Similar to Psalm 22, the psalmist in Psalm 71 acknowledges that dependence on God preceded his birth.

### *Psalm 51:5–6*

Another passage that deepens our understanding of how the Bible sees the unborn is Psalm 51:5–6 where David wrote, "Indeed, I was guilty when I

---

notice that, in the process, they are transmuting imagery and metaphor into causal and propositional modes of discourse." See Harrison, *Our Right to Choose*, 70.

was born; I was sinful when my mother conceived me. Surely you desire integrity in the inner self, and you teach me wisdom deep within." In these verses David is confessing his adultery with Bathsheba; the murder of her husband, Uriah; and the entire web of lies he used to cover up his sin. Confronted by Nathan (2 Samuel 12), David understands his guilt and repents. His heartfelt lament in Psalm 51 shows that he understands most fundamentally he has sinned against God (v. 4). As he pleads for mercy, David acknowledges the profound depth of his own sinfulness. For our purposes, David's probing reflections on his sin underscore a theological truth with pro-life implications. Specifically, in verse 5, David traces his sinfulness to the very beginning of his life—to the very hour of his conception.

As David considers his sin, he recognizes that he has always been a sinner before God, including as an unborn baby in utero (v. 5). Although some scholars have argued that the word in verse 5 translated "sinful" refers to David's mother, the entire context of the passage precludes this interpretation. Psalm 51 is unmistakably a lament by David about his sin against God; no one else is in view.[59] David is saying that from the moment of his conception he possessed a sin nature.

---

[59] In his commentary on Psalm 51, Archdeacon Anthony S. Aglen suggests an alternative interpretation for verse 5, noting, "The later rabbis, combining this verse with the mystery hanging over the origin and nature of David's mother, represent him as born in adultery. . . . The argument for a personal origin to the psalm from this verse seems strong; but in Ps. cxxix. 1, and frequently, the community is personified as an individual growing from youth to age, and so may here speak of its far-back idolatrous ancestry as the mother who conceived it in sin." See Anthony S. Aglen, "Psalms," in *An Old Testament Commentary for English Readers*, ed. Charles John Ellicott (New York: E. P. Dutton, 1884), 4:161. Contra Aglen, Derek Kidner argues, "David is, of course, not speaking against his mother in particular, nor against the process of conception." Derek Kidner, *Psalms 1–72*, Tyndale Old Testament Commentaries (Downers Grove, IL: Inter-Varsity, 1973), 208. Also see Plumer, who notes, "To say that David is here merely publishing the sins of one or both of his parents is trifling with sacred things." Plumer, *Psalms*, 557.

In David's confession, John Calvin sees biblical evidence for the doctrine of original sin: "The passage affords a striking testimony in proof of original sin entailed by Adam upon the whole human family. . . . David does not charge it upon his parents, nor trace his crime to them, but sists [*sic*] himself before the Divine tribunal, confesses that he was formed in sin, and that he was a transgressor ere he saw the light of the world."[60] He adds, "David was far from seeking to invent an apology for his sin, when he traced it back to the period of his conception."[61] For Calvin, Psalm 51:5 suggests that a sin nature is present in every person from the moment of conception. This acknowledgment, by implication, ascribes moral significance to the unborn. In terms of a pro-life ethic, Calvin's insight aligns with John Frame's contention that sin is "never a property of things, only of persons."[62] In other words, the presence of a personal sin nature indicates a person, who, although fallen, is a moral being with inherent value.

Another detail of this passage is David's use, once again, of personal pronouns to refer to himself in utero: "*I* was sinful when *my* mother conceived *me*" (v. 5, emphasis added). The entity in the womb was not impersonal; the psalmist consciously personalized the unborn and saw the baby as a distinct person from the moment of his conception.

---

[60] John Calvin, *Commentary on the Book of Psalms*, vol. 2 (1843; repr., Grand Rapids: Baker, 2005), 290.

[61] Calvin, *Commentary on the Book of Psalms*, 2:292.

[62] According to Frame, "Sin in Scripture is a personal quality, never an impersonal one. It is never a property of things, only of persons. It is personal estrangement from God on account of disobedience." For Frame, like Calvin, these verses provide support for the doctrine of original sin: "The Christian church has found in this text one of the chief Old Testament witnesses to the doctrine of original sin: that each of us inherits the guilt of Adam's sin and his sinful nature." See Frame, *The Doctrine of the Christian Life*, 722. Writing in the nineteenth century, Plumer also saw original sin taught in this passage: "That the doctrine of original and universal depravity was taught from the first is clear from Gen. v. 3; vi. 5; viii. 21; Job xiv. 4; xv. 14; xxv. 4. That David embraced it is clear from his writings, v. 5; Ps. lviii. 3." See Plumer, *Psalms*, 557.

But the unborn David was not only a sinner; he was also the recipient of God's moral instruction in utero. Old Testament scholars agree that the Hebrew words in verse 6 rendered "inner self" (CSB) and "innermost being" (ESV) do not refer to David but to his mother's womb.[63] Old Testament scholar Peter Gentry translates verse 6 as follows: "You desired truth in the smeared-over place, you make me to know wisdom in the bottled-up place." According to Gentry, the Hebrew words he renders "smeared-over place" and "bottled-up place" are obvious references to the human womb.[64]

Gentry argues that the literary structure of verses 5–6 teaches the following: First, David confessed his sin. Then he acknowledged his own impotence—or moral inadequacy—that had been part of his nature since before birth. Next, he prayed for forgiveness. Finally, he prayed for power to overcome his moral impotence. "Apparently the divine image is there in the womb so that moral factors are entailed in the fetus," explains Gentry.[65] In other words, David, even in his embryological state, by virtue of his status as a moral being (distinct in his own personhood from the moment of conception), had the moral law already inscribed within his being. In his mother's womb, David was a moral being and an inheritor of Adam's sin whose relationship to the moral law of God had already begun.[66]

---

[63] Davis, *Abortion and the Christian*, 51.

[64] Personal correspondence with Dr. Peter J. Gentry, August 22, 2019. Gentry served as professor of Old Testament interpretation at The Southern Baptist Theological Seminary in Louisville, Kentucky, for twenty-two years (1999–2021).

[65] Personal correspondence with Gentry. For the full exegesis and proof of Gentry's argument on the literary structure of Psalm 51, see the exhaustive treatment in Edward R. Dalglish, *Psalm Fifty-One in the Light of Ancient Near Eastern Patternism* (Leiden, NL: Brill, 1962), 121.

[66] Some have asked what sin the unborn David could have been guilty of. According to John Frame, it is in these verses that the Christian church has found one of the chief Old Testament witnesses to the doctrine of original sin: that each of us inherits the guilt of Adam's sin and his sinful nature. For the full discussion, see Frame, *The Doctrine of the Christian Life*, 723.

## *Isaiah 49:1*

In addition to texts from the Poetic Books, passages from the Prophetic Books of the Old Testament also contribute to the Bible's overall pro-life message, including Isaiah 49:1. Setting the passage in context will assist in seeing its pro-life dimensions.

Having previously introduced the figure of the "Servant of the Lord," chapters 42–48 rehearse the sinfulness of Israel, predict the rise of a pagan king who will aid in Israel's return out of Babylonian captivity, and prophesy about the fall of Babylon. In chapter 49, Isaiah returns to the theme of the Servant.[67]

Isaiah 49:1 says, "Coasts and islands, listen to me; distant peoples, pay attention. The LORD called me before I was born. He named me while I was in my mother's womb." In context, Isaiah is shifting to a new section (chaps. 49–55) that will focus on the calling and ministry of the Servant of the Lord. Whereas the nation of Israel had been previously referred to as a servant (chaps. 41–48), Isaiah introduces and expands on the role of another Servant, one who will be obedient and faithful. A few specific details of this verse deserve our attention.

First, Isaiah identifies this second Servant as an individual. The language used in verse 1b provides evidence that Isaiah is describing a single figure. Speaking from the perspective of the Servant, Isaiah says God "called me before I was born." The Hebrew word translated "called" is *qârâ'*. Elsewhere in Isaiah the word is translated "summoned" (13:3 ESV) or "named" (14:20 ESV). Context makes the meaning clear: God has appointed the Servant to a special task.[68] The Servant explains that he was called "from the womb"

---

[67] Most scholars see chapters 49–55 as constituting a new section in Isaiah. For example, see John N. Oswalt, *The Book of Isaiah: Chapters 40–66* (Grand Rapids: Eerdmans, 1998), 286.

[68] Evidently, the implications of this mission have far-reaching implications, which is why the "coastlands" and "peoples from afar" are told to listen in verse 1a.

and "from the body of my mother" (ESV). Like Jeremiah (whom we will look at next), the Servant's calling precedes his birth. God has plans for the Servant—understood in an opaque, incomplete way in Isaiah's day—that would usher in God's salvific purposes for Israel and the world. Later in verse 5, the Servant will reiterate that God "formed me from the womb to be his servant."[69] From before birth, the Servant has been marked for special service in God's kingdom.

Second, the Servant says that God "named" him while in utero. The word used here is *zâkar*, which has been translated "spoken" (NIV), "made mention of" (NKJV), and "named" (CSB, ESV, NASB). The term is translated "remember" in other places in Isaiah (17:10; 23:16; 38:3; 46:9). By saying "he named me," the Servant is saying that God designated him. God's "naming" of the Servant implies an appointing or commissioning. As John Oswalt explains, "Thus a name is not merely mentioned, but carefully assigned and recorded."[70] In terms of contributing to the Bible's pro-life ethic, the significance is that the Servant's naming or appointing occurred while he was still "in my mother's womb." In other words, the Servant, while in utero, was a moral being whom God related to personally.

Finally, most commentators believe that the Servant featured in Isaiah 49–55 is the Messiah, who is revealed in the New Testament as the Lord Jesus Christ.[71] If this interpretation is correct, Isaiah 49:1 is referring to Jesus's calling as the Servant of the Lord. Significantly, this means that the Servant of the Lord (i.e., Jesus), is "named" and appointed while in

---

[69] Worth noting is that the word translated "formed" in verse 5 is (יָצַר, yâtsar), which is the same Hebrew word used in Genesis 2:2, Psalm 139:16, and Jeremiah 1:5. The context and word choice lead to the conclusion that the Servant was formed and fashioned in utero for a specific, God-ordained purpose.

[70] Oswalt, *The Book of Isaiah*, 289.

[71] On the Servant's identity, see Oswalt, *The Book of Isaiah*, 289–90. See also the discussions in J. Alec Motyer, *Isaiah: An Introduction and Commentary* (Downers Grove, IL: IVP Academic, 1999), 347–51; and Edward Young, *The Book of Isaiah* (Grand Rapids: Eerdmans, 1972), 266ff.

the womb. Although God's plan of sending his Son originated in eternity past, it is nevertheless noteworthy to see the personal language of calling and naming applied to the Servant, whose identity is none other than Jesus Christ.

## *Jeremiah 1:4–5*

At the onset of Jeremiah, God commissions the Old Testament prophet. The careful wording of the passage reveals God's intimate and personal relationship with the unborn prophet and further illustrates the pro-life perspective of Scripture. In Jeremiah 1:4–5, the prophet wrote, "Now the word of the LORD came to me, saying, 'Before I formed you in the womb I knew you, and before you were born I consecrated you; I appointed you a prophet to the nations'" (ESV).

In its historical context, the book of Jeremiah was written in the years leading up to the Babylonian invasion and the fall of Jerusalem in 586 BC. Living during a time of political, economic, and societal upheaval, Jeremiah's ministry was characterized by opposition, unresponsiveness, and apathy. Aware of the challenges ahead, the Lord provided Jeremiah with a clear mandate at the beginning of his ministry.

Jeremiah recounts his calling in verse 4, noting, "Now the word of the LORD came to me." Readers familiar with Jeremiah's ministry know that the prophet's forthcoming work would be marked by difficulty.[72] Thus, at the onset, God made it clear to Jeremiah that his prophetic ministry was divinely authorized. As the days became demanding and enemies fought against him

---

[72] In the course of his ministry, Jeremiah would be beaten and put in stocks (Jer. 20:1–2), the king would burn Jeremiah's scroll (Jer. 36:23), Jeremiah would be left to die in a mud pit (Jer. 38:6), and those in positions of authority would call him a liar (Jer. 43:2). God even told Jeremiah that the people would not listen to his message (Jer. 7:27).

(see v. 19), Jeremiah's calling would ground and sustain him.[73] For our purposes, this calling continues the Bible's unmistakable pro-life ethic.

In verse 5, God tells Jeremiah: "Before I formed you in the womb I knew you, and before you were born I consecrated you; I appointed you a prophet to the nations" (ESV). This summary of Jeremiah's call is theologically and practically significant. Specifically, four key phrases are used to describe God's relationship with Jeremiah before the prophet's birth. Each of them aids in understanding the pro-life implications of the passage.

First, verse 5 mentions the forming of the prophet: "Before I formed you." The Hebrew term employed here (*yâtsar*) connotes fashioning or molding. In other places throughout Jeremiah's prophecy, the word refers to the care and skill of a potter (Jer. 18:2; 19:11). Like an experienced potter, God fashioned and molded Jeremiah "in the womb." The word for "womb" is the same word David used in Psalm 139:13 when he described his own development. Like David, Jeremiah was the object of God's personal care as he developed in utero.[74]

Second, the text says, "I knew you" (rendered "I chose you" in the CSB). Before God "formed" the prophet, he "chose" or "knew" him. The term used for "knew" (*yâda'*) has a wide range of meaning in the Old Testament. The word often indicates more than simple intellectual knowledge and includes an aspect of personal commitment. In fact, this is the same word used to describe intimate relations between a husband and wife (Gen. 4:1) as well as God's commitment to Israel: "I have known only you out of all the clans of the earth" (Amos 3:2a).

---

[73] As J. A. Thompson explains, "If ever Jeremiah in later days were overtaken by despair he could know that the divine purpose for him reached back before his birth." See Thompson, *The Book of Jeremiah* (Grand Rapids: Eerdmans, 1980), 145.

[74] On this point, Philip Ryken observes, "Jeremiah had biological parents, of course, but God himself fashioned and knit him together in his mother's womb. Telling children who ask where babies come from that they come from God is good theology." Philip Ryken, *Jeremiah and Lamentations* (Wheaton, IL: Crossway, 2001), 20.

In Jeremiah 1:5, God stresses to Jeremiah that before he was born or even conceived, God knew him. As theologian Philip Ryken explains, "In some ineffable way, God has personal knowledge of the individual that precedes conception."[75] In the mind of God, our lives existed before our first breath. As David said in Psalm 139:16, God knew every one of our days "when as yet there was none of them" (ESV). Before our first day, first smile, or first cry, God knew us and, as we will see next, has specific plans and purposes for our lives.[76]

Third, God said, "I set you apart before you were born." The relevant term used here (*qâdash*) means to be set apart, dedicated, or sanctified. Not only had God known Jeremiah before the prophet's birth, but God also set him apart for a specific purpose. The inclusion of the phrase "before you were born"—where the temporal preposition "before" appears for the second time in verse 5—emphasizes that Jeremiah's consecration, his being set apart for special service, occurred before his birth.[77]

Significantly, God's intentional setting apart of Jeremiah is not unique to the Old Testament prophet. In fact, the idea of God choosing and appointing people for various forms of service is a theme present throughout the Bible. Moreover, the doctrine of election teaches that God elects all believers to salvation. As Philip Ryken notes, God's election of Jeremiah to service is like God's election of every believer to salvation. Citing John 15:16 and Ephesians 1:3–4, which both speak of the election of believers, Ryken says,

---

[75] Ryken, *Jeremiah and Lamentations*, 20.

[76] In Jeremiah's case, God knew that a son of a priest from the village of Anathoth would one day stand as Yahweh's mouthpiece before stubborn and unrepentant kings and their sycophants and lackeys.

[77] J. A. Thompson argues that the verb translated "consecrated" by the ESV "gathers about it another aspect of commitment." Thompson explains, "Basically the root *qdš* is concerned with setting something apart from all other uses to a specific use. It is therefore of significance in the religious sphere where persons, places, things, days, seasons can be set apart (consecrated) for Yahweh. Once set apart, these items were for the sole use of Yahweh." See Thompson, *The Book of Jeremiah*, 145–46.

"God not only knows you, he chose you; and he did so long before you were ever conceived."[78]

Fourth, verse 5 concludes, "I appointed you a prophet to the nations." The relevant Hebrew term *nâthan* has been rendered "appointed" (CSB, ESV, NASB, NIV) and "ordained" (NKJV) by English translators. In Hebrew, the word can mean to give, set, ascribe, or assign. In context, the term conveys the idea of God giving Jeremiah to the nations. Jeremiah's ministry—unlike most prophets called in the Old Testament—would extend beyond Judah and Israel and include Gentile nations.[79] Thus, God's setting apart of Jeremiah for service, which God set into place before the prophet's birth, would have international significance.

In summary, Jeremiah's calling provides further proof that God has a personal relationship with developing unborn children. In utero, God "forms," "knows," "sets apart," and "appoints." God had a personal relationship with the unborn prophet, similar to how he would relate to him as an adult. In other words, there was a clear continuity between prenatal and postnatal Jeremiah; the unborn prophet possessed the same calling he would exercise later in life.

---

[78] Ryken, *Jeremiah and Lamentations*, 21. Notably, theologians who defend abortion dismiss Jeremiah's calling as unique. For example, Margaret Kamitsuka argues, "[T]he most [William Kurz] (or other pro-life authors) can succeed in proving is a pattern of biblical 'type scenes' about prenatal commissioning of particular important individuals. However, to extrapolate from this biblical literary motif a claim about God's universal call to all uterine life is an unwarranted hermeneutical leap that would strike many readers as a thinly disguised eisegetical attempt to claim biblical evidence for the idea one brought to one's reading of the text." See Kamitsuka, *Abortion and the Christian Tradition*, 64–65.

[79] On this point, Walter Kaiser observes, "The call to be a prophet to the nations was a distinctive appointment to say the least. Instead of what might otherwise be regarded as a provincial message appropriate only for Israel, here was an appointment and a message for the Gentile nations at large as well." See Walter C. Kaiser Jr., *Walking the Ancient Paths: A Commentary on Jeremiah* (Bellingham, WA: Lexham, 2019), 35.

## *Galatians 1:15–16*

The language of "calling" and "setting apart" from before birth appears in the New Testament as well. For example, Paul noted that God set him apart for service before he was born, explaining, "But when God, who from my mother's womb set me apart and called me by his grace, was pleased to reveal his Son in me, so that I could preach him among the Gentiles, I did not immediately consult with anyone" (Gal. 1:15–16).

In context, Paul was giving a brief biographical sketch explaining his conversion to Christianity. Specifically, Paul was seeking to establish his apostolic independence, especially from the Jerusalem church. In verse 15, he emphasizes that he was set apart and called "from my mother's womb." According to New Testament scholar Douglas Moo, Paul was intentionally drawing on the language of Isaiah 49:1 and Jeremiah 1:5 to explain his own apostolic calling. As Moo explains, "Paul's dependence on these texts makes it very likely that he is claiming to have been 'set apart' 'before he was born.'"[80] Reminiscent of Jeremiah's prenatal appointing, Paul understood that before his birth, God had set him apart and purposed him to preach; before the apostle's own cognizance of the divine plan, God was relating to and working in Paul's life.

As we've observed elsewhere, the personal pronouns in the text are significant. The "me" in utero who is set apart and called by grace is the same "me" who encounters Jesus ("was pleased to reveal his Son in me") and subsequently preaches the gospel to the Gentiles, travels to Arabia, and returns to Damascus (Gal. 1:16–17). This is yet another example of Scripture affirming continuity between the prenatal person in the womb and the adult author of Scripture.

---

[80] Douglas Moo, *Galatians*, Baker Exegetical Commentary on the New Testament (Grand Rapids: Baker Academic, 2013), 104.

## *Ephesians 1:3–4*

Finally, in Ephesians 1, Paul makes a remarkable statement with far-reaching implications for the Bible's pro-life ethic. In verses 3–4, he wrote, "Blessed is the God and Father of our Lord Jesus Christ, who has blessed us with every spiritual blessing in the heavens in Christ. For he chose us in him, before the foundation of the world, to be holy and blameless in love before him."

At the onset of Ephesians, Paul praises God for the spiritual blessings that Christians enjoy (v. 3). According to Paul, Christians now have "every spiritual blessing in the heavens in Christ." How do Christians receive these blessings? Undoubtedly, many would answer that Christians receive these blessings by believing in Christ and repenting of sin. That, of course, is true. But Paul does not begin with faith or repentance. Neither does he start with the work of Christ on behalf of sinners. Instead, as Martyn Lloyd-Jones observes, "[Paul] goes right back into eternity, before the foundation of the world; and he starts with that which has been done by God the Father."[81]

Thus, according to Paul, those who enjoy these spiritual blessings do so because they have been chosen by God. In other words, how is it that anyone escapes the consequences of sin and God's wrath? God chose them. And when did God choose them to be delivered from sin and appoint them unto salvation? Before the "foundation of the world." This means that in a real, yet ineffable, way, God's relationship with each person begins before development in the womb. Rather, as we've seen from our discussion of Psalm 139:13–16 and Jeremiah 1:4–5, God knows and calls us even before conception. The Bible's teaching on election shows that God sovereignly chose those whom he would save before they took their first breath, before they were born, and even before they were conceived. Although the timing and means are debated, God's election of sinners unto salvation in eternity past simply demonstrates, once again,

---

[81] D. Martyn Lloyd-Jones, *God's Ultimate Purpose: An Exposition of Ephesians 1:1–23* (Grand Rapids: Baker, 1995), 82.

that God is intimately and personally involved with each of us from the earliest possible moment.[82]

## Response to Counterarguments

Before concluding the chapter, it is worth responding to four of the most popular claims put forward by pro-abortion theologians and activists. If true, these claims would undermine the thesis that the Bible is pro-life from cover to cover. Although often articulated by learned scholars, these arguments ultimately fail to prove that the Bible is either pro-choice or neutral on abortion.

[82] Although space does not permit for an extended discussion about the doctrine of election, I am simply noting that Scripture teaches that in eternity past, God appointed the elect unto salvation (Acts 4:28; Rom. 8:29, 30; 1 Cor. 2:7). Major evangelical commentators elaborate on this point, including F. F. Bruce, who explains in his commentary, "It was in Christ, then, that God chose his people 'before the world's foundation.' This phrase . . . denotes the divine act of election as taking place in eternity. Time belongs to the created order: believers' present experience of the blessings bestowed by God is the fulfillment on the temporal plane of his purpose of grace toward them conceived in eternity." See F. F. Bruce, *The Epistles to the Colossians, to Philemon, and to the Ephesians*, Eerdmans Classic Biblical Commentaries (1984; repr., Grand Rapids: Eerdmans, 2020), 254. Likewise, Ian Hamilton explains the implications of Ephesians 1:4 by noting, "Salvation does not begin with my choice of Christ, but with God's choice of me. 'Before the foundation of the world,' before you or I or anyone was thought of, far less born, the Father chose us in Christ (v. 4)." See Ian Hamilton, *Ephesians*, The Lectio Continua Expository Commentary on the New Testament (Grand Rapids: Reformation Heritage Books, 2017), 20. Martyn Lloyd-Jones concludes his lengthy discussion of Ephesians 1:4 by drawing attention to the joy it elicits: "Were I to believe that my future is dependent upon myself and my decisions I would tremble in fear; but I thank God that I know that I am in His hand. . . . It is because I know that before time began, before the foundation of the world, He looked at me and saw me and selected me, and in His mind gave me to Christ. . . . That is why all this matters; my sense of security and my joy depend upon it." See Lloyd-Jones, *God's Ultimate Purpose*, 92. For Lloyd-Jones's full discussion on Ephesians 1:4, see 81–105.

### *Claim #1: Noah's Flood and the Conquest of Canaan Prove God Is Not Pro-Life*

One argument leveled against pro-life Christians is that the Bible contains examples of God-sanctioned killings. An article published by the Freedom from Religion Foundation contends:

> We know that God killed millions of unborn children and their pregnant mothers-to-be in the Noachian deluge, the conquest of Canaan, the incineration of Sodom and Gomorrah and in 20 major slaughters described in the bible. . . . It can be concluded from this ghastly program of human annihilation that the God of the bible is the greatest mass murderer in history and that he does not care about unborn children or living children or living adults.[83]

How should Christians respond to these claims? Although space does not allow for an in-depth apologetic of Noah's flood, the conquest of Canaan, or the Old Testament wars, the Bible provides an explanation for these events that does not compromise the pro-life ethic we have seen elsewhere.

First, the Bible presents Noah's flood as God's just judgment on the wickedness of humanity. According to Genesis 6:11, the pre-flood world was "corrupt in God's sight, and the earth was filled with wickedness." Moreover, "every inclination of the human mind was nothing but evil all the time" (Gen. 6:5). Although the concept of sin offends modern sensibilities, the Bible presents humanity's rebellion against God as an egregious affront to his holiness that merits judgment. Given the shocking decadence and depravity of pre-flood culture, the flood—which, admittedly, is one of the most graphic displays of God's judgment in the Bible—was a just response.[84]

---

[83] Brian Bolton, "God Is So Not 'Pro-Life,'" Freedom from Religion Foundation, accessed April 4, 2024, https://ffrf.org/fttoday/november-2015/articles-november-2015/god-is-so-not-pro-life/.

[84] In his commentary on Genesis, Kenneth Mathews notes that Genesis 6:11 makes it clear that "The justification for the calamity is the complete moral

Second, the people of Noah's generation were given many chances to repent. First Peter 3:20 teaches that "God patiently waited in the days of Noah while the ark was being prepared." Additionally, 2 Peter 2:5 indicates Noah preached righteousness in the years before the deluge. These passages suggest that if anyone had repented, they would have been spared judgment alongside Noah and his family. The fact that no one repented is evidence of how corrupt the world had become.

The massive destruction and loss of life brought about by the flood reveal God's holiness, the wickedness of sin, and God's righteous judgment upon sin. The fact that the floodwaters fell on children and unborn babies is heartrending. However, the context of the flood narrative reminds us that all death is a consequence of human sin. Ultimately, every person, including every child and baby drowned in the flood, died because of the pre-flood world's wicked rebellion against God.[85]

Like Noah's flood, the conquest of Canaan is often invoked as evidence that the God of the Old Testament was vengeful and violent.[86] However, the conquest of Canaan must be understood within its place in the biblical

---

corruption of the human family and the defilement of the earth." See Kenneth A. Mathews, *Genesis 1–11:26*, The New American Commentary, vol. 1A (Nashville: B&H, 1996), 359.

[85] Notably, the death of children and unborn babies in the flood is also a form of mercy; given the Bible's teaching about the age of accountability, I believe that children lost in the flood were spared eternal damnation in hell. For a helpful and pastoral article on the age of accountability, see R. Albert Mohler Jr. and Daniel L. Akin, "The Salvation of the 'Little Ones': Do Infants Who Die Go to Heaven?," AlbertMohler.com, July 16, 2009, https://albertmohler.com/2009/07/16/the-salvation-of-the-little-ones-do-infants-who-die-go-to-heaven/.

[86] In recent years, some pastors, including Andy Stanley, have characterized the entire Old Testament as a "stumbling block" to faith. According to Stanley, "The Christian faith doesn't need to be propped up by the Jewish Scriptures. In a post-Christian context, our faith actually does better without old covenant support." He goes on to argue, "When it comes to stumbling blocks to faith, the Old Testament is right up there at the top of the list. It's usually a contender for second place right behind pain and suffering." Andy Stanley, *Irresistible: Reclaiming the New that Jesus Unleashed for the World* (Grands Rapids: Zondervan, 2020), 278, 280.

storyline. In context, the wars against the Canaanites occurred after the exodus and the wilderness wandering. As the Israelites prepared to enter the Promised Land, God instructed them to drive out and "completely destroy" the inhabitants of the land (Deut. 7:1–6 cf. Deut. 6:19; 12:3; Num. 33:51–52).

Although devoting the Canaanites to destruction (i.e., placing them "under the ban") appears ethically problematic, the Bible provides important context and a rationale for the command. First, Scripture reveals that the idolatry of the Canaanites was a long-standing, worsening reality. In Genesis, God explicitly told Abram that his offspring would live in a foreign country and be oppressed for 400 years before returning to the land promised to them. One of the reasons God gave for this lengthy travail was "the iniquity of the Amorites has not yet reached its full measure" (Gen. 15:16). In other words, the sobering reality is that God was patient with the Canaanite nations and that his judgment had been building for centuries. By the time of the conquest, the pagan inhabitants had reached the point of no return and were ripe for judgment.[87] Thus, Israel's conquest of the land was God's means of executing divine justice; it occurred within the moral framework of punishment, not arbitrary violence (Deut. 9:4–6).

Second, up until the moment of the conquest, it appears mercy was available to repentant Canaanites who submitted to God and identified with his people. For example, Rahab and her family were spared because they provided aid to the Israelite spies (Josh. 2:8–24). The lesson is clear: choosing to live as God's enemy results in judgment; submitting to God's

---

[87] As Old Testament scholar Christopher Wright remarks, "[The conquest] was an act of God's justice and punishment on a morally degraded society. The conquest shouldn't be portrayed as random genocide or ethnic cleansing. The wickedness of Canaanite society was anticipated (Gn 15:16) and described in moral and social terms (Lv 18:24; 20:23; Dt 9:5; 12:29–31)." See Christopher Wright, "Is the Old Testament Ethical?," in *The Apologetics Study Bible*, ed. Ted Cabal (Nashville: Holman Bible, 2007), 116.

rule results in blessing (and for Rahab specifically, inclusion in the line of the Messiah—Matt. 1:5).

Third, the Canaanites' continued presence in the land threatened the religious purity of Israel. According to Genesis 18:18, God's intention was to bless the nations of the world through Abraham's descendants. However, the egregious idolatry of the Canaanites—which by this time included child immolation (Deut. 12:31)—would, if allowed to continue, corrupt the witness and integrity of the Israelites by influencing them to adopt wicked, syncretistic forms of worship (Deut. 20:16–18).[88] Thus, eradicating Canaanite religion was a matter of safeguarding God's covenant people through whom he intended to bless the world.

Finally, the conquest of the land was limited and directly sanctioned by God, who personally fought on behalf of Israel (Exodus 14; Joshua 6; Judges 7). Elsewhere in the Old Testament, wars waged for selfish reasons or conducted with unrestrained violence and bloodshed are condemned.[89] The unique purposes of the conquest—to divinely judge the Canaanites and protect the religious purity of Israel—were unique to this period of redemptive history; no other nation or person can claim the same mandate.

---

[88] Tragically, because of their disobedience, it appears that some areas of the land were never fully possessed by Israel (Judg. 1:28; Ps. 106:34–35). Throughout their history, the Israelites repeatedly turned from God and adopted idolatrous practices. Ultimately, the Assyrian exile in 722 BC (2 Kgs. 15:29) and the Babylonian exile in 586 BC (2 Kgs. 24:10–17) were consequences for the people's sin; 2 Kings 17:7–23 provides the theological rationale for the Assyrian exile; Jeremiah 25 gives the reason for the Babylonian captivity.

[89] Ken Magnuson cites the example of Gideon in Judges 8 and some of David's military exploits as wars the Bible does not condone. According to Magnuson, "Israel's warfare policy as authorized by God is limited and not dependent on Israel's military might. When various kings and other leaders go beyond that policy and engage in wars for their own purposes, with unrestrained violence and bloodshed, it is not merely a sign of their disobedience, but of their Canaanization." See Ken Magnuson, *Invitation to Christian Ethics: Moral Reasoning and Contemporary Issues* (Grands Rapids: Kregel Academic, 2020), 430.

## *Claim #2: "Life Begins with Breath"*

A theological argument put forward by some pro-abortion advocates is that "life begins with breath."[90] According to this argument, abortion is morally neutral (and thus permissible) because it ends the life of an unborn child before he or she has taken his or her first breath. Supporters of this position cite Genesis 2:7, which says, "Then the LORD God formed the man out of the dust from the ground and breathed the breath of life into his nostrils, and the man became a living being."

In context, Genesis 2:7 does not teach that life began with Adam's first breath. In fact, the passage says nothing about Adam breathing (although it can be assumed Adam began breathing after receiving life). According to the passage, God breathed into nonliving matter and the first human being became a living being. Adam's creation was unique; he was personally formed by God and given life as a fully adult man. It may appear too obvious to need pointing out, but how God gave Adam life differs from how every other person subsequently born receives life. In other words, Genesis 2:7 does not describe normal human development. Following God's creation of Eve, the normal biological process of reproduction was the means for creating new life. The special circumstances of Adam's creation are not paradigmatic or representative of how the rest of humanity comes into existence. After our first parents, no one has received "the breath of life" directly from God in the same way.

---

[90] For example, the Freedom from Religion Foundation has a section on its website titled "What Does the Bible Say about Abortion?" Under the header "When Does Life Begin?," they write, "According to the bible, life begins at birth—when a baby draws its breath. The bible defines life as 'breath' in several significant passages, including the story of Adam's creation in Genesis 2:7." See Freedom from Religion Foundation, "What Does the Bible Say About Abortion?," FFRF, accessed July 15, 2024, https://ffrf.org/component/k2/item/26087-abortion-nontract#when-does-life-begin. In my critique of this argument, I rely on my analysis in David Closson, "A Closer Look at FRC's Viral Tweet: The Bible Really Is Pro-Life (Part 1)," Family Research Council, September 8, 2021, https://www.frc.org/blog/2021/09/closer-look-frcs-viral-tweet-bible-really-pro-life-part-1.

Additionally, critics who insist the Bible teaches that life began with Adam's first breath should note that the unborn are "breathing" in the sense that they receive the oxygen they need for their cells to function. Adam began breathing through his mouth after receiving life because that is how a person at that stage of development takes in oxygen; unborn children receive oxygen from blood vessels in the umbilical cord.[91]

## *Claim #3: Exodus 21 Demonstrates That the Unborn Are Not Fully Human*

Both sides of the abortion debate recognize Exodus 21 as a relevant text.[92] In context, the passage is found in a portion of the Torah that scholars refer to as the book of the covenant, which includes legal judgments, moral precepts, and other instructions for the Israelites.[93] Exodus 21:22–25 describes a scene in which an out-of-control fight breaks out between men. Tragically, during the fight, a pregnant bystander is injured: "When men get in a fight and hit a pregnant woman so that her children are born prematurely but there is no injury, the one who hit her must be fined as the woman's husband demands from him, and he must pay according to judicial assessment. If there is an injury, then you must give life for life, eye for eye, tooth for tooth, hand for hand, foot for foot, burn for burn, bruise for bruise, wound for wound" (Exod. 21:22–25).

---

[91] For a succinct scientific explanation of fetal breathing, see Zawn Villines, "How Babies Breathe in the Womb," Medical News Today, updated July 12, 2023, https://www.medicalnewstoday.com/articles/318993.

[92] For example, feminist theologian Beverly Harrison says that Exodus 21:22–24 is the "one uncontested reference to abortion in Christian scripture." See Harrison, *Our Right to Choose*, 68.

[93] Although Old Testament scholars debate the scope of the book of the covenant, most, including T. Desmond Alexander and Victor P. Hamilton, demarcate Exodus 20:22–23:33 as the book of the covenant. See T. Desmond Alexander, *Exodus*, Apollos Old Testament Commentary (Downers Grove, IL: InterVarsity, 2017), 439, and Victor P. Hamilton, *Exodus: An Exegetical Commentary* (Grand Rapids: Baker Academic, 2011), 358–61.

Although progressive theologians argue that Exodus 21 "demonstrates that causing the death of a fetus did *not* constitute a major crime at that time," a closer look at the passage reveals that the law provided justice for whoever was injured, whether the mother or her unborn children.[94]

Although Old Testament scholars debate how best to translate the Hebrew grammar and syntax in these verses, a plain reading of the text demonstrates that the law's provision covers both mothers and their unborn children.[95] According to the law, if a woman was hit and premature birth resulted but no harm occurred to the woman or her child, the man at fault would incur a fine (as determined by the woman's husband and the community elders).[96] But if there was harm to either the woman or child, the

---

[94] Harrison, *Our Right to Choose*, 68. Notably, Harrison cautions pro-abortion supporters about uncritically citing this text due to what she refers to as its patriarchal context. According to Harrison, "Biblicist approaches to this text disclose a further limitation of all biblical proof-texting for the purpose of justifying morality. This same text is often cited, appropriately, on the pro-choice side of the debate. Even as we do so, we may bypass a deeper problem. All appeals to this passage obscure the painful fact that the moral ethos revealed in this and many other biblical stories is that of a patriarchal society in which *ownership of women and children by men was not merely assumed but considered morally acceptable*." See Harrison, *Our Right to Choose*, 69, emphasis original. In her discussion of Exodus 21, feminist scholar Margaret Kamitsuka notes, "We see articulated here the notion that the loss of an unformed fetus would only incur a fine rather than a penalty of homicide." See Kamitsuka, *Abortion and the Christian Tradition*, 27.

[95] According to Douglas Stuart, Exodus 21:22 "contains some wording that is without parallel elsewhere in the Old Testament and thus challenging to translate." See Douglas K. Stuart, *Exodus*, The New American Commentary (Nashville: B&H, 2006), 491. Likewise, Victor Hamilton notes, "There are two Hebrew words in this law that are difficult to translate, on which skilled Hebraists have multiple opinions." See Hamilton, *Exodus*, 387. Desmond Alexander provides a detailed discussion of the relevant Hebrew words and translation options in his Exodus commentary. See Alexander, *Exodus*, 483–89.

[96] In his discussion of the passage, Douglas Stuart notes, "Presumed in the logic of the law is that men are inexcusably out of control if they engage in a brawl so wild that a pregnant woman would be hurt in the process. . . . The husband could prosecute the case even if there was no harm to his wife or to his child(ren) since

penalty was the application of the law of retaliation (*lex talionis*), whereby the punishment resembled the offense committed in kind and degree.

Notably, the application of *lex talionis* is unique in this situation. Under similar circumstances—where someone unintentionally caused the death of another person—the penalty was not "life for life." Rather, the person at fault could flee to a city of refuge, where he had to wait until the high priest's death. But in a situation where the mother or child was harmed, the irresponsible brawler received an exacting punishment. Thus, contrary to progressive interpretations, the text indicates that Israel's law pursued justice for unborn children whose lives were unintentionally taken. As Philip Ryken observes, "Another implication of this case is that a fetus is a person who deserves special protection. The law of God imposed strict penalties on anyone who harmed an unborn child. It treated the injury of an unborn child the same way it treated the injury of any other human being. By this standard, performing an abortion is an act of murder, for which the proper penalty is 'life for life' (v. 23).[97]

Finally, it should be obvious that Exodus 21 does not justify elective abortion. Even if the interpretation is granted that the penalty for injuring an unborn child is less severe than for injuring the mother, it does not follow that someone can deliberately terminate a pregnancy. As stipulated in the passage, any injury suffered by the unborn child resulted in arbitration and a penalty imposed on the negligent man.

---

the mere risk and anxiety of facing the possibility of injury to the unborn or the infertility of his wife would warrant it." See Stuart, *Exodus*, 492.

[97] Ryken continues, writing, "To put it bluntly, abortionists deserve the death penalty. It should be emphasized that this is a sentence no private individual ever has the right to execute. Killing a doctor who performs abortions is also murder, because only the proper authorities have the right to use deadly force. Nevertheless, the proper legal category is murder, with all the penalties that apply—never in a private vendetta, but as a matter of public justice." Philip Graham Ryken, *Exodus: Saved for God's Glory*, Preaching the Word Series (Wheaton, IL: Crossway Books, 2015), 674.

### *Claim #4: Numbers 5 Describes a God-Sanctioned Abortion*

In conversations about the Bible and abortion, Numbers 5:11–31 is sometimes cited as proof that God condones abortion.[98] However, a careful look at the admittedly enigmatic passage demonstrates that it does not justify abortion.

According to Numbers 5, if a husband suspected his wife of infidelity, he could take her to the priest for what most commentators call a "trial by ordeal."[99] The ritual, led by the priest, included multiple steps, the most important of which was putting the woman under a vow and having her drink water mixed with dust from the floor of the tabernacle. If the woman was innocent, "she will be unaffected and will be able to conceive children" (Num. 5:28). But if she was guilty, "the water that brings a curse will enter her to cause bitter suffering; her belly will swell, and her womb will shrivel" (5:27).

As noted, some commentators have suggested that the punishment described in verses 21 and 22 is evidence that God endorses abortion. Others have argued that miscarriage was the punishment for the guilty woman.[100]

---

[98] For example, Julius Brewer argues that Numbers 5 "admits of little doubt" that abortion for the guilty woman is in view. See Julius Brewer, "The Ordeal in Numbers Chapter 5," *American Journal of Semitic Languages and Literature* vol. 1 (October 1913): 36–47.

[99] According to Timothy Ashley, "The trial by ordeal was a common feature of the ancient world. . . . The most common ordeals in the ancient world seem to be by water . . . by heat . . . and by the action of some potion. It must be admitted that the current passage is similar to certain features of the trial by ordeal, viz., the imbibing of the liquid and the fact that the verdict is, in effect, left in God's hands. These similarities have led virtually every modern commentator to call the ritual in Num. 5:11–31 a trial by ordeal." Notably, Ashley argues that Numbers 5 differs from a typical trial by ordeal. Specifically, in Numbers 5, the ordeal is not dangerous to the innocent party. See Timothy R. Ashley, *The Book of Numbers*, New International Commentary on the Old Testament (Grand Rapids: Eerdmans, 1993), 123.

[100] "Miscarriage" is the interpretation favored by the NIV, which translates the relevant phrases from verses 21–22, "When he makes your womb miscarry and

However, there are compelling reasons for why neither abortion nor miscarriage are in view. First, the focus of the passage is infidelity. In many cases, a woman would not have become pregnant from an illicit affair; if miscarriage or spontaneous abortion were the punishment, it is unclear how the ordeal punished nonpregnant, adulterous women.

Second, the translation "miscarriage" by some English versions (e.g., NIV, NEB) in verses 21, 22, and 27 is suspect. In fact, most English translations (including the CSB, ESV, NASB, and NKJV) indicate that bodily disfigurement, not miscarriage, was the punishment for guilt. On this point, a closer analysis of the text is illuminating. Whereas the NIV says the guilty woman's "womb" would "miscarry," the CSB translates the relevant Hebrew phrase to say that the woman's "womb" would "shrivel." For its part, the ESV translates the phrase to read that the woman's "thigh" would "fall away."[101] Thus, although scholars debate the best way to translate and interpret the text, the fact that the innocent woman's ability to conceive children was contrasted with the bodily disfigurement of the guilty woman suggests that sterility, not abortion or miscarriage, was the guilty woman's punishment.[102]

---

your abdomen swell . . . so that your abdomen swells or your womb miscarries." R. K. Harrison favors the miscarriage interpretation as well, noting, "The *NEB* seems to afford the most plausible explanation in suggesting miscarriage or spontaneous abortion, but it does not take account of the possibility of death." See R. K. Harrison, *Numbers*, The Wycliffe Exegetical Commentary (Chicago: Moody, 1990), 113.

[101] The CSB translates Numbers 5:21–22 as follows: "[H]e makes your womb shrivel and your belly swell . . . causing your belly to swell and your womb to shrivel." Similarly, the ESV says, "[T]he Lord makes your thigh fall away and your body swell . . . and make your womb swell and your thigh fall away." Contrast these translations with the NIV, which renders Numbers 5:21–22 to say, "[H]e makes your womb miscarry and your abdomen swell . . . so that your abdomen swells or your womb miscarries." For a helpful discussion of the relevant Hebrew words, see Ashley, *The Book of Numbers*, 132.

[102] As the Mishnaic comment on this passage explains, "In the member she sinned with she will be punished." Gordan Wenham quotes the Mishnaic comment (Sotah 1:7) in his Numbers commentary. See Gordan J. Wenham, *Numbers*, Tyndale Old Testament Commentaries (Downers Grove, IL: IVP Academic, 1981),

Finally, even if abortion or miscarriage were included in the punishment of the adulterous woman, Numbers 5 does not justify abortion performed by human agents. Notably, it was the Lord—not the priest or the husband—who brought about the punishment or acquittal. Nothing in the passage delegates God's prerogative over life and death to the couple, and nowhere are conditions provided that allow for a morally permissible abortion.

## Conclusion

In closing, the Bible is explicit in its affirmation of the personhood of the unborn. The Bible's pro-life ethic does not derive from proof-texting or a misreading of an isolated text. From verses that portray God's creative power in the womb (Ps. 139:13–16) to passages where prophets and apostles were called and set apart for ministry while still in utero (e.g., Jeremiah, the Servant of the Lord, and Paul), the Bible sees all human life as precious and possessing inherent worth and dignity.

From a biblical and theological perspective, Christians rightly understand that abortion runs contrary to the Bible's pro-life ethic. But despite the Bible's unmistakable teaching on life, a growing number of pastors, politicians, and activists have argued that the Bible is either neutral on abortion or affirms a pro-abortion stance. Some have even argued that pro-life arguments based on the Bible are motivated by political, rather than theological, considerations.

However, a careful study of church history shows that pastors, theologians, and church leaders have maintained and defended the Bible's pro-life teaching since the first century. In fact, the unbroken tradition of the church has been to affirm, not deny, the Bible's pro-life ethic. To this history we now turn.

95. Commentator R. K. Harrison comes to a similar conclusion, noting, "It is probably safest to conclude that, whatever the true nature of her punishment, it was deemed appropriate to the crime and fell upon the bodily organs that had engendered the woman's sin." See Harrison, *Numbers*, 113.

# 3

# Consistently Pro-Life: The Church's Teaching on Life

On May 20, 2022, San Francisco archbishop Salvatore Cordileone made international news by announcing that then-Speaker of the House Nancy Pelosi was barred from receiving the sacrament of the Eucharist in her hometown diocese because of her outspoken, ongoing advocacy of abortion.[1] The decision amounted to a rare public rebuke of one of the nation's most recognized Catholic politicians.[2]

---

[1] Ramon Antonio Vargas, "San Francisco Archbishop Bars Pelosi from Communion over Abortion Stance," *Guardian*, May 21, 2022, https://www.theguardian.com/us-news/2022/may/21/nancy-pelosi-san-francisco-archbishop-communion-abortion.

[2] About a week after Archbishop Cordileone's decision to bar Speaker Pelosi from Communion, I wrote a short commentary analyzing some of the questions of pastoral authority raised by the story. For this article, see David Closson, "No Communion for Thee: Nancy Pelosi, Abortion, and Pastoral Authority," *Washington Stand*, May 26, 2022, https://washingtonstand.com/commentary/no-communion-for-thee-nancy-pelosi-abortion-and-pastoral-authority.

Cordileone's explosive announcement was covered by every major American news outlet. Not surprisingly, the archbishop was characterized by most reports as extremely conservative. For example, the *New York Times* referred to Cordileone as an "ultraconservative."[3] NPR said the archbishop was among "the most outspoken of U.S. bishops."[4] And in their report, CNN told readers that "The Communion refusal movement is driven by a more conservative wing of the Catholic Church."[5] Clearly, the archbishop's decision to exclude Pelosi from Communion was perceived by many in the media as a step too far.

For his part, however, Archbishop Cordileone believed that Catholic canon law and his pastoral responsibility to Pelosi required drastic measures. As he explained to Pelosi in his letter, "A Catholic legislator who supports procured abortion, after knowing the teaching of the Church, commits a manifestly grave sin which is a cause of most serious scandal to others."[6] According

---

[3] Annie Karni and Ruth Graham, "Archbishop Bars Pelosi from Communion over Abortion Stance," *New York Times*, May 20, 2022, https://www.nytimes.com/2022/05/20/us/politics/pelosi-communion-abortion.html.

[4] Emma Bowman, "An Archbishop Bars Pelosi from Communion over Her Support for Abortion Rights," NPR, last updated May 21, 2022, https://www.npr.org/2022/05/21/1100536547/nancy-pelosi-communion-abortion-rights.

[5] Manu Raju and Melanie Zanona, "Pelosi Banned from Receiving Communion in San Francisco Archdiocese over Her Position on Abortion," CNN, May 20, 2022, https://www.cnn.com/2022/05/20/politics/pelosi-communion-ban-abortion-san-francisco-archdiocese/index.html.

[6] Archbishop Cordileone, "Notification to the Speaker of the House of Representatives of the United States Congress Nancy Pelosi," Archdiocese of San Francisco, May 20, 2022, https://sfarchdiocese.org/notification-to-the-speaker-of-the-house-of-representatives-of-the-united-states-congress-nancy-pelosi/. Cordileone also wrote letters to the broader Catholic community and fellow priests to explain his decision. See Archbishop Cordileone, "Letter to the Faithful on the Notification Sent to Speaker Nancy Pelosi," Archdiocese of San Francisco, May 20, 2022, https://sfarchdiocese.org/letter-to-the-faithful-on-the-notification-sent-to-speaker-nancy-pelosi/, and Archbishop Cordileone, "Letter to Priests of the Archdiocese on the Notification Sent to Speaker Nancy Pelosi," Archdiocese of San Francisco, May 20, 2022, https://sfarchdiocese.org/letter-to-priests-of-the-archdiocese-on-the-notification-sent-to-speaker-nancy-pelosi/.

to the archbishop, Pelosi's "extreme position" on abortion alongside her public identification as a Roman Catholic necessitated pastoral action.

In his letter, Cordileone emphasized the "scandal" caused by Pelosi's public support for abortion. In Catholicism, a scandal refers to behavior that leads others to do evil.[7] For Cordileone, Pelosi's energetic support of abortion not only endangered her own soul but caused harmful confusion among practicing Catholics about the Church's teaching.

Additionally, Cordileone explained how the Speaker's efforts in September 2021 to codify *Roe v. Wade* into federal law were antithetical to Catholic moral teaching.[8] For the archbishop, Pelosi's active support of abortion and refusal even to discuss the matter with him represented "resistance to pastoral counsel."[9] Thus, after years of praying, searching his conscience for how to respond pastorally, and engaging in unsuccessful attempts to speak privately with Pelosi on at least six occasions, Cordileone felt he had no choice but to bar the Speaker from Communion.

Despite the archbishop's pleas, Pelosi refused to change course. In an interview shortly after the publication of the archbishop's letter, Pelosi

---

[7] See Libreria Editrice Vaticana, *Catechism of the Catholic Church*, 2nd ed., revised in accordance with the official Latin text promulgated by Pope John Paul II (Washington, DC: United States Council of Catholic Bishops, 2023), art. 5, II.2284. https://www.usccb.org/sites/default/files/flipbooks/catechism/553/.

[8] Under Pelosi's leadership, the House of Representatives passed the Women's Health Protection Act on September 24, 2021. If enacted into law, this proposed legislation would weaken conscience protections for medical professionals, jeopardize prohibitions on taxpayer funding for abortion, enshrine late-term abortion into law, strike down many pro-life laws passed in the states, and equate the death of unborn children with routine medical procedures.

[9] For Catholics, barring someone from receiving the Eucharist carries significant theological implications. The Catholic Church holds to a sacramental theology, which teaches that to be in a state of grace members must regularly receive the sacraments. Among the seven sacraments recognized in Catholicism, the Eucharist (known as the Lord's Supper or Communion in other Christian traditions) is seen as the most important, as members encounter and receive the literal body and blood of Jesus in Communion. However, Catholics may not receive the Eucharist if they are conscious that they have committed a grave sin and have not first made a sacramental confession.

dismissed Cordileone's concerns, noting, "So these same people [Catholic Church officials] are against contraception, family planning, in vitro fertilization—it's a blanket thing. And they use abortion as the front man for it while they try to undo so much."[10] Evidently in no mood to repent, Pelosi doubled down on her support for abortion and led the House to pass the Women's Health Protection Act once again in July 2022. The bill, if passed into law, would strike down nearly every state-level pro-life law.

Although the disagreement between Archbishop Salvatore Cordileone and then Speaker of the House Nancy Pelosi has largely receded from public memory, the incident raises significant questions about church teaching, discipline, and pastoral authority. Shortly after the archbishop's letter was published, *The View* cohost Whoopi Goldberg blasted Cordileone, saying, "This is not your job, dude. That is not up to you to make that decision."[11]

How should Christians evaluate Goldberg's claim that Archbishop Cordileone was stepping outside of his "job" by disciplining Nancy Pelosi? A helpful place to begin answering this question is church history. Although critics were quick to claim that Cordileone had "weaponized" the sacrament by wading into politics, a survey of church history demonstrates that the archbishop's actions follow the example of the church's most influential leaders who have defended the Bible's teaching on abortion and, when necessary, exercised pastoral care for wayward members.

The interpretation of biblical texts and themes related to life and abortion presented in chapter 2 is not a minority opinion or the view of an isolated denomination. Christians have been clear and consistent on abortion

---

[10] Nancy Pelosi, "Transcript of Speaker Pelosi Interview on MSNBC's Morning Joe with Joe Scarborough, Mika Brzezinski and Willie Geist," press release, Speaker's Press Office, May 24, 2022, https://pelosi.house.gov/news/press-releases/transcript-of-speaker-pelosi-interview-on-msnbcs-morning-joe-with-joe.

[11] *Washington Free Beacon* (@FreeBeacon), "Whoopi: 'The archbishop of San Francisco is calling for speaker Nancy Pelosi to be denied receiving Communion because of her pro-choice stance . . . This is not your job, dude. That is not up to you to make that decision.'" Twitter, May 23, 2022, 10:07 a.m., https://twitter.com/FreeBeacon/status/1528754587498434560.

since the first century. Despite disagreements on a wide variety of subjects, nearly every prominent authority in the history of Christianity—including theologians, pastors, and church councils—has opposed abortion and affirmed the personhood of the unborn. Beginning with the early church, this chapter will demonstrate that, with very few exceptions, the Christian church has been pro-life since its inception. Awareness of this historic teaching can equip current generations to articulate a faithful pro-life witness.

## Early Church

The Bible's teaching on the sanctity of life, and specifically the personhood of the unborn, contradicted the practices of the Greco-Roman culture in which Christianity arose. In fact, abortion was widely accepted and practiced in Roman society during the first three centuries after Christ. Soranos (c. AD 98–138), a second-century gynecologist, explained that Roman women sought abortion for three main reasons: a desire to conceal the consequences of adultery, to maintain feminine beauty, and to avoid danger to the mother when her uterus was thought too small to accommodate the full embryo.[12]

---

[12] John T. Noonan Jr., "An Almost Absolute Value in History," in *The Morality of Abortion: Legal and Historical Perspectives*, ed. John T. Noonan Jr. (Cambridge, MA: Harvard University Press, 1970), 4. It's worth noting that Noonan's chapter has long generated discussion amongst scholars. For example, in her 1983 book, Beverly Harrison notes, "John Noonan's statement that fetal life has been granted 'an almost absolute value in Christian history,' . . . has enjoyed a credibility which, in my view, it in no way deserves. It is easy enough to compile statements that anathematize abortion written by Christian theologians over the centuries. But it is quite another thing to suggest that the moral justification for these theologians' opposition to abortion stemmed from their deep concern for the value of fetal life." See Beverly Harrison, *Our Right to Choose*, 125. Margaret Kamitsuka also takes issue with Noonan and claims that he and others "obscure the complex, varied, and contested ways the church historically tried to address not only the idea of abortion but also actual instances of women with unwanted pregnancies attempting an abortion." Kamitsuka argues that the early church's objections to abortion ought to be read against a backdrop of sexism and "outright pleasure-phobic attitudes directed especially toward women's sexuality." She also points to the "relatively lenient

Reasons not too different from some given today—overpopulation and a desire to be childless—were also frequently cited as justifications for abortion.[13] In other words, the average Roman had such a low view of fetal and infant life that infanticide, child abandonment, and abortion remained common in the Roman Empire until these practices were outlawed at the urging of Christians in 374.[14]

It was against this morally dark backdrop that the early church opposed abortion. Christians were convinced by two biblical themes that the Bible expressly condemned feticide. The first was the priority of love in Jesus's teaching. According to Jesus, second only to love for God was loving one's neighbor (Mark 12:31). This emphasis on love motivated Christians to care for society's vulnerable, including discarded infants and unborn children.[15]

The second biblical theme that informed the church's teaching on abortion was Jesus's high view of children. Christians could not help but notice how often Jesus included children in his ministry (Matt. 19:14; cf. Mark 10:14; Luke 18:16). Often to the chagrin of his own disciples, Jesus attended to the needs of children. As we observed previously, Jesus specifically condemned those who tempt children to sin, saying, "It would be

---

ecclesial stances in the penitential material regarding the sin of abortion," suggesting that there "never was a univocal sanctity-of-fetal-life message in Christianity." See Margaret Kamitsuka, *Abortion and the Christian Tradition: A Pro-Choice Theological Ethic* (Louisville: Westminster John Knox, 2019), 18, 22, 46–47. As we will see in this chapter, evidence for a consistent pro-life ethic in the early church is overwhelming. For a concurring view, see Christopher A. Hall, *Living Wisely with the Church Fathers* (Downers Grove, IL: IVP Academic, 2017), 179–93.

[13] Alvin J. Schmidt, *Under the Influence: How Christianity Transformed Civilization* (Grand Rapids: Zondervan, 2001), 56.

[14] Schmidt notes that Basil of Caesarea was active in the fourth century in mobilizing Christians to minister to women facing unwanted pregnancies. He also notes that Basil's "efforts reportedly inspired Emperor Valentinian to outlaw abortion, along with infanticide and child abandonment, in 374." For a brief study on Roman culture and the wide acceptance of abortion during the first three centuries of the church, see Schmidt, *Under the Influence*, 55–60.

[15] Noonan highlights both of these themes in his discussion of the early church's attitude toward abortion. See Noonan, *The Morality of Abortion*, 7–8.

better for him if a millstone were hung around his neck and he were thrown into the sea than for him to cause one of these little ones to stumble" (Luke 17:2). From these texts, an ethic of responsibility toward children developed in the early church.

In short, the general themes of love and care for children, combined with the Bible's teaching on the personhood of the unborn, motivated clear pronouncements from church leaders against abortion. Living and ministering in a culture with a low view of life, pastors in the early centuries of the church taught that abortion was unbiblical and sinful.

## Patristics

The earliest Christian text to mention abortion is the Didache (AD 50–120). In a section listing proscribed acts such as murder, adultery, sodomy, fornication, and stealing, the Didache states, "You shall not murder a child by abortion nor kill that which is begotten."[16] Elsewhere in the Didache, the author contrasts the "Way of Life" with the "Way of Death," noting that the latter is followed by sinners, including "murderers of children, destroyers of the handiwork of God."[17] A commentary on the Didache, the Epistle of Barnabas (written between AD 70 and 132), notes, "You shall not slay the child by abortions. You shall not kill what is generated."[18] Children—born and unborn—were considered neighbors who merited protection, love, and care. As the antithesis of love of neighbor, abortion was decisively rejected. As we will see, this categorical rejection of abortion in the Didache and Epistle of Barnabas remained the consensus view of the early church.

Another early Christian document, the Apocalypse of Peter, conveys the church's negative attitude toward abortion through apocalyptic imagery.

---

[16] Didache 2.2, online at New Advent, accessed May 20, 2024, https://newadvent.org/fathers/0714.htm.

[17] Didache 5.2. John Noonan renders this phrase "killers of the child, who abort the mold [plasma] of God." See Noonan, *The Morality of Abortion*, 10.

[18] Barnabas 19.5. Cited in Noonan, *The Morality of Abortion*, 10.

In this early second-century text, aborted children are depicted as confronting their parents in hell. Among the sinners who are punished are women who "have caused their children to be born untimely, and have corrupted the work of God that created them."[19] The passage goes on to explain that both men and women who are responsible for killing their children "shall be tormented eternally" while the children are taken care of by an angel.[20] Although the Apocalypse of Peter was not regarded as canonical, it underscored the early church's disapproval of abortion.

Clement of Alexandria (155–215) addressed abortion in his teaching. He explained that Christians should not, in an effort to hide sexual sin, "take away human nature, which is generated from the providence of God, by hastening abortions and applying abortifacient drugs to destroy utterly the embryo and, with it, the love of man."[21] Although someone may be motivated by shame to cover up an illicit relationship, abortifacient drugs only introduce additional layers of sin to the situation. God is responsible for the generation of new human life, and adults can claim no prerogative to end an unborn child's life, even if, humanly speaking, the child is the result of an embarrassing sinful liaison.

Further support for the early church's pro-life ethic is found in the writings of Athenagoras (133–190), a second-century Christian apologist. Writing to the emperor, Athenagoras defended the church against spurious accusations

---

[19] Apocalypse of Peter, The Ethiopic Text, accessed June 18, 2024, earlychristianwritings.com/text/apocalypsepeter-mrjames.html.

[20] The children in view are likely those killed by exposure. However, O. M. Bakke thinks children killed by abortion may be in view as well, noting "This means that small children who were killed (a category that may also include unborn children who were aborted) are seen as individuals on whom God will bestow immortality." See O. M. Bakke, *When Children Became People: The Birth of Childhood in Early Christianity* (Minneapolis, MN: Fortress, 2005), 118. Bakke argues that Clement of Alexandria understood this text to include unborn children. See discussion in Bakke, 118.

[21] Clement of Alexandria, *Pedagogus* 2.10.96.1, *Die grieschen christlichen Schriftsteller der ersten drei Jahrhundert* [The Greek Christian Writers of the First Three Centuries]. Cited in Noonan, *The Morality of Abortion*, 11.

of cannibalism that arose from misunderstandings about the Lord's Supper. According to Athenagoras, the charge of cannibalism was groundless because Christians denounce violence. Christians, in contrast to those in the broader culture, oppose all forms of cruelty and exploitation, including gladiatorial games and abortion. Athenagoras explicitly connects abortion with murder, explaining, "And when we say that those women who use drugs to bring on abortion commit murder, and will have to give an account to God for the abortion, on what principle should we commit murder?"[22] He mentions that Christians believe unborn children are objects of God's care, noting:

> For it does not belong to the same person to regard the very fœtus in the womb as a created being, and therefore an object of God's care, and when it has passed into life, to kill it; and not to expose an infant, because those who expose them are chargeable with child-murder, and on the other hand, when it has been reared to destroy it. But we are in all things always alike and the same, submitting ourselves to reason, and not ruling over it.[23]

In short, the church's abhorrence of abortion was informed by the convictions that unborn children are created beings, abortion is murder, and the guilty must give an account to God. As we will see, these beliefs exerted an enormous influence on subsequent generations of Christians.[24]

---

[22] Athenagoras, *A Plea for the Christians*, 35, *Ante-Nicene Fathers: The Writings of the Fathers down to A.D. 325*, ed. Alexander Roberts and James Donaldson, 9 vols. (1885; repr., Peabody, MA: Hendrickson, 2004) [hereinafter *ANF*], 2.147.

[23] Athenagoras, 35.

[24] Athenagoras, 35. Concerning Athenagoras's letter, Michael Gorman notes, "[Athenagoras] writes that Christians have renounced murder in all its forms—mentioning the common Roman practices of gladiator contests, animal fights, exposure, and abortion—in order to avoid becoming polluted and defiled. It is this absolute abhorrence to bloodshed in any form which drives them away from even looking at practices such as gladiator fights and criminal executions. This view stood in stark contrast to the prevailing Roman lifestyle." See Michael Gorman, *Abortion and the Early Church: Christian, Jewish and Pagan Attitudes in the Greco-Roman World* (Downers Grove, IL: InterVarsity, 1982), 54.

Tertullian (155–220) also made compelling arguments against abortion. Responding to accusations that the church secretly practiced cannibalism, Tertullian explained that child sacrifice and exposure were features of the Greco-Roman world. For Christians, however, all forms of killing are prohibited, including abortion and infanticide. As Tertullian explained, "In our case, murder being once for all forbidden, we may not destroy even the fœtus in the womb, while as yet the human being derives blood from other parts of the body for its sustenance. To hinder a birth is merely a speedier man-killing; nor does it matter whether you take away a life that is born, or destroy one that is coming to the birth. That is a man which is going to be one; you have the fruit already in its seed."[25]

For Tertullian, the general prohibition against murder applies to the unborn. Although the victim may be small and dependent on its mother, abortion is nevertheless homicide because the unborn child has a life of its own.

In another text, *A Treatise on the Soul*, Tertullian explains his view that ensoulment occurs before birth (a view that contrasted sharply with Roman law). Tertullian argues that unborn children, although within their mother's womb, are independent human beings. According to Tertullian:

> Now, in such a question as this, no one can be so useful a teacher, judge, or witness, as the sex itself which is so intimately concerned. Give us your testimony, then, ye mothers, whether yet pregnant, or after delivery. . . . (Tell us, then,) whether you feel in the embryo within you any vital force other than your own, with which your bowels tremble, your sides shake, your entire womb throbs, and the burden which oppresses you constantly changes its position? Are these movements a joy to you, and a positive removal of anxiety, as making you confident that your infant both possesses vitality and

[25] Tertullian, *Apology*, 1.9 (*ANF* 3:25). See Gorman's discussion of this passage in Gorman, *Abortion and the Early Church*, 54–55.

enjoys it? Or, should his restlessness cease, your first fear would be for him?[26]

Although Tertullian's main concern in the *Treatise on the Soul* was that unborn children have a soul before birth, his description of fetal movements underscores the inherently pro-life worldview of early Christian leaders.[27] Simply put, the experience of pregnant mothers testifies to the humanity of the developing child.

Another early Christian apologist, Marcus Minucius Felix (d. 250), included a reference to abortion in his book *Octavius*. Felix contends that pagans, not Christians, practiced infanticide by exposing their children to wild beasts and birds. Moreover, among the pagans, "There are some women who, by drinking medical preparations, extinguish the source of

---

[26] Tertullian, *A Treatise on the Soul*, 25 (*ANF* 3:205).

[27] In the same passage, Tertullian talked about instances where abortion is necessary to save the mother's life. He writes, "But sometimes by cruel necessity, whilst yet in the womb, an infant is put to death, when lying awry in the orifice of the womb he impedes parturition, and kills his mother, if he is not to die himself." Tertullian goes on to describe the surgical instruments used in abortion and how "the entire fœtus is extracted by a violent delivery." Although Tertullian believed there are instances where the life of the unborn baby must be forfeited to save the mother, he left no doubt about the moral value of the baby. Doctors in these situations "all knew well enough that a living being had been conceived, and pitied this most luckless infant state, which had first to be put to death, to escape being tortured alive." In other words, because abortion ends the life of an innocent human being, it is a last resort in only extreme situations (to save the life of a mother). See Tertullian, *A Treatise on the Soul*, 25 (*ANF* 3:206). A few pages later, Tertullian connects the Bible and abortion. Arguing against the view that life begins at "first breath," Tertullian cites Luke 1:41–46 and Jeremiah 1:5. For Tertullian, Elizabeth's and Mary's recognition of the personhood of their unborn children and Jeremiah's declaration that God forms and imparts life to humanity within the womb offered strong biblical support that unborn babies are worthy of respect and care. See Tertullian, *A Treatise on the Soul*, 25 (*ANF* 3:207). A few chapters later, Tertullian applies the Bible's teaching in Exodus 21 to abortion, noting, "The law of Moses, indeed, punishes with due penalties the man who shall cause abortion." See Tertullian, *A Treatise on the Soul*, 25 (*ANF* 3:217).

the future man in their very bowels, and thus commit a parricide before they bring forth."[28] The term "parricide" is the Roman legal word for the homicide of near relatives.[29] For Felix, abortion was the equivalent of killing a near relative, which was unthinkable for Christians.

Although Christian leaders were clear in their disapproval of abortion, some Christians still sought to terminate unwanted pregnancies. In fact, one of the church's leading theologians in the first half of the third century, Hippolytus (c. 170–c. 235), seemed to be aware that abortion was occurring among Christians influenced by lax moral standards and what he claimed was Pope Callixtus's lenient policy of extending absolution to those guilty of sexual sin. In a polemic directed against Pope Callixtus I, Hippolytus describes the consequences of lax moral standards: "Whence women, reputed believers, began to resort to drugs for producing sterility, and to gird themselves round, so to expel what was being conceived on account of their not wishing to have a child either by a slave or by any paltry fellow, for the sake of their family and excessive wealth. Behold, into how great impiety that lawless one has proceeded, by inculcating adultery and murder at the same time."[30] According to Hippolytus, Callixtus's permissive measures led to an increase in two related vices: sexual immorality and abortion, the latter of which he condemned as "murder."

Cyprian (c. 210–c. 258), another third-century church leader, also condemned abortion. Cyprian's view of abortion surfaced in his scathing critique of Novatian, a theologian whose schismatic beliefs resulted in his

---

[28] Minucius Felix, *Octavius* (*ANF* 4:192). Suggestively, Felix adds, "And these things assuredly come down from the teaching of your gods. For Saturn did not expose his children, but devoured them." For Felix, pagan theology was a contributing factor behind the rationale for getting an abortion.

[29] For further discussion, see Noonan, *The Morality of Abortion*, 12, and Germain G. Grisez, *Abortion: The Myths, The Realities, and the Arguments* (New York: Corpus Books, 1970), 141.

[30] Hippolytus, *The Refutation of All Heresies*, 7 (*ANF* 5:131). For further discussion, see Bakke, *When Children Became People*, 126–27.

eventual excommunication. According to Cyprian, Novatian's heretical views were accompanied by gross immorality, which included despoiling orphans, defrauding widows, withholding money from the church, not caring for his father, and causing his wife to miscarry their son. In graphic terms, Cyprian wrote about Novatian's violent outburst, noting, "The womb of his wife was smitten by a blow of his heel; and in the miscarriage that soon followed, the offspring was brought forth, the fruit of a father's murder."[31] For his reckless actions, church officials had planned to investigate Novatian but were prevented by the outbreak of the Decian persecution (AD 250).[32]

In the fourth century, two church councils formalized what individual pastors and theologians had been teaching about abortion for 300 years. In the West, the Council of Elvira (AD 305/6) became the first Christian body to enact punishment for abortion. According to canon 63, "If a woman, while her husband is away, conceives by adultery and after that crime commits abortion, she shall not be given communion even at the approach of death, since she has doubled her crime."[33] In the situation described, the woman "doubled her crime" by adding to adultery the sin of abortion. The fact that no penance was offered to the woman who aborted her child demonstrates the gravity of the sin.

---

[31] Cyprian, *The Epistles of Cyprian*, 48.3 (*ANF* 5:326). In the next sentence, Cyprian asks, "And now does he [Novatian] dare to condemn the hands of those who sacrifice, when he himself is more guilty in his feet, by which the son, who was about to be born, was slain?"

[32] According to Cyprian, "[Novatian] long ago feared this consciousness of crime. On account of this he regarded it as certain that he would not only be turned out of the presbytery, but restrained from communion; and by the urgency of the brethren, the day of investigation was coming on, on which his cause was to be dealt with before us, if the persecution had not prevented." See Cyprian, *The Epistles of Cyprian*, 48.4 (*ANF* 5:326).

[33] Council of Elvira, canon 63, https://strannikjournal.wordpress.com/historic-confessions/81-canons-of-the-synod-of-elvira/.

Additionally, canon 68 states, "If a catechumen [a convert preparing for baptism and confirmation in the church] should conceive by an adulterer, and should procure the death of the child, she can be baptized only at the end of her life."[34] According to the council, abortion was such a flagrant departure from Christian morals that it constituted grounds for disqualifying a woman from full inclusion in the church until the very end of her life.

In the East, the Council of Ancyra (AD 314) once again confirmed the church's opposition to abortion. According to canon 21 of the council, women who "commit fornication, and destroy that which they have conceived, or who are employed in making drugs for abortion" were to be excluded from the church but readmitted after ten years of penance.[35] Although the punishment imposed by Ancyra was less severe than what the bishops at Elvira required, the stiff penalty further illustrates how Christians thought about abortion.[36]

Two leading fourth-century theologians in the Eastern church, John Chrysostom (c. 349–407) and Basil of Caesarea (330–379), also provided clear statements about abortion. In a stirring sermon on Romans 13:11–14, Chrysostom equated abortion with murder. According to Chrysostom, men who engage in illicit sex increase the likelihood of abortion, which he describes as "something even worse than murder."[37] Chrysostom grounds his opposition to abortion in the theological principle that the unborn child

---

[34] Council of Elvira, canon 68. I have followed the translation rendered by Michael Gorman in Gorman, *Abortion and the Early Church*, 64.

[35] Council of Ancyra, canon 21, https://newadvent.org/fathers/3802.htm.

[36] It is worth noting how the penalty for abortion compared to the punishment for other sins. According to the bishops at Ancyra, unintentional killing and fornication required various forms of penance for five to seven years. Intentional murder was punished with excommunication for life. Thus, abortion was considered more serious than unintentional murder, but not as serious as intentional murder. For a lengthier discussion, see Bakke, *When Children Became People*, 130.

[37] John Chrysostom, *Homily 24 on Romans*, https://newadvent.org/fathers/210224.htm.

is a gift from God, explaining, "Why then dost thou abuse the gift of God, and fight with His laws, and follow after what is a curse as if a blessing, and make the chamber of procreation a chamber for murder, and arm the woman that was given for childbearing unto slaughter?" Moreover, men who encourage or pressure women to get an abortion compound the sin of adultery with murder: "You do not let a harlot remain only a harlot but make her a murderess as well."[38]

Likewise, Basil of Caesarea stated his opinion succinctly in a letter to Amphilochius of Iconium: "The woman who purposely destroys her unborn child is guilty of murder."[39] Although some theologians made distinctions between embryos that were "formed" or "unformed," Basil saw these distinctions as irrelevant, noting, "With us there is no nice enquiry as to its being formed or unformed. In this case it is not only the being about to be born who is vindicated, but the woman in her attack upon herself; because in most cases women who make such attempts die. The destruction of the embryo is an additional crime, a second murder, at all events if we regard it as done with intent."[40] Basil went on to propose that those guilty of abortion should observe ten years of penance. For Basil, abortion was a serious sin; often, it resulted in two deaths, the mother and her child. But abortion was not unforgivable. For the truly penitent, grace should be extended.

In the same letter, Basil makes the distinction between intentional and unintentional killing. In the category of intentional killing is abortion, of which Basil said, "Women also who administer drugs to cause abortion, as well as those who take poisons to destroy unborn children, are murderesses."[41] Abortion is wrong because abortion is murder; those who participate in abortion are morally culpable.

---

[38] This follows the translation provided by John Noonan in *The Morality of Abortion*, 17.

[39] Basil, *Letters* 188, II (*Nicene and Post-Nicene Fathers* [hereinafter *NPNF*] 2/8:225).

[40] Basil, *Letters* 188, II.

[41] Basil, 188, VIII (*NPNF* 2/8:227).

In the West, Ambrose (340–397), Jerome (347–420), and Augustine (354–430) contributed to the church's moral appraisal of abortion. In 387, Ambrose preached a sermon in which he criticized the wealthy for their complicity in abortion. "Even the wealthy, in order that their inheritance may not be divided among several, deny in the very womb their own progeny," Ambrose lamented. "By the use of parricidal mixtures they snuff out the fruit of their wombs in the genital organs themselves. In this way life is taken away before it is given," he added.[42] According to Ambrose, parents violate the rights of their offspring if they allow some to live and consign others to die.

For his part, Jerome articulated a clear position on abortion. In 384, Jerome composed his most well-known letter, which vividly portrayed Roman society as morally bankrupt. Among those guilty of sexual immorality were those who "go as far as to take potions, that they may insure barrenness, and thus murder human beings almost before their conception."[43] Additionally,

---

[42] Ambrose, *Hexaemeron*, 5, 18, 58. Online at https://www.scribd.com/doc/46349268/Hexaemeron-of-Saint-Ambrose-of-Milan. In another place, Ambrose connected God's calling of Jeremiah to his creation of other unborn children. According to Ambrose, "It is written: 'Before I formed you in the womb I knew you, and in the genitals of your mother I sanctified you' (Jer 1:5). To inhibit your rashness, you are made to notice that the hands of your maker are forming something in the womb into a man. He is at work—and you would violate by your passion the secret of that sacred womb? Either imitate brute animals or respect God." Cited in Germain Grisez, *Abortion: The Myths, the Realities, and the Arguments* (New York: Corpus Books, 1970), 143. Worth noting is how Ambrose used Jeremiah 1 to highlight the presence of God working in the womb. As Grisez notes, "To violate the womb is to interfere with the supreme craftsman at his work." See Grisez, *Abortion*, 143.

[43] Jerome, *Letter* 22.13 (To Eustochium) (*NPNF* 2/6:27). In *Letter* 22, Jerome does not mention the age of the fetus or make the distinction between a "formed" or "unformed" fetus. Elsewhere, however, Jerome made the distinction between a formed and unformed fetus (see *Letter* 121 to Algasiam). According to Jerome, a fetus needed to reach a certain stage of development before it received a soul and could be considered a person. From this perspective, abortion is not murder unless the fetus is "formed." As we will see, this was also the view held by Augustine, who, nevertheless, believed the abortion of an unformed fetus was immoral.

"Some, when they find themselves with child through their sin, use drugs to procure abortion, and when (as often happens) they die with their offspring, they enter the lower world laden with the guilt not only of adultery against Christ but also of suicide and child murder."[44] Notably, Jerome made the linkage between illicit sex and abortion. He also called a woman's abortion-induced death "suicide" and referred to abortion as "child murder."

Finally, Augustine, the early church's foremost thinker, also opposed abortion. For the bishop of Hippo, contraception, sterilizing drugs, and abortion were immoral because they denied the procreative purpose of sex. According to Augustine, "Sometimes, indeed, this lustful cruelty, or, if you please, cruel lust, resorts to such extravagant methods as to use poisonous drugs to secure barrenness; or else, if unsuccessful in this, to destroy the conceived seed by some means previous to birth, preferring that its offspring should rather perish than receive vitality; or if it was advancing to life within the womb, should be slain before it was born."[45]

Although Augustine made the distinction between a "formed" and "unformed" fetus (in his thinking a formed fetus had reached the point in development when it received a soul), abortion was denounced in both instances.[46] For Augustine, decoupling sex from a commitment to the procreation of new life—whether through contraception or abortion—was morally wrong.

Augustine's view on abortion was further explored in the *Enchiridion* (written in 421). Although the bishop was inclined to believe that an unformed fetus perishes "like seeds that have never fructified," he conceded,

---

[44] Jerome, *Letter* 22.13 (To Eustochium) (*NPNF* 2/6:27).

[45] Augustine, *On Marriage and Concupiscence*, 1.17 (*NPNF* 1/5:271).

[46] In this passage, "preferring that its offspring should rather perish than receive vitality" refers to an unformed fetus, whereas "if it was advancing to life within the womb" refers to a formed fetus. In another translation, this sentence reads, ". . . preferring that their offspring die before it lives, or if it was already alive in the womb, to kill it before it was born." See Noonan, *The Morality of Abortion*, 16. Augustine's distinction between a "formed" and "unformed" fetus is clear in his discussion of Exodus 21:22. See Augustine, *Questions on Exodus*, 21, question 80.

"But who will dare to deny . . . that at the resurrection every defect in the form shall be supplied, and that thus the perfection which time would have brought shall not be wanting, any more than the blemishes which did bring shall be present."[47] Thus, despite his uncertainty about "whether life exists in a latent form before it manifests itself in the motions of the living being," Augustine seems convinced that unborn babies aborted early in pregnancy were alive at one point and will be included in the resurrection.[48] In summary, the early church's most prolific theologian affirmed what a long line of theologians had taught before him: abortion is immoral and contrary to Christian faithfulness.

By the fifth century, the church's opposition to abortion had been expressed clearly and consistently. Despite the surrounding culture of death, where abortion and infanticide were common, Christians taught that all people, born and unborn, deserve dignity and love. Guided by Scripture, the early church saw abortion for what it truly is: a vicious assault on human beings bearing the image of God.

The consistent pro-life ethic articulated by the early church continued uninterrupted for centuries and was adopted by government leaders as the church's influence spread. For example, in the eighth century, the Frankish kingdom of Charlemagne adopted the decision of the Council of Ancyra (AD 314) as the law of the land.[49] Recall that Ancyra had condemned abortion and imposed ten years of penance on those who sought abortion as well as those who made abortifacient drugs.

---

[47] Augustine, *Enchiridion*, 85 (*NPNF* 1/3:265).

[48] Augustine, 86. In context, Augustine asks, "To deny that the young who are cut out limb by limb from the womb, lest if they were left there dead the mother should die too, have never been alive, seems too audacious. Now, from the time that a man begins to live, from that time it is possible for him to die. And if he die, wheresoever death may overtake him, I cannot discover on what principle he can be denied an interest in the resurrection of the dead."

[49] Noonan, *The Morality of Abortion*, 18.

Further discussion of abortion occurred in the medieval period. From 450 to 1100, when monks and bishops took on an important role in transmitting church doctrine, the patristic teaching on abortion was reiterated.[50] For example, in 1234, Pope Gregory IX published a decretal collection that set out the teachings and laws of the church. Included in this decretal was a tenth-century penitential titled *Si aliguis*, which stated, "If anyone for the sake of fulfilling lust or in meditated hatred does something to a man or a woman, or gives them to drink, so that he cannot generate, or she conceive, or offspring be born, let it be held as homicide."[51] In other words, the canon, which had the force of law for the entire church, says that using contraception and seeking abortion are violations of church law and should be considered morally equivalent to homicide. The Decretals of Gregory IX remained an authoritative source of law for nearly 700 years until the Catholic Church adopted a new code of canon law in 1917 (which continued to uphold the Catholic Church's pro-life position).

Finally, Thomas Aquinas (1225–1274) discussed the moral status of the embryo and the act of abortion in his *Summa Theologica*. Like Augustine, Aquinas was concerned about ensoulment (when human beings receive a soul). Although he was unclear when ensoulment occurs—Thomas did not believe the rational human soul was present in the first few weeks of pregnancy—he said that once it occurs, it is homicide to kill the unborn

---

[50] In his discussion of the "Later Christian Tradition," Grisez provides examples from the seventh, eighth, ninth, and tenth centuries that show how Christians continued to follow the common teaching on abortion we have discussed so far. See Grisez, *Abortion*, 150–53.

[51] *Decretales* 5.12.5. Cited in Noonan, *The Morality of Abortion*, 21. The Latin text reads, "*Si aliquis causa explendae libidinis vel odii meditatione homini aut mulieri aliquid fecerit, vel ad potandum dederit, ut non possit generare, aut concipere, vel nasci soboles, ut homicida teneatur.*" Available online at http://thelatinlibrary.com /gregdecretals5.html.

baby.[52] Notably, Aquinas never offered a defense for abortion at any stage of pregnancy and said it is a sin "against nature" to reject God's gift of new life.[53]

## Reformation and Post-Reformation Protestants

In the sixteenth century, the Protestant Reformation, led by Martin Luther (1483–1546), resulted in far-reaching changes to Europe's religious landscape. For our purposes, although Protestants and Roman Catholics diverged on scores of doctrinal issues, leaders in both theological camps maintained Christianity's unbroken opposition to abortion.

For example, in several of his sermons, Luther refers to abortion as murder. In a sermon on Genesis 30, Luther sharply criticized men who "vent their rage on pregnant women even with blows," explaining that "those who pay no attention to pregnant women and do not spare the tender fetus become murderers and parricides."[54] Elsewhere, Luther says, "How great,

[52] Aquinas, *Summa Theologica* II-II, Q. 64, Art. 8, ad. 2. Online at https://www.ccel.org/a/aquinas/summa/SS/SS064.html#SSQ64A8THEP1. In a consideration of Thomas Aquinas, it is worth mentioning the principle of double effect, which he articulated in *Summa Theologica*. In Catholic moral theory, the principle of double effect lays out guidelines for determining when it is morally permissible to pursue an act with regrettable yet foreseeable harmful effects. For example, if a pregnant woman has an aggressive form of uterine cancer, the principle of double effect will allow, as the last possible resort, the doctor to save the mother's life even though the unintended result of the cancer treatment would be the loss of the unborn child. See Aquinas's discussion in *Summa Theologica*, II-II, Q. 64, Art. 7, It should be noted that instances in which the doctrine of double effect can legitimately be applied to abortion are incredibly rare. See Matthew A. C. Newsome, "Abortion and Double Effect," *Catholic Answers*, September 1, 2006, https://www.catholic.com/magazine/print-edition/abortion-and-double-effect.

[53] Quoted in United States Conference of Catholic Bishops, "Respect for Unborn Human Life: The Church's Constant Teaching," accessed August 14, 2023, https://usccb.org/issues-and-action/human-life-and-dignity/abortion/respect-for-unborn-human-life.

[54] Martin Luther, *Luther's Works*, ed. James Pelikan and Walter A. Hansen (St. Louis: Concordia, 1968), 5:381.

therefore, the wickedness of human nature is! How many girls there are who prevent conception and kill and expel tender fetuses, although procreation is the work of God!"[55] For Luther, the reality of abortion was evidence of humanity's depravity and rebellion against God.

In another sermon, Luther reflects on Jesus's omnipresence. In an aside, he notes, "Moreover, when Christ, the Son of God, was to be conceived in his mother's womb and become incarnate, he certainly had to be already present in essence and in person in the Virgin's womb, and had to assume humanity there."[56] Luther's comment that Jesus "had to assume humanity" in Mary's womb demonstrates the Reformer's belief that Jesus's incarnation began well before the first Christmas. Likewise, Luther stated that John the Baptist "was a child in his mother's womb [Luke 1:41] but, as I believe, could have faith."[57] Based on his reading of Luke 1, Luther believed John, although in utero, could have had faith in Jesus.[58]

In yet another sermon, Luther directly affirms the personhood of the unborn. Speaking on Genesis 26, the Reformer discusses life after death. In a brief digression on soul sleep, Luther acknowledges the limits of human reason and memory. As he explains, "Look at your infancy, and give thought to whether you remember that you were in your mother's womb, that you lay in a cradle, that you sucked your mother's breasts, cried, ate pap, grew, etc. Yet we are certainly alive even during the first year, when the fetus is carried in the mother's womb . . . frequent movements show that there is certain and vigorous life of the fetus in the womb."[59] In con-

---

[55] Martin Luther, *Luther's Works*, ed. James Pelikan and Walter A. Hansen (St. Louis: Concordia, 1964), 4:304.

[56] Martin Luther, *Luther's Works*, ed. Robert H. Fischer and Helmut T. Lehmann (St. Louis: Concordia, 1961), 37:62.

[57] Martin Luther, *Luther's Works*, ed. Conrad Bergendoff and Helmut T. Lehmann (St. Louis: Concordia, 1958), 40:242.

[58] For a discussion on Luke 1:39–45, see chapter 2.

[59] Luther, *Luther's Works*, 5:75. In the same passage, Luther states confidently, "I also lived in my mother's womb." Elsewhere, Luther says something similar in a sermon on Genesis 49:33, noting, "For no one of those who are alive today knows

text, Luther's point is that man's limited knowledge and memory related to one's personal history ought to produce humility when considering the topic of life after death. For our purposes, the text also effectively illustrates Luther's high regard for pre-born life, which is how his denunciations of abortion elsewhere should be read. For Luther, the unborn child's personhood is not in question. Consequently, abortion is a wicked interference in God's creative work.

Another Reformer, Martin Bucer (1491–1551), wrote at length about marriage and divorce. According to Bucer, divorce is permissible if one of the spouses has committed a serious crime. Included in his list of crimes is abortion, which "is so profoundly contrary to the divine institution of marriage that by it the nuptial agreement is totally dissolved."[60] Although marriage is designed to be an inviolable covenant, the criminality of abortion demonstrates that the woman no longer meets the biblical requirements of a Christian spouse. As a result, the marriage can be dissolved.

Likewise, French Reformer John Calvin (1509–1564) also opposed abortion in his teaching. In his commentary on Exodus 21:22, Calvin affirms fetal personhood, explaining, "For the fœtus, though enclosed in the womb of its mother, is already a human being, and it is almost a monstrous crime to rob it of the life which it has not yet begun to enjoy."[61] Calvin goes on to explain that it is "atrocious to destroy a fœtus in the womb before it has come to life" because the Old Testament law provided protections for

---

where he was during the first two years, when he lived either in the womb, or when, after being brought into the light of day, he sucked his mother's milk. He knows nothing about the days, the nights, the times, and the rulers. Yet he lived at that time, and he was a body to a soul—a body adapted to all natural functions." See Martin Luther, *Luther's Works*, ed. Jaroslav Pelikan and Walter A. Hansen (St. Louis: Concordia, 1966), 8:316–7.

[60] This quotation appears in H. J. Selderhuis, *Marriage and Divorce in the Thought of Martin Bucer*, trans. John Vriend and Lyle D. Bierma (Kirksville, MO: Thomas Jefferson University Press, 1999), 311.

[61] John Calvin, *Calvin's Commentaries*, trans. Charles Bingham (Grand Rapids: Baker, 1981), 3:41–2.

both the pregnant mother and unborn child. As he explains, "It would be a crime punishable with death, not only when the mother died from the effects of abortion, but also if the infant should be killed; whether it should die from the wound abortively, or soon after its birth."[62]

In his 1673 book, *Christian Directory*, the English Puritan Richard Baxter (1615–1691) included a lengthy discussion on murder. According to Baxter, some people, desperate to conceal a crime and save face, will resort to murder. He notes that sexually promiscuous women will often seek abortion "to prevent the shame" of fornication.[63] Baxter believed that those responsible for abortion would face judgment; even if the guilty party evaded detection in this life, "the righteous Judge will make them know, that all their wicked shifts will be their confusion, because there is no hiding them from him."[64]

In colonial America, ministers continued to speak against abortion. For example, in 1712, Benjamin Wadsworth, a minister and future president of Harvard College, published a series of sermons in a book titled *The Well-Ordered Family*. Wadsworth prefaces his comments on abortion by noting, "Here I might say, as soon as the Mother perceives her self with Child, she should be careful, not to do any thing, injurious to her self or to the Child God has formed in her. A conscientious regard to the Sixth Commandment, (which is, *Thou shalt not kill*) should make her thus careful." He adds, "If any purposely indeavour to destroy the fruit of their Womb (whether they actually do it or not) they [a]re guilty of Murder in God's account."[65]

---

[62] Calvin, *Calvin's Commentaries*, 3:42.

[63] Richard Baxter, *A Christian Directory or a Sum of Practical Case of Conscience* (London: Robert White, 1673), pt. 4, chap. 8, 7. Online at https://www.gutenberg.org/cache/epub/43967/pg43967-images.html.

[64] Baxter, *A Christian Directory or a Sum of Practical Case of Conscience.*

[65] Benjamin Wadsworth, *The Well-Ordered Family; or, Relative Duties* (Boston: B. Green, 1712), 45, emphasis in original. The essay is printed in *The Colonial American Family: Collected Essays*, ed. David J. Rothman and Sheila M. Rothman (New York: Arno, 1972).

Seven years later, in 1719, Wadsworth wrote a treatise on the Ten Commandments. In his discussion about the Decalogue's prohibition against murder, Wadsworth explains, "Those break this Command, who purposely give poison to others, or unwholesome Meats or Drinks, with a design to hurt their bodies. And so do those, who purposely indeavor to destroy the Life of a *Child in the Womb*, whether the Woman *her self*, or *another*, does it."[66] For Wadsworth, those responsible for abortion—whether the mother or an abortionist—were guilty of breaking the sixth commandment.

## Roman Catholic Church

After the Reformation, the Roman Catholic Church continued to oppose abortion. In 1588, Pope Sixtus V published a papal bull titled, "Against Those Who Procure Abortion," known by its opening word, *Effraenatam*.[67] Understanding abortion to be a common and socially accepted practice, Sixtus wanted to "eradicate" it. For Sixtus, there was no distinction between an "animated" or "unanimated" fetus; all abortion was homicide. According to Sixtus, the purpose of abortion was "to kill . . . immature fetuses in the maternal viscera through medicines, poisons, violence, or work imposed on the pregnant mother." Sixtus consciously directed the bull to men, asking, "Who will not condemn . . . those men who with poisons, potions, and evil deeds sterilize women or prevent them from conceiving and giving birth with evil medicines?" As Professor John Christopoulos observes, Sixtus "sought to control the practice of abortion by disciplining the men

---

[66] Benjamin Wadsworth, *An Essay on the Decalogue, or Ten Commandments* (Boston: B. Green, 1719), 89, italics original.

[67] Evidently, there are no reliable English translations of *Effraenatam*. Quotes are taken from John Christopoulos's article, which relied on the Latin original. For his full discussion, see John Christopoulos, "Abortion and the Confessional in Counter-Reformation Italy," *Renaissance Quarterly* 65, no. 2 (2012): 443–84. For a summary of the document, see Katherine Brind'Amour, "'Effraenatam' (1588), by Pope Sixtus V," *Embryo Project Encyclopedia*, November 11, 2007, https://embryo.asu.edu/pages/effraenatam-1588-pope-sixtus-v.

who put women in this situation."[68] Women who "knowingly" took abortifacients were also condemned. In short, Sixtus hoped, as philosopher Germain Grisez puts it, "to wipe out attacks on incipient life, and so he invoked all the legal penalties of homicide against all abortion and even against contraception."[69]

Under *Effraenatam*, those who procured an abortion as well as those who aided in abortion were to be treated as murderers. Additionally, they were to be automatically excommunicated from the church with the right to extend absolution reserved to the pope alone.[70]

Sixtus's successor, Gregory XIV, believed *Effraenatam* was too severe and ineffective. Thus, acting on the advice of the cardinals, he issued a new papal constitution titled *Sedes apostolica* in 1591. Gregory's constitution returned to making distinctions between animated and unanimated fetuses. Abortion of an animated fetus was still met with excommunication, while abortion of an unanimated fetus received lesser penalties.[71] He also allowed absolution to be given by local priests and bishops (as opposed to solely the pontiff). This constitution remained in effect until it was revised by Pope Pius IX in 1869.

In response to the Protestant Reformation, the Council of Trent commissioned a compendium of Catholic doctrine to expound the church's teaching. Known as the Catechism of the Council of Trent (1566), this catechism describes abortion as a "heinous crime" and says couples who procure an abortion are guilty of "nothing less than a premeditated conspiracy to murder."[72]

---

[68] Christopoulos, "Abortion and the Confessional in Counter-Reformation Italy," 467.

[69] Grisez, *Abortion*, 168.

[70] Christopoulos, "Abortion and the Confessional in Counter-Reformation Italy," 467.

[71] Christopoulos, 474; Grisez, *Abortion*, 167–68.

[72] "The Catechism of the Council of Trent," accessed June 19, 2024, https://fisheaters.com/srpdf/xcatechismoftrent.pdf?bcs-agent-scanner=6fe57841-1265-c840-91da-06722a6dc724.

In 1869, Pope Pius IX once again removed the distinction between an animated and unanimated fetus from canon law. According to Pius IX in his *Apostolic Sedis* encyclical, this distinction was grounded in neither evidence nor reason. Thus, the unscientific marker of "quickening" was removed as a standard for determining the right to life.[73]

In the last hundred years, the Catholic Church has reiterated its teaching on life. In 1930, Pope Pius XI released an encyclical titled *Casti Connubii*, affirming that the lives of both a mother and her unborn child are "equally sacred, and no one has the power, not even the public authority, to destroy it."[74] Pius charged civil governments to "defend the lives of the innocent . . . among whom we must mention in the first place infants hidden in the mother's womb." Governments who fail to protect unborn children from "death at the hands of doctors or of others" should remember that God is the "Judge and Avenger of innocent blood."[75]

At the Second Vatican Council (1962–1965), the Roman Catholic Church released a series of documents, including a constitution titled *Gaudium et Spes*. Promulgated by Pope Paul VI in 1965, the constitution aims at explaining the church's mission to those outside the church. The document includes two mentions of abortion, both of which reaffirm the church's historic teaching. First, abortion is mentioned alongside murder, genocide, and euthanasia as a practice "opposed to life itself" that "poison[s] human society."[76] Second, in a section dealing with family life, *Gaudium*

---

[73] See Katherine Brind'Amour, "Roman Catholic Church Quickening," *Embryo Project Encyclopedia*, November 11, 2007, https://embryo.asu.edu/pages/roman-catholic-church-quickening, and Grisez, *Abortion*, 177.

[74] Pius XI, *Casti Connubii*, December 31, 1930, para. 64, https://www.vatican.va/content/pius-xi/en/encyclicals/documents/hf_p-xi_enc_19301231_casti-connubii.html.

[75] Pius XI, para. 67.

[76] Paul VI, *Gaudium et Spes*, December 7, 1965, section 27, https://www.vatican.va/archive/hist_councils/ii_vatican_council/documents/vat-ii_const_19651207_gaudium-et-spes_en.html.

*et Spes* explains, "For God, the Lord of life, has conferred on men the surpassing ministry of safeguarding life in a manner which is worthy of man. Therefore from the moment of its conception life must be guarded with the greatest care while abortion and infanticide are unspeakable crimes."[77] Although Vatican II significantly adjusted aspects of Catholic liturgy and practice, the church's teaching on abortion did not change.

Additionally, the Catholic Church's canon law books of 1917 and 1983 provide severe penalties for abortion. Canon 2350 of the 1917 law book states that "Procurers of abortion, the mother not excepted, incur, upon the effect being secured, automatic excommunication reserved to the Ordinary, and if they are clerics, they are also deposed."[78] The 1983 canon law, promulgated by Pope John Paul II and edited slightly in 2021 by Pope Francis, reads, "A person who actually procures an abortion incurs a *latae sententiae* excommunication."[79] In Catholic theology, a *latae sententiae* excommunication occurs automatically upon the commission of the offense (rather than a *ferendae sententiae* penalty, which is not binding until imposed by a third party). The Catholic Church imposes the severe penalty of excommunication on anyone complicit in abortion, including the woman, the abortionist, the boyfriend who encourages the abortion, and the parent or friend who pays for the abortion.

---

[77] Paul VI, *Gaudium et Spes*, section 51.

[78] *The 1917 or Pio-Benedictine Code of Canon Law* (New York: P. J. Kennedy & Sons, 1918), Canon 2350.

[79] *Apostolic Constitution Sacrae Disciplinae Leges* (Rome: Vatican, 1983), Book VI, Part II, Title VI, Canon 1397, emphasis original. Online at https://www.vatican.va/archive/cod-iuris-canonici/eng/documents/cic_lib6_en.pdf. In December 2021, Pope Francis edited Book VI of the Code of Canon Law, which deals with penal law. Before 2021, canon 1397, which had previously been numbered canon 1398, referred to "a person who procures a completed abortion." The new English version adds the word "actually." For a discussion of the change, see Ed Condon and J. D. Flynn, "The Church's New Penal Canon Law: The Good, the Bad, and the Ugly," *The Pillar*, June 1, 2021, https://www.pillarcatholic.com/p/the-churchs-new-penal-canon-law-the.

Finally, the most recent pontiffs, John Paul II, Benedict XVI, and Francis, have maintained the Roman Catholic Church's teaching on life. In 1995, Pope John Paul II stated, "Among all the crimes which can be committed against life, procured abortion has characteristics making it particularly serious and deplorable . . . procured abortion is the deliberate and direct killing, by whatever means it is carried out, of a human being in the initial phase of his or her existence, extending from conception to birth."[80]

In 2008, Pope Benedict XVI addressed members of Italy's pro-life movement. According to the pope, "defending human life today has become more difficult because a mindset has developed, entrusted to the opinion of the individual, which has gradually debased its value."[81] Despite the challenges, Benedict reminded his audience that "permitting recourse to the termination of pregnancy [has] not solved the problems that afflict many women and a fair number of families." The pope encouraged those in the pro-life movement to work "in the contexts of education, culture, and political debate" to end abortion and create a culture that honors life.

Likewise, Pope Francis, in a 2021 interview, explained, "Abortion is murder. . . . Those who carry out abortions kill."[82] Francis's comment was similar to remarks he made in 2016, when he stated, "Abortion is not a 'lesser evil.' It is a crime. . . . That is what the mafia does. It is a crime, it is absolutely evil. . . . It is against the Hippocratic Oath that physicians

---

[80] John Paul II, "*Evangelium Vitae*," Vatican, March 25, 1995, https://www.vatican.va/content/john-paul-ii/en/encyclicals/documents/hf_jp-ii_enc_25031995_evangelium-vitae.html.

[81] Benedict XVI, "Address of His Holiness Benedict XVI to the Members of Italy's Pro-Life Movement," Vatican, May 12, 2008, https://www.vatican.va/content/benedict-xvi/en/speeches/2008/may/documents/hf_ben-xvi_spe_20080512_movimento-vita.html.

[82] Quoted in Philip Pullella, "Pope Says Abortion Is 'Murder' but U.S. Bishops Should Not Be Political," Reuters, September 15, 2021, https://www.reuters.com/world/europe/pope-says-abortion-is-murder-us-bishops-should-not-be-political-2021-09-15/.

take. It is an evil in and of itself. It is not a 'religious' evil, to start with, no, it is a human evil. Evidently, as it is a human evil—like all killing—it is condemned."[83] Finally, in 2024, the Dicastery for the Doctrine of the Faith—the department of the church responsible for promulgating and defending doctrine—released a declaration on human dignity, which explained, "It must, therefore, be stated with all force and clarity, even in our time, that 'this defense of unborn life is closely linked to the defense of each and every other human right. It involves the conviction that a human being is always sacred and inviolable, in any situation and at every stage of development.'"[84]

## Eastern Orthodox Church

The Eastern Orthodox Church has also consistently opposed abortion.[85] This opposition has been stated by Orthodox church leaders in encyclicals and sermons. For example, in his Christmas encyclical in 1976, former Archbishop Iakovos described abortion as a "moral alienation."[86] In 1985, Greek Orthodox priest Stanley Harakas summarized the church's position on abortion, noting, "The Orthodox Church brands abortion as murder;

---

[83] Francis, "In-Flight Press Conference of His Holiness Pope Francis from Mexico to Rome," Vatican, February 17, 2016, https://www.vatican.va/content/francesco/en/speeches/2016/february/documents/papa-francesco_20160217_messico-conferenza-stampa.html.

[84] Dicastery for the Doctrine of the Faith, "Dignitas Infinita," Vatican, April, 8, 2024, https://press.vatican.va/content/salastampa/en/bollettino/pubblico/2024/04/08/240408c.html. In this quotation, the document is quoting Pope Francis, "Apostolic Exhortation *Evangelii Gaudium*," Vatican, November 24, 2013, para. 213.

[85] The Eastern Orthodox Church shared communion with the Roman Catholic Church until the East-West Schism. The schism was the result of theological, political, and cultural differences that came to a head in 1054.

[86] Cited in Stanley S. Harakas, "The Stand of the Orthodox Church on Controversial Issues," Greek Orthodox Archdiocese of America, August 12, 1985, https://www.goarch.org/-/the-stand-of-the-orthodox-church-on-controversial-issues.

that is, as a premeditated termination of the life of a human being. The only time the Orthodox Church will reluctantly acquiesce to abortion is when the preponderance of medical opinion determines that unless the embryo or fetus is aborted, the mother will die."[87]

In 2021, on the eve of oral arguments in the *Dobbs* case (the case that eventually led to the overturning of *Roe v. Wade*), Metropolitan Tikhon, the Primate of the Orthodox Church in America, participated in a pro-life event for ministry leaders. According to the Orthodox leader, "The sanctity of life is not only a social issue, it is a spiritual issue that must be addressed constantly and clearly because it touches the very fabric of humanity and salvation."[88] From the perspective of the Orthodox Church, abortion ends human life. Consequently, Orthodox Christians believe abortion is immoral and that Christians should work for and promote a pro-life ethic.

## The Modern Church

Christian opposition to abortion—whether Protestant, Roman Catholic, or Orthodox—remained unbroken into the twentieth century. For example, in 1945, German pastor Dietrich Bonhoeffer said, "To kill the fruit in the mother's womb is to injure the right to life that God has bestowed on the developing life."[89] In 1982, the founding editor of *Christianity Today*,

---

[87] Harakas, "The Stand of the Orthodox Church on Controversial Issues."

[88] See "Pray for *Dobbs* Prayer Event: Metropolitan Tikhon," YouTube video, November 30, 2021, https://www.youtube.com/watch?v=VXSgaXj1Nuw. Metropolitan Tikhon made these comments during the Pray for *Dobbs* webinar I helped organize on October 14, 2021. See chapter 4 for more details on the Pray for *Dobbs* initiative.

[89] Dietrich Bonhoeffer, *Ethics*, vol. 6, Dietrich Bonhoeffer Works (Minneapolis: Fortress, 2009), 206. The full quotation reads, "To kill the fruit in the mother's womb is to injure the right to life that God has bestowed on the developing life. Discussion of the question whether a human being is already present confuses the simple fact that, in any case, God wills to create a human being and that the life

Carl F. H. Henry (1913–2003), wrote, "Where the living God is clouded as the transcendent source of human life and dignity, respect for the meaning and worth of personal existence tends to vanish. . . . Nowhere is this more evident than in the callous modern attitude toward abortion."[90] Of course, the position of Bonhoeffer and Henry had been the position of Christians since the first century. In fact, there were virtually no dissenting voices on abortion within the church until the middle of the twentieth century. Only then, under the influence of theological liberalism and at the height of the sexual revolution, did many mainline Protestant denominations such as the Episcopal Church, Presbyterian Church (USA), and United Methodist Church change their position on abortion.[91] Significantly, the

---

of this developing human being has been deliberately taken. And this is nothing but murder."

[90] Carl F. H. Henry, *God, Revelation and Authority*, vol. 5 (Wheaton, IL: Crossway, 1982), 150. Henry went on to say, "The disregard for the value of fetal life prepares a mood of growing acceptance of euthanasia, and possibly even of infanticide as in the destruction rather than salvaging of malformed infants." It is worth noting that in discussions about church history and abortion, the November 1968 issue of *Christianity Today* is often brought up because of its focus on abortion. Articles by theologians, including Paul Jewett, attempted to offer a nuanced Christian position that allowed for abortion in some circumstances. I briefly discuss this well-known issue of the publication in the next chapter.

[91] The following denominations have historically been considered part of mainline Protestantism: the United Methodist Church, the Evangelical Lutheran Church in America, the Presbyterian Church (USA), the Episcopal Church, the American Baptist Churches, the United Church of Christ, and the Disciples of Christ. Some of these denominations, such as the Episcopal Church (TEC), Presbyterian Church (USA), and United Church of Christ, are decidedly pro-choice (demonstrated by their membership in the Religious Coalition for Reproductive Choice). Others, such as the United Methodist Church and Evangelical Lutheran Church in America, support abortion rights with some limits. Worth noting is that within a five-year window (2019-2023), over 7,600 churches disaffiliated from the United Methodist Church (UMC) (over 4,200 in 2023 alone). This represents about 25% of churches within the UMC. Although most of these churches left the denomination over issues related to gender and sexuality, thousands of former UMC churches have joined the new Global Methodist Church, a denomination with a pro-life doctrinal statement. On abortion, the Global Methodist Church states, "The sacredness of all

churches that adjusted their theology on abortion were the same churches that had embraced theological liberalism in the first decades of the twentieth century.[92]

Although a lengthy discussion of theological liberalism is outside the scope of this book, it is worth noting a few features of this movement as it relates to abortion. With its emphasis on critical rationality and religious experience, theological liberalism departed from the authority-based orthodoxy of traditional Christian theology. In liberal theology, the Bible may record aspirational principles, but it is not infallible or inspired.[93] In other words, a liberal approach to the Bible allows modern readers to experience the spiritual message of Jesus without divisive doctrinal debates on matters like the Trinity, the deity of Christ, original sin, etc. From the vantage point of liberal theology, modern readers can dispense with a literal interpretation of the miraculous events recorded in Scripture. Additionally,

---

life compels us to resist the practice of abortion except in the cases of tragic conflicts of life against life when the wellbeing of the mother and the child are at stake. We do not accept abortion as a means of birth control or gender selection, and we call upon all Christians as disciples of the Lord of Life to prayerfully consider how we can support those women facing unintended pregnancies without adequate care, counsel, or resources (Exodus 22:23–23, Psalm 139:13–16, James 1:27)." Global Methodist Church website, accessed August 12, 2024, https://globalmethodist.org/the-global-methodist-church-in-the-public-square-restraint-and-modesty/.

[92] For further discussion on theological liberalism and abortion, see chapter 4.

[93] This approach to the Bible was famously articulated by Henry Emerson Fosdick. Here are a few examples from his well-known book *The Modern Use of the Bible*: "Fortunately for us, spiritual efficiency in the use of the Bible is not entirely dependent upon correctness of exegesis" (11). And: "Moreover, the new approach to the Bible saves us from the necessity of apologizing for immature stages in the development of the Biblical revelation" (27). And: "So we used to think of inspiration as a procedure which produced a book guaranteed in all its parts against error, and containing from beginning to end a unanimous system of truth. No well-instructed mind, I think, can hold that now. . . . Our ideas of the method of inspiration have changed; verbal dictation, inerrant manuscripts, uniformity of doctrine between 1000 B.C. and 70 A.D.—all such ideas have become incredible in the face of facts" (30–31). See Henry Emerson Fosdick, *The Modern Use of the Bible* (New York: MacMillan, 1924).

liberal theology emphasizes the natural sciences, a social gospel ethos, and cultural optimism and is committed to the authority of individual reason and experience.[94]

The correlation between churches and denominations that embraced theological liberalism and subsequently changed their position on abortion is striking. As culture shifted in the middle of the twentieth century, churches that rejected the Bible as God's infallible and authoritative Word were the same churches that accepted and endorsed abortion. Conversely, the churches and denominations that continued to believe in the trustworthiness and reliability of the Bible remained committed to Christianity's historic teaching on the personhood of the unborn.

For example, as we have previously discussed, the Roman Catholic Church has remained committed to its teaching on abortion.[95] The same is true for theologically conservative Protestant denominations such as the

---

[94] According to Roger Olson, the "essence of liberal Protestant theology" is the "maximal acknowledgment of the claims of modernity within a Christian framework." See Roger E. Olson, *The Story of Christian Theology: Twenty Centuries of Tradition & Reform* (Downers Grove, IL: InterVarsity, 1999), 549–50. For two twenty-first-century defenses of liberal theology, see Gary Dorrien, *The Making of American Liberal Theology: Imagining Progressive Religion* (Louisville: Westminster John Knox, 2001), xix–xxiii, and Michael J. Langford, *The Tradition of Liberal Theology* (Grand Rapids: Eerdmans, 2014). Langford identifies eleven characteristics of liberal theology: a use of the Bible that is not always literal; reason and revelation in harmony; a nonlegalist account of redemption; the possibility of salvation outside a narrow path; toleration; original sin but not original guilt; belief in free will; a view of providence that respects the integrity of the natural order; the joint need of faith and works; a minimal number of basic teachings; and a range of acceptable lifestyles. See Langford, *The Tradition of Liberal Theology*, 19–59.

[95] The official position of the Roman Catholic Church on abortion is articulated in the *Catechism of the Catholic Church*. In part 3, section 2, chapter 2, article 5, line 2271, it states: "Since the first century the Church has affirmed the moral evil of every procured abortion. This teaching has not changed and remains unchangeable. Direct abortion, that is to say, abortion willed either as an end or a means, is gravely contrary to the moral law." See http://www.vatican.va/archive/ENG0015/__P7Z.HTM.

Lutheran Church-Missouri Synod, Presbyterian Church in America (PCA), Assemblies of God, and many others that remain committed to the Bible's teaching on abortion.[96]

Finally, the correlation between theological liberalism and accepting abortion as morally permissible is helpfully illustrated in the recent history of the Southern Baptist Convention (SBC), the largest Protestant denomination in the United States. Although the SBC was founded as a theologically conservative denomination in 1845, by the 1950s, leaders and professors within the denomination's seminaries and entities were publishing and teaching modernist views on the Bible.[97] For example, in 1961,

---

[96] Reverend Dr. Matthew Harrison, the president of the Lutheran Church–Missouri Synod, released the following statement in 2019 after governors in New York and Virginia expanded abortion in their states. Harrison said, "The Lutheran Church—Missouri Synod advocates strong citizenship and active participation in government. We obey the laws of our land and encourage those around us to do so. We are, however, bound by our conscience to speak against those laws that are unjust and, especially, those laws that violate God's law and the natural law that binds all mankind. Abortion and other means through which humans kill humans violate these natural and moral laws that form the foundation of society." See Matthew Harrison, "LCMS President's Statement Regarding Gubernatorial Actions Expanding Abortion in New York, Illinois," *Reporter*, January 24, 2019, https://reporter.lcms.org/2019/lcms-presidents-statement-regarding-gubernatorial-actions-expanding-abortion-in-new-york-and-illinois/. The official position of the Presbyterian Church (PCA) is presented in TE Carl Bogue, "Report of the Ad Interim Committee on Abortion," PCA Historical Center, 1978, https://www.pcahistory.org/pca/digest/studies/2-015.pdf?bcs-agent-scanner=5f9dff27-37f3-d146-b07d0bbc3b6c4418. For the Assemblies of God's official statement, see "Sanctity of Human Life: Abortion and Reproductive Issues (Adopted by the General Presbytery in Session August 9–11, 2010)," https://ag.org/Beliefs/Position-Papers/Abortion-Sanctity-of-Human-Life.

[97] When the original charter for The Southern Baptist Theological Seminary was adopted in 1858, it included a statement of belief known as the Abstract of Principles. In its article on the Bible, it states, "The Scriptures of the Old and New Testaments were given by inspiration of God, and are the only sufficient, certain and authoritative rule of all saving knowledge, faith, and obedience." Although every professor since the founding of the seminary has been required

Professor Ralph Elliott of Midwestern Seminary published a commentary with Broadman Press, the denomination's publishing house, that questioned the historicity of Genesis 1–11.[98] Additionally, in 1969, Broadman Press published the first volume in a commentary set written by G. Henton Davies that applied higher critical methodology, rejected Mosaic authorship of the Pentateuch, and contested details of Noah's flood.[99]

The influence of theologically liberal professors and denominational leaders became increasingly evident in the 1960s and '70s as the denomination passed a series of politically liberal resolutions (nonbinding statements that express the opinion or concern of the SBC). For example, in 1971, the SBC passed their first resolution on abortion, calling for the legalization of abortion in certain cases including rape, incest, fetal deformity, and the life

---

to sign the Abstract of Principles and commit to "teach in accordance with, and not contrary to" the document, professors throughout the mid-twentieth century signed the statement despite maintaining unspoken reservations about certain articles.

[98] In the introduction of his commentary, Elliott states, "Critical study must be, not an end in itself, but a tool to help us go from the basic historical situation to a positive theological emphasis which challenges the people of one's own day. In other words, one must come to the place that he sees the parabolic and symbolic nature of much of the Old Testament Scriptures. Genesis is to be understood in this light. It is not science. In the material attributed to J and P, the early writers were in no way trying to give a scientific or literal explanation." In his comments on Noah's flood, Elliott opts for a "local flood" explanation: "All of this suggests that the compiler of Genesis was using a local flood account only as a means of introducing the background and culture out of which the need arose for Abraham to serve as the representative of God." Finally, Elliott questions some of the factual details about God's destruction of Sodom and Gomorrah, noting, "That something drastic happened, there can be no doubt. . . . The theological theme and purpose of judgement has been established. This is in no way injured when one asks, from a physical standpoint, whether there is any explanation possible for the physical phenomenon which became the vehicle of the religious theme." See Ralph Elliott, *The Message of Genesis* (Nashville: Broadman, 1961), 15, 67, 134–35.

[99] Adam Winters, "The Broadman Bible Commentary Controversy: From Genesis to the Conservative Resurgence," *Towers* 14, no. 10 (June–July 2016): 22.

of the mother.[100] Additional resolutions on abortion passed in the 1970s took the same view.[101]

However, starting in 1979, theologically conservative Southern Baptists successfully elected a succession of conservative presidents, which led to the resignation (or firing) and replacement of liberal seminary presidents, professors, and agency leaders.[102] As liberal leaders departed, the convention's seminaries and entities returned to upholding inerrancy and rejected theological liberalism. Not surprisingly, starting in 1980, the convention adopted resolutions more aligned with the denomination's historically conservative roots.[103]

---

[100] See "Resolution on Abortion," Southern Baptist Convention, June 1, 1971, https://www.sbc.net/resource-library/resolutions/resolution-on-abortion-2/. Mainstream publications including the *New York Times* reported on the SBC resolution. See "Southern Baptists Approve Abortion in Certain Cases," *New York Times*, June 3, 1971, https://www.nytimes.com/1971/06/03/archives/southern-baptists-approve-abortion-in-certain-cases.html.

[101] See "Resolution on Abortion and Sanctity of Human Life," Southern Baptist Convention, June 1, 1974, https://www.sbc.net/resource-library/resolutions/resolution-on-abortion-and-sanctity-of-human-life/; "Resolution on Abortion," Southern Baptist Convention, June 1, 1976, https://www.sbc.net/resource-library/resolutions/resolution-on-abortion-3/; "Resolution on Abortion," Southern Baptist Convention, June 1, 1977, https://www.sbc.net/resource-library/resolutions/resolution-on-abortion-4/; and "Resolution on Abortion," Southern Baptist Convention, June 1, 1978, https://www.sbc.net/resource-library/resolutions/resolution-on-abortion-5/.

[102] This movement became known as the Conservative Resurgence. Starting with the election of Adrian Rodgers in 1979, Southern Baptist messengers at the Annual Meeting voted for inerrantists to serve as the denomination's president. Within the SBC, the president appoints people to serve on the Committee of Committees, which in turn is responsible for appointing the members of the Committee of Nominations. This committee is responsible for electing the trustees that oversee the denomination's entities, including the six seminaries (the source of much of the liberal theology).

[103] The first strong pro-life resolution was passed in 1980. The resolution called for a constitutional amendment to prohibit abortion with an exception for the life of the mother. See "Resolution on Abortion," Southern Baptist Convention, June 1, 1980, https://www.sbc.net/resource-library/resolutions/resolution-on-abortion-6/. Since 1980, Southern Baptists have passed dozens of pro-life resolutions. The latest

Despite the rise of theological liberalism in the twentieth century, pastors, theologians, and evangelists committed to the authority of the Bible continued to affirm a pro-life ethic. To conclude our overview of church history, consider what some of the twentieth century's most influential Protestant ministers taught about abortion: Billy Graham (1918–2018), J. I. Packer (1926–2020), and John MacArthur.[104]

---

resolution, passed in 2022 (nine days before the *Dobbs* decision), states, "The Bible affirms that the preborn child is a person, bearing the image of God, from the moment of conception." For the full text of the resolution, see "On Anticipation of a Historic Moment in the Pro-life Movement," Southern Baptist Convention, June 15, 2022, https://www.sbc.net/resource-library/resolutions/on-anticipation-of-a-historic-moment-in-the-pro-life-movement/. In 2021, the SBC passed another pro-life resolution that states, "We affirm that the murder of the preborn children is a crime against humanity that must be punished equally under the law." For full text of the resolution, see "On Abolishing Abortion," Southern Baptist Convention, June 21, 2021, https://www.sbc.net/resource-library/resolutions/on-abolishing-abortion/. Another resolution, passed by messengers at the 2018 convention states, "We affirm the full dignity of every unborn child and denounce every act of abortion except to save the mother's physical life." For the text of this resolution, see "On Reaffirming the Full Dignity of Every Human Being," Southern Baptist Convention, June 12, 2018, https://www.sbc.net/resource-library/resolutions/on-reaffirming-the-full-dignity-of-every-human-being/.

[104] It is worth noting that some scholars, like ethicist David Gushee, have shifted toward a more abortion-affirming position. For example, in 2008, Gushee criticized the evangelical Left for their refusal to take a clear stand on abortion:

> [The evangelical Left] does not signal that it takes fully seriously the sanctity of *all* human life, including those lives developing in the womb. It is not just that the left is far softer on its preferred abortion policy measures than the right (or the center) would be, but that the matter simply does not seem to rise very high on their moral agenda. . . . There is no visible analysis of the complex but significant issue of the moral status of fetal life. . . . Evangelical left authors proclaim that they are pro-life, but this does not seem to cash out in a real significant way on the abortion issue.

David P. Gushee, *The Future of Faith in American Politics: The Public Witness of the Evangelical Center* (Waco, TX: Baylor University Press, 2008), 80.

## *Billy Graham*

Evangelist Billy Graham (1918–2018) was the defining figure of twentieth-century American evangelism. During his career, Graham preached to more than 215 million people in more than 185 countries and territories.[105] Although Graham provided spiritual counsel to U.S. presi-

In 2013, Gushee discussed abortion in his book *The Sacredness of Human Life*. According to Gushee, "There is certainly support in Christian tradition for profound moral discomfort with abortion." However, he states, "The biblical basis for opposition to abortion is disputed, because there is no explicit condemnation of abortion in the canon." Gushee, *The Sacredness of Human Life: Why an Ancient Biblical Vision Is Key to the World's Future* (Grand Rapids: Eerdmans, 2013), 357. Despite this comment, Gushee affirms the "unbroken daily continuity of the development process" and rejects personhood theory. He also argues, "It should be hard to avoid the commonsense conclusion that the prenatal human being is indeed human from the beginning of her precarious journey, and this fragile humanity simply continues to blossom over the entire course of her life span, with birth one very significant milestone in the journey" (358).

Despite these relatively strong pro-life statements, Gushee has come out more recently in favor of abortion. For example, following the 2022 midterms, he wrote, "My view long has been that the Republican game on abortion was clear, for many elections: gain voters by promising to roll back abortion, and then fail to deliver. . . . This strategy worked from Ronald Reagan through George W. Bush. But it ended with the *Dobbs* decision." Gushee then states, "Watching legislation develop since this summer and listening closely to women and couples in states where abortion (and related health care) access has been restricted, has made it more clear to me than ever that women's health care choices during pregnancy are too vital, personal, and complex to be taken away from them by legislators sitting in capitol buildings." Gushee concludes his article by observing how pro-abortion political mobilization affected the outcome of the election. Significantly, Gushee celebrated this development, noting, "A fever has gripped our national politics for a while now. It has been a frightening time. . . . At least as of the morning after the midterms, I am more hopeful than I have been since 2016." David Gushee, "Trump's Toxicity: A First Take on the Midterm Elections," *Baptist News Global*, November 9, 2022, https://baptistnews.com/article/trumps-toxicity-a-first-take-on-the-midterm-elections/.

[105] "Billy Graham, Evangelist to the World, Dead at Age 99," Billy Graham: Official Obituary, February 21, 2018, https://memorial.billygraham.org/official-obituary/.

dents, the focus of his worldview ministry was evangelism, not politics.[106] However, Graham did write about abortion, including in one of his widely published "My Answer" columns in 1961. In response to a writer who confessed to feeling guilty of murder after an abortion, Graham responded, "Abortion is as violent a sin against God, nature, and one's self as one can commit. Granted also that there is an element of murder in it." He went on to add, "The worst effect of abortion is upon the soul of the would-be mother."[107] According to Graham, abortion was a "violent" sin against God that harmed the mother and her unborn baby.

## *J. I. Packer*

Puritan scholar J. I. Packer (1926–2020) was one of the most well-known and influential evangelicals in the twentieth century. He served as the

---

[106] Billy Graham famously did not join the Moral Majority, led by Jerry Falwell. That Graham did not make politics a focus of his public ministry is reflected in the fact that the word "abortion" does not appear in the index in William Martin's 698-page biography of Graham. See William Martin, *A Prophet with Honor: The Billy Graham Story* (Grand Rapids: Zondervan, 2018). Abortion also does not appear in the index of biographies written by John Pollock or Marshall Frady. See John Pollock, *Billy Graham: Evangelist to the World* (New York: Harper & Row, 1979), and Marshall Frady, *Billy Graham: A Parable of American Righteousness* (1979; New York: Simon & Schuster, 2006). In his biography, Grant Wacker includes one mention of abortion, noting that Graham recognized that Christians hold differing views on contentious issues "including justifiable reasons for abortion." See Grant Wacker, *America's Pastor: Billy Graham and the Shaping of a Nation* (Cambridge, MA: Belknap, 2014), 53. Although Graham certainly recognized that Christians held different views on the issue, it is inaccurate to suggest Graham did not have strong personal convictions on the subject as seen in his "My Answer" response in 1961.

[107] Billy Graham, "My Answer," *Clarion-Ledger,* August 28, 1961, p. 8. Graham concluded his column by reminding his reader about the offer of forgiveness in Christ, noting, "If abortion is 'murder,' then you must remember that Peter, who tried to murder a Roman soldier, became a pillar of Christ's church. Paul, who participated in the murder of Stephen, became the greatest Christian missionary of all time. There is forgiveness in Christ, and there is strength to face life with a new and fresh sense of purpose. No one in history has ever trusted wholly in Him who ever had the least regret."

general editor for the English Standard Version (ESV) of the Bible and was the author of the bestseller *Knowing God*. Although Packer did not often wade into politics, his participation in the "Evangelicals and Catholics Together" (ECT) initiative underscored his pro-life convictions. According to the 1994 document, which he signed, "Abortion is the leading edge of an encroaching culture of death."[108]

Shortly after signing the statement, Packer was criticized by fellow evangelicals for his endorsement of ECT. In response to the criticism, Packer penned an article in *Christianity Today* where he outlined his rationale for signing the document. Packer drew attention to ECT's resolve to uphold religious freedom and the sanctity of life, commitments he knows are widely held by evangelicals. He specifically commends Francis Schaeffer's understanding of "co-belligerence," noting, "The late Francis Schaeffer focused [on] the concept of co-belligerence, that is, joint action for agreed objectives by people who disagree on other things, and then implemented it by leading evangelicals into battle alongside Roman Catholics on the abortion front, where—thank God!—they remain."[109] Although the theological differences between Protestants and Roman Catholics are significant, Packer believed the two groups should be able to fight together against anti-Christian statism and abortion.

### *John MacArthur*

Since 1969, John MacArthur has served as the pastor of Grace Community Church. The author of over 150 books, MacArthur is recognized as one of

---

[108] "Evangelicals & Catholics Together: The Christian Mission in the Third Millennium," *First Things*, May 1994, https://www.firstthings.com/article/1994/05/evangelicals-catholics-together-the-christian-mission-in-the-third-millennium. Related to abortion, the document also notes, "Abortion on demand, which is the current rule in America, must be recognized as a massive attack on the dignity, rights and needs of women."

[109] J. I. Packer, "Why I Signed 'Evangelicals and Catholics Together,'" *Christianity Today*, December 12, 1994, https://www.christianitytoday.com/ct/1994/december12/j-i-packer-why-i-signed-evangelical-and-catholics-together.html.

the most influential expository preachers in the United States. In a 1992 sermon, MacArthur explained his view on abortion succinctly, noting, "To sum up what we are experiencing with regard to abortion in America, we could simply say America as a nation is highly committed by law and by practice to a form of mass murder. And that is really the bottom line. This nation, which certainly prides itself on its humanitarianism, is in a murderous cycle of violence that makes the Nazi Holocaust look mild by comparison."[110] For MacArthur, abortion is a moral stain on the United States and constitutes a "form of mass murder."

Additionally, in his 2017 systematic theology book, MacArthur addresses the question of personhood and when life begins, explaining, "When does personhood begin? Various views concerning the beginning of personhood have been offered. Only one is biblical. Personhood begins at conception."[111] Arguing that life begins at conception, MacArthur points to Exodus 21:22–25, Psalm 139:13–16, Jeremiah 1:5, and Luke 1:44 as evidence of the Bible's pro-life worldview.

## Conclusion

Outside the National Archives Building in Washington, DC, there is a statue with the inscription: "What Is Past Is Prologue." Originally employed in Shakespeare's play *The Tempest*, the phrase captures the idea that history sets the context for the present day. Positioned near the entrance of the building holding America's Declaration of Independence and Constitution, the statue beckons visitors to view these aging documents and consider how the ideals expressed in them have affected and continue to shape the history of the United States.

---

[110] John MacArthur, "The Biblical View on Abortion, Part 1" (sermon at Grace Community Church, Sun Valley, CA, August 30, 1992), https://www.gty.org/library/sermons-library/90-67/the-biblical-view-on-abortion-part-1.

[111] John MacArthur and Richard Mayhue, *Biblical Doctrine: A Systematic Summary of Biblical Truth* (Wheaton, IL: Crossway, 2017), 433.

In a similar way, studying church history reveals what generations of Christians before us have believed about the Bible, theology, and ethics. A benefit of studying church history is that insights from the church's past can shed new light on modern questions. The study of the church's past is also an exercise in humility, helping believers recognize that the modern age does not have a monopoly on knowledge and that today's Christians can benefit from the accumulated wisdom of the past.

But as we close a chapter on the church's historic teaching on abortion, we must remember that even if the past is prologue, the church is not infallible. Although various leaders have served Christ's church wisely, no one is inerrant or beyond making a mistake. Yet the reality that the church's most prominent, respected, and influential teachers have interpreted the Bible similarly on the topic of abortion carries weight.

In his 2001 book, *Under the Influence: How Christianity Transformed Civilization*, Professor Alvin Schmidt (1932–2022) reflects on how Christians have affected positive change in the world.[112] Contributions he ascribes to Christianity include opposing the Greco-Roman practices of infanticide and child abandonment, advocating for the dignity of women, founding the first hospitals, opening the first universities and colleges, bringing honor to work, working for the abolition of slavery, and producing major contributions in the fields of art, architecture, music, and literature. According to Schmidt, an additional, often unrecognized contribution made by Christians is their opposition to abortion. Guided by their reading and interpretation of Scripture, early Christians were willing to oppose the prevailing attitudes of their day to champion a culture of life.

As we have seen in this chapter, a deeply rooted conviction in the sanctity of human life has distinguished the Christian church for two millennia. From the beginning, Christians have opposed abortion and advocated for the dignity of families, mothers, and unborn children. However, despite the

---

[112] Alvin Schmidt, *Under the Influence: How Christianity Transformed Civilization* (Grand Rapids: Zondervan, 2001).

church's longstanding teaching on life, some denominations have recently shifted away from or downplayed their pro-life convictions. The result has been growing confusion in the church about what Christians should believe regarding abortion.[113]

Reflecting on the church and abortion at the onset of the twenty-first century, Schmidt observed, "Only a few of the larger denominations . . . continue to walk in the path of their Christian ancestor, reaching back to the pristine church." He lamented that in contrast to the early church, "there is really no Christian admonition or discipline regarding abortion when some of their members—for instance, legislators—promote pro-abortion laws."[114] According to Schmidt, although theologically conservative churches have formally retained a biblically orthodox position on abortion, few are willing to publicly correct or discipline members who endorse or support abortion.

Although recent history supports Schmidt's contention that there is a general unwillingness in the church to address abortion with vigor and clarity, recent high-profile incidents, including Archbishop Cordileone's reprimand of Pelosi in 2022, demonstrate that there are still churches and pastors willing to bear public scorn and ridicule to affirm pro-life convictions.

---

[113] Notably, in 2024, political commentators, including Joe Scarborough, argued publicly that Christians are latecomers to a pro-life ethic. According to Scarborough, Christians have been "pro-choice from the time of Jesus through the time the Beatles broke up." Shortly after Scarborough's comments, *Politico* published a piece by Bradley Onishi that claimed "The idea that life begins at conception is far from a universally agreed upon matter of historical Christian doctrine. When viewed in the long history of the Christian tradition, it is actually a minority opinion." Notably, Scarborough and Onishi made their comments in the lead-up to the 2024 presidential election, amid what appeared to be an intentional effort to convince Christians that the Bible is either neutral on abortion or even pro-choice. For a response to these comments, see David Closson, "Recent Claims about Abortion and the Church Fail Biblical and Historical Scrutiny," *Washington Stand*, March 27, 2024, https://washingtonstand.com/commentary/recent-claims-about-abortion-and-the-church-fail-biblical-and-historical-scrutiny-.

[114] Schmidt, *Under the Influence*, 60.

Of course, because Christianity's teaching on abortion is grounded in the Bible, gospel-believing churches ought to joyfully embrace, teach, and affirm what the Scripture teaches about life. A reluctance to affirm anything taught in Scripture should call into question a church's actual commitment to the Bible. Likewise, when professing Christians energetically support policies that contradict clear biblical teaching, it brings into question the authenticity of their faith, or at least it should. As we have seen in this chapter, Christians have confessed for 2,000 years that all human life is valuable and that abortion is antithetical to the faith. For the sake of the church's witness, pastors, theologians, and church members must insist, as their forebearers did, that Christian faithfulness requires upholding and living out the church's historic pro-life ethic.

As we now shift our attention to the United States in the twentieth and twenty-first centuries, we will review the religious and legal landscape before and after the infamous *Roe v. Wade* decision. The story of the modern pro-life movement in America is a riveting tale that includes heartbreaking disappointments, astonishing victories, and countless unseen acts of courage and love.

# 4

# A Brief History of Abortion in America

As oral argument in *Dobbs v. Jackson Women's Health Organization* approached, pro-lifers were cautiously optimistic. With six justices appointed by Republican presidents, the composition of the Supreme Court suggested a favorable decision. However, pro-lifers had been disappointed before, and as oral arguments approached, Christians around the country began praying for the upcoming case.

In the months leading up to oral arguments, many pro-life organizations and churches talked about the case and encouraged people to pray for a pro-life outcome. One example was the Pray for *Dobbs* coalition organized by Alliance Defending Freedom (ADF), Family Research Council (FRC), and the United States Conference of Catholic Bishops (USCCB). On October 14, 2021, the Pray for *Dobbs* team hosted an informational webinar attended by over 4,000 pastors, priests, and ministry leaders.[1] During the webinar, national pro-life leaders including Adam Greenway (president, Southwestern Seminary), Albert Mohler (president, Southern Seminary), Joseph F. Naumann (Archbishop, Kansas City, and chairman of the USCCB's Committee on Pro-Life Activities), and Bishop Vincent Mathews (president, Church of God in Christ World Missions) shared practical ways for ministry leaders to educate their congregations about the case. Additionally, speakers stressed the importance of prayer and provided specific ways to pray.

Allotted a few minutes to speak myself, I underscored the Bible's fundamentally pro-life message, noting, "The witness of Scripture and the teaching of the church for two thousand years is clear on the dignity and value of the unborn." Because the Bible is "profoundly pro-life," I encouraged pastors to preach and teach about abortion as the nation awaited the Court's decision.

On November 18, the Pray for *Dobbs* coalition hosted a national, ecumenical online prayer event. Over 18,000 people joined the broadcast, praying alongside national leaders including Tony Evans, Metropolitan Tikhon (Primate of the Orthodox Church in America), Archbishop Joseph F. Naumann, Benjamin Watson, Lou Engle, Mother Agnes Mary Donovan, and Kathy Branzell.[2]

Additionally, on November 28, Family Research Council hosted a prayer rally in Jackson, Mississippi.[3] Prayer leaders included Michele Bachmann, Marjorie Dannenfelser, Mike Farris, Jack Hibbs, Alveda King, Monica Sparks, and Tony Perkins. Mississippi governor Tate Reeves also spoke at the event and encouraged believers across the nation to continue

---

[1] Pray for *Dobbs*, "Pray for *Dobbs*: Informational Webinar," YouTube video, October 19, 2021, https://www.youtube.com/watch?v=Jm7g9O6fD9E.

[2] Pray for *Dobbs*, "Pray for *Dobbs*: Prayer Event," YouTube video, November 23, 2021, https://www.youtube.com/watch?v=YxxvfMNAyAE.

[3] "Pray Together for Life," Pray Together for Life, November 28, 2021, https://web.archive.org/web/20211201065102/https:/praytogetherforlife.com/.

praying for the outcome of the case. As we cried out to God in prayer just a few blocks away from the abortion clinic at the center of the *Dobbs* case, the gravity of the moment was palpable. As I left Jackson the following day, it was evident to me that Christians around the country understood the stakes of the *Dobbs* case and that scores of believers across the country were asking God to overturn *Roe*.[4]

Following oral arguments, the nation waited, the media speculated, and Christians continued to pray. With a decision expected in June 2022, the Pray for *Dobbs* coalition continued its work by organizing monthly prayer calls and sending over 125,000 emails with information about the case and reminders to pray.

At the heart of *Dobbs* was the Supreme Court's decision in *Roe v. Wade*. Decided in 1973, *Roe*, along with its companion case, *Doe v. Bolton*, effectively legalized abortion through all nine months of pregnancy. Authored by Justice Harry Blackmun, the decision supercharged cultural, political, and moral debates about abortion and thrust the issue into the center of American public discourse, where it has stayed ever since.

In addition to the perpetual electioneering and campaigning over abortion policy, fifty years of abortion on demand has had a corrosive effect on the morality of our culture. Law is inherently pedagogical, and two generations of Americans have been conditioned to see abortion through the lens of health care and equality.

From today's vantage point, the fruit of these ideas—seeing abortion as morally permissible health care and a feature of women's empowerment—has

---

[4] Two days before oral arguments, Tessa Longbons and I coauthored an article for The Gospel Coalition about *Dobbs*. In the article, which trended on TGC's site for weeks, we encouraged Christians to pray for the Supreme Court justices, their law clerks, Mississippi's lawyers who would be arguing the case, honest media coverage, women facing unplanned pregnancies, pregnancy resource centers, and lawmakers. See David Closson and Tessa Longbons, "The Supreme Court Case That Could Overturn *Roe v. Wade*: How Pastors Can Think and Lead Well," The Gospel Coalition, November 29, 2021, https://www.thegospelcoalition.org/article/overturn-roe-wade/.

been moral decay and carnage on an unimaginable scale. The killing of over 60 million babies since 1973 is the most obvious result of America's permissive abortion regime, but the incalculable emotional and psychological harm to mothers and fathers is also a lasting, ruinous consequence of *Roe* and the nation's commitment to abortion on demand.

Surprisingly, the current divisiveness around abortion is largely a phenomenon of the twentieth century. Before *Roe*, most people opposed abortion and believed that unborn children deserved legal protection. A brief review of the relevant history demonstrates that the modern era, despite all its purported sophistication, has digressed in appalling ways when it comes to appreciating and respecting the dignity and value of human life.

Thus, in this chapter, we will review a brief history of abortion in America, starting with the common law tradition. After demonstrating that the common law viewed abortion as a criminal offense, the chapter will examine how doctors in the nineteenth century led the successful effort to codify state-level protections for the unborn. We will then analyze trends in the early and middle parts of the twentieth century that led to the liberalization of America's abortion laws, culminating in the Supreme Court's infamous *Roe v. Wade* decision, which galvanized the fledgling modern pro-life movement. The successes and setbacks of this movement will be briefly recounted as will the political implications of abortion politics on America's two major political parties. Finally, the chapter will conclude by providing background on *Dobbs v. Jackson Women's Health Organization*, the case that ultimately led to the overturning of *Roe* and the next chapter in America's abortion history.

## Common Law and Early American History

In the majority opinion in *Roe*, Justice Harry Blackmun asserted, "It is undisputed that, at common law, abortion performed before 'quickening'—the first recognizable movement of the fetus in utero, appearing usually from the sixteenth to the eighteenth week of pregnancy—was not an indictable offense."[5] According to Blackmun's reading of history, abortion was entirely permissible before the mother's first sensation of fetal movement. However, Blackmun was willing to go further, explaining, "A recent review of common law precedents argues . . . that even post-quickening abortion was never established as a common law crime . . . it now appears doubtful that abortion was ever firmly established as a common law crime even with respect to the destruction of a quick fetus."[6]

Although the central holding of Blackmun's decision in *Roe* was ostensibly grounded in legal theory, the justice's analysis of history provided a supporting rationale for striking down the nation's pro-life laws.[7] However, as historians have since demonstrated, Blackmun's analysis was inaccurate, relying heavily on the work of Cyril Means. Means, a professor who served as the general counsel to a major abortion rights advocacy group during the *Roe* litigation, was hardly an objective arbiter.[8] Yet his work was cited in Blackmun's final opinion seven times.

---

[5] Roe v. Wad*e*, 410 U.S. 113 (1973).

[6] *Roe*.

[7] At the onset of Part VI of his argument, Justice Blackmun wrote, "It perhaps is not generally appreciated that the restrictive criminal abortion laws in effect in a majority of States today are of relatively recent vintage." See Roe v. Wade, 410 U.S. 113 (1973). From there Blackmun went on to argue that the common law did not treat abortion as a crime.

[8] For more on the discredited historical revisionism of Cyril Means, see Clarke D. Forsythe, *Abuse of Discretion: The Inside Story of Roe v. Wade* (New York: Encounter, 2013), 186–89, and Justin Dyer, "Wrong Then, Wrong Now: The Fake Abortion History of *Roe v. Wade*," *Public Discourse*, September 29, 2021, https://www.thepublicdiscourse.com/2021/09/78200/. See also Joseph Dellapenna's brief in the *Dobbs* case, where he argued that the historical record shows that "abortion was a common-law crime from the earliest recorded days, and the common law was followed and codified in the states and territories in order to protect the life of the unborn child." See Joseph W. Dellapenna, *Brief of Amicus Curiae in Support of Petitioners,* Supreme Court of the United States, July 29, 2021, 2–3, https://www.supremecourt.gov/DocketPDF/19/19-1392/185316/20210806173754092_19-1392%20Amicus%20Br%20Joseph%20Dellapenna.pdf. Incredibly, the lawyers working on the *Roe* case knew they were misrepresenting history. A memo sent to Roy Lucas, an attorney assisting lead attorneys Sarah Weddington and Linda Coffee,

## *Common Law*

A faithful recounting of the historical record reveals the exact opposite of what Blackmun alleged in *Roe*. In fact, common law theorists Henry de Bracton (c. 1210–c. 1268), Edward Coke (1552–1634), Matthew Hale (1609–1676), and William Blackstone (1723–1780) all described abortion as a crime.[9]

According to law historian Joseph Dellapenna, the earliest recorded common law proceeding to address abortion dates around 1200. The abortion alleged in this case involved the battering of a woman named Agnes, who lost her child as a result. Although the outcome of the specific case is unknown, it demonstrates that courts spoke in terms of killing a child, not just in terms of harming the mother.[10]

A survey of common law theorists demonstrates conclusively that abortion was viewed as a crime. Writing around 1250, Henry de Bracton explained, "If one strikes a pregnant woman or gives her a potion in order

---

stated that the conclusions of Means's scholarship "sometime strain credibility." The memo went on to state, "Where the important thing is to win the case no matter how, however, I suppose I agree with Means's technique: begin with a scholarly attempt at historical research; if it doesn't work, fudge it as necessary; write a piece so long that others will read only your introduction and conclusion; then keep citing it until courts begin picking it up. This preserves the guise of impartial scholarship while advancing the proper ideological goals." See "David Tundermann memo to Roy Lucas, Re Legislative Purpose," August 5, 1971, www.thepublicdiscourse.com/wp-content/uploads/2021/09/Tundermann-Lucas-Memo-19711.pdf?bcs-agent-scanner=57fde80d-1a2c-e14b-9792-e38c0a768154.

[9] See Joseph W. Dellapenna, *Dispelling the Myths of Abortion History* (Durham, NC: Carolina Academic, 2006). For a discussion of Edward Coke, see 189–203. For a summary of Matthew Hale's writing, see 203–11. Notably, Dellapenna himself identifies as "moderate" on abortion; he personally favors allowing abortion up to eight weeks of gestation. However, his exhaustive history of abortion law in England and America demonstrates that courts, since the beginning of the common law tradition, have consistently condemned abortion and that from *Roe* on, courts have relied on a deliberately distorted history of abortion law. See Dellapenna, *Dispelling the Myths of Abortion History*, x.

[10] Dellapenna, 135.

to procure an abortion, if the foetus is already formed or animated, especially if it is animated, he commits homicide."[11] Another early writer on the common law, known as "Fleta," who wrote around 1290, stated, "He, too, in strictness is a homicide who has pressed upon a pregnant woman or has given her poison or has struck her in order to procure an abortion or to prevent conception, if the foetus is already formed and animated. . . . A woman also commits a homicide if, by potion or the like, she destroys a quickened child in her womb."[12] Similar to what theologians had been arguing for centuries, Bracton and Fleta maintained that aborting a quickened baby was murder and, therefore, impermissible under English criminal law. (Recall that "quickening" is the point in pregnancy when a mother can feel fetal movement.)

Beginning in 1628, Edward Coke published a series of legal treatises that are widely regarded as foundational documents for the common law. In 1644, Coke published the third volume of his commentary on English law. As part of his discussion on murder, Coke explained that abortion of a "quick" child by a potion, battery, or other cause constituted murder. As he put it, "If a woman be quick with childe, and by a Potion or otherwise killeth it in her wombe; or if a man beat her, whereby the childe dieth in her body, and she is delivered of a dead childe, that is a great misprision, and no murder: but if the childe be born alive, and dieth of the Potion, battery, or other cause, this is murder."[13] Although Coke distinguished between

[11] Quoted in Dellapenna, 132.

[12] Quoted in Dellapenna, 133.

[13] Cited in *Dobbs v. Jackson Women's Health Organization*, 597 U.S. 215 (2022), 242. Hereinafter, *Dobbs*. The original source is Edward Coke, *The Third Part of the Institutes of the Laws of England: Concerning High Treason, and Other Pleas of the Crown* (London: Printed for E. and R. Brooke, Bell-Yard, near Temple-Bar, 1797), 50. The Law Library at the Library of Congress has a 1797 edition of Coke's work, which was originally published in 1644. In his discussion about abortion, Coke goes on to note, "If a man counsel a woman to kill the childe within her wombe, when it shall be born, and after she is delivered of the childe, she killeth it; the councellor is an accessory to the murder."

pre-quickening and post-quickening, abortion in either case was viewed as a criminal offense. In fact, Coke defines "misprision" as a "heynous offence under the degree of felony."[14]

Likewise, Sir Matthew Hale mentioned abortion in his treatises on the law. Writing in 1670, Hale explained, "If a Woman quick with Child take a potion to kill it, and accordingly it is destroyed without being born alive, a great misprision, but no Felony; but if born alive, and after dies of that potion, it is Murder."[15]

In the eighteenth century, William Blackstone also taught that abortion was a crime. In his commentary on the laws of England, Blackstone explained:

> Life is the immediate gift of God, a right inherent by nature in every individual; and it begins in contemplation of law as soon as an infant is able to stir in the mother's womb. For if a woman is quick with child, and by a potion or otherwise, killeth it in her womb; or if any one beat her, whereby the child dieth in her body, and she is delivered of a dead child; this, though not murder, was by the antient law homicide or manslaughter. But Sir Edward Coke doth not look upon this offence in quite so atrocious a light, but merely as a heinous misdemeanor.[16]

In colonial America, abortion was considered murder after quickening.[17] But even before quickening, abortion was often treated as a crime.

---

[14] Coke, *The Third Part of the Institutes of the Laws of England*, 139.

[15] Sir Matthew Hale, *Pleas of the Crown. Or a Brief, but Full Account of whatsoever can be found Relating to that Subject* (London: 1678), 44. Accessed at the Law Library at the Library of Congress.

[16] William Blackstone, *Commentaries on the Laws of England in Four Books*, 7th ed. (Oxford: Clarendon, 1775), 129–30.

[17] In his discussion of quickening, Clarke Forsythe notes, "It is clear that the mere detection of pregnancy early in gestation was quite difficult from the fourteenth to the nineteenth century. . . . The English common law developed

As Marvin Olasky and Leah Savas have documented in their book, *The Story of Abortion in America*, men responsible for causing or facilitating an abortion were often tried for murder. For example, in 1652, Captain William Mitchell was charged for plotting "to destroy or Murther the Child by him begotten in the womb of the Said Susan Warren."[18] Another man, Francis Brooke, was charged in 1656 with murdering his unborn child of three months (a point in pregnancy before quickening).[19] Still another man, Jacob Lumbrozo, was jailed in 1663 on murder charges for administering an abortifacient to Elizabeth Weales.[20]

In summary, the historical record demonstrates that Justice Blackmun's assertion in 1973 that abortion was never "firmly established as a common law crime" relied on a distorted and specious reading of history.[21] Instead, abortion was condemned by every respectable authority since the start of the common law in England. Additionally, abortion, which was widely seen as immoral, was prohibited in the American colonial era.

---

at a time of both primitive medical conditions and high infant mortality. . . . Consequently, the common law fixed upon the mother's first sensation of fetal movement—quickening—as the first true sign of pregnancy for purposes of legal proof. . . . Since quickening does not usually occur until sixteen to eighteen weeks of pregnancy, it was therefore very difficult, if not impossible, for medicine to prove a live pregnancy before sixteen weeks of gestation, and it was thus impossible for the law to apply the homicide law before that time. Quickening was an evidentiary distinction, not a moral one." Forsythe, *Abuse of Discretion*, 184.

[18] The story of William Mitchell and Susan Warren is told in chapter 2 of *Story of Abortion in America*. See Marvin Olasky and Leah Savas, *The Story of Abortion in America: A Street-Level History, 1652–2022* (Wheaton, IL: Crossway, 2023), 17–23. Justice Samuel Alito cited this story in *Dobbs*. See Dobbs v. Jackson Women's Health Organization, 597 U.S. 215 (2022), 246.

[19] Olasky and Savas, *The Story of Abortion in America*, 26.

[20] Olasky and Savas, 34.

[21] Notably, Justice Blackmun did not invoke the historical record in his concurring opinion in *Planned Parenthood v. Casey*, the 1992 case that reaffirmed *Roe*.

## Nineteenth Century: Doctors Lead the Campaign for Pro-Life Laws

Shortly after the verdict in the Ammi Rogers case, Connecticut passed the first state law against abortion.[22] The law, passed in 1821, criminalized administering "any deadly poison, or other noxious and destructive substance, with an intention . . . to murder, or thereby to cause or procure the miscarriage of any woman, then being quick with child."[23] Other states quickly followed Connecticut's example.

By 1868, twenty-eight out of thirty-seven states had enacted statutes making abortion a crime. Of the remaining nine states, all but one would criminalize abortion by 1910; the outlier, Mississippi, would criminalize abortion in 1952. The trend toward criminalization continued in the territories that would become the final thirteen states. All of them criminalized abortion between 1850 and 1919.[24] The District of Columbia criminalized abortion in 1901.[25]

---

[22] Ammi Rogers was an Episcopal minister accused of administering abortifacient drugs to Asenath Smith. Although he adamantly denied the accusation, Rogers received a two-year jail sentence. According to Rogers, the charges against him represented the "most dreadful plot, plan, stratagem and conspiracy, that ever was formed against any man in any country." Ammi Rogers, *Memoirs of the Rev. Ammi Rogers* (Watertown, 1846), 84. Rogers's full account of the trial and prosecution against him is on pages 81–126. Online at https://tile.loc.gov/storage-services/public/gdcmassbookdig/memoirsofrevammi01roge/memoirsofrevammi01roge.pdf.

[23] Cited in Olasky and Savas, *The Story of Abortion in America*, 73.

[24] Justice Alito reviews much of this history in his majority opinion in *Dobbs*. See *Dobbs*, 248–49, appendices A and B, 302–30.

[25] For an example of state statutes criminalizing abortion, consider Missouri and California. Missouri's law, passed in 1825, stated, "That every person who shall wilfully and maliciously administer or cause to be administered to or taken by any person, any poison, or other noxious, poisonous or destructive substance or liquid, with an intention to harm him or her thereby to murder, or thereby to cause or procure the miscarriage of any woman then being with child, and shall thereof be duly convicted, shall suffer imprisonment not exceeding seven years, and be fined not exceeding three thousand dollars." See Act of July 4, 1925, ch. 1, §12, 1 Mo. Laws (*Revised Statutes of Missouri*) 283 (1825), https://mdh.contentdm.oclc

Many pro-life laws were enacted following the advocacy of doctors in the middle of the nineteenth century. Advancements in science and medicine had increased knowledge about fetal development and convinced scores of doctors—including the first woman to receive a medical degree from an American medical school—that abortion at any stage in pregnancy ended the life of an unborn child. These convictions prompted doctors, including Hugh Hodge (1796–1873), Horatio Storer (1830–1922), Stephen Tracy (1810–1873), and Andrew Nebinger (1819–1886), to forcefully oppose abortion at meetings of regional and national medical associations. Their efforts motivated the medical community to lobby state legislatures to pass laws protecting unborn children.[26]

---

.org/digital/collection/p16795coll26/id/289/. California's law, passed in 1850, stated, "And every person who shall administer or cause to be administered or taken, any medical substances, or shall use or cause to be used any instruments whatever, with the intention to procure the miscarriage of any woman then being with child, and shall be thereof duly convicted, shall be punished by imprisonment in the State Prison for a term not less than two years, nor more than five years: Provided, that no physician shall be affected by the last clause of this section, who, in the discharge of his professional duties, deems it necessary to produce the miscarriage of any woman in order to save her life." See *Digest of Laws of California*, 1857, art. 1905, 9. 334. Both statutes were cited in Justice Alito's opinion in *Dobbs*. See *Dobbs*, 302, 309–10.

[26] Although no one disputes the point that nineteenth-century physicians led the campaign for pro-life laws, recent writers have questioned their motives. For example, Kira Schlesinger writes, "Suddenly male physicians with formal medical training found themselves in competition with irregular medical practitioners like midwives and abortionists, who were overwhelmingly female. So in 1847 physicians formed the American Medical Association (AMA). By requiring a medical license to practice, the AMA put the irregular doctors out of business and subsequently took a strict abortion stance." Schlesinger argues that pro-life doctors were also motivated by racism: "In addition to protecting their profession, there were racial motivations for their position on abortion. Physicians perceived that as more middle- and upper-class white women successfully limited the size of their families, the proportion of the white population in America would decline, and they were afraid that free blacks and immigrants entering the country would outpace the more desirable American-born white population." See Kira Schlesinger, *Pro-Choice and Christian: Reconciling Faith, Politics, and Justice* (Louisville: Westminster John Knox, 2017), 23. Likewise, Ignacio Castuera, who for

For example, in 1839, Professor Hugh Hodge gave a series of lectures on obstetrics, where he admitted that medical experts had previously "undervalued the importance of foetal life." However, equipped with a better understanding of physiology, Hodge called upon "the legislators of our land, upon the ecclesiastical profession and upon every one whose mind and conscience are open to conviction, to stay the progress of this destructive evil of criminal abortion."[27]

According to Hodge, the discipline of obstetrics is distinguished because it is always concerned with the "welfare of two individuals."

---

six years served as the national chaplain for Planned Parenthood (2001–2007), claims that pro-life doctors like Horatio Storer were motivated, at least in part, by racism and misogyny. As Castuera notes, "The ideal of 'womanhood' espoused by the AMA [American Medical Association] was a prison, since it relegated women to the home in a manner not too dissimilar to the Taliban's policies. . . . According to this vision of a gendered world, white, upper-class women were supposed to have children while men ran the world." See Ignacio Castuera, "A Social History of Christian Thought on Abortion: Ambiguity vs. Certainty in Moral Debate," *The American Journal of Economics and Sociology* 76, no. 1 (2017): 194. According to Castuera, "racist, misogynist, and economic factors . . . motivated the doctors of the American Medical Association to launch a crusade against abortion in 1857." However, he concedes that "the nominal reason the AMA strongly opposed both early- and late-stage abortions was entirely on moral grounds: to protect the unborn." See Castuera, "A Social History of Christian Thought on Abortion," 197. Contrary to Castuera, the historical record, which includes documents from AMA meetings and private correspondence between doctors involved in the campaign, demonstrates that efforts to curb abortion were motivated by a sincere desire to protect unborn children. For an in-depth examination of the nineteenth century campaign against abortion, including a rebuttal to the idea that pro-life doctors were merely motivated by economic, misogynistic, or racist considerations, see Joseph W. Dellapenna, *Dispelling the Myths of Abortion History*, 342–70. As Dellapenna summarizes, "The historical record is clear. Only by impugning the integrity of innumerable social and professional leaders can one argue that protection of unborn children from the rising numbers of abortions was not a significant concern." See Dellapena, 372.

[27] Hugh Hodge, *Fœticide or Criminal Abortion: A Lecture Introductory to the Course of Obstetrics, and Diseases of Women and Children* (Philadelphia: Lindsay and Blakiston, 1869), 5.

Doctors, therefore, "must regard the infant, as well as the mother, from the period of conception to delivery."[28] For Hodge, the science was decisive: an unborn child is a person from the moment of conception. "There can be no reasonable doubt that human existence . . . commences not with the birth of the foetus and the first inspiration, but at conception," Hodge wrote. Although doctors must always be attentive to mothers, "we must not forget her *offspring*, in the various stages of its existence, from the moment of conception to delivery."[29] Hodge's understanding of embryology led him to see that unborn children maintain an independent existence from their mother. As he explained, "Invisible to the naked eye, the embryo is nevertheless endowed, at once, with the principles of vitality; and, although retained within the system of its mother, it has, in a strict sense, an independent existence."[30]

Hodge also dispensed with the long-standing belief that "quickening" marks the beginning of life. For Hodge, quickening was an unscientific marker that had led to a faulty understanding of when human life begins. According to Hodge, "The usual impression, and one which is probably still maintained by the mass of the community, is that the embryo is perfected at the period of quickening. . . . These and similar suppositions are, as has been already shown, contrary to all fact, to analogy, to reason; and if it were not for the high authorities, medical, legal, and theological, in opposition,

[28] Hodge, 12.

[29] Hodge, 28–29, 14, emphasis original.

[30] Hodge, 15. Hodge makes this point throughout the book. In another place he explains, "The embryo generated by germs from each parent has henceforth an independent existence. As regards its *vital properties*, it is as perfect as it ever will be; its subsequent nutrition, growth, susceptibilities, are but the successive manifestations of these vital properties." He also states, "Physiologically, therefore, the infant at birth, while deriving all its nourishment and means of support from the breasts of its mother, cannot be regarded as more independent than the fœtus in utero." See Hodge, 16–17.

we might add, to common sense."[31] Simply put, at any stage in pregnancy, abortion is "murder."[32]

In 1857, the American Medical Association (AMA) appointed a committee of physicians to investigate abortion and provide a report with legislative recommendations. Dr. Horatio Storer, the chairman of the committee, wrote the report, and Dr. Thomas Blatchford presented it at the 1859 annual meeting of the AMA in Louisville. Hugh Hodge also served on the eight-person committee. The report, which was adopted unanimously, summarized the position of the nation's leading physicians on abortion. According to the report, "The heinous guilt of criminal abortion, however viewed by the community, is everywhere acknowledged by medical men." The report acknowledged that abortion was common among all classes of society and suggested three reasons for the high incidence of abortion. The first reason was "wide-spread popular ignorance of the true character of the crime." In short, the doctors believed that even among mothers, the belief persisted that "the fœtus is not alive till after the period of quickening." Second, too many physicians are "careless of fœtal life." Third, abortion was readily available because of "grave defects of our laws . . . as regards the independent and actual existence of the child before birth, as a living being."[33]

---

[31] Hodge, *Fœticide or Criminal Abortion*, 21. Elsewhere, Hodge asks, "What, it may be asked, have the sensations of the mother to do with the vitality of the child? Is it not alive because the mother does not feel it? Every practitioner of Obstetrics can bear witness that the child lives and moves and thrives long before the mother is conscious of its existence. . . . The supposition of inanimate embryos capable of being developed, is, at the present day, an absurdity. From the moment of conception it must be alive, for immediately it begins to be developed." See Hodge, 21–22.

[32] Hodge mourned that Christians were active participants in abortion. As he explained, "It is, however, a mournful fact, which ought to be promulgated, that this crime, this mode of committing murder, is prevalent among the most intelligent, refined, moral, and Christian communities." See Hodge, *Fœticide or Criminal Abortion*, 31.

[33] *The Transactions of the American Medical Association* 12 (1859): 75–76.

For Storer and the committee, the nation's doctors had a moral and professional responsibility to address the scourge of abortion. Their report urged the AMA to adopt three resolutions: first, a resolution that physicians make an "earnest and solemn protest against such unwarrantable destruction of human life." Second, a resolution calling for doctors to lobby legislators to strengthen the nation's laws against "the crime of procuring abortion." Finally, the report calls on the association to "request the zealous co-operation of the various State Medical Societies in pressing this subject" upon lawmakers.[34]

Another nineteenth-century physician who wrote with conviction about abortion was Dr. Stephen Tracy. Writing in 1853, Tracy carefully described the development of a baby in utero. After describing the size of a baby around three to four gestational weeks, he noted how the unborn child, even at this size, is "one of the human family as really and truly as if it had lived six months or six years."[35] "Consequently," said Tracy, "its life should be as carefully and tenderly cherished." Unfortunately, not every unborn child is treated with care, and Tracy paused his description of fetal development to address abortion, noting, "I shudder when I think that women sometimes designedly endeavor to bring on abortion."[36] For Tracy, a basic scientific fact is that life begins at conception: "Its life commenced at the time of the formation of the embryonic cell—at the moment of

---

[34] *The Transactions of the American Medical Association*, 76–78. For the background of the AMA's 1859 meeting and Horatio Storer's involvement, see Frederick N. Dyer, *Champion of Women and the Unborn: Horatio Robinson Storer, M.D.* (Canton, MA: Watson, 1999), 146–51. In a letter to Storer about a month before the AMA's meeting in Louisville, Hugh Hodge wrote, "Perhaps the probability of success might be increased, if the general association would strongly recommend that each state med. association would press the subject on the legislative bodies of their respective states." Hodge's letter was dated March 30, 1859. See Dyer, *Champion of Women and the Unborn*, 148.

[35] Stephen Tracy, *The Mother and Her Offspring* (New York: Harper & Brothers, 1853), 108.

[36] Tracy, 109.

conception." Thus, abortion is "wholly and entirely inadmissible," and whoever commits this "most awful crime" will be called "to give an account therefor at the judgment of the Great Day." Simply put, "The *life of this new human being* is sacred, and no one but God himself" can take away life.[37]

Another doctor who campaigned against abortion was Andrew Nebinger. Although many states had criminalized abortion by the late 1870s, Nebinger observed that these laws were rarely enforced. After researching abortion, Nebinger wrote a short book for the Medical Society in Pennsylvania in 1876. For the book, Nebinger interviewed fifty-nine doctors in Philadelphia and concluded that "Criminal abortion is now and has been steadily, for a long series of years, on the increase in this country."[38] For Nebinger, criminal abortion in the 1870s was "epidemic" and "of such magnitude as to 'out-Herod Herod.'" His research demonstrated that abortion affected every class, including the "refined, the learned, [and] the higher classes." According to Nebinger, abortion is "mainly committed to avoid the labor and expense of rearing children," but there is also "ignorance of the true physiology of gestation." Even women of "education and respectable position in society" believe "the fœtus is not alive, but only has . . . a capacity for living." The "almost universally erroneous belief that the fœtus *is not* viable until the fourth and half month of its development, the usual period of '*quickening*'" had contributed to widespread confusion about fetal development and the nature of abortion.[39]

At the conclusion of his report, Nebinger argues that legislation with stronger enforcement provisions is needed to curb abortion, an "evil of such gigantic proportions." However, to effect lasting change, Nebinger says that doctors should partner with Christian ministers to ensure that "intellectual, moral, and religious light shall be shed upon the subject in all its phases."[40]

---

[37] Tracy, 109, emphasis original.

[38] Andrew Nebinger, *Criminal Abortion; Its Extent and Prevention* (Philadelphia: Collins, 1876), 4.

[39] Nebinger, 4, 24, 11–12.

[40] Nebinger, 24, 20.

In 1880, Dr. Winslow Ayer published a book on abortion titled *The Great Crime of the Nineteenth Century*. In his book, Ayer argues, "It is moral cowardice and false delicacy that shrinks from rational consideration of so terrible a crime." According to Ayer, "In the present stage of science, it is folly to pretend to believe that while the germ of being is yet incomplete, and the evolution going on that will develop perfect organism, there is not life." Ayer notes that a person's physical structure continues growing into adulthood, "and the reason that would justify killing in the one case, must surely do it in the other."[41]

Finally, opposition to abortion was a major factor in motivating Elizabeth Blackwell to enter the medical profession. Blackwell, who was the first woman to receive a medical degree from an American medical school, was disgusted by the then-common association of female physicians with abortion. In her memoirs, she recounts an incident that made a strong impression on her. According to Blackwell, "There was at that time a certain Madame Restell flourishing in New York. This person was a noted abortionist, and known all over the country. . . . She made a large fortune, drove a fine carriage, had a pew in a fashionable church, and though often arrested, was always bailed out by her patrons."[42] For Blackwell, the plying of the abortion trade by Restell and other abortionists was scandalous. As she recalls, "The gross perversion and destruction of motherhood by the

---

[41] J. Winslow Ayer, *The Great Crime of the Nineteenth Century, and Perils of Child Life, Physical and Moral* (Grands Rapids: Central, 1880), 57, 6. Like other nineteenth-century physicians, Ayer pleaded with Christian ministers to address the topic of abortion, writing, "'Thou shalt not kill,' is a Divine command, imperative, final and complete, and does not admit of the interpretation, 'Thou shalt not kill unless the killing be for the sake of convenience, or to serve fashion.' If one command is to be ignored, why not ignore the ten? If the infraction of one command is to be passed over in silence, by the professed man of God, why demand the acceptance of the other nine, or of any? No Christian minister can or will seek to evade even one; no Christian man or woman will desire silence upon even one." Ayer, 4–5.

[42] Elizabeth Blackwell, *Pioneer Work in Opening the Medical Profession to Women: Autobiographical Sketches* (London: Longmans, Green, 1895), 29–30.

abortionist filled me with indignation, and awakened active antagonism. That the honorable term 'female physician' should be exclusively applied to those women who carried on this shocking trade seemed to me a horror. It was an utter degradation of what might and should become a noble position for women."[43]

Blackwell's convictions about life were also rooted in her understanding of fetal development. In her 1852 book *The Laws of Life*, she wrote, "Look at the first faint gleam of life, the life of the embryo, the commencement of human existence. We see a tiny cell, so small that it may easily be overlooked. . . . And yet there is in that simple germ-cell something most wonderful—life!—it is a living cell."[44] For Blackwell, the development of the baby in utero was a source of wonder: "Throughout this period of early life we remain spectators merely of the wonderful growth; it would be impious folly to attempt to interfere directly with this act of creation; but even here, in this early stage of existence, we have *important* aid to render."[45] Because the unborn child is a person from the moment of conception, expectant mothers should take appropriate measures to ensure their baby develops in a safe and comfortable environment.

Other female physicians in the late nineteenth and early twentieth centuries spoke out against abortion. For example, in 1911, Dr. Mary Melendy wrote, "Intentional abortion is to all purposes murder." According

---

[43] Blackwell, *Pioneer Work in Opening the Medical Profession to Women*, 30. In the next paragraph, Blackwell writes, "Being at that time a reader of Swedenborg, and strongly impressed by his vivid representations of the unseen world, I finally determined to do what I could to 'redeem the hells,' and especially the one form of hell thus forced upon my notice." According to some reports, upon graduation from medical school, Blackwell was shunned by other doctors and potential landlords because she was mistaken for an abortionist. See Mary Krane Derr, Rachel MacNair, and Linda Naranjo-Hubel, *ProLife Feminism: Yesterday and Today*, 2nd ed. (Kansas City, MO: Feminism and Nonviolence Studies Association, 2005), 36–38.

[44] Elizabeth Blackwell, *The Laws of Life, with Special Reference to the Physical Education of Girls* (New York: George P. Putnam, 1852), 70–71.

[45] Blackwell, 72, emphasis original.

to Melendy, advances in embryology had removed all doubt as to when life begins. As she explained, "Among the ancients the distinction was made that before the time of quickening the child had no life, and therefore there was no sin in its destruction. This statement has, however[,] been proven to be false." Melendy continued, noting, "The embryo is alive and hence quick from the moment of conception. Modern science has abundantly proven this to be a fact."[46]

Another female physician, Dr. Mary Hood, writing in 1914, explained fetal development by noting, "The two cells unite, and become one, much as two drops of water, when they come in contact, merge and become one drop. Thus, the two cells, which in their origin come from two different living beings, unite to form the new cell which will result in a completely new and different human being." For Hood, the question of when human life begins was settled by science: "From the moment when the sperm enters the ovum—from the moment that fertilization is thus accomplished—life begins." Hood categorically rejected the notion that life begins at quickening, explaining, "This phrase gives undue importance to the first feelings of the mother, for life has been present for eighteen weeks, and motion has been going on for seven or eight weeks."[47]

## Twentieth Century

Although abortion had been prohibited and condemned by civil and ecclesiastical authorities for centuries, gradual changes in culture, law, and policy shifted the proverbial Overton window (i.e., the range of policies that are acceptable to the majority of people at a given time) on how Americans

---

[46] Mary R. Melendy, *The Ideal Woman for Maidens—Wives—Mothers: A Book Giving Full Information on All the Mysterious and Complex Matters Pertaining to Women* (Chicago: J. R. Peper, 1911), 155–56.

[47] Mary G. Hood, *For Girls and the Mothers of Girls: A Book for the Home and the School Concerning the Beginnings of Life* (Indianapolis: Bobbs-Merrill, 1914), 67–68, 77.

viewed abortion. As various changes took place, what was once considered unthinkable soon became acceptable and then even popular among a broad swath of the American people.

Thus, as we consider the history of abortion in America, a few of the most consequential developments from the last century merit our attention: weak enforcement of pro-life laws, an increasingly sympathetic press, the championing of contraception and abortion by feminists, liberalizing churches, a changing legal landscape, and the mainstreaming of secular philosophical assumptions about identity and personhood. Taken together, these shifts provide the historical context for the current abortion debate in America.

### *Weak Enforcement of Pro-Life Laws*

Despite remarkably clear explanations by doctors and medical associations about the barbarity of abortion since the mid-1850s, enforcement of pro-life laws was inconsistent in the early decades of the twentieth century. According to Marvin Olasky, "weak-kneed enforcement" and the short attention span of the press ensured that abortionists could operate with little fear of recrimination.[48] For example, Inez Burns (1886–1976) performed an estimated 50,000 abortions in San Francisco from 1922 to 1945 with minimal interference from authorities.[49] According to one account, by the early 1960s, abortion was the third most extensive criminal activity in the country, surpassed only by narcotics and gambling.[50] However, prosecution of abortionists was sporadic and infrequent.

---

[48] For further discussion, see Olasky and Savas, *The Story of Abortion in America*, 225.

[49] Olasky and Savas devote a chapter to Burns in their book. See Olasky and Savas, 243–51.

[50] Mary Frances Berry, *The Pig Farmer's Daughter and Other Tales of American Justice: Episodes of Racism and Sexism in the Courts from 1865 to the Present* (New York: Alfred A. Knopf, 1999), 159.

Over time, uneven enforcement of abortion laws undermined efforts to stem criminal abortion. Intermittent efforts to enforce laws drove some abortionists underground and led to new concerns about maternal safety and class inequality. Additionally, psychiatric reasons for abortion were increasingly accepted as loopholes around state laws. As this became more common, middle-class white women found it easier to access abortion compared to poor minority women. This disparity led to the perception that abortion laws were discriminatory and dangerous, which prompted a growing number of public-health officials, lawyers, and second-wave feminists to demand changes to the law.[51]

### *Sympathetic Press*

In the years leading up to *Roe*, the news media increasingly took a sympathetic view toward abortion seekers and painted abortion regulations as unfair and discriminatory. Additionally, newspapers allowed abortionists to advertise their services. Although abortion advertisements appeared in American newspapers as early as 1836, Anna Lohman (1812–1878), known

[51] According to Leslie Reagan, between 1943 and 1962, white women had over 91% of the abortions performed in New York City. For Reagan's discussion on the growing acceptance of psychiatric reasons for abortion as well as the class divide, see Leslie J. Reagan, *When Abortion Was a Crime: Women, Medicine, and Law in the United States, 1867–1973* (Berkeley: University of California Press, 1997), 203–7, 211–13, 217, 229. In their book, *Abortion Counseling and Social Change*, Arlene Carmen and Howard Moody discuss how perceived racial and economic inequalities in accessing abortion motivated the Clergy Consultation Service on Abortion to help women find low-cost abortion before they were legal. See Arlene Carmen and Howard Moody, *Abortion Counseling and Social Change: From Illegal Act to Medical Practice* (Valley Forge, PA: Judson, 1973), 13–14. Finally, influential abortion advocate Lawrence Lader also highlighted what he perceived was the "economic and social discrimination" in who was allowed to procure a legal abortion. According to Lader, from 1960 to 1962, 93% of hospital abortions in New York City were for white women; 7% were for non-whites. See Lawrence Lader, *Abortion* (Indianapolis, IN: Bobbs-Merrill, 1966), 29.

by her trade name "Madame Restell," was the first to sell the idea of abortion.[52] Restell's ads were effective, and the abortionist, who had no formal medical training, made a fortune throughout the middle part of the nineteenth century.

As Marvin Olasky has demonstrated, newspapers in the nineteenth century periodically published stories that described the depravity of abortionists and the misery of young women who sought abortion. Some stories even highlighted the victimization of the unborn child. However, toward the close of the nineteenth century, newspapers leery of losing advertisers began shying away from hard-hitting exposés. According to Olasky, the *New York Times*, which had previously covered abortion through the early 1890s, did not mention the topic a single time from 1898 through 1916.[53]

When the press did cover abortion, reporters in the early twentieth century focused primarily on the greed of abortionists (and their political allies) rather than the evil of abortion.[54] Additionally, coverage shifted from concern for the unborn child to issues of corruption. From the mid-century onward, coverage of abortion in the press was overwhelmingly favorable to those seeking to liberalize abortion laws.

A significant media event occurred in 1962. Sherri Finkbine, a married mother of four, learned that she had inadvertently ingested thalidomide, a drug associated with fetal deformities. Although Finkbine was approved for an abortion by her doctor and a hospital medical board, a public outcry erupted when she spoke to a reporter about the drug she had unwittingly taken. Following the publicity of her case, the hospital canceled the scheduled abortion, and Finkbine subsequently traveled to Sweden for

---

[52] As Marvin Olasky explains, Restell sold the idea of abortion in five ways: "Her ads made abortion seem loving to husbands, kind to children already born, easy to accomplish, fair to women, and maybe not even an abortion at all." See Marvin Olasky, *The Press and Abortion, 1838–1988* (Hillsdale, NJ: Lawrence Erlabaum Associates, 1988), 5.

[53] Olasky, 46.

[54] Olasky, 67–75.

an abortion. The coverage of the Finkbines' plight attracted international attention. Afterward, a Gallup poll showed that 52% of Americans thought she had "done the right thing" in getting an abortion; 32% thought she had done wrong; and 16% had no opinion.[55]

The influence of the press in shaping (and shifting) public opinion on abortion has been acknowledged by abortion advocates. For example, Lawrence Lader, the cofounder of the National Association for the Repeal of Abortion Laws (which would later be renamed NARAL Pro-Choice America), admitted that a sympathetic press was crucial for the early accomplishments of the abortion rights movement. In the ultimately successful campaign to liberalize New York's abortion laws in the early 1970s, the press was initially seen as a hurdle. As Lader explained, "The obvious hurdle was that the press had become so immured to reform debate for years, they had no grasp of the meaning or potential of repeal [of abortion laws]." However, after an early press conference, Lader found that most reporters were sympathetic to the abortion cause, and he developed a "reasonable assurance that repeal could stir some excitement in the press."[56]

## *Feminist Support for Contraception and Abortion*

By the mid-1960s, the movement to legalize abortion had steadily gained traction among feminists. Before this time, the leading issue for most feminists was birth control. For example, Margaret Sanger (1879–1966), the founder of the American Birth Control League (which later became the

---

[55] Lawrence Lader devoted an entire chapter to the Finkbine incident, titled "A Farce in Phoenix," in his book *Abortion*. See Lader, 10–16. Jessica Waters also mentions the Finkbine story in her brief discussion of abortion history before *Roe*. See Jessica Waters, "Women's Leadership in the Reproductive Rights Movement," in *Gender and Women's Leadership: A Reference Handbook*, ed. Karen O'Connor (Thousand Oaks, CA: SAGE, 2010), 743–44. Olasky and Savas also discuss it in their book, *The Story of Abortion in America*, 278–80.

[56] Lawrence Lader, *Abortion II: Making the Revolution* (Boston: Beacon, 1973), 92.

Planned Parenthood Federation of America), focused her energies and activism on legalizing contraception.[57] In 1917, she started her own publication, *The Birth Control Review* (published from 1917 to 1940), which advocated for expanding access to contraception.[58]

Contraception remained the focus of early second-wave feminists in the 1960s. In fact, when the National Organization of Women (NOW) was founded in 1966, abortion was not included in the organization's initial statement of purpose. However, as efforts to legalize contraception made progress (the Supreme Court legalized contraception for married women in

[57] Although Sanger is mostly remembered as the founder of Planned Parenthood, she devoted most of her time to advocating for access to contraception. In 1916, Sanger opened a family planning and birth control clinic in Brooklyn, New York. Nine days after the clinic opened, Sanger was arrested for distributing contraceptives, a violation of New York's Comstock law. A subsequent arrest and thirty-day prison sentence attracted widespread publicity and garnered support for the fledgling birth control movement. In her autobiography, published in 1938, Sanger actually speaks negatively about abortion. In recounting the opening of the first birth control clinic in America in 1916, Sanger recalls speaking to at least 150 women. She notes, "To each group we explained simply what contraception was; that abortion was the wrong way—no matter how early it was performed it was taking life; that contraception was the better way, the safer way—it took a little time, a little trouble, but was well worth while in the long run, because life had not yet begun." See Margaret Sanger, *Margaret Sanger: An Autobiography* (New York: W. W. Norton, 1938), 217. In another place, Sanger says abortion leaves women "physically damaged and spiritually crippled." See Sanger, *Margaret Sanger*, 185.

[58] In her efforts to promote birth control, Sanger often tapped into widespread anti-Catholic sentiment in the 1920s. For example, the leading article in *The Birth Control Review* for the issue published in December 1921 stated, "All who resent this sinister Church Control of life and conduct—this interference of the Roman Church in attempting to dictate the conduct and behavior of non-Catholics, must now choose between Church Control or Birth Control. You can no longer remain neutral. You must make a declaration of independence, of self-reliance, or submit to the dictatorship of the Roman Catholic hierarchy. This is a dictatorship of celibates who presume to decide on the morality of a question upon which they professedly have had and cannot have any basis of experience." See Margaret Sanger, "Church Control?," *Birth Control Review* 5, no. 12 (December 1921).

1965 and unmarried women in 1972), the battle for contraception turned into a campaign for abortion.[59]

In the 1960s, activists such as Lawrence Lader argued that abortion was a civil rights issue for women. In his influential book *Abortion*, Lader argued, "The laws that force a woman to bear a child against her will are the sickly heritage of feminine degradation and male supremacy."[60] He believed that laws against abortion were rooted in a "primeval past" when women were expected to "breed until exhaustion." For Lader, the "triumph of reason over blind instinct" can come only when the state, church, and every "instrument of authority" allow women to make their own decisions about procreation.

In 1967, NOW included abortion in their "Bill of Rights for Women."[61] Other liberal national organizations followed their lead: the ACLU called for abortion law repeal in 1968, and Planned Parenthood did the same in 1969. At the First National Conference on Abortion Laws in Chicago, Lawrence Lader, NOW president Betty Friedan, and other abortion activists founded the National Association for the Repeal of Abortion Laws (NARAL), which advocated for the complete repeal of state abortion laws. By 1971, fourteen states had liberalized their abortion laws. However, most state legislatures resisted the aggressive lobbying effort, making it clear to activists that wide-ranging, comprehensive change would need to come from the courts.[62]

---

[59] Marvin Olasky documents this history in Olasky and Savas, *The Story of Abortion in America*, 260, 294. According to Olasky, the linkage between contraception and abortion made it seem to many liberals that the debate on such matters was about sex, not killing.

[60] Lader, *Abortion*, 167–68. Significantly, Lader's book *Abortion* was cited seven times in Justice Blackmun's *Roe v. Wade* majority decision. Lader crowed about this achievement in the preface of his second book, *Abortion II*, published in 1973.

[61] Waters, "Women's Leadership in the Reproductive Rights Movement," 744. See also Deirdre Carmody, "General Strike by U.S. Women Urged to Mark 19th Amendment," *New York Times*, March 21, 1970.

[62] Nancy McGlen et al. provide a helpful summary of how national feminist groups began to work for the repeal of abortion laws before *Roe*. See Nancy E. McGlen et al., eds., *Women, Politics, and American Society*, 5th ed. (London: Longman, 2011), 269.

### *Influence of Theological Liberalism*

Theological liberalism, which we briefly examined in the previous chapter, affected how some Protestant ministers thought about abortion. In fact, those belonging to mainline Protestant denominations were the first professing Christians to deviate from Christianity's historic pro-life ethic. In 1962, the Episcopal Church adopted a resolution that permitted "the termination of pregnancy" for a variety of reasons, including the mental health of the mother.[63] Similarly, the Presbyterian Church (USA) changed their official position in 1970, arguing that abortion should be a "matter of the careful ethical decision of a woman, her physician and her pastor or other counselor."[64]

In 1967, the Clergy Consultation Service on Abortion (CCS) was founded by mainline Protestant ministers and Jewish rabbis. The group lobbied against state abortion laws and referred pregnant women to

---

[63] *Journal of the General Convention of the Protestant Episcopal Church in the United States of America: Otherwise Known as The Episcopal Church*, Seattle, Washington, 1967, 307, https://www.episcopalarchives.org/sites/default/files/publications/1967_GC_Journal.pdf. In 1976, the Episcopal Church passed another resolution on abortion that stated in part, "That the Episcopal Church express its unequivocal opposition to any legislation on the part of the national or state governments which would abridge or deny the right of individuals to reach informed decisions in this matter [i.e., abortion] and to act upon them." See *Journal of the General Convention of the Protestant Episcopal Church in the United States of American—Otherwise Known as The Episcopal Church*, Minneapolis, Minnesota, 1976, 474, https://www.episcopalarchives.org/sites/default/files/publications/1976_GC_Journal.pdf.

[64] In 1972, the Presbyterian Church (USA) went even further, declaring, "Women should have full freedom of personal choice concerning the completion or termination of their pregnancies and that the artificial or induced termination of pregnancy, therefore, should not be restricted by law, except that it be performed under the direction and control of a properly licensed physician." For a brief history of the denomination's history on abortion, see Nick Skaggs and David Staniunas, "Reproductive justice and the PC(USA)," *Presbyterian Historical Society*, May 17, 2022, https://www.pcusa.org/news/2022/5/17/reproductive-justice-and-pcusa/.

abortion providers. An estimated 3,000 clergy members were part of the group.[65] Additionally, in 1971, the United Church of Christ adopted a proposal titled "Freedom of Choice Concerning Abortion," in which the denomination called for the "repeal of all legal prohibitions of physician-performed abortions."[66]

In the late 1960s, a handful of evangelical leaders joined their mainline counterparts in adopting a more pro-abortion position. Evidence of this shift can be discerned in a 1968 edition of *Christianity Today*. In one article, "25 evangelical scholars" summarize their view on abortion and contraception by explaining, "The Bible does not expressly prohibit either contraception or abortion but it does set forth certain governing principles." The scholars go on to argue, "The Christian physician will advise induced abortion only to safeguard greater values sanctioned by Scripture." Among these "greater values" are those of an "individual, familial, or societal" nature.[67] In the same issue of the magazine, theologian Paul Jewett observes that the "paucity of biblical references to pre-natal life" has led to "a spectrum of opinion" regarding the morality of abortion.[68] Relying on personhood theory, Jewett argues, "[A] fetus is a potential person, and maybe a primordial person, that is, a person in the most

---

[65] In a book documenting the history of the Clergy Consultation Service on Abortion (CCS), authors Arlene Carmen and Howard Moody provide a firsthand account of the pro-abortion clergy movement. Carmen and Moody note that the founders of the organization recruited clergy known for their "liberal attitudes and commitments." These ministers formed the "original nucleus" of the CCS. See Carmen and Moody, *Abortion Counseling and Social Change*, 21.

[66] See "Freedom of Choice Concerning Abortion: A Proposal for Action adopted by the Eighth General Synod," June 29, 1971. Additional statements from the United Church of Christ on abortion, including the text of the 1971 resolution, can be found at https://new.uccfiles.com/pdf/GS-Resolutions-Freedom-of-Choice.pdf?bcs-agent-scanner=48cc911b-4698-974f-9cc3-87c81002e45f.

[67] "A Protestant Affirmation on the Control of Human Reproduction," *Christianity Today*, November 8, 1968, 18–19.

[68] Paul K. Jewett, "The Relation of the Soul to the Fetus," *Christianity Today*, November 8, 1968, 8–9.

elementary form."[69] Although acknowledging the difficulties in justifying abortion, Jewett contends that for Christians abortion "will always remain a last recourse, ventured in emergency and burdened with uncertainty." Likewise, as we noted previously, the nation's largest Protestant denomination, the Southern Baptist Convention, approved a resolution in 1971 that permitted the "possibility of abortion under such conditions as rape, incest, clear evidence of severe fetal deformity, and carefully ascertained evidence of the likelihood of damage to the emotional, mental and physical health of the mother."[70]

Although evangelicals would rally to the pro-life cause in the late 1970s and early '80s (more on this in a moment), the shift toward affirming the morality and legality of abortion by mainline Protestants and some evangelicals in the mid-twentieth century was appreciated and appropriated by abortion supporters. By 1968, enough churches and clergy members publicly backed abortion that the *New York Times* inferred that "the Protestant position" on abortion was trending toward the "total repeal of abortion laws."[71]

## *Changing Legal and Moral Landscape*

Attitudes toward abortion were affected by the replacing and overturning of laws that restricted certain sexual behaviors and conduct. For example, access to and use of birth control expanded dramatically following two U.S. Supreme Court cases, *Griswold v. Connecticut* (1965) and *Eisenstadt v. Baird* (1972).

---

[69] Jewett, 8–9. Jewett goes on to note, "The primordial person, if that is what the fetus is, can never become a full-orbed person apart from another person, the mother in whose womb it is conceived and in whose body it is nourished. And while we may question the humanity of the fetus, we cannot question the humanity of the mother who conceives it."

[70] See "Resolution on Abortion," Southern Baptist Convention, June 1, 1971, https://www.sbc.net/resource-library/resolutions/resolution-on-abortion-2/.

[71] *New York Times*, December 29, 1968, VI-10, cited in Olasky and Savas, *The Story of Abortion in America*, 301.

In *Griswold*, the Court overturned a state law that prevented married women from accessing birth control. A few years later, the Court extended contraceptive access to unmarried couples in *Eisenstadt*.

These court decisions—combined with shifting sexual mores and advances in contraceptive technology, such as "the Pill" (first approved by the FDA in 1969)—helped separate sex from its consequences in the minds of many Americans. Previously, the prospect of conceiving a child had deterred many people from engaging in premarital or extramarital sex. But contraceptive technologies and laws that authorized their unfettered use allowed for seemingly consequence-free sexual activity. As sex and the possibility of pregnancy were separated, the notion of individual liberty was expanded to include a wider range of personal decisions. This expansion gradually but inexorably led to the elevation of sexual expression to the level of a quasi-virtue. Meanwhile, traditional sexual mores, and even parenthood, were increasingly dismissed as restraints on personal freedom.

Laws governing intimate behavior typically reflect a society's moral consensus. Thus, changes to a society's laws are indicative of changes in that consensus. However, changes in the law also drive the new consensus. In recent decades, permissive abortion laws have reshaped the moral imagination and the intuitions of tens of millions of Americans. In fact, in ways that will be explored in the next section, these laws have contributed to the perception that men and women are autonomous beings who can shape their own identities. As this thinking took hold, the ability to legally end an unwanted pregnancy became an unquestioned right and a moral good. This is entirely unsurprising. A society that elevates sexual license as the highest good of existence demands the availability of abortion because an unborn child's right to life is secondary to the perceived sexual needs and desires of the adult.

As both an indicator and source of the moral revolution, new laws related to contraception, divorce, and sexual behavior have ensured that the priorities of family formation—and even the right to life—would take a back seat to the demands of expressive individualism, the prevailing mindset in the West that sees the expression of personal identity, self-definition, and self-expression as the highest good.

### *Shifting Assumptions about Identity and Personhood*

Although the biological question about when life begins has been definitively settled by embryology, the adoption of secular philosophical ideas in the twentieth century has contributed to the acceptance of abortion in the broader American culture. These ideas have been articulated in recent books by Nancy Pearcey and Carl Trueman.

In her book *Love Thy Body*, Nancy Pearcey outlines what she sees as one of the guiding philosophical underpinnings of secular thought: personhood theory, a dualistic understanding of the human person that conceptually divides the physical body from the authentic person. As we discussed in chapter 2, personhood theory accepts the underlying worldview premise that the body has no inherent design or purpose. The mind, with its subjective perceptions, feelings, and intuitions, determines reality. In this framework, if there is tension or dysphoria between what the mind perceives and the physical body reveals, it is morally permissible, and, in some cases, morally obligatory to conform the body to the perceptions of the mind.

In Pearcey's view, personhood theory's dualistic view of the person is the unspoken yet animating premise behind pro-abortion arguments. To support abortion, Pearcey argues, "we must decide that human life in its earliest stages has no real value—so little that it may be killed for any reason."[72] Merely being alive in a biological sense does not confer moral standing that warrants legal protection. Thus, there is the creation of the category of "human non-person," which allows for the killing of those

---

[72] Nancy Pearcey, *Love Thy Body: Answering Hard Questions about Life and Sexuality* (Grand Rapids: Baker, 2018), 14, 20, 51–52.

deemed non-persons. Emblematic of the influence of personhood theory on the abortion debate, Pearcey cites one professor who states, "The question is not really about life in any biological sense. . . . It is instead asking about the magical moment at which a cluster of cells becomes more than a mere physical thing."[73]

Although personhood theory is not typically at the forefront for a woman facing an unplanned pregnancy or the activist protesting outside the Supreme Court, it is nonetheless the intellectual framework operating in the background. In an era when ultrasound technology is readily available, personhood theory's unscientific approach to embryology would presumably struggle to gain traction or credibility; the fact that it continues to be cited and embraced demonstrates the commitment of a secular age to find and use any possible justification for abortion.

Likewise, Carl Trueman, in his influential book *The Rise and Triumph of the Modern Self*, argues that the philosophical developments of the last few centuries have resulted in a popular conception of personhood, which is untethered from tradition, revelation, or moral restraint. According to Trueman, expressive individualism, with its elevation of self-actualization and deconstruction of tradition, religion, and received wisdom, has contributed to the overall philosophical framework that makes abortion plausible. As human selfhood is redefined in terms of personal identity, individual freedom, and self-definition, "the only moral criterion that can be applied to behavior is whether it conduces to the feeling of well-being in the individuals concerned."[74] Abortion is permissible because

---

[73] Pearcey, 60. Pearcey uses this example to note, "Put bluntly, abortion supporters have lost the argument on the scientific level. They can no longer deny that an embryo is biologically human. As a result, they have switched tactics to an argument based on personhood, defined ultimately by their own personal views and values."

[74] Carl Trueman, *The Rise and Triumph of the Modern Self: Cultural Amnesia, Expressive Individualism, and the Road to Sexual Revolution* (Wheaton, IL: Crossway, 2020), 79. Trueman's discussion of abortion on pages 101–2 is insightful as well.

individual preference and taste are more important than anything religion, tradition, or even science may tell us about the personhood of the unborn child.

### *Growing Understanding of Fetal Anatomy*

Finally, although the foregoing developments contributed to the liberalization of abortion laws in the lead-up to *Roe*, another development with significant pro-life consequences entered the picture in the second half of the twentieth century: a growing understanding of fetal anatomy. In short, Americans' awareness of fetal anatomy and development grew substantially from the 1930s to the 1960s. For example, in 1939, the Maternity Center Association commissioned a series of realistic sculptures of unborn children to display at the World's Fair in Queens, New York. More than two million people viewed the Birth Series sculptures. After the World's Fair, the sculptures toured the country and exposed more Americans to the science of fetal development. In 1965, *Life Magazine* astonished readers by publishing Lennart Nilsson's "Drama of Life" series, which featured the first published image of a living fetus inside its mother's womb. Additional images showed fetal development at several points throughout pregnancy. One stunning image shows an 18-week unborn child sucking its thumb. The issue sold 8 million copies, the second most during the publication's 89-year run as a weekly magazine.[75]

A related technological advancement that personalized unborn children was the invention of ultrasound technology in the 1950s. In 1985, a U.S.-based pregnancy center used an ultrasound to confirm pregnancy for the first time. The widespread availability of this technology in subsequent years has allowed millions of women to see and hear their unborn

[75] To view the images, see Ben Cosgrove, "'Drama of Life Before Birth': Lennart Nilsson's Landmark 1965 Photo Essay," *Life*, https://www.life.com/lifestyle/drama-of-life-before-birth-landmark-work-five-decades-later/.

babies.[76] According to pregnancy resource centers, seeing an ultrasound image of one's child has led many women in unplanned pregnancies to keep their child. In short, a growing understanding of fetal development is another important trend in the twentieth century. In fact, after the Supreme Court's decision in *Roe v. Wade*, the humanity and personhood of unborn children would become the central focus of the decades-long pro-life movement.

## *Roe v. Wade*

The abortion decisions of the U.S. Supreme Court in 1973 did not emerge in a vacuum. Rather, they followed liberalizing trends seen in churches, state legislatures, professional organizations, and public opinion. However, even as abortion advocates were making progress, thirty-one states resisted efforts at liberalizing their laws. In 1972, the year before the Court decided *Roe*, voters in Michigan and North Dakota rejected initiatives to allow physicians to perform abortions before twenty weeks.[77] Thus, even as abortion advocates succeeded in passing pro-abortion laws in liberal states—California passed a permissive abortion law in 1967 and New York passed a similar law in 1970—activists knew that overturning pro-life laws in the Midwest and South would not be easy. By the late-1960s, efforts at loosening state abortion laws had turned to the courts, a venue where abortion supporters increasingly found success.[78]

---

[76] Marvin Olasky and Leah Savas provide a brief history of ultrasound technology and discuss its effect on the abortion rate. In short, ultrasounds make a difference. This was demonstrated by one study that showed 78% of women at risk for an abortion who saw an ultrasound image chose not to abort. See Olasky and Savas, *The Story of Abortion in America*, 341–48.

[77] In Michigan, the referendum failed 60.7% to 39.4%. The vote in North Dakota was 76.6% against liberalization; only 23.4% of voters were in favor of permitting physicians to perform abortions before twenty weeks' gestation.

[78] Writing in 1973 after the Supreme Court's decision in *Roe v. Wade*, abortion advocate Lawrence Lader summarized recent abortion history in his book

In 1970, attorneys Sarah Weddington and Linda Coffee filed suit in the U.S. District Court for the North District of Texas, challenging the constitutionality of Texas's abortion laws. The plaintiff in the case was Norma McCorvey, who went under the legal pseudonym "Jane Roe." On June 17, 1970, a three-judge panel unanimously declared Texas's abortion laws unconstitutional, finding they violated the right to privacy secured by the Ninth Amendment.[79] After both parties appealed the decision, the Supreme Court granted certiorari, and oral arguments were heard before seven justices on December 13, 1971 (justices Hugo Black and John Marshall Harlan had retired in September 1971). In May 1972, the decision was made to rehear the case, in part, because of the poor quality of the first oral arguments and the arrival of two new justices (justices Lewis Powell and William Rehnquist).[80] Oral arguments before the full Court took place on October 11, 1972.

On January 22, 1973, the U.S. Supreme Court issued its decision in *Roe v. Wade*. Authored by Justice Harry Blackmun, the majority opinion established that a state could impose few restrictions on abortion until the third trimester. Blackmun grounded the right to abortion in a "right to privacy"

---

*Abortion II*. In a chapter titled "Overturning the Old Abortion Laws in Federal and State Supreme Courts," he conceded, "It was the courts, however, that produced even more sweeping gains for abortion in this period." See Lader, *Abortion II*, 187. Notably, between 1968 and 1973, almost thirty abortion-related cases were resolved or pending before the U.S. Supreme Court alone; dozens more were before lower federal and state courts. For a list, see Lee Epstein and Joseph F. Kobylka, *The Supreme Court and Legal Change: Abortion and the Death Penalty* (Chapel Hill, NC: The University of North Carolina Press, 1992), 164–66.

[79] *Roe v. Wade*, 314 F. Supp. 1217, 1221 (N.D. Tex. 1970). According to the U.S. District Court, "On the merits, plaintiffs argue as their principal contention that the Texas Abortion Laws must be declared unconstitutional because they deprive single women and married couples of their right, secured by the Ninth Amendment, to choose whether to have children. We agree." In explaining their reasoning, the judges wrote, "Not only are the Texas Abortion Laws unconstitutionally overbroad, they are also unconstitutionally vague."

[80] For a detailed recounting of the Supreme Court's deliberations on *Roe*, see Epstein and Kobylka, *The Supreme Court and Legal Change*, 137–202.

that he located in the Fourteenth Amendment. However, Blackmun stated that although the "right to privacy includes the abortion decision," a right to abortion "is not unqualified." According to Blackmun, a state's interest in protecting "potential life" increases as the "woman approaches term." States could regulate and even prohibit abortion in the third trimester, so long as exceptions for the woman's life or health were included.[81]

Despite Blackmun's assertion that a right to abortion "must be considered against important state interests in regulation," another case, *Doe v. Bolton* (also authored by Blackmun and released on the same day as *Roe*), provided a broad health exception that in theory and practice allowed abortion into the third trimester of pregnancy. Specifically, the Court in *Doe* held that a determination of maternal health should be made by a physician (often the abortionist with a profit motive) "in the light of all factors—physical, emotional, psychological, familial, and the woman's age—relevant to the wellbeing of the patient. All these factors may relate to health." This intentionally broad definition of "health" meant that in practice very little could be done to limit abortion at any point during pregnancy.

In summary, Justice Blackmun's twin abortion rulings dramatically liberalized abortion policy in the United States. In fact, the scope and rationale of Blackmun's ruling surprised even ardent supporters of abortion. Abortion activist Lawrence Lader, whose 1966 abortion book was cited seven times in *Roe*, declared that the ruling was "more conclusive than any of us had dared to hope." According to Lader, Blackmun's decision "climaxed a social

---

[81] In addition to claiming that a right to abortion was grounded in a right to privacy guaranteed by the Fourteenth Amendment, Justice Blackmun claimed that the common law tradition permitted a woman to terminate a pregnancy before quickening. For Blackmun, it was apparent "that at common law, at the time of the adoption of our Constitution, and throughout the major portion of the nineteenth century, abortion was viewed with less disfavor than under most American statutes currently in effect." Blackmun argued that new scholarship even shows that "post-quickening abortion was never established as a common law crime." As his source, Blackmun cited Cyril C. Means Jr., the legal counsel for the National Association for the Repeal of Abortion Laws (NARAL).

revolution whose magnitude and speed were probably unequaled in United States history."[82] In other words, the breadth of the decision was so far-reaching that even those who supported permissive abortion laws recognized that Blackmun might have gone too far. In 1992, soon-to-be Supreme Court Justice Ruth Bader Ginsburg conceded that *Roe* "prolonged divisiveness" and "deferred stable settlement on the issue" of abortion.[83] According to Ginsburg, *Roe* "halted a political process that was moving in a reform direction." The future justice even blamed Blackmun's opinion for triggering a "well-organized and vocal" movement that "succeeded, for a considerable time, in turning the legislative tide" in a pro-life direction.[84]

## Elephants and Donkeys: America's Political Parties Respond to *Roe*

Legislators from both political parties responded to the Supreme Court's decision in *Roe v. Wade* by introducing Human Life Amendments in 1973.

[82] Lader, *Abortion II*, inside cover.

[83] Ruth Bader Ginsburg, "Speaking in a Judicial Voice," *New York University Law Review* 67, no. 6, December 1992, https://www.law.nyu.edu/sites/default/files/ECM_PRO_059254.pdf.

[84] In her address, then-Circuit Judge Ginsburg also stated, "*Roe v. Wade* . . . invited no dialogue with legislators. Instead, it seemed entirely to remove the ball from the legislators' court. In 1973, when *Roe* was issued, abortion law was in a state of change across the nation. As the Supreme Court itself noted, there was a marked trend in state legislatures 'toward liberalization of abortion statutes.' . . . No measured motion, the *Roe* decision left virtually no state with laws fully conforming to the Court's delineation of abortion regulation still permissible."

Over twenty years later, Justice Ginsburg would repeat her criticism of *Roe* in a 2013 talk at the Law School of the University of Chicago. According to Ginsburg, *Roe* was too far-reaching and too sweeping. "My criticism of *Roe* is that it seemed to have stopped the momentum on the side of change," Ginsburg explained. See Meredith Heagney, "Justice Ruth Bader Ginsburg Offers Critique of *Roe v. Wade* During Law School Visit," University of Chicago, May 15, 2013, https://www.law.uchicago.edu/news/justice-ruth-bader-ginsburg-offers-critique-roe-v-wade-during-law-school-visit.

Eight days after the *Roe* decision, Rep. Lawrence Hogan (R-MD) introduced House Joint Resolution 261 that called for a constitutional amendment to protect unborn children "from the moment of conception."[85] Later in the year, Rep. James Burke (D-MA) introduced an amendment that stated, "With respect to the right to life, the word 'person' . . . applies to all human beings, including their unborn offspring at every stage of their biological development, irrespective of age, health, function, or condition of dependency."[86] In total, eight Democrats and fourteen Republicans introduced Human Life Amendments in 1973.[87]

Although Republicans and Democrats have taken widely divergent positions on abortion since the 2000s, it is important to note that national Democrats were not always aggressively pro-abortion. From the period of 1973–2003, there were 332 Human Life Amendments introduced in the United States Congress. Of these, 151 were introduced by Democrats.

In fact, some of the most well-known Democrats in the 1980s and '90s held pro-life views before flipping on the issue. For example, former House Majority Leader Richard Gephardt (D-MO), who served in the House of Representatives from 1977 to 2015, wrote in 1977, "Life is the division of human cells, a process that begins with conception. . . . The [Supreme Court's abortion] ruling was unjust, and it is incumbent on the Congress to correct this injustice."[88] In a 1977 op-ed, activist Jesse Jackson

---

[85] United States, Congress, House. H.R. Res 261, 93rd Congress, January 30, 1973, https://www.congress.gov/bill/93rd-congress/house-joint-resolution/261.

[86] United States, Congress, House. H.R. Res 769, 93rd Congress, October 12, 1973, https://www.congress.gov/bill/93rd-congress/house-joint-resolution/769?overview=closed.

[87] Human Life Amendments, National Committee for a Human Life Amendment, accessed September 30, 2023, https://web.archive.org/web/20070927034423/http:/www.nchla.org/datasource/idocuments/HLAlst7303.pdf.

[88] Cited in Mark Collette, "Pangs of Conscience: Five Modern Benedict Arnolds of the Pro-Life Movement," *World*, January 17, 1998, https://wng.org/articles/pang-of-conscience-1618010375. When running for president in 1987, Gephardt switched positions, telling the National Right to Life Committee, "I do not support any Constitutional Amendment pertaining to the legality of abortion."

stated, "In the abortion debate one of the crucial questions is when does life begin. Anything growing is living. Therefore human life begins when the sperm and egg join and drop into the fallopian tube and the pulsation of life take place."[89] Although life may be described differently at various states (as an embryo, baby, child, adult), Jackson maintained that the "essence is the same."[90] Notably, when he ran for president in 1988, Jackson reversed course, stating, "Women must have freedom of choice over what to do over their bodies."[91]

Perhaps most famously, then-governor Bill Clinton wrote in 1986, "I am opposed to abortion and to government funding of abortions. We should not spend state funds on abortions because so many people believe abortion is wrong."[92] Clinton's future vice president, then-Senator Al Gore (D-TN), expressed similar sentiments in 1983, writing, "I have strongly opposed Federal funding of abortions. In my opinion, it is wrong to spend Federal funds for what is arguably the taking of a human life. It is my deep personal conviction that abortion is wrong."[93] As the 1992 presidential election approached, Clinton and Gore flipped their positions, expressing support for abortion.

---

[89] Jesse Jackson, "How We Respect Life Is the Over-Riding Moral Question," *Right to Life News*, January 1977, https://groups.csail.mit.edu/mac/users/rauch/nvp/consistent/jackson.html.

[90] Jackson, "How We Respect Life Is the Over-Riding Moral Question." Jackson concludes his essay by asking, "What happens to the mind of a person, and the moral fabric of a nation, that accepts the aborting of the life of a baby without a pang of conscience? What kind of a person, and what kind of a society will we have 20 years hence if life can be taken so casually?"

[91] Colman McCarthy, "Jackson's Reversal on Abortion," *Washington Post*, May 21, 1988, https://www.washingtonpost.com/archive/opinions/1988/05/21/jacksons-reversal-on-abortion/dd9e1637-020d-447b-9329-95ec67e41fd5/.

[92] Felicity Barringer, "The 1992 Campaign: Campaign Issues; Clinton and Gore Shifted on Abortion," *New York Times*, July 20, 1992, https://www.nytimes.com/1992/07/20/us/the-1992-campaign-campaign-issues-clinton-and-gore-shifted-on-abortion.html.

[93] Barringer, "The 1992 Campaign."

Finally, in 1973, Senator Joe Biden (D-DE), then in his first term, stated the Supreme Court had gone "too far" in its *Roe* ruling.[94] The next year, Biden told a reporter that a woman should not have the "sole right to say what should happen to her body."[95] In 1984, Biden penned a letter explaining his opposition to taxpayer funding for abortion. According to Biden, "I will continue to abide by the same principle that has guided me throughout my 21 years in the Senate: those of us who are opposed to abortion should not be compelled to pay for them."[96] The future president went on to say, "I have consistently—on no fewer than 50 occasions—voted against federal funding of abortions." Biden concluded the 1984 letter by noting, "[T]he government should not tell those with strong convictions against abortion, such as you and I, that we must pay for them." Furthermore, in 1996, 1997, 1998, 1999, and 2003, then-Senator Biden voted to prohibit partial-birth and late-term abortions.[97]

## *The Pro-Life Movement Grows*

While Democrats at the national level were beginning to abandon their pro-life convictions, Republicans took notice of the burgeoning pro-life movement. In the lead-up to the 1980 presidential election, Jerry Falwell organized the Moral Majority to mobilize voters to support pro-family, conservative candidates, including former governor Ronald Reagan (R-CA).

---

[94] Maggie Astor, "Joe Biden on Abortion and the Hyde Amendment," *New York Times*, June 27, 2019, https://www.nytimes.com/2019/06/27/us/politics/joe-biden-abortion-hyde-amendment.html.

[95] Lisa Lerer, "When Joe Biden Voted to Let States Overturn *Roe v. Wade*," *New York Times*, March 29, 2019, https://www.nytimes.com/2019/03/29/us/politics/biden-abortion-rights.html.

[96] Joe Biden to Michael Gregg, Letter, April 7, 1994, https://www.documentcloud.org/documents/6127592-biden94letter.html.

[97] For an overview of Joe Biden's record on abortion, see David Closson, "The 2020 Election: A Clear Distinction on Abortion," Public Discourse, September 20, 2020, https://www.thepublicdiscourse.com/2020/09/71555/.

Although Reagan had liberalized California's abortion laws as governor, evangelical Christians rallied to his campaign, in part because of his pro-life platform.[98] These voters were rewarded as Reagan championed pro-life policies throughout his two terms.[99]

In the aftermath of *Roe*, abortion became an animating issue for evangelical voters; before 1973, the most vocal and consistent opponents of abortion had been Roman Catholics. However, as abortion clinics sprang up throughout the Bible Belt and legal abortions skyrocketed from fewer

---

[98] Notably, as governor, Reagan signed the Therapeutic Abortion Act of 1967 into law on June 14, 1967. The law allowed abortions in cases of rape, incest, or when a doctor deemed that giving birth was likely to impair the physical or mental health of the mother. In 1967, when the measure was enacted, there were only 518 legal abortions in California. In 1980, there were 199,089 abortions. From 1968 to 1980, there were a total of 1,444,778 abortions in California. For more on Reagan's decision to sign the 1967 law, see Lou Cannon, *Governor Reagan: His Rise to Power* (New York: PublicAffairs, 2003), 208–14. Significantly, Reagan expressed regret for liberalizing California's abortion laws as early as 1976 when he challenged President Gerald Ford for the Republican nomination for president. During one campaign stop, he stated, "If I had it to do all over again I would have more restrictions than I agreed to. . . . I placed too much faith in those who were entrusted with insuring that the patient met the terms of the bill." See "Reagan Affirms Anti-Abortion Stand," *New York Times*, February 8, 1976, https://www.nytimes.com/1976/02/08/archives/reagan-affirms-antiabortion-stand.html.

[99] In addition to pursuing pro-life policies, President Reagan published a short pro-life book during his first term and addressed the March for Life in 1988. See Ronald Reagan, *Abortion and the Conscience of the Nation* (Nashville: Thomas Nelson, 1984). President Reagan's book initially appeared as an essay in *The Human Life Review* in 1983. In one poignant passage, Reagan notes, "The real question today is not when human life begins, but, *What is the value of human life*? The abortionist who reassembles the arms and legs of a tiny baby to make sure all its parts have been torn from its mother's body can hardly doubt whether it is a human being. The real question for him and for all of us is whether that tiny human life has a God-given right to be protected by the law—the same right we have." See Reagan, *Abortion and the Conscience of the Nation*, 22, emphasis original. For President Reagan's 1988 address to the March for Life, see Ronald Reagan, "Remarks to Participants in the March for Life Rally," Reagan Foundation, January 22, 1988, https://www.reaganfoundation.org/media/51185/pdf-012288.pdf?bcs-agent-scanner=f7c9c9f0-e690-3a40-ae43-d95c4e4ef925.

than 750,000 in 1973 to more than 1.5 million in 1980, evangelicals took notice. Under the influential leadership of Falwell, Francis Schaeffer, D. James Kennedy, and others, abortion was presented as a moral imperative, and many evangelicals turned to political action to effect change.[100]

Writing in 1979, Schaeffer urged evangelical Christians to live under the "Lordship of Christ," which included using "every constitutional practice to offset the rise of authoritarian governments and the loss of humanness in our society."[101] For Schaeffer, permissive abortion laws demonstrated that the United States was secularizing, and he believed that Christians should use everything at their disposal to return Christian values to government and society. Likewise, Falwell argued that "abortion, the drug traffic, pornography, child abuse, and immorality" were tearing the country apart. For Falwell, "to stop the killing of 1.5 million unborn infants every year," evangelicals needed to work alongside Roman Catholics, Jews, Mormons, and nonbelievers to win the "war" over "shared moral issues."[102] In the lead-up to the 1980 presidential election, the Moral Majority registered 3 to 4 million voters, published voter guides, held rallies and parades, produced television and radio promotions, and mailed millions of brochures and letters. Their efforts were largely credited with helping Reagan defeat incumbent Jimmy Carter.[103]

---

[100] Daniel K. Williams, "The Partisan Trajectory of the American Pro-Life Movement: How a Liberal Catholic Campaign Became a Conservative Evangelical Cause," *Religions* 6, no. 2 (April 16, 2015): 463, https://doi.org/10.3390/rel6020451.

[101] Francis A. Schaeffer and C. Everett Koop, *Whatever Happened to the Human Race?* (Old Tappan, NJ: Revell, 1979), 194.

[102] Jerry Falwell, *Strength for the Journey: An Autobiography* (New York: Simon & Schuster, 1987), 362, 364.

[103] In his 1987 biography, Falwell explained that the Moral Majority worked "to raise the moral conscience of the nation and to mobilize people of like mind to take political action. And in the process, we helped elect a President." See Falwell, *Strength for the Journey*, 365. In a diary entry for September 26, 1980, President Jimmy Carter refers to the Moral Majority as "religious nuts," yet acknowledges their growing influence. Carter's diary, published with the former president's annotations in 2010, notes Falwell's influence in the 1980 campaign. According to

## After *Roe*: Party Platforms and Legislative Developments

Although space does not allow for an extended analysis of federal and state abortion law in the half century between *Roe* and its eventual overturning, a brief survey of relevant events can provide insight into how the political landscape changed from 1973 to 2022. Specifically, a review of the party platforms—quadrennial documents produced before each presidential election—provides a window into how elected officials and the electorate as a whole has thought about abortion over the last five decades.

### *History of Party Platforms on Abortion*

In 1976, the first presidential election year after *Roe*, Democrats included two sentences about abortion in their platform. The platform stated: "We fully recognize the religious and ethical nature of the concerns which many Americans have on the subject of abortion. We feel, however, that it is undesirable to attempt to amend the U.S. Constitution to overturn the Supreme Court decision in this area."[104]

Similarly, in 1976, Republicans stated, "The question of abortion is one of the most difficult and controversial of our time. It is undoubtedly a moral and personal issue but it also involves complex questions relating to

---

Carter, "As one indication of the power wielded by this new alliance, that autumn a group headed by Jerry Falwell purchased $10 million in commercials on southern radio and TV to brand me as a traitor to the South and no longer a Christian." See Jimmy Carter, *White House Diary* (New York: Farrar, Straus and Giroux, 2010), 468–69. Outlets like the *Washington Post* regularly covered the Moral Majority and acknowledged that abortion was a motivating concern for the organization. See Nicholas D. Kristof, "Jerry Falwell Plans 'Massive Effort' To Register Million New Voters by Fall," *Washington Post*, July 30, 1982, https://www.washingtonpost.com/archive/politics/1982/07/30/jerry-falwell-plans-massive-effort-to-register-million-new-voters-by-fall/89bef675-7b47-485d-baa4-f98dfee8fa43/.

[104] 1976 Democratic Party Platform, The American Presidency Project, July 12, 1976, https://www.presidency.ucsb.edu/documents/1976-democratic-party-platform.

medical science and criminal justice."[105] The platform acknowledged that there were those in the party who favored *Roe* as well as those who wanted to enact a constitutional amendment "prohibiting all abortions." Although the platform stated that it supported those seeking a constitutional amendment to restore protections for unborn children, it sought to strike a moderate position, explaining, "The Republican Party favors a continuance of the public dialogue on abortion."

In 1980, Democrats once again publicly supported *Roe*.[106] However, Democrats acknowledged "the religious and ethical concerns which many Americans have about abortion." Significantly, incumbent President Jimmy Carter did not approve of the abortion language in the 1980 platform. A week after the Democratic Convention, Carter admitted to Archbishop John Quinn that he disagreed with the "platform plank on abortion."[107]

In the lead-up to Ronald Reagan's ultimately successful campaign, Republicans in 1980 included a short section on abortion, affirming the party's support for a pro-life constitutional amendment.[108] While acknowledging "differing views" on abortion within the country and party, the

---

[105] 1976 Republican Party Platform, The American Presidency Project, August 18, 1976, https://www.presidency.ucsb.edu/documents/republican-party-platform-1976.

[106] 1980 Democratic Party Platform, The American Presidency Project, August 11, 1980, https://www.presidency.ucsb.edu/documents/1980-democratic-party-platform.

[107] In his diary, Carter wrote on August 20, 1980, "In the evening I talked to Archbishop [John R.] Quinn about the Democratic convention platform plank on abortion. I told him that my position had not changed; that I disagree with the platform and had expressed my disapproval specifically in my last Wednesday's remarks." President Carter's diary, published in 2010, contains an explanatory note in which he explains, "Because of my religious beliefs I have never supported abortions, except to protect the life and health of the mother or in cases where pregnancies resulted from rape or incest. But as president I had to comply with *Roe v. Wade*." See Jimmy Carter, *White House Diary*, 459, 71.

[108] 1980 Republican Party Platform, The American Presidency Project, July 15, 1980, https://www.presidency.ucsb.edu/documents/republican-party-platform-1980.

platform voiced support for congressional efforts aimed at restricting the use of taxpayer funding for abortion.

Four years later, in 1984, the word "abortion" disappeared from the Democratic Party platform. The only reference to abortion was a sentence warning about the consequences of "a Supreme Court chosen by Ronald Reagan," which Democrats feared would threaten "the fundamental right of a woman to reproductive freedom."[109]

For their part, Republicans strengthened their pro-life position in 1984.[110] According to the platform, "The unborn child has a fundamental individual right to life which cannot be infringed." The platform endorses legislation to clarify that the Fourteenth Amendment's protections apply to unborn children. Unlike the previous two platforms, the 1984 platform does not acknowledge dissenting views within the party. Additionally, the platform refers to President Reagan's commitment to eliminate funding for organizations that "advocate or support abortion." Following his reelection, President Reagan fulfilled this promise by implementing the Mexico City Policy, a policy that prohibited funding for international nongovernmental organizations that perform or promote abortion.

In 1988, Democrats once again did not use the word "abortion" in their platform.[111] Instead, the platform affirmed that "the fundamental right of reproductive choice should be guaranteed regardless of ability to pay."

---

[109] 1984 Democratic Party Platform, The American Presidency Project, July 16, 1984, https://www.presidency.ucsb.edu/documents/1984-democratic-party-platform. Although Democratic nominee Walter Mondale eventually lost in a landslide to Reagan, he earned the endorsement of the National Organization of Women (NOW). See Past and Current Presidents, National Organization for Women, accessed September 30, 2023, https://now.org/about/history/presidents/.

[110] 1984 Republican Party Platform, The American Presidency Project, August 20, 1984, https://www.presidency.ucsb.edu/documents/republican-party-platform-1984. From 1984 onward, national Republicans were unapologetic in their support of pro-life policies and sought to embrace their reputation as the pro-life party.

[111] 1988 Democratic Party Platform, The American Presidency Project, July 18, 1988, https://www.presidency.ucsb.edu/documents/1988-democratic-party-platform.

Although Michael Dukakis, the Democratic nominee, lost the election to Vice President George H. W. Bush, he earned the endorsement of the National Abortion Rights Action League (NARAL).[112]

Republicans, meanwhile, reaffirmed their support for legislation clarifying that the Fourteenth Amendment applies to unborn children and restated their opposition to the use of taxpayer dollars for organizations that fund or support abortion.[113]

The 1992 Republican platform reused the abortion language from the 1988 platform almost verbatim.[114] Democrats, however, reintroduced the word "abortion" in their 1992 platform. After twelve years out of power, Democrats sought to offer a moderate position to the American people. According to their platform, Democrats supported "the right to a safe, legal abortion."[115] In a section titled "Choice," Democrats affirmed their support for *Roe* but noted, "The goal of our nation must be to make abortion less necessary, not more difficult or more dangerous."

In the lead-up to the 1992 presidential election, the Supreme Court handed down decisions in two abortion cases: *Webster v. Reproductive Health Services* (1989) and *Planned Parenthood v. Casey* (1992). In *Webster*,

---

[112] David Anderson, "Abortion Supporters Back Dukakis," United Press International, September 13, 1988, https://www.upi.com/Archives/1988/09/13/Abortion-supporters-back-Dukakis/6234590126400/.

[113] 1988 Republican Party Platform, The American Presidency Project, August 16, 1988, https://www.presidency.ucsb.edu/documents/republican-party-platform-1988. Additionally, the 1988 platform included a commendation of religious and private organizations that provide alternatives to abortion and expressed opposition to programs in public schools that provide birth control or "abortion services or referrals."

[114] 1992 Republican Party Platform, The American Presidency Project, August 17, 1992, https://www.presidency.ucsb.edu/documents/republican-party-platform-1992.

[115] 1992 Democratic Party Platform, The American Presidency Project, July 13, 1992, https://www.presidency.ucsb.edu/documents/1992-democratic-party-platform. Worth noting is that the 1992 Democratic platform included, for the first time, support for "a national law to protect" abortion.

the Court upheld the constitutionality of a Missouri law that prohibited public employees, facilities, or funds from being used to perform an abortion. Although *Roe* was upheld, the 5–4 decision revealed that four justices wanted to overturn it. In response to *Webster*, conservative states were emboldened to pass new pro-life legislation. In *Casey*, the Court again upheld *Roe*, but replaced the trimester framework with a prohibition against states creating an "undue burden" on women seeking an abortion before viability (the gestational age at which an unborn child is thought to be capable of surviving outside the womb). The 5–4 decision left in place the "health exception" that enabled states to permit elective abortion late in pregnancy.[116]

In his first term, President Bill Clinton reversed several of his predecessor's pro-life policies, including a ban on federal funding of fetal tissue research, a prohibition on privately funded abortions at military facilities, and the Mexico City Policy.[117] Additionally, Clinton vetoed the Partial-Birth

---

[116] In his *Casey* concurrence, Justice Harry Blackmun, the author of *Roe*, noted his displeasure and fear that the *Casey* decision was decided by a close, 5-4 vote, writing, "I do not underestimate the significance of today's joint opinion. Yet I remain steadfast in my belief that the right to reproductive choice is entitled to the full protection afforded by this Court before *Webster*. And I fear for the darkness as four Justices anxiously await the single vote necessary to extinguish the light." He concluded his concurrence by signaling his concern about the future of legalized abortion: "In one sense, the Court's [majority] approach is worlds apart from that of The Chief Justice and Justice Scalia. And yet, in another sense, the distance between the two approaches is short—the distance is but a single vote. I am 83 years old. I cannot remain on this Court forever, and when I do step down, the confirmation process for my successor well may focus on the issue before us today. That, I regret, may be exactly where the choice between the two worlds will be made." See Blackmun's concurring opinion in Planned Parenthood of Southeastern Pa. v. Casey, 505 U.S. 833 (1992).

[117] Memorandum on the Mexico City Policy, The American Presidency Project, January 22, 1993, https://www.presidency.ucsb.edu/documents/memorandum-the-mexico-city-policy-0; David Burrelli, "Services and Military Medical Facilities," *Defense Technical Information Center*, December 16, 2010, https://apps.dtic.mil/sti/citations/ADA535851.

Abortion Act of 1995 and appointed Ruth Bader Ginsburg, a former ACLU lawyer, to the U.S. Supreme Court.[118]

In 1996, Republicans offered their most detailed section yet on abortion.[119] After reiterating portions of previous platforms, the new platform noted that Republicans are not "punitive" toward women facing unplanned pregnancies. "We oppose abortion, but our pro-life agenda does not include punitive action against women who have an abortion," the platform read. The 1996 platform also condemned President Clinton's veto of a partial-birth abortion bill.

For their part, Democrats devoted three paragraphs to abortion in their 1996 platform.[120] Although pledging support for *Roe*, the platform stated, "The Democratic Party is a party of inclusion. We respect the individual conscience of each American on this difficult issue, and we welcome all our members to participate at every level of our party." Significantly, the platform celebrated the decreasing abortion rate and called on Americans "to take personal responsibility" to "reduce unintended pregnancies." Although supportive of abortion, the platform sought middle ground, acknowledging, "Our goal is to make abortion less necessary and more rare."

The 2000 Republican platform repeated much of its abortion language from the '96 platform. It also included a rebuke of the Supreme Court's decision in *Stenberg v. Carhart*, a 2000 decision that invalidated a state law

---

[118] The Clinton Presidency: Timeline of Major Actions, The White House Archives, accessed October 1, 2023, https://clintonwhitehouse5.archives.gov/WH/Accomplishments/eightyears-02.html; United States, Congress, House, H.R. Res 1833, 104th Congress, June 14, 1995, https://www.congress.gov/bill/104th-congress/house-bill/1833.

[119] 1996 Republican Party Platform, The American Presidency Project, August 12, 1996, https://www.presidency.ucsb.edu/documents/republican-party-platform-1996.

[120] 1996 Democratic Party Platform, The American Presidency Project, August 26, 1996, https://www.presidency.ucsb.edu/documents/1996-democratic-party-platform.

that had made partial-birth abortion illegal.[121] The platform reiterated the party's opposition for using tax money to support abortion.

In 2000, the Democrats' national platform recycled much of the same language from the previous platform. Once again, the stated goal was "to make abortion less necessary." Significantly, Democrats chided Republicans for making opposition to abortion a purity test for the party.[122]

Not surprisingly, the Republican platform in 2004 focused on combatting terrorism, ongoing wars in Afghanistan and Iraq, and al-Qaeda.[123] Although abortion was moved to the end of the platform, Republicans offered their lengthiest section yet on "Promoting a Culture of Life." The 2004 platform highlighted President George Bush's support for crisis pregnancy centers and the party's support for parental notification laws.

Like Republicans, Democrats focused their 2004 platform on national security.[124] In one paragraph devoted to abortion, the party pledged to uphold *Roe*. Noticeably, the appeal to pro-lifers from the 2000 platform was dropped. In the lone sentence where the word "abortion" appeared, Democrats stated, "Abortion should be safe, legal, and rare."

The 2008 Republican platform included a section on abortion that once again pledged the party's support for pro-life policies. Specifically, the platform celebrated the Supreme Court's 2007 decision that upheld

---

[121] 2000 Republican Party Platform, The American Presidency Project, July 31, 2000, https://www.presidency.ucsb.edu/documents/2000-republican-party-platform.

[122] To this end, Democrats quoted Bob Dole, the Republicans' nominee for president in 1996, who urged his party to recognize that "members of our party have deeply held and sometimes differing views on issues of personal conscience like abortion." In short, Democrats in 2000 sought to show that although the party was committed to abortion, they were, as the "party of inclusion," a big-tent party for pro-life and pro-choice voters. See 2000 Democratic Party Platform, The American Presidency Project, August 14, 2000, https://www.presidency.ucsb.edu/documents/2000-democratic-party-platform.

[123] 2004 Republican Party Platform, The American Presidency Project, August 30, 2004, https://www.presidency.ucsb.edu/documents/2004-republican-party-platform.

[124] 2004 Democratic Party Platform, The American Presidency Project, July 27, 2004, https://www.presidency.ucsb.edu/documents/2004-democratic-party-platform.

the Partial-Birth Abortion Ban Act of 2003 and affirmed pregnancy care centers.[125] For their part, Democrats included a short section on abortion in their 2008 platform that reaffirmed the party's support of *Roe*.[126] The platform also trumpeted the party's support of "comprehensive affordable family planning services" that would "reduce the need for abortions."

In 2012, Republicans voiced support for several pro-life policies within their platform, including legislation to prohibit sex-selective abortion, protections for babies "who are capable of feeling pain," a ban on the "use of body parts from aborted fetuses for research," and a prohibition on killing embryos for their stem cells.[127]

Conversely, Democrats in 2012 affirmed their support of *Roe* and stated their opposition to "all efforts to weaken or undermine" a right to abortion.[128] The platform noted that abortion is an "intensely personal decision between a woman, her family, her doctor, and her clergy" and that the government has no place "to get in the way." The platform also highlighted President Obama's decision to end the Mexico City Policy.

As we have seen, from 1980 to 2012, Democrats and Republicans approached abortion from increasingly different perspectives. By the 2016 election, the respective party platforms offered the starkest contrast yet.

---

[125] The 2008 platform also supported a human life amendment to the Constitution and stated that society has a moral obligation to "assist, not to penalize" women facing an unplanned pregnancy. 2008 Republican Party Platform, The American Presidency Project, September 1, 2008, https://www.presidency.ucsb.edu/documents/2008-republican-party-platform.

[126] 2008 Democratic Party Platform, The American Presidency Project, August 25, 2008, https://www.presidency.ucsb.edu/documents/2008-democratic-party-platform.

[127] The platform also called for strengthening the Born Alive Infant Protection Act and praised states for passing informed consent, mandatory waiting periods, and health-protective clinic regulations. See 2012 Republican Party Platform, The American Presidency Project, August 27, 2012, https://www.presidency.ucsb.edu/documents/2012-republican-party-platform.

[128] 2012 Democratic Party Platform, The American Presidency Project, September 3, 2012, https://www.presidency.ucsb.edu/documents/2012-democratic-party-platform.

Before the summer conventions, the Democratic nominee, former secretary of state Hillary Clinton, campaigned vigorously as a defender of abortion. In fact, Clinton became the first candidate to receive Planned Parenthood's endorsement in a presidential primary.[129] On the Republican side, Donald Trump made a variety of pro-life commitments, even promising in the final presidential debate with Clinton to appoint pro-life justices to the Supreme Court.[130] Although Trump had previously referred to himself as "totally pro-choice" as recently as 1999, he earned the backing of trusted pro-life leaders, including Marjorie Dannenfelser (president, Susan B. Anthony List) and James Dobson (founder, Focus on the Family) by campaigning on a pro-life platform and selecting then governor Mike Pence as his running mate.[131]

---

[129] Amy Chozick, "Planned Parenthood, in Its First Primary Endorsement, Backs Hillary Clinton," *New York Times*, January 7, 2016, https://archive.nytimes.com/www.nytimes.com/politics/first-draft/2016/01/07/planned-parenthood-in-its-first-primary-endorsement-backs-hillary-clinton/. Throughout the 2016 campaign, Clinton campaigned as an enthusiastic supporter of abortion. About a month before the Democratic National Convention, Clinton spoke at Planned Parenthood Action Fund's membership event in Washington, DC. In her address, Clinton sought to portray Donald Trump, the presumptive Republican nominee for president, as extreme on abortion. She also embraced abortion, noting, "And, it is worth saying again: defending women's health means defending access to abortion—not just in theory, but in reality." See Katie Reilly, "Read Hillary Clinton's Speech Hitting Donald Trump on Women's Issues," *Time,* June 10, 2016, https://time.com/4364631/hillary-clinton-planned-parenthood-speech-transcript/.

[130] Dan Mangan, "Trump: I'll Appoint Supreme Court Justices to Overturn *Roe v. Wade* Abortion Case," CNBC, October 19, 2016, https://www.cnbc.com/2016/10/19/trump-ill-appoint-supreme-court-justices-to-overturn-roe-v-wade-abortion-case.html.

[131] In the 1999 *Meet the Press* interview, Trump stated his opposition to prohibitions on abortion as late as the third trimester, stating "I am pro-choice in every respect." See Meet the Press, "Trump in 1999: 'I Am Very Pro-Choice,'" NBC News, July 8, 2015, https://www.nbcnews.com/meet-the-press/video/trump-in-1999-i-am-very-pro-choice-480297539914; Katie Glueck, "Trump taps top abortion foe to chair anti-abortion coalition," *Politico*, September 16, 2016, https://www.politico.com/story/2016/09/donald-trump-marjorie-dannenfelser-abortion-228252; "James Dobson: Why I Am Voting for Donald Trump," *Christianity Today*,

In terms of platforms, the Democrats' 2016 platform stated that "reproductive health" is core to the "health and wellbeing" of Americans.[132] Additionally, the platform praised Planned Parenthood and promised to defend the abortion provider from Republican defunding attempts. The platform also noted the party's opposition to "federal and state laws and policies that impede a woman's access to abortion." Significantly, the platform called for the repealing of the Hyde Amendment, the legislative provision that blocks federal tax dollars from funding abortion. This marked the first time a major American political party had endorsed, as a matter of party policy, direct government funding for abortion.

Republicans, on the other hand, set forth in their 2016 platform a vision for the country that included robust protections for the unborn.[133] Notably, the section on abortion appears much earlier in the document, signaling the party's prioritization of the issue. The 2016 platform supports the defunding of Planned Parenthood, criticizes the Supreme Court for striking down health and safety standards for abortion clinics in Texas, calls on Congress to pass the Born-Alive Abortion Survivors Protection Act and Pain-Capable Unborn Child Protection Act, praises states for enacting laws to protect unborn babies who can feel pain, and endorses legislation to prohibit sex-selective abortion as well as dismemberment abortion procedures.

---

September 23, 2016, https://www.christianitytoday.com/ct/2016/october/james-dobson-why-i-am-voting-for-donald-trump.html.

[132] 2016 Democratic Party Platform, The American Presidency Project, July 21, 2016, https://www.presidency.ucsb.edu/documents/2016-democratic-party-platform.

[133] 2016 Republican Party Platform, The American Presidency Project, July 16, 2016, https://www.presidency.ucsb.edu/documents/2016-republican-party-platform. Significantly, the Republican platform chastised national Democrats, stating, "The Democratic Party is extreme on abortion. Democrats' almost limitless support for abortion, and their strident opposition to even the most basic restrictions on abortion, put them dramatically out of step with the American people." The section concludes by noting, "the old Clinton mantra of 'safe, legal, and rare' has been reduced to just 'legal.' We are proud to be the party that protects human life and offers real solutions for women."

Following his victory in the 2016 election, President Trump honored his pro-life campaign commitments by reinstating and expanding the Mexico City Policy, rescinding an Obama-era administration letter that restricted the states' flexibility in removing abortion providers from federal health care programs, and requiring recipients of Title X family planning money to be financially and physically separate from facilities that either perform or refer for abortion. Additionally, the Trump administration spearheaded the Geneva Consensus Declaration, an international declaration signed by thirty-four countries that reaffirmed the conviction that "there is no international right to abortion."[134]

Due to challenges attributed to the COVID-19 pandemic, Republicans did not write a new platform for the 2020 election. Democrats, however, drafted a new platform in 2020 that restated their view on abortion.[135] Once again, Democrats called for the repeal of the Hyde Amendment. Additionally, for the first time, the platform affirmed the party's opposition to restrictions on "medication abortion care" (i.e., abortion pills) and formally opposed the Helms Amendment, a legislative provision that prohibits using American foreign assistance funds for abortion.

Although the 2020 presidential election was marked by discussion about the COVID-19 pandemic, abortion was a fiercely contested issue that separated the major candidates. For his part, President Trump reminded voters of his administration's pro-life record, which included an unprecedented willingness to use the bully pulpit of the presidency to highlight pro-life concerns. Notably, Trump was the first sitting president to attend the March

---

[134] Ambassador Kelly Craft, "Geneva Consensus Declaration on Promoting Women's Health and Strengthening the Family," United States Mission to the United Nations, December 2, 2020, https://web.archive.org/web/20210123201856/https:/usun.usmission.gov/geneva-consensus-declaration-on-promoting-womens-health-and-strengthening-the-family/.

[135] 2020 Democratic Platform, The American Presidency Platform, August 17, 2020, https://www.presidency.ucsb.edu/documents/2020-democratic-party-platform.

for Life (which he did in January 2020). Additionally, he called on Congress to ban late-term abortion in his 2020 State of the Union address.

For his part, Joe Biden reiterated his support for what he described as "a woman's right to choose" throughout the campaign. Despite voting for the Hyde Amendment for decades, Biden reversed course in June 2019 and vowed to work for its removal.[136] Biden also pledged to restore additional federal funding for Planned Parenthood, end the Mexico City Policy, and vowed to instruct the Justice Department to do "everything in its power" to counteract state laws that limited abortion, including parental notification requirements, mandatory waiting periods, and ultrasound requirements. The selection of Kamala Harris as a running mate also underscored the Democratic nominee's support for abortion rights. As California's junior senator, Harris had voted against the Born-Alive Abortion Survivors Protection Act and Pain-Capable Unborn Child Protection Act.[137]

Following his victory in 2020, President Biden supported an array of pro-abortion policies. These included repealing the Mexico City Policy; withdrawing from the U.S.-led Geneva Consensus Declaration; rewriting rules governing the Title X family planning program to allow taxpayer dollars to subsidize abortion clinics, including Planned Parenthood; issuing an executive order that, among other directives, ordered the attorney general and White House Counsel to convene a group of pro bono lawyers to defend abortion seekers and providers; and issuing a memorandum affirming the FDA's decision to allow pharmacies to fulfill prescriptions for the chemical

---

[136] Maggie Astor, "Joe Biden on Abortion and the Hyde Amendment," *New York Times*, June 27, 2019, https://www.nytimes.com/2019/06/27/us/politics/joe-biden-abortion-hyde-amendment.html.

[137] In the lead-up to the 2020 presidential election, I published an article featuring an in-depth comparison of then-President Trump and then-former Vice President Joe Biden on abortion. See David Closson, "The 2020 Election: A Clear Distinction on Abortion," *Public Discourse*, September 20, 2020, https://www.thepublicdiscourse.com/2020/09/71555/.

abortion drug mifepristone.[138] Additionally, the president appointed abortion activist Julie Rikelman to the federal judiciary (Rikelman had represented the Mississippi abortion clinic in the *Dobbs* case); staffed his cabinet with ardent abortion defenders, including Xavier Becerra (secretary of health and human services); and vowed to reinstate *Roe v. Wade* in his 2024 State of the Union.

In summary, the party platforms of America's two major political parties and recent national campaigns demonstrate an increasing divide between Democrats and Republicans on abortion. National Democrats have moved away from their former position that abortion should be "safe, legal, and rare" and now consider abortion to be a fundamental right that the government should fund. Republicans, meanwhile, support pro-life policies and generally oppose abortion. These dueling positions on abortion would be at the center of much of American political discourse in the years leading up to *Dobbs*.

## Abortion History in the Lead-Up to *Dobbs*

Before the overturning of *Roe v. Wade* in 2022, the U.S. Congress voted on a handful of abortion-related bills. These votes further underscored the growing partisan divide on abortion and set the stage for the *Dobbs* decision.

In 2021, Congress considered the Women's Health Protection Act, legislation that would eliminate nearly every state-level restriction on abortion and codify *Roe* into federal law. If passed, the bill would weaken conscience

---

[138] These actions, among others, were tracked by FRC Action, the legislative affiliate of Family Research Council. See FRCAction.org/BidenActions. Additionally, ahead of President Biden's 2024 State of the Union address, the White House released a lengthy list of abortion-related actions. See "FACT SHEET: Biden-Harris Administration Continues the Fight for Reproductive Freedom," The White House, March 7, 2024, https://www.whitehouse.gov/briefing-room/statements-releases/2024/03/07/fact-sheet-biden-harris-administration-continues-the-fight-for-reproductive-freedom/.

protections for medical professionals, jeopardize prohibitions on taxpayer funding for abortion, and enshrine late-term abortion into law.[139] In September 2021, the bill passed the House of Representatives on a near-party line vote (218–211) with Rep. Henry Cuellar of Texas as the lone Democrat joining every Republican in voting "no."[140] In the Senate, the bill failed by a 51–49 vote with Sen. Joe Manchin (D-WV) joining a unanimous Republican caucus in voting "no."[141]

Other abortion votes took place in the Senate in 2019 and 2020. In response to states such as New York and Virginia liberalizing their abortion laws to include late-term abortion, Sen. Ben Sasse (R-NE) introduced the Born-Alive Abortion Survivors Protection Act in January 2019.[142]

---

[139] For a more thorough analysis of the bill, see David Closson, "Unconscionable: New Bill Proves Democrats Are Okay with Abortion up until Birth," *FRC Blog*, September 28, 2021, https://www.frc.org/blog/2021/09/unconscionable-democrats-are-okay-killing-babies-day-birth.

[140] U.S. Congress, House, Women's Health Protection Act of 2021, H.R. 3755, 117th Congress, introduced in House June 8, 2021, https://www.congress.gov/bill/117th-congress/house-bill/3755.

[141] U.S. Congress, Senate, Women's Health Protection Act of 2022, S.B. 4132, 117th Congress, introduced in Senate May 3, 2022, https://www.congress.gov/bill/117th-congress/senate-bill/4132. As we will see in the next chapter, Democrats forced another vote on the Women's Health Protection Act after the *Dobbs* decision. Once again, every Democrat except Representative Cuellar voted in favor of the bill. Further discussion of the bill can be found in David Closson, "Senate Democrats Fail to Federally Enshrine Abortion on Demand Until Birth," *FRC Blog*, March 3, 2022, https://www.frc.org/blog/2022/03/senate-democrats-fail-federally-enshrine-abortion-demand-until-birth.

[142] U.S. Congress, Senate, Born-Alive Abortion Survivors Protection Act, S. 311 (2019), 116th Congress, introduced in Senate January 31, 2019, https://www.congress.gov/bill/116th-congress/senate-bill/311. The issue of infanticide became part of the political conversation in 2019 when New York repealed a section of the state's public health law that had protected children born alive during failed abortions. The updated law allows abortion after twenty-four weeks of pregnancy if the mother's health is in jeopardy. However, the "exception to health" provision is not restricted to a physical definition and can include psychological and emotional health (subject to the medical judgment of the abortion provider). Thus, the 2019 law is so broad that abortion is now legal until the moment of birth in New York.

The proposed legislation would require doctors present during a failed abortion—an abortion that results in the birth of a living infant—to provide the same level of care that would be offered to any other baby born at that stage of development. Doctors who did not provide proper care would be subject to criminal prosecution. Senate Democrats refused to support the bill and, on February 25, 2019, denied cloture (i.e., end debate and move to vote on the bill) on the motion to proceed. Only three Senate Democrats voted to advance the bill to a final vote.[143] Democrats in the House refused to consider the bill, despite Republicans asking then-Speaker Nancy Pelosi eighty times to schedule a vote.

The refusal by House Democrats to even acknowledge the fact that some infants survive botched abortions received national attention when

---

Following the passage of New York's law, Delegate Kathy Tran (D) introduced a similar bill in Virginia to legalize abortion through the third trimester. When asked if her bill would allow for an abortion even after a woman showed "physical signs she is about to give birth," Tran responded, "My bill would allow that, yes." For video of Tran's admission, see *The Republican Standard*, "Kathy Tran Presents Virginia Third Trimester Abortion Bill in Committee," YouTube video, January 29, 2019, https://www.youtube.com/watch?v=OMFzZ5I30dg. Responding to these comments and the public outrage that ensued, then-Virginia Governor Ralph Northam (D), a former pediatric neurologist, was asked what would happen to a baby who survived a late-term abortion under the proposed legislation. His response shocked the nation: "The infant would be delivered. The infant would be kept comfortable. The infant would be resuscitated if that's what the mother and family desired. And then a discussion would ensue between the physicians and the mother." For Northam's comments, see Hannah Cortez, "VA Gov on Abortion: 'Infant Would Be Resuscitated If That's What the Mother and the Family Desired,'" January 30, 2019, https://www.youtube.com/watch?v=SkTopSKo1xs.

[143] Several Democrats, including Senate Minority Leader Chuck Schumer (D-NY), spread outright lies about the bill, arguing it would infringe on a woman's right to get an abortion. However, as Sen. Ben Sasse (R-NE), the bill's sponsor, noted several times, the bill applied only to infants who survived a botched abortion. The final roll call vote was 53–44 (60 yea votes needed). No Republican senator voted against the bill, while three Democrat senators (Manchin, Jones, and Casey) voted for it. See Alex Swoyer, "Senate Democrats Block Republicans' Anti-Infanticide Bill," *Washington Times*, February 25, 2019, https://www.washingtontimes.com/news/2019/feb/25/senate-democrats-block-republicans-anti-infanticid/.

House Republicans requested a hearing to bring in witnesses to investigate the depth of the issue. Since none of the Democrat-led committees were willing to hold a hearing on the topic, congressional Republicans were forced to hold their own hearing in the basement of the Capitol on September 10, 2019. At the hearing, researcher Tessa Longbons shared data from the Centers for Disease Control (CDC) that revealed at least 143 newborn infants died after attempted abortions from 2003 to 2014, a statistic the CDC acknowledged was likely an underestimate.[144]

In February 2020, the U.S. Senate considered two bills to protect unborn children: the Pain-Capable Unborn Child Protection Act and, once again, the Born Alive Abortion Survivors Protection Act. Although a majority of senators supported the bills, both fell short of the sixty votes needed to invoke cloture and overcome a Democrat-led filibuster.[145] If passed, Pain-Capable would have protected unborn children from abortion procedures late in pregnancy when they can feel pain. However, only two Democrats voted for Pain-Capable, and only three voted for Born-Alive. Both bills would have become federal law had Democrats not filibustered them as the Trump administration had pledged to sign them into law.[146]

---

[144] The hearing was chaired by then House Minority Whip Steve Scalise. For a news report on the hearing, see Alexandra DeSanctis, "House Republicans Hold a Hearing on the Born-Alive Bill," *National Review*, September 11, 2019, https://www.nationalreview.com/2019/09/born-alive-bill-hearing-house-republicans/.

[145] The Senate voted 53–44 on the Pain-Capable cloture vote and 56–41 on the Born-Alive cloture vote. The votes were largely along party lines. Two Democrats (Casey and Manchin) voted in favor of Pain-Capable, and three (Casey, Manchin, and Jones) voted in favor of Born-Alive. All Republicans voted for Born-Alive, while two Republicans (Collins and Murkowski) voted against Pain-Capable. See David Closson, "Callous and Cruel: The Senate Fails to Uphold Human Dignity," Family Research Council, February 26, 2020, https://www.frc.org/blog/2020/02/callous-and-cruel-senate-fails-uphold-human-dignity.

[146] "Statement of Administrative Policy," Executive Office of the President: Office of Management and Budget, February 25, 2020, https://trumpwhitehouse.archives.gov/wp-content/uploads/2020/02/SAP_S-3275-and-S-311.pdf.

## *Dobbs v. Jackson Women's Health Organization*

For the Supreme Court to review a case, four justices must agree to take it. Thus, on May 17, 2021, when the Court granted certiorari in *Dobbs v. Jackson Women's Health Organization*, a case involving a Mississippi pro-life law, there was optimism among pro-lifers.[147] Although the state of Mississippi asked the Court to consider three questions related to its case, the Court limited its grant of review to the first and potentially most crucial question, namely, "whether all pre-viability elective-abortion prohibitions are unconstitutional."[148]

Only a year earlier, in *June Medical Services, LLC v. Russo*, the Court struck down a Louisiana law requiring abortionists to have admitting privileges at nearby hospitals.[149] Many legal observers were surprised by the Court's 5–4 decision, which found that the state's admitting requirement imposed an undue burden on a woman's right to obtain an abortion.[150] Conservatives had hoped the addition of two justices appointed by former president Trump—Neil Gorsuch and Brett Kavanaugh—would be enough to swing the Court in a pro-life direction.

But lingering disappointment among conservatives was replaced by measured optimism with word that the Court would review the Mississippi case and consider whether all pre-viability abortion prohibitions were constitutional. Crucially, the Court's composition had changed since the last

---

[147] Dobbs v. Jackson Women's Health Organization, cert. Order List: 593 U.S., May 17, 2021, https://www.supremecourt.gov/orders/courtorders/051721zor_6537.pdf?bcs-agent-scanner=dcc95891-5283-1a47-8f55-f1c32cfcb21b.

[148] Dobbs v. Jackson Women's Health Organization, Petition for a Writ of Certiorari, June 15, 2020, https://www.supremecourt.gov/DocketPDF/19/19-1392/145658/20200615170733513_FINAL%20Petition.pdf.

[149] Adam Liptak, "Supreme Court to Hear Abortion Case Challenging *Roe v. Wade*," *New York Times*, May 17, 2021, https://www.nytimes.com/2021/05/17/us/politics/supreme-court-roe-wade.html.

[150] June Medical Services, *LLC v. Russo*, 591 U.S. (2020), https://www.supremecourt.gov/opinions/19pdf/18-1323_c07d.pdf?bcs-agent-scanner=354e4170-babe-1243-9d73-12691b8d5bc0.

abortion decision (*June Medical Services, LLC v. Russo*) with the death of Justice Ruth Bader Ginsburg in September 2020. Ginsburg, a longtime defender of abortion rights, had been replaced by Justice Amy Coney Barrett, President Trump's third appointment to the Court.

Both sides understood the significance of the Court's decision to grant certiorari in *Dobbs*. On the day the Court agreed to hear the case, Family Research Council president Tony Perkins wrote, "After 29 long years, the justices just took a case that every pro-lifer has been waiting for: a direct challenge to *Roe v. Wade*. For the first time since 1992, the highest court in the land has a chance to deal a death blow to the precedent that's tied this country in judicial knots—and robbed us of 62 million unique, irreplaceable lives."[151]

Similarly, on the opposite side of the ideological spectrum, Nancy Northup, president and CEO of the Center for Reproductive Rights, acknowledged the potential significance of the case. According to Northup, "Alarm bells are ringing loudly about the threat to reproductive rights. The Supreme Court just agreed to review an abortion ban that unquestionably violates nearly 50 years of Supreme Court precedent and is a test case to overturn *Roe v. Wade*."[152]

At the heart of *Dobbs* was the constitutionality of Mississippi's Gestational Age Act, a bipartisan law that prohibited elective abortion after fifteen weeks' gestation.[153] According to the law, the United States is "one of only seven nations in the world that permits nontherapeutic or elective abortion on demand after the twentieth week of gestation." The law further

---

[151] Tony Perkins, "A Supreme Chance at an Abortion Fix," Family Research Council, May 17, 2021, https://web.archive.org/web/20210518152104/https:/www.frc.org/updatearticle/20210517/supreme-chance.

[152] "Supreme Court to Hear Abortion Ban Case Challenging *Roe v. Wade*," Center for Reproductive Rights, May 17, 2021, https://reproductiverights.org/supreme-court-to-hear-abortion-ban-case-challenging-roe-v-wade/.

[153] H.B. 1510, Sess. of 2018 (Miss. 2018), http://billstatus.ls.state.ms.us/documents/2018/html/HB/1500-1599/HB1510IN.htm.

explains that 75% of nations do not permit abortion after twelve weeks' gestation unless the mother's physical health is in danger.

On March 19, 2018, Mississippi governor Phil Bryant signed the Gestational Age Act into law. On the same day, Dr. Sacheen Carr-Ellis filed a suit on behalf of Jackson Women's Health Organization, the only abortion facility in Mississippi. Predictably, on November 20, 2018, the U.S. District Court for the Southern District of Mississippi declared the law unconstitutional. Citing the precedent of *Roe* and *Casey*, Judge Carlton W. Reeves explained that viability was the earliest point at which the state could justify legislative measures to protect fetal life.

Judge Reeves, a district judge appointed by President Barack Obama in 2010, offered a stinging rebuke to the Mississippi legislature, writing, "The State chose to pass a law it knew was unconstitutional to endorse a decades-long campaign, fueled by national interest groups, to ask the Supreme Court to overturn *Roe v. Wade.*"[154] Judge Reeves characterized the legislature's professed concern for women's health as "pure gaslighting" and "disingenuous." The judge also claimed that the Gestational Age Act reminded him of the "old Mississippi—the Mississippi bent on controlling women and minorities."

Following the district court's permanent injunction, the state appealed to the U.S. Court of Appeals for the Fifth Circuit. On December 13, 2019, the circuit court affirmed the district court's ruling. However, Judge James C. Ho, one of three circuit judges who heard the appeal, took exception to Judge Reeves's handling of the case. In a concurring opinion to the Fifth Circuit's order, Judge Ho explained, "The opinion issued by the district court displays an alarming disrespect for the millions of Americans who believe that babies deserve legal protection during pregnancy as well as after

---

[154] Jackson Women's Health v. Currier, Order Granting Permanent Injunction, November 20, 2018, https://s3.documentcloud.org/documents/5205137/11-20-18-Jackson-Women-s-Health-v-Currier.pdf?bcs-agent-scanner=967345d7-a88c-174f-ad3a-591440437111.

birth, and that abortion is the immoral, tragic, and violent taking of innocent human life."[155] After losing at the Fifth Circuit, Mississippi officials appealed the case to the Supreme Court, which, as we noted, agreed to hear the case during the Court's October 2021–2022 term.

In the lead-up to the oral arguments, Mississippi, led by Attorney General Lynn Fitch, changed its position on whether they wanted the Supreme Court to deal with *Roe* in their case. In their initial request for certiorari, Mississippi noted that the case did "not require the Court to overturn *Roe* and *Casey*."[156] However, in her brief submitted on July 22, 2021, Fitch wrote, "*Roe* and *Casey* are egregiously wrong. The conclusion that abortion is a constitutional right has no basis in text, structure, or tradition."[157] As oral arguments approached, the stakes were high; both sides knew that *Dobbs* offered the best chance of overturning *Roe* in a generation. In the event that *Dobbs* failed and *Roe* was upheld, it would likely be years, perhaps even decades, before the Court would accept a similar challenge.

---

[155] Dobbs v. Jackson Women's Health Organization, U.S. Court of Appeals for the Fifth Circuit No. 18-60868, December 13, 2019, https://www.ca5.uscourts.gov/opinions/pub/18/18-60868-CV0.pdf?bcs-agent-scanner=86e78518-c7af-654f-b351-ad745ff4d366; Judge Ho went on to note, "I find it deeply disquieting that a federal court would disparage the millions of Americans who believe in the sanctity of life as nothing more than 'bent on controlling women and minorities' and 'disregarding their rights as citizens.' Those insults not only directly conflict with the Supreme Court's admonitions that both sides of the debate deserve respect—they are also demonstrably incorrect." Judge Ho also took Judge Reeves to task for the latter's suggestion that pro-life legislators were racist, writing, "What's more, the district court's claim that it is racist to believe in the sanctity of life is particularly noxious, considering the racial history of abortion advocacy as a tool of the eugenics movement."

[156] Dobbs v. Jackson Women's Health Organization, Petition for a Writ of Certiorari, June 15, 2020, https://www.supremecourt.gov/DocketPDF/19/19-1392/145658/20200615170733513_FINAL%20Petition.pdf.

[157] Dobbs v. Jackson Women's Health Organization, Brief for Petitioners, July 22, 2021, https://opencasebook.org/casebooks/11069-sexual-orientation-gender-identity-and-expression-and-the-law/resources/20.1-brief-for-petitioners-dobbs-v-jackson-womens-health-organization/.

## Conclusion

As spring bloomed in 2022, Americans prepared for a summer decision in *Dobbs*. The question on everyone's mind was whether the Supreme Court would finally overturn *Roe v. Wade*. Some legal commentators suggested the Court would take a modest approach by upholding Mississippi's fifteen-week law while keeping *Roe* intact. Still others, including some pro-lifers, feared the justices might reaffirm the central holding of *Roe* and *Casey* and once again assert that abortion is protected by the United States Constitution.

Although Court observers expected the *Dobbs* decision toward the end of June, an unprecedented leak stunned advocates on both sides of the abortion debate. According to a leaked version of the decision obtained and published by *Politico* on May 2, 2022, at least five members of the U.S. Supreme Court were poised to overturn *Roe* and return the authority to decide abortion policy to the people and their elected representatives.

From coast to coast, the furor and outrage from the pro-abortion side was immediate; protestors took to the streets in droves to voice their indignation. On the pro-life side, astonishment turned into fervent prayer as the nation anxiously waited to see how the leak would affect the ultimate decision.

# 5

# The *Dobbs* Decision: The States Respond to the Overturning of *Roe*

*Held:* The Constitution does not confer a right to abortion; *Roe* and *Casey* are overruled; and the authority to regulate abortion is returned to the people and their elected representatives."[1]

## Introduction

After weeks of anticipation, the U.S. Supreme Court released its opinion in *Dobbs v. Jackson Women's Health Organization* on June 24, 2022. The final vote was 6–3 to uphold Mississippi's fifteen-week protection law and 5–4 to overturn *Roe* and *Casey*. The majority opinion, authored by

[1] Dobbs v. Jackson Women's Health Organization, 597 U.S. 215 (2022), 215.

Justice Samuel Alito, was largely the same as the leaked opinion published by *Politico* seven weeks earlier.

One cannot overstate the significance of *Dobbs*. Overturning *Roe* had been the rallying cry and animating force behind the pro-life movement for half a century. Now, after decades of prayer, lobbying, campaigning, and legislating—not to mention a few heartbreaking disappointments—the Supreme Court admitted they had erred in 1973 by determining that a right to abortion was protected by an implied right to privacy in the U.S. Constitution.

In *Dobbs*, Justice Alito dismantled the historical and legal rationale of *Roe* and *Casey*. Because abortion "is not a fundamental constitutional right," these precedents were "egregiously wrong" from the day they were handed down.[2] As Alito explained, nothing in the Constitution, the nation's history, or Court precedent supports the logic of *Roe* or *Casey*. An exercise in "raw judicial power," *Roe* short-circuited the democratic process by overriding scores of state laws and usurping "the power to address a question of profound moral and social importance that the Constitution unequivocally leaves for the people."[3] Acknowledging that "abortion presents a profound moral question," Alito insisted that the Court overstepped in both *Roe* and *Casey* and that the Constitution empowers the American people, not the courts, to decide these types of questions.[4]

With *Roe v. Wade* overturned, lawmakers at all levels of government now have the power to legally protect the unborn. Although it is still too early to fully appreciate or quantify the impact of *Dobbs*, the response to the decision by lawmakers, the media, voters, and even foreign governments demonstrates the opportunities as well as the challenges facing the

---

[2] *Dobbs*, 300, 231.

[3] *Dobbs*, 269.

[4] *Dobbs*, 223.

pro-life movement after *Roe*. Already, encouraging trends have emerged as elected officials in many states have acted decisively to codify protections for unborn children. But troubling signs have emerged as well, including an emboldened pro-abortion movement that has successfully passed abortion measures across the country.

As stated in the preface, this book exists to help Christians engage thoughtfully on the subject of abortion. To this end, it is important to understand the logic of the Supreme Court's decision in *Dobbs* as well as the relevant policy and political developments that occurred in response. Thus, in this chapter, we will take a closer look at *Dobbs* and the national reaction it provoked. Predictably, political leaders on both sides of the aisle responded swiftly, as did state legislatures, attorneys general, and state courts. American voters have also weighed in, and their decisions illustrate the challenges facing pro-lifers. Finally, the chapter will examine how many states responded legislatively to *Dobbs*. To provide an accurate account, I interviewed over a dozen state legislators. Their stories are both encouraging and sobering. Whether encountering protestors at their homes or navigating death threats against their children, many pro-life legislators paid a high personal price for their convictions. Thankfully, despite the threats, many were successful in passing meaningful protections for the unborn. Others, given the political realities in their state, fought an ultimately losing battle. From these experiences, the pro-life movement can learn valuable lessons as it navigates a post-*Roe* world and grapples with the lingering effects of fifty years of abortion on demand.

## Response to the *Dobbs* Leak

The interlude between the leaked opinion and the release of *Dobbs* was fraught with anxiety and anticipation. In response to the unprecedented May 2 leak, pro-abortion protestors rallied in major American cities, activists interrupted dozens of church services, pro-life organizations were firebombed, and pregnancy resource centers were burglarized and attacked.[5] Abortion activists even held protests outside the private residences of Supreme Court justices.[6]

Outrage over the leak reached a fever pitch in early June when a man attempted to assassinate Justice Brett Kavanaugh. On June 8, police arrested a man who admitted to authorities that he had purchased a firearm and traveled from California to Maryland because he was "upset" about the *Dobbs* leak and believed killing Justice Kavanaugh would "give his life a purpose."[7]

Within this highly charged context, the nation waited for *Dobbs*. For just under two months (May 2 to June 24), the press talked continually about the leak. Because the Supreme Court does not announce in advance when they will publish decisions, supporters from both sides gathered

---

[5] Luke Vander Ploeg and Addison Lathers, "Anti-Abortion Group in Wisconsin Is Hit by Arson, Authorities Say," *New York Times*, May 8, 2022, https://www.nytimes.com/2022/05/08/us/madison-anti-abortion-center-vandalized.html; "Thousands Gather for Pro-Abortion Rights Protests across U.S.," CBS News, May 14, 2022, https://www.cbsnews.com/news/abortion-rights-protests-supreme-court-leaked-draft-opinion-roe-v-wade/; Louis Casiano, "Washington, DC Pro-Life Pregnancy Center Vandalized with Red. Paint, Eggs, 'Revenge' Message," Fox News, June 3, 2022, https://www.foxnews.com/us/washington-dc-abortion-pregnancy-vandalized; Emma Colton, "Pro-Choice Activists Strip during Joel Osteen Church service: 'Overturn Roe, Hell No,'" Fox News, June 6, 2022, https://www.foxnews.com/us/abortion-activists-interrupt-joel-osteen-lakewood-church.

[6] In response to these unlawful demonstrations, the governors of Maryland and Virginia wrote a joint letter to the Department of Justice, urging Attorney General Merrick Garland to enforce laws that prohibit intimidating federal judges and provide resources to protect the justices and their families. See Glenn Youngkin and Larry Hogan to Merrick Garland, May 11, 2022, 4:00 p.m., https://twitter.com/GovLarryHogan/status/1524494786031280128/photo/1.

[7] United States of America v. Nicholas John Roske, 18 U.S.C. 115 (June 8, 2022), 2–3, https://www.documentcloud.org/documents/22056087-criminal-complaint-in-kavanaugh-threat. In response to the incident, the House of Representatives passed a bill previously passed by the Senate to provide additional protection for the justices, their families, and Court employees. See U.S. Congress, "S.4160—117th Congress (2021–2022): Supreme Court Police Parity Act of 2022," June 16, 2022, https://www.congress.gov/bill/117th-congress/senate-bill/4160.

outside the Court on every scheduled opinion day throughout May and June. Significantly, while Court watchers debated and activists protested, Christians continued to pray earnestly for life to win at the Court.

Before the leak, Christians had been praying for the Court to overturn *Roe*. Individual Christians, as well as those inspired by the Pray for *Dobbs* initiative, were praying actively for God's mercy and a favorable decision. Following the leak on May 2, safety and courage became a primary prayer focus. This concern was highlighted in a Pray for *Dobbs* prayer update published shortly after the leak: "Prayer for the safety and wellbeing of the Supreme Court justices, clerks, and staff, and their families. Prayer also for courage and resolve for the justices to issue a final decision to overturn *Roe v. Wade* and *Planned Parenthood v. Casey*."[8]

In a note sent to around 20,000 prayer partners, I explained:

> Abortion is one of the most contentious issues in America. It should come as no surprise that people have responded strongly to the possibility that *Roe* and *Casey* may be overturned. As Christians observing the unfolding events, we must pray that the justices will not be influenced by the outside pressure or public scrutiny. We must pray that they have courage and resolve to stay the course and overturn *Roe*. Evidently, based on the leaked draft opinion written by Justice Alito, there were at least five justices in February ready to overturn *Roe* and *Casey*. Pray for resolve among the justices in the majority.[9]

On May 26, 2022, the Pray for *Dobbs* coalition hosted another prayer call.[10] Five hundred prayer partners joined the conference call to pray for the safety of the justices and their families. When it was my turn to lead in prayer, I asked God to protect the justices, their clerks, and their families.

---

[8] "Monthly Highlights," Pray for *Dobbs*, https://www.prayfordobbs.com/copy-of-monthly-highlights.

[9] "Monthly Highlights," Pray for *Dobbs*.

[10] "Resources," Pray for *Dobbs*, https://www.prayfordobbs.com/resources.

I also prayed and encouraged those on the call to pray that the justices would have the courage of their convictions and not be swayed from doing their constitutional and moral duty in the case.

On this side of eternity, we will not know the impact of our prayers. But when the decision was released on Friday, June 24, it was evident God had heard and answered the prayers of Christians who had prayed earnestly for his intervention and mercy.

## *Dobbs* Decision: Analysis of the Opinion, Concurrences, and Dissent

Although most Americans are aware that *Dobbs v. Jackson Women's Health Organization* overturned *Roe v. Wade*, it is likely that few have read Justice Alito's opinion. However, to understand the scope of the Court's action, it is important to understand Alito's argument, which makes a compelling historical and legal case for why *Roe* was "egregiously wrong" and needed to be overturned. After surveying Alito's opinion, we will turn to the concurrences and the dissent.

### *Opinion of the Court*

In the introduction of his opinion, Justice Alito begins dismantling the historical and legal arguments put forth by *Roe* and *Casey*.[11] According to Alito, "The Constitution makes no reference to abortion, and no such right is implicitly protected by any constitutional provision."[12] He explains that for

[11] At the Supreme Court, protocol dictates that after oral arguments, justices meet to take a preliminary vote on the case. After all justices have given their thoughts on the case, the chief justice casts the first vote, and then each justice, in descending order of seniority, does likewise. After everyone has voted, the chief justice (or the most senior justice in the majority if the chief justice is in the dissent), assigns a justice in the majority to write the opinion of the Court. For the *Dobbs* case, Justice Samuel Alito was chosen to write the majority opinion.

[12] *Dobbs*, 231.

the first 185 years of the nation's history, each state was permitted to address the issue in accordance with the views of its citizens. Significantly, *Roe* circumvented the democratic process by using "raw judicial power" to foreclose the debate.[13] Likewise, the Court's decision in *Casey*, though intended by its authors to end the national debate around abortion, only inflamed and deepened division. Alito concludes the introduction by noting that the legal principle of *stare decisis* is not absolute, especially in cases where the Court was "egregiously wrong from the start."[14]

In Part I of the opinion, Alito recites the facts of Mississippi's Gestational Age Act and notes that the question before the Court is whether "all pre-viability prohibitions on elective abortion are unconstitutional."[15] For Alito, the question concerning pre-viability prohibitions requires the Court to finally return to the underlying question of whether *Roe* and *Casey* are sound decisions that ought to be upheld.

In Part II, Alito argues that the Constitution does not confer a right to an abortion. Since abortion is not mentioned in the Constitution, abortion advocates must prove that the right is somehow implicit in the Constitution. According to Alito, this task is impossible because *Roe* itself "was remarkably loose in its treatment of the constitutional text." Alito explains how *Roe*

---

[13] *Dobbs*, 228. Ironically, Alito's critique of *Roe* was shared in part by the late Justice Ruth Bader Ginsburg, who repeatedly criticized *Roe* despite her support of abortion. As far back as 1984, Ginsburg claimed the Court "ventured too far in the change it ordered and presented an incomplete justification for its action." See David J. Garrow, "A Look at . . . Roe v. Wade v. Ginsburg: History Lesson for the Judge," *Washington Post*, June 20, 1993, https://www.washingtonpost.com/archive/opinions/1993/06/20/a-look-at-rove-v-wade-v-ginsburg-history-lesson-for-the-judge/6a8b1b10-0089-4b17-aec4-a17fc8d4bcf4/. In 2013, Ginsburg stated, "My criticism of *Roe* is that it seemed to have stopped the momentum on the side of change." See Meredith Heagney, "Justice Ruth Bader Ginsburg Offers Critique of Roe v. Wade During Law School Visit," University of Chicago Law School, May 15, 2013, https://www.law.uchicago.edu/news/justice-ruth-bader-ginsburg-offers-critique-roe-v-wade-during-law-school-visit.

[14] *Dobbs*, 231.

[15] *Dobbs*, 234.

claimed the right to abortion was based on the right to privacy, a right not mentioned in the Constitution but that nonetheless could be located in the First, Fourth, Fifth, Ninth, or Fourteenth Amendments. For its part, *Casey* provided an entirely different rationale for abortion rights, i.e., a right to abortion is part of the "liberty" protected by the Due Process Clause of the Fourteenth Amendment.

Alito notes that in deciding whether the Due Process Clause covers unenumerated or substantive rights, the Court typically asks whether that right is "deeply rooted in our history and tradition" and whether it is essential to our nation's "scheme of ordered liberty." In response, Alito reviews the historical record and demonstrates that a legal right to abortion is not rooted in the nation's laws or the common law tradition. In an insightful historical section, Alito shows from common law theorists such as Bracton, Coke, Hale, and Blackstone that abortion has been criminalized by the common law since the thirteenth century.

Focusing on the nineteenth century, Alito explains that "the vast majority of the States enacted statutes criminalizing abortion at all stages of pregnancy." He notes that when the Fourteenth Amendment was ratified in 1868, twenty-eight out of thirty-seven states had enacted statutes against abortion. This observation poses a problem for abortion advocates who locate a right to abortion in the Fourteenth Amendment. As Alito demonstrates, there is no evidence that the amendment's ratifiers had abortion in mind; conversely, most states had already criminalized abortion when the amendment was passed. Additionally, Alito notes that of the nine states that had not criminalized abortion by 1868, all but one did so by 1910.

According to Alito, although laws regulating abortion had begun to liberalize in some states by the time *Roe* was decided in 1973, thirty states "still prohibited abortion at all stages except to save the life of the mother." In short, Alito's overview of history leads to the "inescapable conclusion" that "a right to abortion is not deeply rooted in the Nation's history and traditions."[16]

[16] *Dobbs*, 250.

Toward the end of Part II, Alito addresses the question of whether abortion is part of a "broader entrenched right" to autonomy secured by the Constitution. Arguing that it is not, Alito explains that unenumerated rights recognized by the Court, such as the right to marry someone of a different race (*Loving v. Virginia*) or the right to not be sterilized without consent (*Skinner v. Oklahoma*), are categorically different from abortion, which uniquely involves the "critical moral question" of terminating "potential life" (the term used in *Roe* and *Casey*).

In Part III, Alito turns to the question of *stare decisis*, the legal principle that says courts should honor past decisions. Although *stare decisis* plays an important role in the legal system, Alito contends that it is "not an inexorable command." To support his claim, Alito cites dozens of instances where the Court has overruled past decisions, including *Brown v. Board of Education* (1954), which reversed *Plessy v. Ferguson* (1896) (the decision that had sanctioned legal racial segregation).

According to Alito, five factors weighed strongly for overruling *Roe* and *Casey*: the nature of the Court's error, the quality of reasoning behind the Court's abortion precedents, workability, the effect on other areas of law, and the absence of concrete reliance.

First, Alito discusses the nature of the Court's mistake in both *Roe* and *Casey*. As he explains, *Roe* was "egregiously wrong" on the day it was decided because the Court "usurped the power to address a question of profound moral and social importance that the Constitution unequivocally leaves for the people."[17] In other words, the Court short-circuited the democratic process and illegitimately usurped power. This abuse of power demanded redress.

Second, the reasoning behind *Roe* and *Casey* was specious. Without any grounding in constitutional text, history, or precedent, *Roe* was essentially Court-imposed legislation that relied on "an erroneous historical narrative."[18]

[17] *Dobbs*, 269.

[18] *Dobbs*, 270. According to Alito, "*Roe*'s failure even to note the overwhelming consensus of state laws in effect in 1868 is striking, and what it said of the common

Alito notes that when *Casey* revisited *Roe,* "very little of *Roe*'s reasoning was defended or preserved."[19] In fact, although *Casey* endorsed *Roe*'s central holding, it rejected much of *Roe*'s analysis and deployed what Alito termed a "novel version" of *stare decisis.*[20] In short, because *Casey* ignored the "profound wrongness" of *Roe*, it does not meet the Court's typical standard for *stare decisis* and therefore cannot be upheld.[21]

Third, Alito argues that *Roe* and *Casey* ought to be overturned because the rules they proposed were unworkable. Alito notes that *Casey* itself abandoned *Roe*'s trimester framework. However, *Casey*'s own "undue burden" test was equally obscure and impossible to apply consistently.[22] Fourth, *Roe* and *Casey* led to the distortion of other legal doctrines. For example, Alito notes that the Court's abortion cases have repeatedly ignored the third-party standing rule.[23] And fifth, Alito explains that overturning *Roe* and

---

law was simply wrong. . . . After surveying history, the opinion spent many paragraphs conducting the sort of fact-finding that might be undertaken by a legislative committee." See *Dobbs*, 272.

[19] *Dobbs*, 279. Alito notes that the *Casey* decision abandoned any reliance on privacy and instead "grounded the abortion right entirely on the Fourteenth Amendment's Due Process Clause."

[20] *Dobbs*, 280.

[21] *Dobbs*, 280.

[22] *Dobbs*, 280–81. Alito outlines *Casey*'s three subsidiary rules, which state that abortion regulations cannot impose a "substantial obstacle," an "undue burden on the right" to abortion, or an "unnecessary health regulation." Alito explains how these subsidiary rules were vague, undefined, and resulted in confusion in lower courts. According to *Casey*, an "undue burden" refers to a state regulation that "has the purpose or effect of placing a substantial obstacle in the path of a woman seeking an abortion of a nonviable fetus." See Planned Parenthood of Southeastern Pa. v. Casey, 505 U.S. 833 (1992).

[23] Standing relates to the question of who has a sufficient stake in a case to sue in court. Third-party standing refers to when a party may file a lawsuit or assert a defense on behalf of a third party. In the United States, third-party standing is generally not allowed. However, as Alito notes, much of the Court's previous abortion jurisprudence ignored the third-party standing rule by allowing abortion clinics to bring suit over abortion laws. Justice Clarence Thomas made this argument in his dissent in Whole Woman's Health v. Hellerstedt, 579 U.S. 582 (2016), 631, where

*Casey* will not substantially upend reliance interests (reliance is a legal concept referring to one's ability to depend on the law). Whereas the *Casey* plurality argued that women had come to rely on the availability of abortion, Alito explains that the Court is ill-equipped to assess "the effect of the abortion right on society and in particular on the lives of women." Justice Alito also notes that "contending sides in this case make impassioned and conflicting arguments about the effects of the abortion right on the lives of women," which he argues the Court does not have the authority or expertise to adjudicate.[24]

In Part IV, Alito addresses the issue of the Court's public perception. If the Court overturns *Roe* and *Casey*, will the American people deem the justices to be acting politically? Although "it is important for the public to perceive that our decisions are based on principle," Alito explains that the role of the Court is to judge and interpret the law; political concerns should not factor into any of the Court's decisions. "[W]e cannot exceed the scope of our authority under the Constitution, and we cannot allow our decisions to be affected by any extraneous influences such as concern about the public's reaction to our work," Alito maintains.[25] Notably, in light of all the discussion about the Court's reputation, Alito points out that twenty-six states expressly asked the justices to overturn *Roe* and *Casey*, suggesting

---

he wrote, "[T]he Court has been especially forgiving of third-party standing criteria for one particular category of cases: those involving the purported substantive due process right of a woman to abort her unborn child." By mentioning the Court's third-party standing doctrine, Alito is arguing that the Court has essentially bent over backwards and ignored many well-established legal principles to allow abortion clinics to sue on behalf of pregnant women.

[24] In *Casey*, the Court had stated that "people have organized intimate relationships and made choices that define their views of themselves and their places in society, in reliance on the availability of abortion in the event that contraception should fail." Additionally, the Court had said, "The ability of women to participate equally in the economic and social life of the Nation has been facilitated by their ability to control their reproductive lives." According to Alito, these rationales constitute a more "intangible form of reliance." See *Dobbs v. Jackson*, 288.

[25] *Dobbs*, 291.

that although the Court's detractors are loud, many Americans support the overturning of *Roe*.

In Part V, Alito responds to Chief Justice Roberts's concurrence and the dissent. Notably, Alito rejects the suggestion that *Dobbs* could be used to overturn precedents related to contraception and same-sex marriage. "It is hard to see how we could be clearer," Alito explains, reiterating that "rights regarding contraception and same-sex relationships are inherently different from the right to abortion" because only abortion ends what even *Roe* and *Casey* acknowledged is "potential life."[26]

Finally, in Part VI, Justice Alito lays out a new standard for reviewing state abortion laws. According to Alito, a law regulating abortion is entitled to a "strong presumption of validity." Practically, this means that states can pass meaningful protections for unborn children. Alito explains that a legitimate state interest can include "respect for and preservation of prenatal life at all stages of development," "the elimination of particularly gruesome or barbaric medical procedures," and "the mitigation of fetal pain," among others.

Alito's opinion was joined by justices Amy Coney Barrett, Neil Gorsuch, Brett Kavanaugh, and Clarence Thomas. Chief Justice John Roberts concurred with the majority's opinion in judgment but did not sign on to Alito's opinion.

## *Concurrences*

In a concurring opinion, Justice Clarence Thomas praises the Court for rejecting the "fabrication of a constitutional right to abortion."[27] For Thomas, because the Due Process Clause of the Fourteenth Amendment does not secure unenumerated rights, there is no right to abortion. Although Thomas agrees with Alito that nothing in *Dobbs* should be

[26] *Dobbs*, 295.
[27] *Dobbs*, 336.

understood to cast doubt on precedents that do not concern abortion, the justice argues that the Court "should reconsider all of this Court's substantive due process precedents" and eliminate substantive due process "at the earliest opportunity." Thomas specifically mentions cases dealing with contraception and same-sex marriage as substantive due process precedents that should be reconsidered.

In his concurrence, Justice Brett Kavanaugh affirmed the majority's opinion, noting that the Constitution "does not take sides on the issue of abortion."[28]Agreeing with Alito, Kavanaugh notes that *stare decisis* is "not absolute." He notes that since 1921, every one of the forty-eight justices appointed to the Supreme Court "has voted to overrule precedent" at some point. For Kavanaugh, the *Dobbs* decision returns the Court to a "position of judicial neutrality on the issue of abortion" and "restores the people's authority to resolve the issue of abortion" through democratic self-government. Furthermore, Kavanaugh argues that pro-life laws should not be dismissed as "political stunts or outlier laws," but rather as the "sincere and deeply held views of tens of millions of Americans" who believe that allowing abortion up to twenty-four weeks is "far too radical and far too extreme." Kavanaugh concludes his concurrence by noting that "the Constitution is neither pro-life nor pro-choice," which is why the Court must likewise be "scrupulously neutral."

Chief Justice John Roberts, concurring in judgment only, wrote separately to explain why he would have taken a "more measured course" of upholding Mississippi's law without overturning *Roe* and *Casey.*[29] For Roberts, although the viability line established by *Roe* "came out of thin air" and should be discarded, the right to "terminate a pregnancy," as determined by Court precedent, should "extend far enough to ensure a reasonable opportunity" to obtain an abortion. Roberts explains that in the present case he would prefer a course of "judicial restraint" and

---

[28] *Dobbs*, 337.

[29] *Dobbs*, 348.

chastises the majority for what he believes is a "dramatic and consequential ruling." Roberts notes that the Court had initially granted review in *Dobbs* to determine whether abortion prohibitions before viability are always unconstitutional. He explains that only after the Court granted review did the state more aggressively advocate for the overturning of *Roe* and *Casey*. According to Roberts, the Court should have ruled on the initial question about the lawfulness of pre-viability abortion regulations and refused to go further.

### *Dissent*

For their part, justices Stephen Breyer, Elena Kagan, and Sonia Sotomayor published a rare joint dissent that strongly criticized the majority opinion.[30] Over the course of sixty pages, the liberal justices argue that *Roe* and *Casey* were embedded in "core constitutional concepts of individual freedom." They explain that the concept of individual freedom has helped define "what it means to be an American" and that the Court's abortion precedents honored this principle by properly weighing a woman's right to an abortion and a state's interest in protecting potential life. Additionally, the dissent questions the majority's understanding of history by claiming that early law (including the common law) provides "some support for abortion rights."

The dissenters agree with the majority's claim that the authors of the Fourteenth Amendment would not have recognized that the amendment conferred a right to abortion. However, they claim that the men who authored the Fourteenth Amendment "did not perceive women as equals" and "did not recognize women's rights."[31] Thus, according to justices Breyer, Kagan, and Sotomayor, the Court's insistence that the Constitution be read as it was

---

[30] *Dobbs*, 359–423.

[31] *Dobbs*, 373.

understood at the time of the amendment's ratification "consigns women to second-class citizenship." The dissent rejects the majority's "pinched view" of how to read the Constitution and advocates for an approach that accommodates "new societal understandings and conditions." According to the dissent, a more expansive approach to interpreting the Constitution overcomes the patriarchal prejudices of the Founders and those who ratified the Fourteenth Amendment.

Additionally, the dissent rejects the majority's understanding of *stare decisis*, arguing that *Roe* and *Casey* are embedded in constitutional law and that "neither law nor facts nor attitudes" provide valid reasons for reaching a different result than *Roe* or *Casey*. "All that has changed is this Court," the minority claims, implying that politics, not a good faith interpretation of the Constitution, led to the overturning of *Roe*.

Finally, the dissent claims that because of the majority opinion, "young women will come of age with fewer rights than their mothers and grandmothers had" and that the Court has undermined its legitimacy by betraying its "guiding principles." Notably, the dissenters conclude by stating only that they dissent, omitting the word "respectfully," which typically appears at the end of a dissent.

## Reaction to *Dobbs*

Predictably, *Dobbs* elicited an immediate reaction from across the political spectrum. Almost unanimously, elected Republicans celebrated the decision. Democrats, on the other hand, were apoplectic about *Roe*'s reversal.

Former president Donald J. Trump, who appointed three of the justices in the *Dobbs* majority, praised the Court and sought to take credit for the decision, noting, "Today's decision, which is the biggest WIN for LIFE in a generation, along with other decisions that have been announced recently, were only made possible because I delivered everything as promised, including nominating and getting three highly respected and strong

Constitutionalists confirmed to the United States Supreme Court. It was my great honor to do so!"[32]

Former vice president Mike Pence also celebrated the opinion, tweeting, "Today, Life Won. By overturning Roe v. Wade, the Supreme Court of the United States has given the American people a new beginning for life and I commend the Justices in the majority for having the courage of their convictions."[33] Florida governor and 2024 presidential candidate Ron DeSantis tweeted his response, noting, "The prayers of millions have been answered. For nearly fifty years, the U.S. Supreme Court has prohibited virtually any meaningful pro-life protection, but this was not grounded in the text, history or structure of the Constitution. By properly interpreting the Constitution, the Dobbs majority has restored the people's role in our republic and a sense of hope that every life counts."[34]

Other Republican leaders responded with equal excitement and gratitude, including Senate Minority Leader Mitch McConnell (R-KY), who stated, "The Supreme Court's landmark ruling in Dobbs is courageous and correct. This is an historic victory for the Constitution and for the most vulnerable in our society.[35]

---

[32] Donald J. Trump, "Statement by Donald J. Trump, 45th President of the United States of America," June 24, 2022, Save America, https://saveamerica.nucleusemail.com/amplify/v/pSr52dKErQ.

[33] Mike Pence (@Mike_Pence), "Today, Life Won. By overturning Roe v. Wade, the Supreme Court of the United States has given the American people a new beginning for life and I commend the Justices in the majority for having the courage of their convictions," Twitter, June 24, 2022, 9:15 a.m., https://twitter.com/Mike_Pence/status/1540337828873154560.

[34] Ron DeSantis (@GovRonDeSantis), "By properly interpreting the Constitution, the Supreme Court has answered the prayers of millions upon millions of Americans," Twitter, June 24, 2022, 11:59 a.m., https://twitter.com/GovRonDeSantis/status/1540378975251341315.

[35] "'The Supreme Court's Landmark Ruling Is Courageous and Correct,'" press release, Republican Leader, June 24, 2022, https://www.republicanleader.senate.gov/newsroom/press-releases/the-supreme-courts-landmark-ruling-is-courageous-and-correct.

In contrast to the euphoric celebrations among elected Republicans, Democrats denounced the decision. Following the release of *Dobbs*, President Biden, speaking from the White House just hours after the decision was released, stated that the overturning of *Roe* "casts a dark shadow over a large swath of the land."[36] A few days later, the president called for a change in the Senate's filibuster rules in order to codify a right to abortion into federal law.[37]

Former president Barack Obama expressed outrage as well, lamenting, "Today, the Supreme Court not only reversed nearly 50 years of precedent, it relegated the most intensely personal decision someone can make to the whims of politicians and ideologues—attacking the essential freedoms of millions of Americans."[38] Hillary Clinton also blasted the decision, writing, "Today's Supreme Court opinion will live in infamy as a step backward for women's rights and human rights."[39]

On July 19, 2022, Congresswoman Alexandria Ocasio-Cortez, along with sixteen other Democrat members of Congress, were arrested for

---

[36] "Remarks by President Biden on the Supreme Court Decision to Overturn Roe v. Wade," The White House, June 24, 2022, https://www.whitehouse.gov/briefing-room/speeches-remarks/2022/06/24/remarks-by-president-biden-on-the-supreme-court-decision-to-overturn-roe-v-wade/.

[37] "Remarks by President Biden in Press Conference," The White House, June 30, 2022, https://www.whitehouse.gov/briefing-room/speeches-remarks/2022/06/30/remarks-by-president-biden-in-press-conference-madrid-spain/.

[38] Barack Obama (@BarackObama), "Today, the Supreme Court not only reversed nearly 50 years of precedent, it relegated the most intensely personal decision someone can make to the whims of politicians and ideologues—attacking the essential freedoms of millions of Americans," Twitter, June 24, 2022, 9:26 a.m., https://twitter.com/BarackObama/status/1540340642848690176?s=20.

[39] Hillary Clinton (@HillaryClinton), "Most Americans believe the decision to have a child is one of the most sacred decisions there is, and that such decisions should remain between patients and their doctors. Today's Supreme Court opinion will live in infamy as a step backward for women's rights and human rights," Twitter, June 24, 2022, 9:45 a.m., https://twitter.com/HillaryClinton/status/1540345482186309632.

engaging in a pro-abortion demonstration that illegally blocked the street in front of the Supreme Court.[40] Ocasio-Cortez and the other members were arrested, ticketed, and released on site.[41] Although the demonstration was panned by critics as performative, it previewed how Democrats would seek to keep abortion in the news leading up to the 2022 midterm elections.[42]

## Post-*Dobbs* America: The First Year after *Roe*

Before *Dobbs*, twenty-two states had unenforceable laws or constitutional amendments that would protect fetal life if *Roe* was overturned or weakened. On the eve of *Dobbs*, nine states had pre-*Roe* laws still on the books, thirteen states had trigger laws tied to *Roe* being overturned, eleven states had six-week protection laws in place (although only Texas's law was enforceable), and four states had enshrined protection for unborn children into their state's constitution.[43]

---

[40] Dareh Gregorian, "Reps. Ocasio-Cortez and Omar among Democrats Arrested at Abortion Rights Protest," NBC News, July 19, 2022, https://www.nbcnews.com/politics/congress/reps-ocasio-cortez-omar-democrats-arrested-abortion-rights-protest-rcna38956.

[41] The U.S. Capitol Police (@CapitolPolice), "Correction: We made a total of 35 arrests for Crowding, Obstructing or Incommoding (DC Code § 22–1307). That arrest number includes 17 Members of Congress," Twitter, July 19, 2022, 2:35 p.m., https://twitter.com/CapitolPolice/status/1549477982187700227.

[42] Nancy Mace (@NancyMace), "Politics has become performative art. So of course @aoc fakes being in handcuffs. Performance, not policy, is the name of the game up here," Twitter, July 20, 2022, 12:16 p.m., https://twitter.com/NancyMace/status/1549805361074511872.

[43] In a report published in October 2021, researchers at the Guttmacher Institute, a pro-abortion think tank, predicted that twenty-six states were "certain or likely to ban abortion" if *Roe* was overturned. See Elizabeth Nash and Lauren Cross, "26 States Are Certain or Likely to Ban Abortion without Roe: Here's Which Ones and Why," Guttmacher Institute, October 28, 2021, https://www.guttmacher.org/article/2021/10/26-states-are-certain-or-likely-ban-abortion-without-roe-heres-which-ones-and-why.

After *Dobbs*, attention immediately shifted to the newly empowered state legislatures. Previously, state lawmakers were largely constrained in their ability to limit abortion and pass pro-life legislation. However, with the overturning of *Roe*, state laws that had been dormant for decades were now back in play. Additionally, conditional laws (known as "trigger" laws) could now be enforced in many states.

## *Immediate Reaction in the States*

Within six minutes of the Court's *Dobbs* decision, then-Missouri Attorney General Eric Schmitt announced the certification of his state's trigger law. "With the Dobbs decision just handed down and a stroke of my pen—Missouri became the first state to effectively end abortion and has become the most Pro Life state in America," Schmitt declared.[44]

Other states, including Alabama, Arkansas, Idaho, Louisiana, Mississippi, Oklahoma, South Dakota, Tennessee, and Texas saw their conditional laws take effect immediately or within a few weeks of the decision. Pre-*Roe* laws in states such as West Virginia and Wisconsin also took effect.

Attorneys general in Alabama, Arkansas, and Oklahoma also certified their states' conditional laws within hours of *Dobbs*. In his statement, Alabama attorney general Steve Marshall explained, "Any abortionist or abortion clinic operating in the State of Alabama in violation of Alabama law should immediately cease and desist operations."[45]

[44] Eric Schmitt (@Eric_Schmitt), "BREAKING: With the Dobbs decision just handed down and a stroke of my pen—Missouri became the first state to effectively end abortion and has become the most Pro Life state in America," Twitter, June 24, 2022, 9:28 a.m., https://twitter.com/Eric_Schmitt/status/1540341139156439040.

[45] "Alabama Attorney General Steve Marshall Statement on Overturn of Roe v. Wade," press release, Attorney General Steve Marshall, June 24, 2022, https://www.alabamaag.gov/alabama-attorney-general-steve-marshall-statement-on-overturn-of-roe-v-wade/.

Likewise, Arkansas attorney general Leslie Rutledge moved to immediately certify her state's 2019 pro-life law.[46] Certifying his state's law, Oklahoma attorney general John O'Connor published a letter on June 24, stating, "As a result of *Dobbs*, the authority of the State of Oklahoma to prohibit abortion has been confirmed, and the State of Oklahoma may enforce Section 861 of Title 21 of the Oklahoma Statutes or enact a similar statute prohibiting abortion throughout pregnancy."[47]

As predicted, the overturning of *Roe v. Wade* set off a flurry of activity in the states. Within a year of the decision, legislation related to abortion had been introduced in all fifty states. Whereas pro-abortion legislators worked to promote and expand access to abortion, pro-life lawmakers labored to enact pro-life protections.

By the one-year anniversary of *Dobbs*, fourteen states protected life at conception.[48] Four additional states (Arizona, Indiana, Utah, and Wyoming) had similar laws in place that were unenforceable while litigation played out in the courts. Five states (Georgia, Florida, Iowa, Ohio, and South Carolina) had either passed heartbeat bills or already had a pre-*Dobbs* heartbeat bill on the books (though only Georgia's law was in effect on the one-year anniversary of *Dobbs*). An additional seven states protected unborn life based on gestational age (at the point when unborn children can feel pain or at the point an unborn child is believed to be viable outside the womb), though some were unenforceable due to ongoing litigation.

On the pro-abortion side, abortion was legal in twenty-one states at the one-year anniversary of *Dobbs*. These states either lacked pro-life protections

---

[46] Jerry Cox, "Arkansas Attorney General Certifies That Abortion Is Prohibited," Family Council, June 24, 2022, https://familycouncil.org/?p=24531.

[47] Office of the Attorney General State of Oklahoma, "For Publication," June 24, 2022, 1, https://www.oag.ok.gov/sites/g/files/gmc766/f/certification.pdf?bcs-agent-scanner=6e928ebd-ac6f-6c47-b030-09ce8e09d9b9.

[48] "Pro-Life Laws in the States," Family Research Council, accessed June 24, 2023, https://FRC.org/ProLifeMaps.

or had abortion laws that contained broad health exceptions that effectively allowed abortion until the moment of birth.[49]

In legislatures across the country, those who had campaigned on pro-life platforms were put to the test. The backlash to *Dobbs* was fierce; the media, entertainment industry, and business world castigated the decision.[50] Professional sports leagues, celebrities, and foreign leaders released statements of opposition. For example, the National Basketball Association (NBA) put out a statement that read, "The NBA and WNBA believe that women should be able to make their own decisions concerning their health and future, and we believe that freedom should be protected. We will continue to advocate for gender and health equity, including ensuring our employees have access to reproductive healthcare, regardless of their location."[51] Even the U.S. military, under the direction of the Biden administration, responded with a controversial policy that provided three weeks of leave and paid travel expenses for military members and their dependents to receive "reproductive health care."[52]

---

[49] In these states, "health" can include the mental and emotional health of the mother.

[50] Taylor Telford and Todd C. Frankel, "Disney Says It Will Cover Employee Travel Costs for Abortions," *Washington Post*, June 24, 2022, https://www.washingtonpost.com/business/2022/06/24/abortion-supreme-court-corporate-reaction/.

[51] NBA (@NBA), "NBA AND WNBA STATEMENT REGARDING ROE V. WADE DECISIO [sic] NBA Commissioner Adam Silver and WNBA Commissioner Cathy Engelbert issued the following statement regarding today's decision in Dobbs v. Jackson Women's Health Organization," Twitter, June 24, 2022, 4:25 p.m., https://twitter.com/NBA/status/1540446153854132225.

[52] "DoD Releases Policies to Ensure Access to Non-Covered Reproductive Health Care," press release, U.S. Department of Defense, February 16, 2023, https://www.defense.gov/News/Releases/Release/Article/3301006/dod-releases-policies-to-ensure-access-to-non-covered-reproductive-health-care/. In response to the Defense Department policy, Sen. Tommy Tuberville (R-AL) put a hold on military promotions in the United States Senate. Typically, military promotions are grouped together and approved by voice vote. With Tuberville's hold in place, the Senate could not approve nominees in bulk. Although the Senate could hold an individual roll call vote for each nominee, the process would be time-consuming,

Within this broader context, pro-life lawmakers faced significant pressure to compromise their convictions. But principled leaders in many states made courageous decisions to move forward with pro-life bills. Their efforts resulted in the successful passage of laws that saved tens of thousands of lives.

## *Kansas Defeat Foreshadows Difficulty for Pro-Life Movement*

The first opportunity for Americans to vote on an abortion-related measure after the Supreme Court's decision was a referendum in Kansas. The vote on the proposed amendment, named by supporters as the "Value Them Both Amendment," had been scheduled for over a year before *Dobbs* was decided. If passed, the amendment would have overturned a 2019 Kansas Supreme Court ruling that declared that abortion is protected under the state constitution. Due in large part to the heightened focus on abortion after *Dobbs*, Kansans rejected the pro-life amendment.[53]

"Amendments like 'Value Them Both,' ensuring the question of abortion stayed in the hands of legislators, had passed in multiple states with significantly less organization and spending in prior years," explained Brittany Jones, Director of Policy and Engagement at Kansas Family Voice.[54] According to Jones, the election's proximity to *Dobbs* affected the outcome.

---

and Senate Majority Leader Chuck Schumer (D-NY) refused to call for individual votes for more than just a handful of the nominees. Thus, by November 2023, there were 400 nominations pending before the Senate. When I asked Senator Tuberville about the holds and the DoD's abortion policy, he said, "The lack of answers from the Pentagon has only reaffirmed to me that I'm doing the right thing. It's never easy to go against the grain, but I think if we the American people do not stand up to this government overreach by the radical left, our children and grandchildren will pay the price."

[53] Dylan Lysen et al., "Voters in Kansas Decide to Keep Abortion Legal in the State, Rejecting an Amendment," NPR, August 2, 2022, https://www.npr.org/sections/2022-live-primary-election-race-results/2022/08/02/1115317596/kansas-voters-abortion-legal-reject-constitutional-amendment.

[54] Brittany Jones (Director of Policy and Engagement, Kansas Family Voice), in discussion with the author, July 17, 2023.

"The abortion landscape got turned upside down just five weeks before Kansans went to the ballot box," she noted. "People were scared and did not have time to absorb the meaning of the *Dobbs* decision and so the lies of the abortion industry were easier to believe than they had ever been in the past," Jones reflected.

The August 2 vote signaled that the abortion lobby and their supporters were galvanized and eager to engage politically after *Dobbs*.[55] In fact, despite the generally unfavorable political environment for Democrats in the forthcoming midterms, the Kansas vote indicated that abortion would be a significant factor in November. The vast spending of pro-abortion groups such as Planned Parenthood Action Fund (which alone committed $50 million to the midterms) also suggested that pro-abortion allies were highly motivated.[56]

## *2022 Midterms*

On November 8, five states asked their citizens to vote on abortion-related amendments. Voters in California, Michigan, and Vermont overwhelmingly approved ballot initiatives to enshrine a right to abortion in their state's constitution. When the votes were counted, the margin in each state was decisive (66.9 to 33.1% in California, 56.7 to 43.3% in Michigan, and 76.8 to 23.2% in Vermont).[57] In Kentucky, voters rejected a proposed amendment that would

---

[55] "Kansas Abortion Amendment Election Results," *New York Times*, last updated September 28, 2022, https://www.nytimes.com/interactive/2022/08/02/us/elections/results-kansas-abortion-amendment.html.

[56] "Planned Parenthood Advocacy and Political Organizations Launch Largest-Ever Electoral Program," Planned Parenthood, August 17, 2022, https://www.plannedparenthoodaction.org/pressroom/planned-parenthood-advocacy-and-political-organizations-launch-largest-ever-electoral-program.

[57] "California Proposition 1 Election Results: Constitutional Right to Reproductive Freedom," *New York Times*, last updated December 20, 2022, https://www.nytimes.com/interactive/2022/11/08/us/elections/results-california-proposition-1-constitutional-right-to-reproductive-freedom.html; "Vermont Proposal 5 Election Results: Constitutional Right to Reproductive Freedom," *New York Times*, last updated November 30, 2022, https://www.nytimes.com/interactive/2022/11/08

have ensured the state's constitution could not be "construed to secure or protect a right to abortion or require the funding of abortion."[58] In a surprise to many, the amendment failed in the conservative state 52.3 to 47.7%.[59]

Finally, in Montana, voters weighed in on a legislative referendum known as the Born Alive Infant Protection Act, a referendum that would have required medical professionals to provide medical care to babies who are born alive following botched abortions. Once again, the pro-abortion side won, with the referendum failing 52.6 to 47.4%.[60]

Although pro-life ballot initiatives failed across the country, voters nevertheless handed a narrow majority to Republicans in the U.S. House of Representatives, ensuring that pro-abortion federal legislation would not advance in the 118th Congress. Voters also elected hundreds of pro-life state legislators, and pro-life governors such as Greg Abbott (R-TX), Ron DeSantis (R-FL), Brian Kemp (R-GA), and Mike DeWine (R-OH) cruised to reelection, setting up opportunities across the nation for new pro-life legislation.

In summary, the results of the 2022 midterm elections were undoubtedly mixed and constituted a setback for the pro-life movement in some

---

/us/elections/results-vermont-proposal-5-constitutional-right-to-reproductive-autonomy.html; "Michigan Proposal 3 Election Results: Constitutional Right to Reproductive Freedom," *New York Times*, last updated November 28, 2022, https://www.nytimes.com/interactive/2022/11/08/us/elections/results-michigan-proposal-3-constitutional-right-to-reproductive-freedom.html.

[58] Chapter 174, HB 91, Kentucky Legislature, accessed November 12, 2023, https://apps.legislature.ky.gov/law/acts/21RS/documents/0174.pdf?bcs-agent-scanner=8851e30a-9da6-1049-a71b-94b9b9915a1b.

[59] "Kentucky Constitutional Amendment 2 Election Results: No Right to Abortion," *New York Times*, last updated November 29, 2022, https://www.nytimes.com/interactive/2022/11/08/us/elections/results-kentucky-constitutional-amendment-2-no-right-to-abortion.html.

[60] Aubrie Spady, "Montana Rejects Ballot Measure to Require Medical Care for 'Infants Who Are Born Alive,'" Fox News, November 10, 2022, https://www.foxnews.com/politics/montana-rejects-ballot-measure-require-medical-care-infants-born-alive.

states. Of course, most pro-lifers would gladly accept a poor midterm election result in exchange for *Dobbs*, but the election results underscored some of the long-term challenges facing the pro-life community.

## Pro-Life Victories

Following *Dobbs*, conservative states moved quickly to enforce preexisting but previously unenforceable pro-life laws. In some states, legislators worked to pass new pro-life protections. For example, following *Dobbs*, lawmakers in Indiana met in a special session to pass a pro-life bill. On August 5, 2022, Governor Eric Holcomb signed Senate Bill 1 into law.[61] The law prohibits abortion except in the case of a fatal fetal anomaly or in cases of serious health risk to the mother. Although the law was temporarily enjoined in September 2022, the Indiana Supreme Court upheld the law on June 30, 2023, allowing pro-life protections to go back into effect.[62]

In West Virginia, lawmakers responded to *Dobbs* by passing an expansive pro-life law in a special legislative session held in September 2022.[63] Governor Jim Justice asked lawmakers to clarify and modernize an 1849 law that prohibited abortion.[64] The new law prohibits abortion at all stages of pregnancy with exceptions for rape and incest victims.

---

[61] "Senate Bill 1," Indiana Statehouse, https://iga.in.gov/legislative/2022ss1/bills/senate/1/details.

[62] Casey Smith, "Indiana Supreme Court Upholds Abortion Ban, but Leaves Door Open for Other Legal Challenges," *Indiana Capital Chronicle*, June 30, 2023, https://indianacapitalchronicle.com/2023/06/30/indiana-supreme-court-upholds-abortion-ban-but-leaves-door-open-for-other-legal-challenges/.

[63] West Virginia Legislature, 86th Legislature, House Bill 302, September 13, 2022, https://www.wvlegislature.gov/Bill_Status/bills_text.cfm?billdoc=HB302%20ENR.htm&yr=2022&sesstype=3X&i=302.

[64] Jim Justice, "A Proclamation by the Governor," Office of the Governor (WV), https://governor.wv.gov/Documents/2022%20Proclamations/07%20JULY%202022/072522-Extraordinary-Session-Call-for-July-25-2022-Amended.pdf?bcs-agent-scanner=eed8edc0-6212-bc4e-b2d5-ad986779eba7. On June 25, 2022, West Virginia Attorney General Patrick Morrisey issued a memorandum that

In the 2023 legislative session, conservative states passed a raft of pro-life legislation. For example, Wyoming passed two pro-life laws in March 2023, including a first-of-its-kind prohibition on abortion drugs (also known as chemical abortion or abortion pills).[65] On April 5, 2023, Idaho passed House Bill 242, legislation that criminalizes helping minors procure an abortion in another state.[66] The bill, signed into law by Governor Brad Little, was also the first of its kind.[67]

In March 2023, Utah passed a law prohibiting the state from licensing new abortion clinics.[68] The law also stipulates that it is a crime to procure an abortion anywhere other than a hospital. Since 95% of the roughly 2,800 abortions in the state take place at four clinics, the new law would significantly limit abortion in the state.[69]

---

explained West Virginia's 1849 law could be enforced. See Office of the Attorney General, "Memorandum Concerning the Effects of *Dobbs v. Jackson Women's Health Organization*," Attorney General Office West Virginia, June 29, 2022, https://ago.wv.gov/Documents/Final%20Dobbs%20Memorandum.pdf?bcs-agent-scanner=7b1f2754-3500-a64c-9c2a-013fac360233.

[65] Jay Croft, "Wyoming Outlaws Abortion Pills," CNN, March 18, 2023, https://www.cnn.com/2023/03/18/us/wyoming-bans-abortion-pills/index.html.

[66] Idaho Legislature, State Affairs Committee, 67th Legislature, House Bill 242, Idaho Legislature, https://legislature.idaho.gov/sessioninfo/2023/legislation/h0242/.

[67] Aria Bendix, "Idaho becomes one of the most extreme anti-abortion states with law restricting travel for abortions," NBC News, April 6, 2023, https://www.nbcnews.com/health/womens-health/idaho-most-extreme-anti-abortion-state-law-restricts-travel-rcna78225.

[68] Utah State Legislature, H.B. 467, 2023, https://le.utah.gov/~2023/bills/static/HB0467.html.

[69] "Utah Governor Signs Legislation Banning Clinics from Providing Abortions," NBC News, March 15, 2023, https://www.nbcnews.com/news/us-news/utah-governor-signs-legislation-banning-clinics-providing-abortions-rcna75206; David W. Chen, "Judge Allows Abortion Clinics to Remain Open in Utah for Now," *New York Times*, May 2, 2023, https://www.nytimes.com/2023/05/02/us/utah-abortion-clinics.html#:~:text=Abortion%20is%20legal%20in%20Utah,that%20only%20in%20limited%20circumstances. The law, House Bill 467, was enjoined on May 2, 2023. See Sam Metz, "Utah Judge Delays Implementing Statewide Abortion Clinic Ban," PBS, May 2, 2023, https://www.pbs.org/news hour/politics/utah-judge-delays-implementing-statewide-abortion-clinic-ban.

Finally, in North Dakota, legislators passed Senate Bill 2150 in April 2023, an expansive pro-life law that contains exceptions for rape, incest, and the health of the mother.[70] Although the state had a trigger law that went into effect after *Dobbs*, Governor Doug Burgum wanted the new law to reaffirm that "North Dakota is a pro-life state."[71]

## Stories from Key States

Before examining how progressive states reacted to the Supreme Court's decision, it is instructive to examine how lawmakers with pro-life convictions responded to *Dobbs*. Despite fierce opposition from a hostile culture, lobbyists, and pro-abortion colleagues within the legislature, pro-life lawmakers worked tirelessly to codify protections for unborn children.

Based on personal conversations with lawmakers and those engaged with the legislative process, the following accounts offer a behind-the-scenes look at the often chaotic and emotionally charged battle over abortion that played out in state capitals in 2022 and 2023. These stories are important because successful efforts at passing pro-life legislation can inform lawmakers, advocacy groups, and individuals about the political realities and pressures facing pro-lifers in the legislative arena. Standing for life requires courage; these accounts offer insight and hope for life after *Roe*.

### *Florida*

In the years leading up to *Dobbs*, the Florida legislature passed several pro-life laws, including a prohibition on partial-birth abortion (2000), protections

---

[70] 68th Legislative Assembly of North Dakota, SB 2150, April 2024, https://ndlegis.gov/assembly/68-2023/regular/bill-overview/bo2150.html?bill_year=2023&bill_number=2150.

[71] Shawna Mizelle, "North Dakota Governor Signs Law Banning Nearly All Abortions in the State," CNN, April 25, 2023, https://www.cnn.com/2023/04/25/politics/north-dakota-abortion-ban/index.html.

for infants born alive during a failed abortion attempt (2013), and requirements for informed patient consent (2015).[72] In 2022, Florida passed a law protecting the unborn at fifteen weeks' gestation, replacing the previous law that allowed abortion until viability (interpreted by abortionists at around twenty-four weeks).[73]

Florida's fifteen-week bill, which was similar to Mississippi's law at the heart of the *Dobbs* case, was set to go into effect on July 1, 2022. However, on June 30, 2022, a state judge ruled the law unconstitutional.[74] The state of Florida appealed the ruling, and the law was temporarily allowed to take effect while the Florida Supreme Court reviewed its provisions.

Thus, within a week, Florida's pro-life community received the thrilling news about *Dobbs* but was left wondering about the fate of their fifteen-week law. With midterms looming, Florida's pro-life leaders decided to forego a special session and reevaluate their options after the election.

On November 8, 2022, Florida voters overwhelmingly elected pro-life candidates. Strong statewide campaigns by Gov. Ron DeSantis and Sen. Marco Rubio boosted turnout, and Republicans at all levels fared well. Republicans in the state House expanded their majority from 78 to 85 seats, and Republicans in the state Senate went from 24 to 28 seats.

Empowered by supermajorities in both legislative chambers, Republican lawmakers decided to advance a stronger pro-life bill in 2023, even as they waited for the Florida Supreme Court to decide the constitutionality of the fifteen-week law.

---

[72] Office Secretary of State, "Committee Substitute for Committee Substitute for Committee Substitute House Bill No. 1129," Laws of Florida, June 5, 2013, https://laws.flrules.org/2013/121; "Laws of Florida," State Library and Archives of Florida, https://laws.flrules.org/2000/142; Florida Legislature, House Bill No. 633, Laws of Florida, 2015, https://laws.flrules.org/2015/118.

[73] Senate, CS/HB 5: Reducing Fetal and Infant Mortality, The Florida Senate, 2022 Legislature, https://www.flsenate.gov/Session/Bill/2022/5/ByCategory.

[74] John Kennedy, "Leon County Judge Rules Florida's 15-Week Abortion Law Unconstitutional," *Tallahassee Democrat*, June 30, 2022, https://www.tallahassee.com/story/news/politics/2022/06/30/florida-abortion-law-blocked-leon-county-judge/7773131001/.

Following months of negotiations, Sen. Erin Grall filed a heartbeat bill on March 7, 2023.[75] "After winning supermajorities, those of us who campaigned as pro-life candidates knew we had a responsibility to pass a meaningful bill," Grall explained.[76] According to the senator, "With *Dobbs*, legislative supermajorities, and a supportive governor, pro-lifers were given a gift, a historic opportunity, to save babies and make a difference. We knew we couldn't squander the moment."[77]

Grall's bill offered legal protection for unborn babies after six weeks' gestation. The bill included exceptions for the health of the mother and the victims of rape, incest, and human trafficking (so long as reporting requirements aimed at bringing perpetrators to justice are met).[78] The bill also included $30 million for pregnant women and their families. Additionally, sending chemical abortion pills through the mail was prohibited.

The Senate passed the bill on April 3, with the House following suit and passing it on April 13. Even with pro-life supermajorities, the bill encountered opposition. During debate in the Senate, pro-abortion activists filled the galleries and shouted whenever a pro-life senator attempted to speak. Eventually, the galleries were cleared, and protests, led by Senate Minority Leader Lauren Book, continued outside.[79]

In response to activists protesting the fifteen-week bill in 2022, police in Tallahassee implemented heightened security protocols, including the

---

[75] Florida Legislature, Senate, SB 300: Pregnancy and Parenting Support, Chapter. No. 2023-21, https://www.flsenate.gov/Session/Bill/2023/300/?Tab=BillText.

[76] Erin Grall (Sen., District 29, Florida Legislature), in discussion with the author, July 6, 2023.

[77] Grall, discussion.

[78] "Florida Senate Passes Heartbeat Protection Act," press release, The Florida Senate, April 3, 2023, https://www.flsenate.gov/Media/PressReleases/show/4437.

[79] Senator Book was eventually arrested for failing to comply with repeated orders from law enforcement to vacate the plaza in front of City Hall. See C. A. Bridges, "Florida DemLeaders Nikki Fried, Lauren Book Arrested at Abortion Ban Protest: What We Know," *Tallahassee Democrat*, April 4, 2023, https://www.tallahassee.com/story/news/politics/2023/04/04/nikki-fried-lauren-book-arrested-in-florida-6-week-abortion-ban-protest/70078878007/.

installation of new cameras around the capitol complex and the occasional use of protective details for lawmakers. As the six-week bill made its way through the legislative process, Senator Grall and her family received death threats due to her sponsorship and advocacy for the bill. As the heartbeat bill was debated, police insisted on escorting Grall to and from her office. "You really feel the anger and vitriol from the other side when you work on pro-life legislation," Grall explained as she described the backlash to her work on the heartbeat bill.[80] "This job puts a lot of stress on your family, but my husband and I view this work as worth it."[81]

When Governor Ron DeSantis signed the bill into law on April 13, 2023, Senator Grall stood at the governor's right hand.[82] "This is by far the most meaningful work I've ever done," Grall recounted.[83] "It is a brutal process, but there's no ranking for me. Without life, none of the other issues matter. Passing a heartbeat bill into law is the most important thing I've ever done or accomplished."[84]

After nearly two years of litigation, the Florida Supreme Court decided on April 1, 2024, that the state's fifteen-week protection law did not violate the state constitution's privacy clause. The decision allowed the Heartbeat Protection Act to take effect as well.[85]

In summary, Florida's pro-life success is due, in part, to the election of legislators who were willing to fight for pro-life legislation. A perennial

---

[80] Grall, discussion.

[81] Grall, discussion.

[82] "Governor Ron DeSantis Signs Bill to Protect the Lives of Florida's Most Vulnerable," news release, Ron Desantis, April 14, 2023, https://www.flgov.com/2022/04/14/governor-ron-desantis-signs-bill-to-protect-the-lives-of-floridas-most-vulnerable/.

[83] Grall, discussion.

[84] Grall, discussion.

[85] Planned Parenthood of Southwest and Central Florida v. State of Florida, No. SC2022-1127 (April 1, 2024), https://supremecourt.flcourts.gov/content/download/2285280/opinion/Opinion_SC2022-1050%20&%20SC2022-1127.pdf.

swing state for years, Florida voters have increasingly voted in a pro-life, conservative direction. The adage "elections have consequences" is appropriate in this instance; the state's years-long journey to a strong pro-life law underscores how elections have a direct effect on a state's ability to protect the unborn through legislation.

## *Iowa*

Before 2017, there were few pro-life protections in Iowa. However, following the 2016 elections when Republicans took control of the legislature and governor's office for the first time since 1998, pro-life lawmakers saw an opportunity.[86] Shortly after taking office, the Republican majority passed a twenty-week bill that prohibited abortion when an unborn child can feel pain.[87]

In 2018, Iowa legislators went further and passed a heartbeat bill.[88] With *Roe* still in place, Gov. Kim Reynolds acknowledged the new law would likely be struck down but explained, "I understand and anticipate that this will likely be challenged in court, and that courts may even put a hold on the law until it reaches the Supreme Court. However, this is bigger than just a law. This is about life."[89]

---

[86] William Petroski and Brianne Pfannenstiel, "2017 Iowa Legislature Convenes amid Pomp, Speeches," *Des Moines Register*, January 9, 2017, https://www.desmoinesregister.com/story/news/politics/2017/01/09/2017-iowa-legislature-convenes-amid-pomp-color/96338210/.

[87] Iowa Legislature, Senate, SF 471, https://www.legis.iowa.gov/legislation/BillBook?ga=87&ba=sf471. The bill also specified that those seeking an abortion are required to get an ultrasound and must be given information regarding other available options (such as adoption).

[88] Iowa Legislature, Senate, SF 359, https://www.legis.iowa.gov/docs/publications/LGE/87/SF359.pdf?bcs-agent-scanner=60ec4043-b552-d345-b0e1-d5df8d87e606.

[89] "Gov. Reynolds releases statement after signing heartbeat bill," Office of the Governor of Iowa, May 4, 2018, https://web.archive.org/web/20180509223152/https://governor.iowa.gov/2018/05/gov-reynolds-releases-statement-after-signing-heartbeat-bill.

Within a few weeks the new law was enjoined by state courts and subsequently struck down in 2019.[90] However, following *Dobbs*, Reynolds asked the state's supreme court to reinstate the heartbeat law. In her view, the rationale for the permanent injunction against the heartbeat law had been removed.

"After *Dobbs*, we expected our law to be enforced," explained State Senate President Amy Sinclair.[91] "Those of us in Iowa had already done work to protect unborn life in our state. With the overturning of *Roe*, we just needed the court to let our heartbeat law take effect."[92]

Despite the governor's request for the Iowa Supreme Court to lift the injunction on the 2018 law, the court refused, issuing a 3–3 decision on June 16, 2023, that kept the heartbeat law enjoined. Incredibly, in his ruling, Justice Thomas Waterman described the 2018 legislation as "a hypothetical law" and claimed that when it was passed, legislators did not think it would ever actually be enforced. Waterman also questioned whether the legislature would pass a heartbeat law in 2023 given the changed legal landscape.[93]

---

[90] Tony Leys, "Iowa 'Fetal Heartbeat' Abortion Restriction Declared Unconstitutional, Struck Down by Polk County Judge," *Des Moines Register*, January 22, 2019, https://www.desmoinesregister.com/story/news/2019/01/22/iowa-fetal-heartbeat-abortion-law-struck-down-injunction-planned-parenthood-supreme-court-fetus/2650491002/.

[91] Amy Sinclair (State Senate President, District 12, Iowa Legislature), in discussion with the author, July 25, 2023.

[92] Sinclair, discussion.

[93] Planned Parenthood of the Heartland, Inc., Emma Goldman Clinic, and Jill Meadows v. Kim Reynolds ex rel. State of Iowa and Iowa Board of Medicine, 22-2036, (2023), https://www.courtlistener.com/opinion/9407300/planned-parenthood-of-the-heartland-inc-emma-goldman-clinic-and-jill/. Because the Iowa Supreme Court deadlocked, the 2018 heartbeat law could not go into effect. Justice Thomas Waterman explained his decision, noting, "To put it politely, the legislature was enacting a hypothetical law. Today, such a statute might take effect given the change in the constitutional law landscape. But uncertainty exists about whether a fetal heartbeat bill would be passed today. To begin, a different general assembly is in place than was in place in 2018, with significant turnover of membership in the intervening three election cycles." Despite Waterman's suggestion

Sinclair and her colleagues were shocked. "With all due respect to Justice Waterman, it's not his job to speculate on the intent of legislators. Our intent has nothing to do with the enforceability of a duly enacted law. There is no such thing as a 'hypothetical law,'" she explained to me.[94]

In response to the court's refusal to enforce the law, Governor Reynolds convened the legislature for a special session with the goal of passing a new heartbeat law. "If the justices truly believe the 2018 law is 'hypothetical,' we will pass it again so they can do their job, which is to weigh the merits of the actual law, not speculate on the mindset or opinions of legislators," Sinclair said.

In July 2023, the legislature passed the heartbeat bill again.[95] In the Senate, Senator Sinclair served as the floor manager at the request of the governor. On July 14, Governor Reynolds signed the bill into law.[96] Notably, the law passed the legislature by large margins, defying Justice Waterman's contention that the current legislature might not pass another heartbeat bill.

The passage of pro-life legislation in Iowa was not without personal cost to the state's legislators. During debate over the bill, activists protested at the personal residences of pro-life lawmakers, including Senator Sinclair. Enraged at Sinclair's support for the heartbeat bill, protestors

---

that a heartbeat bill might not be able to pass the legislature in 2023, the legislature responded on July 11, 2023, by passing a new heartbeat bill (known as House File 732) by wide margins (56–34 in the House, 32–17 in the Senate). See Jay Waagmeester and Kathie Obradovich, "Iowa Legislature Passes Legislation to Outlaw Most Abortions after Six Weeks," *Iowa Capital Dispatch*, July 11, 2023, https://iowacapitaldispatch.com/2023/07/11/hundreds-gather-at-capitol-for-abortion-special-session/; Kim Reynolds, Office of the Governor, July 14, 2023, https://www.legis.iowa.gov/legislation/BillBook?ga=90&ba=HF732,

[94] Sinclair, discussion.

[95] Shania Shelton, "Iowa Governor Signs 6-Week Abortion Ban into Law," CNN, last updated July 14, 2023, https://www.cnn.com/2023/07/14/politics/iowa-abortion-ban-reynolds-sign/index.html#:~:text=The%20bill%2C%20which%20passed%20the,women%20know%20they%20are%20pregnant.

[96] Iowa Legislature, House, SF 732, https://www.legis.iowa.gov/legislation/BillBook?ga=90&ba=HF%20732.

filmed themselves casting a hex on her house and uploaded it to TikTok. "I try to be understanding of what's driving these individuals. I will hear your viewpoint, but there's a line that gets crossed sometimes. And it's not okay to hex someone's house or threaten a lawmaker's children," Sinclair explained.[97]

Iowa's post-*Dobbs* experience is a reminder that in many states, passing pro-life legislation is not enough. Even in traditionally conservative states, activist courts can thwart duly passed pro-life legislation. Thus, moving forward, those committed to protecting the unborn must pay attention to the judiciary. In some states, judges are appointed; in other states they are elected. Although judges should impartially interpret and apply the law, this is often not the case, and accountability and oversight are needed, even in conservative states.

## *North Carolina*

Following the Supreme Court's *Roe v. Wade* decision in 1973, North Carolina enacted legislation that prohibited many abortions after twenty weeks.[98] Over the years, the legislature enacted additional pro-life laws, including parental consent for minors to obtain an abortion (1995), a twenty-four-hour waiting period (2011), and a prohibition on sex-selective abortion (2013).[99]

---

[97] Additionally, pro-abortion protestors traveled to the house of another pro-life representative's house and threatened to kidnap his children. Other lawmakers received similar threatening messages.

[98] North Carolina General Assembly, House Bill 615, 1973 Session, https://www.ncleg.gov/enactedlegislation/sessionlaws/html/1973-1974/sl1973-711.html.

[99] See Woman's Right to Know Act, 2011-405, s. 1, https://www.ncleg.gov/EnactedLegislation/Statutes/PDF/ByArticle/Chapter_90/Article_1I.pdf?bcs-agent-scanner=0c99dff0-732b-f340-a828-3db1cea9f50b; Woman's Right to Know Act, § 90-21.82, https://www.ncleg.gov/enactedlegislation/statutes/pdf/bysection/chapter_90/gs_90-21.82.pdf, and General Assembly of North Carolina, Senate Bill 353, https://www.ncleg.gov/Sessions/2013/Bills/Senate/PDF/S353v5.pdf?bcs-agent-scanner=5d912cfe-ef0b-e348-824d-94d49b738d13. The twenty-four-hour waiting

However, in 2019, a federal judge declared portions of the state's decades-old pro-life law unconstitutional.[100] With the twenty-week law overturned, abortions could be legally performed up to viability. However, following *Dobbs*, the same federal judge reinstated the twenty-week law on August 17, 2022.[101] Despite reinstatement of the law, North Carolina quickly became an outlier in the Southeast.

"Even with the reinstatement of our 20-week law, we became a destination state for abortion as our neighbors passed stronger pro-life protections," explained state Senator Jim Burgin.[102] "After *Dobbs*, estimates were that our abortion rate would double as out-of-state residents came to North Carolina to get an abortion," Burgin said.[103]

But with Democrat Roy Cooper in the governor's office, Republican majorities in the state legislature could not change the law by themselves. To pass pro-life legislation—and override the expected veto—the voters would need to elect a Republican supermajority in the 2022 election, or a handful of Democratic lawmakers would need to cross their party and vote pro-life.

---

period was changed to seventy-two hours in 2015. Additionally, the 2013 law allowed doctors to object to performing an abortion on moral, ethical, and religious grounds.

[100] Eli Watkins, "Judge Rules against North Carolina's 20-Week Abortion Ban," CNN, March 26, 2019, https://www.cnn.com/2019/03/26/politics/north-carolina-abortion-ruling/index.html. According to U.S. District Judge William Osteen, Supreme Court precedent dictates that "A state is never allowed to prohibit any swath of pre-viability abortions outright, no matter how strenuously it may believe that such a ban is in the best interests of its citizens or how minimal it may find the burden to women seeking an abortion." See "Federal Judge Ends North Carolina Ban on Abortions after 20 Weeks," Reuters, last updated March 26, 2019, https://www.reuters.com/article/us-north-carolina-abortion/federal-judge-ends-north-carolina-ban-on-abortions-after-20-weeks-idUSKCN1R7263.

[101] Hannah Schoenbaum, "Judge Reinstates North Carolina's 20-Week Abortion Ban," AP News, August 17, 2022, https://apnews.com/article/abortion-health-north-carolina-government-and-politics-59ec5074eb84f16aa614276c7c3fa24d.

[102] Jim Burgin (Sen., District 12, North Carolina Legislature), in discussion with the author, July 11, 2023.

[103] Burgin, discussion.

Following the 2022 election, Republicans picked up two seats in the Senate, securing a supermajority. They also picked up two seats in the House but were one seat short of a supermajority in the lower chamber. Consequently, pro-life lawmakers entered the 2023 legislative session uncertain of what they could accomplish in terms of pro-life legislation.

After working on the bill for months, pro-life lawmakers coalesced around Senate Bill 20, a twelve-week protection bill co-sponsored by Senator Burgin.[104] However, with Governor Cooper opposed to expanding pro-life protections, the proposed legislation faced an uncertain future. But on April 5, 2023, a political earthquake rocked Raleigh when Rep. Tricia Cotham announced a party-switch. Cotham's switch gave Republicans a supermajority in the House and the ability to override the governor's veto.

"The party switch was one of those things where God confirmed that things could move on," Burgin recounted.[105] With their new supermajorities, the House and Senate passed the twelve-week bill on May 4. As expected, Cooper vetoed Senate Bill 20 on May 13. Significantly, Cooper vetoed the bill at a large public rally, described by the press as "electric" and "exuberant."[106] Designed to exert pressure on the legislature, the unconventional public display thrust the state in the national spotlight as lawmakers considered their next move.

"It was a show of force, a very public spectacle" recalled John Rustin, president and executive director of the North Carolina Family Policy Council. "Standing with the leaders of Planned Parenthood and NARAL, the governor wanted to send a clear message with his public veto. The subsequent media coverage was distorted, even untruthful," he added.[107]

---

[104] North Carolina General Assembly, Care for Women, Children, and Families Act, SL 2023-14, https://ncleg.gov/BillLookUp/2023/S20.

[105] Burgin, discussion.

[106] "North Carolina's Governor Vetoed a 12-Week Abortion Ban, Setting up an Override Fight," NPR, May 14, 2023, https://www.npr.org/2023/05/14/1176064846/north-carolinas-governor-vetoed-a-12-week-abortion-ban-setting-up-an-override-fi.

[107] John Rustin, interview with author, April 1, 2024.

Knowing that they could not lose a single vote, Republicans moved to override the veto. "For someone with higher political ambitions, I understand the governor's public veto. But it was a shame to see a good bill, one that provided a lot of services to women and children get pilloried like that," Burgin recounted.[108]

Despite the abortion lobby's best efforts to sink the bill, the Senate and House overrode the governor on May 16 and officially enacted a twelve-week protection law in North Carolina. "It was a great moment for the state," Burgin explained.[109] "I wish we could have done more; we need a heartbeat bill, but we did make some difference, and more babies will be alive in North Carolina because of our bill."[110]

As a politically purple state, North Carolina's efforts to pass a pro-life law are instructive. In fact, there are at least four lessons to learn from the Tar Heel state. First, efforts to pass pro-life legislation will encounter massive resistance, particularly from politicians supported by the abortion lobby. Notably, Governor Cooper's veto of Senate Bill 20 was the seventy-seventh veto of his governorship, yet it was the first bill to be vetoed on a stage in front of hundreds of cheering supporters. "When it comes to abortion, you need to anticipate that your opponents will pull out all the stops," Rustin reflected. "Even if they can't stop the legislation, they will exert a tremendous amount of pressure on you," he added.[111] As pro-lifers around the country work to advance commonsense legislation to protect women and their children, the opposition will be fierce, and it is helpful to prepare for it beforehand.

Second, pro-lifers must anticipate how both politicians and the media will misrepresent their bills. For example, at his raucous veto rally, Cooper stated that the twelve-week protection bill "has nothing to do with making

---

[108] Burgin, interview.
[109] Burgin, interview.
[110] Burgin, interview.
[111] Burgin, interview.

women safe" despite the inclusion of millions of dollars in the bill for maternal care and other services for women. Similarly, on May 3, the *Charlotte Observer* published a piece that spread outright lies about the bill, alleging, for example, that the bill "will restrict access to all abortions."[112] A third lesson is the importance of coupling pro-life protections with enhanced services and care for women. As Rustin explained, "Our lawmakers recognized that if they limited abortion, more women would carry their pregnancy to term. They also understood that there would be more women in levels of greater need who may require additional social services. They wisely addressed these needs in the bill." In fact, the new law includes over $160 million in funding for foster care, adoption care, maternity homes, and maternal care. Although opponents still lampooned the bill, pro-life lawmakers in North Carolina provided significant support for women, counteracting the narrative that pro-lifers are only "pro-birth."

Finally, the effort in North Carolina illustrates the importance of not letting the perfect become the enemy of the good. Although many lawmakers wanted to pass a heartbeat bill, a supermajority of lawmakers in both chambers were unfortunately unwilling to vote for heartbeat. Instead of resigning themselves to the status quo—where abortion was legal through twenty weeks—legislators worked to protect as many babies as they could. In fact, within the twelve-week law are provisions that prohibit partial-birth abortion, that prohibit eugenic abortion (based on the race, sex, or diagnosis of Down syndrome), and that make it more difficult to acquire and dispense abortion-inducing drugs. In short, although North Carolina's new law did not give pro-lifers everything they wanted, it moved the law in a more pro-life direction and set the stage for stronger pro-life protections in the future.

---

[112] Paige Masten, "North Carolina's 12-Week Abortion Ban Is Worse Than You Think. Here's Why," *Charlotte Observer*, May 3, 2023, https://www.charlotteobserver.com/opinion/article275027951.html.

## *South Carolina*

In 2021, South Carolina passed a fetal heartbeat law.[113] Predictably, the law was enjoined by a federal judge in March 2021.[114] At the time, many legislators hoped the new law would lead to the overturning of *Roe*. But before challenges to South Carolina's law could work their way through the courts, the justices agreed to hear the *Dobbs* case. Legislators in the Palmetto state thus waited to see how the Court's ruling in *Dobbs* would affect their state's hitherto unenforceable law.

Following the overturning of *Roe*, the state's attorney general announced on June 27, 2022, that the state's heartbeat law was in effect.[115] In response, Planned Parenthood sued, alleging that the law violated the state constitution's right to privacy.[116] On August 17, the South Carolina Supreme Court enjoined enforcement of the heartbeat law.

Anticipating the *Dobbs* decision, the legislature had adjourned in May 2022 with a resolution in place that would allow legislators to come back into session if *Roe* was overturned.[117] In a special session held in August and September, the Senate passed a revised heartbeat bill that members believed addressed the concerns of the state Supreme Court. But conservative lawmakers in the House insisted on passing a stronger bill, known as

---

[113] Amanda Watts and Caroline Kelly, "South Carolina Governor Signs Bill Prohibiting Most Abortions When a Fetal Heartbeat Is Detected," CNN, February 18, 2021, https://www.cnn.com/2021/02/18/politics/south-carolina-abortion/index.html.

[114] "Federal Judge Blocks SC Fetal Heartbeat Abortion Ban Law," News 19, March 19, 2021, https://www.wltx.com/article/news/local/judge-blocks-south-carolina-fetal-heartbeat-abortion-law/101-19b9855f-22bb-488d-a104-9f2751e90db3.

[115] Nevin Smith, "Fetal Heartbeat Law Now in Effect in South Carolina," WIS News 10, June 27, 2022, https://www.wistv.com/2022/06/27/fetal-heartbeat-law-now-effect-south-carolina/.

[116] James Pollard, "S.C. Court Blocks Abortion Law as Senate Considers New One," AP News, August 17, 2022, https://apnews.com/article/abortion-us-supreme-court-health-government-and-politics-south-carolina-2d1807549d5e4442904d98860f217869.

[117] South Carolina General Assembly, Bill 1325, 124th Session, introduced May 10, 2022, https://www.scstatehouse.gov/sess124_2021-2022/bills/1325.htm.

the Human Life Protection Act, legislation that protected life at conception with exceptions for rape, incest, and fatal fetal anomalies.

"The Human Life Protection Act, as originally written, was the strongest piece of pro-life legislation ever introduced in this nation's history. Even with the exceptions that were added in before the House passed it, it was a very strong bill," explained Rep. John McCravy, who authored the bill.[118]

Throughout the late summer and into the fall, pro-life legislators in the two chambers tried to find agreement. However, the Senate lacked the votes to pass the House's more conservative bill. "The votes for a stronger bill were just not there in the Senate," argued Sen. Larry Grooms, a pro-life senator who was first elected in 1997.[119]

As a result of deadlock between pro-life legislators, the special session adjourned without a new pro-life law. Grooms, speaking for many of his Senate colleagues, was frustrated. "The Senate voted on the House bill several times. It was clear we couldn't pass it. The House was listening to the wrong people, and as a result, South Carolina became an abortion destination in the South," he recounted.[120]

With the legislature at an impasse, the South Carolina Supreme Court ruled on January 5, 2023, that the 2021 Fetal Heartbeat and Protection from Abortion law was unconstitutional.[121] "I wasn't surprised," Grooms explained.[122] "We hadn't addressed the concerns of the Court and as a result the state now had the weakest pro-life laws in the region."[123]

---

[118] John McCravy (Rep., District 13, South Carolina Legislature), in discussion with the author, July 6, 2023.

[119] Larry Grooms (Sen., District 37, South Carolina Legislature), in discussion with the author, July 5, 2023.

[120] Grooms, discussion.

[121] Tierney Sneed and Devan Cole, "South Carolina's Six-Week Abortion Ban Struck Down by State Supreme Court," CNN, last updated January 5, 2023, https://www.cnn.com/2023/01/05/politics/south-carolina-abortion-ban-ruling-unconstitutional/index.html.

[122] Grooms, discussion.

[123] Grooms, discussion.

In February 2023, the Senate passed a revised heartbeat bill.[124] But once again, the House wanted a stronger bill. "In my opinion, the Senate bill wasn't very strong," McCravy explained.[125] Thus, Republicans in the two chambers remained at odds, and pro-life legislation stalled.

In a meeting convened among pro-life groups in the spring, Grooms pleaded with his House colleagues to pass the heartbeat bill. The House, led by Representative McCravy, refused again, insisting that the Senate vote for a seventh time on the Human Life Protection Act.

As debate dragged on throughout the spring, tensions grew between conservative lawmakers. The national press drew attention to the standoff, spotlighting the "Sister Senators" in the Senate—three Republicans, one Independent, and one Democrat—who opposed the House's full-protection bill.[126] On April 27, the Senate agreed to hold another vote on the House's Human Life Protection Act. The vote failed 22–21.[127] Once again, the legislature adjourned without passing a pro-life bill. "We knew it would fail, but a handful of pro-life groups and House members insisted on another vote," explained Grooms.[128]

On May 12, Gov. Henry McMaster called for a special session to address, among other topics, the heartbeat bill.[129] Just four days later, on

---

[124] James Pollard, "South Carolina Senate Passes New Abortion Ban after Ruling," AP News, February 9, 2023, https://apnews.com/article/abortion-politics-south-carolina-state-government-health-5d0e6e63c15173db4c82f15fbd9a0540.

[125] McCravy, discussion.

[126] Kate Zernike, "The Unexpected Women Blocking South Carolina's Near-Total Abortion Ban," *New York Times*, May 7, 2023, https://www.nytimes.com/2023/05/07/us/south-carolina-abortion-ban.html.

[127] Margery A. Beck and James Pollard, "Abortion Bans Fail in Conservative South Carolina, Nebraska," AP News, April 28, 2023, https://apnews.com/article/abortion-nebraska-south-carolina-c78ec68b095180a9b53f6e136ba3e045.

[128] Grooms, discussion.

[129] South Carolina Executive Department, Executive Order No. 2023-13, May 11, 2023, https://governor.sc.gov/sites/governor/files/Documents/2023-05-11%20FILED%20Executive%20Order%20No.%202023-13%20-%20Convening%20General%20Assembly%20in%20Extra%20Session.pdf?bcs-agent-scanner=9d35723b-a162-3847-b006-34b6627312da.

May 16, the special session began. Although McCravy wanted a stronger bill, he agreed to champion the heartbeat bill in the special session. "I didn't want our state to become an abortion destination," McCravy explained. "I knew we needed to do something; doing anything would be better than the status quo."[130]

Intent on slowing down the process, Democrats in the House introduced over 900 amendments during debate on the heartbeat bill. "The Democrats did everything they could to derail the process, but Republicans and one pro-life Democrat held together. It took a while, but we defeated the amendments and passed the bill," McCravy explained.[131]

After multiple days of debate, the House passed the heartbeat bill 82–33. However, an unforeseen roadblock almost derailed it in the Senate, where an initial cloture vote was needed to break a filibuster. Although she supported the heartbeat bill, Senator Katrina Shealy, one of the "Sister Senators," had grown increasingly frustrated at having to vote repeatedly on the issue. When the roll was called to invoke cloture, Shealy initially did not vote.

"We really needed her vote," Grooms recalled.[132] At the last moment, Shealy voted "Aye," allowing the bill to proceed. According to Grooms, the fact that South Carolina had become a destination state for abortion bothered his colleague. "We were having around 1,000 abortions a month with half of them coming from out of state," Grooms explained.[133]

On May 23, the Senate passed the heartbeat bill by a 27–19 vote. Governor McMaster signed the Fetal Heartbeat and Protection from Abortion Act into law on May 25, 2023.[134]

---

[130] McCravy, discussion.

[131] McCravy, discussion.

[132] Grooms, discussion.

[133] Grooms, discussion.

[134] South Carolina General Assembly, Fetal Heartbeat and Protection from Abortion Act, 125th Session, introduced in the Senate February 1, 2023, https://www.scstatehouse.gov/sess125_2023-2024/bills/474.htm.

Although it took almost a year to pass, South Carolina's successful passage of a heartbeat law ensured that the state would not become an abortion destination. "If I had accomplished nothing else in my twenty-five-year legislative career, I would still be happy," Grooms told me shortly after passage of the heartbeat bill. "Helping pass heartbeat, knowing that we've saved babies, is the highest calling and perhaps the most important thing I'll ever do," he added.[135]

Although he wanted a stronger bill, McCravy agreed that passing a pro-life bill in the wake of *Dobbs* was important. "There is nothing greater than to advocate for life. I'm grateful the Lord gave me an opportunity to help pass this bill. It certainly ranks at the top of my legislative accomplishments," McCravy reflected.[136]

South Carolina's nearly yearlong journey to passing a strong pro-life law is instructive. First, although differences among political allies is not unusual, strong disagreement within the Republican caucus exposed deep divides. Among pro-life lawmakers, the inclusion of specific legislative exceptions (e.g., rape, incest, health of the mother, etc.) is a point of tension. Although opposing pro-life factions in South Carolina were able to find consensus on heartbeat, the battle to find consensus continues in other states.

A second lesson from South Carolina is one that Senator Grooms emphasized to me repeatedly: good bills often fail because of those who insist on perfection. "In the legislative arena, when someone has an all-or-nothing approach the result is always the same: nothing. If it is all or nothing, nothing wins every time. That's almost where we ended up again in South Carolina," cautioned Grooms.[137] This point underscores an ongoing debate within the pro-life community about strategy, one which we will return to in the final chapter.

---

[135] Grooms, discussion.

[136] McCravy, discussion.

[137] Grooms, discussion.

## *Nebraska*

In terms of advancing pro-life legislation, one of the most gripping stories in the nation comes from the center of the American heartland. In the nation's only unicameral legislature, pro-life legislators responded enthusiastically to *Dobbs,* but strident opposition from pro-abortion lawmakers, an unexpected conservative defection, and a hospitalized senator on the day of the final vote almost derailed a twelve-week protection bill. The successful passage of Nebraska's new pro-life law is a remarkable story that demonstrates how even in reliably conservative states, nothing can be taken for granted in the fight for life.

For context, in 2010, Nebraska passed the Pain-Capable Unborn Child Protection Act, legislation that protects unborn children who can feel pain in the womb.[138] The legislation was the first in the nation that considered fetal pain and prohibited abortion after twenty weeks' gestation.[139] In the ensuing years, lawmakers passed additional pro-life bills, including a parental consent requirement for minors seeking an abortion (2011); a provision that provides resources for families who receive a diagnosis of lethal fetal anomalies (2017); a revision of the informed consent laws, requiring doctors to inform women how to reverse the effects of medication abortion (2019); and a ban on dismemberment abortion procedures (2020).[140]

---

[138] Nebraska Legislature, Legislative Bill 103, 2010, https://nebraskalegislature.gov/FloorDocs/101/PDF/Slip/LB1103.pdf?bcs-agent-scanner=0495b6c8-499c-6f4c-ab34-78e6fc1471e0.

[139] An impetus for the law was Dr. LeRoy Carhart, an abortionist who provided late-term abortions in the state. After the assassination of abortionist George Tiller in 2009 in nearby Kansas, Carhart promised to carry on Tiller's legacy of performing late-term abortions in Bellevue, Nebraska. Not wanting to become the late-term abortion capital of the Midwest, Nebraska lawmakers were eager to pass a pain-capable bill. See Monica Davey, "Nebraska Law Sets Limits on Abortion," *New York Times*, April 13, 2010, https://www.nytimes.com/2010/04/14/us/14abortion.html.

[140] Nebraska Legislature, Legislative Bill 690, 2011, https://nebraskalegislature.gov/FloorDocs/102/PDF/Slip/LB690.pdf?bcs-agent-scanner=d0ccf440-285e-204d-8ad8-5ccf1ebfff9e; "Compassion and Care for Medically Challenging

At the onset of the 2022 legislative session, pro-life lawmakers introduced legislation to prohibit abortion in the event *Roe v. Wade* was overturned. Introduced by Sen. Joni Albrecht, the legislation faced uncertain prospects. Although Republicans held a majority in the legislature, thirty-three votes are needed in Nebraska to break a filibuster.

"I knew we had thirty-one votes," Albrecht explained.[141] "I had hoped we could get the bill over the finish line, but the votes were just not there."[142] Albrecht's bill faltered as conservatives failed by two votes to break a Democrat-led filibuster.[143] Disappointed, pro-life lawmakers concluded the 2022 legislative session without a pro-life bill.

But disappointment turned into joy on June 24 with the *Dobbs* decision. "With *Roe* overturned, we can really make a difference," Albrecht thought as she read the opinion.[144]

Although Nebraska's pro-life leaders were thrilled with *Dobbs*, failure to pass pro-life legislation in the spring tempered expectations. Although some pro-life supporters wanted Governor Pete Ricketts to call a special session to work on a pro-life bill, longtime pro-life advocates such as Karen Bowling urged caution. Bowling, who leads the influential Nebraska Family Alliance (NFA), believed failure in a special session would send the wrong message

---

Pregnancies Act," Nebraska Department of Health and Human Services, last updated May 1, 2018, https://dhhs.ne.gov/MCAH/MI-LB506-InformationSupportSheet.pdf?bcs-agent-scanner=2bed619a-fe41-8e4a-a93c-03edbb00670b; Nebraska Legislature, Legislative Bill 209, 106th Legislature, https:// nebraskalegislature.gov/FloorDocs/106/PDF/Intro/LB209.pdf?bcs-agent-scanner=ff482ef6-f8b3-234c-a16d-aac73ba06ee9; Nebraska Legislature, Legislative Bill 814, 2020, https://nebraskalegislature.gov/FloorDocs/106/PDF/Slip/LB814.pdf?bcs-agent-scanner=1baf7297-dccd-a344-81fb-446528453191.

[141] Joni Albrecht (Sen., District 17, Nebraska Legislature), in discussion with the author, July 10, 2023.

[142] Albrecht, discussion.

[143] Grant Schulte, "Abortion Rights Backers Block 'Trigger' Law in Nebraska," AP News, April 7, 2022, https://apnews.com/article/voting-rights-us-supreme-court-health-nebraska-legislature-0b8e1e93be48c9e3fd7264c94da7b786.

[144] Albrecht, discussion.

to the rest of the nation. "If we failed in the special session, the message would be 'Even conservative Nebraska doesn't want to eliminate abortion,'" explained Bowling.[145]

Knowing the legislature lacked the votes to overcome a filibuster, Governor Ricketts announced on August 8 that he would not call the legislature back into a special session to work on a pro-life bill.[146] The announcement came five days after Kansas voters rejected a pro-life amendment to their state's constitution.

With a special session off the table, pro-life supporters focused their attention on the upcoming fall elections. In the lead-up to the election, NFA partnered with Susan B. Anthony Pro-Life America, an influential national pro-life organization, to conduct research on what Nebraskans believed about abortion. Their research revealed that 58% of Nebraskans believed babies should receive legal protections when a heartbeat can be detected.[147]

"If the elections went well, we really felt like we could do a heartbeat bill," Bowling recounted.[148] Although the national press predicted the political environment would boost candidates who supported liberal abortion laws, pro-life candidates performed well in Nebraska. When the votes were counted, there were thirty-three pro-life votes, which was just enough to break a potential filibuster. "This is what we've all been waiting for," exclaimed Senator Albrecht after the election. "We are going to be able to protect babies in the spring!"[149]

---

[145] Karen Bowling (executive director, Nebraska Family Alliance), in discussion with the author, July 7, 2023.

[146] Margery A. Beck, "Nebraska Won't Hold Special Legislative Session on Abortion," AP News, August 8, 2022, https://apnews.com/article/abortion-legislature-nebraska-omaha-pete-ricketts-8e4be716151ac772c608ea2ad80e3130.

[147] Trevor K. Smith to Nebraska Right to Life, Nebraska Catholic Conference, and Nebraska Family Alliance, January 5, 2023, https://nebraskafamilyalliance.org/wp-content/uploads/2023/02/2023-Nebraska-Poll-Results-Memo.pdf?bcs-agent-scanner=1f185925-7237-f449-8fc8-8962d8236a1b.

[148] Bowling, discussion.

[149] Albrecht, discussion.

In Nebraska, the state legislature meets for ninety days in odd-numbered years. Anticipating this compressed time frame, pro-life legislators and their allies worked throughout the winter. Although some legislators, including Albrecht, wanted a bill protecting the unborn at conception, the consensus among pro-life allies was that a heartbeat bill was achievable. After drafting the bill and securing cosponsors, Senator Albrecht announced on January 11, 2023, that she would be introducing the Nebraska Heartbeat Act (LB 626).[150] In a press conference about the bill, Albrecht shared the NFA commissioned research, showing that LB 626 was supported by 58% of Nebraskans.[151] Before the bill's introduction, NFA distributed a fifty-one-page information package to legislators about the bill.[152]

In Nebraska, a bill is assigned to a committee after introduction. From committee it proceeds to general file and eight hours of debate. The next stage is select file and an additional four hours of debate. Finally, a bill receives a final reading and a final vote. At each stage, thirty-three votes are needed to advance. After passing the Health and Human Services Committee, LB 626 proceeded to general file. With thirty-three cosponsors, it moved to select file. However, as the bill was set to be debated in select file, something unexpected occurred.

Although he had appeared at the January 11 press conference and had cosponsored the bill, Sen. Merv Riepe began having doubts about

---

[150] LB 626 proposed providing legal protections for babies when a heartbeat can be detected. An example of how the national media covered Albrecht's announcement can be seen at Margery A. Beck, "New Push to Restrict Abortions to Be Introduced in Nebraska," AP News, January 11, 2023, https://apnews.com/article/abortion-politics-health-nebraska-omaha-06b7febb41715e7e0b28ae3a2b62c6ca.

[151] Smith to Nebraska Right to Life, Nebraska Catholic Conference, and Nebraska Family Alliance.

[152] Anticipating the usual attacks, NFA's materials underscored how LB 626 served women and their families. "Being pro-life means so much more than being pro-birth," Bowling explained to me. "But the narrative is that we are only pro-birth. Through our messaging, we wanted to help senators communicate how this legislation helps build strong families and communities."

the proposed legislation. Shaken by his narrow election margin, Riepe, an eighty-year-old former hospital administrator, suggested to his colleagues that they consider a twelve-week bill instead of heartbeat.[153]

"I consider myself pro-life, but I've found there are many definitions of what that means," Riepe explained.[154] "And one of the reasons I had a change of thought, is that we're a democracy, not a theocracy, and we need to act accordingly," the senator said.[155]

Riepe's about-face stunned the bill's supporters and surprised his colleagues. "Joni, I'm not going to let this bill fail," Albrecht recalled Riepe promising her less than a week before select file.[156] Riepe, who served on the Health and Human Services Committee, had advanced the bill out of committee without voicing any objections.[157]

But now Riepe seemed determined to stop the bill.

"People shouldn't have been so surprised," Riepe recounted to me. "They should have seen this was a significant amendment [Riepe's twelve-week bill]."[158] Defending his decision, Riepe argued that he waited until select file because he did not believe he could get a hearing in general file.

---

[153] Riepe drafted his amendment, officially known as AM626, for LB 626 on February 28, 2023. See Nebraska Legislature, Amendments to LB626, February 28, 2023, https://nebraskalegislature.gov/FloorDocs/108/PDF/AM/AM626.pdf?bcs-agent-scanner=822495e4-d45b-3348-938b-977f9848b464. However, Riepe did not officially file AM 626 until March 15, 2023. See "LB626—Adopt the Nebraska Heartbeat Act," Nebraska Legislature, https://nebraskalegislature.gov/bills/view_bill.php?DocumentID=50641.

[154] Merv Riepe (Sen. District 12, Nebraska Legislature), in discussion with the author, July 17, 2023.

[155] Riepe, discussion.

[156] Albrecht, discussion.

[157] When I asked him why he voted for the bill in committee and general file, Riepe explained, "I was in a tough spot. Had I voted to kill it there, I would have been villainized. I voted 'yes' for it in part, because I felt it deserved a discussion of the entire chamber."

[158] Riepe, discussion.

After voting "yes" on LB 626 in general file, Riepe anticipated a fair hearing and a vote on his amendment in select file.

"My early support and earlier votes on LB 626 may have been misread," Riepe conceded. However, when pressed on why he changed his vote, he replied, "I read my voters and the general sense was that a total ban was too restrictive in a pluralistic society."[159]

For Riepe, backlash to *Dobbs* also factored into his calculation. "I easily won my primary election. But for the general election, after the *Dobbs* decision was made, I won by 4.6%. That means I lost over 23 percentage points," explained Riepe.[160]

Despite pleas from colleagues and even the governor, Riepe held firm. When his amendment was blocked, Riepe withheld what would have been the thirty-third vote for LB 626. On April 27, Senator Riepe voted "present, not voting." The Heartbeat Act was officially dead.

"For Merv, in the end, to not vote with us, it was a gut punch to all Nebraskans," Albrecht recalled.[161] "It is still unfathomable to me that he would go with us as far as he did to only back out at the last minute," she added.[162]

Riepe's decision disappointed pro-life groups in the state. "He was there for the photo ops. He was there with the bill's other cosponsors at a rally on the steps of the capital two days before select file," Marilyn Newland,

---

[159] Riepe. In our conversation, I asked Riepe, "Just to be really clear, you ultimately made the decision you did because you felt that best represented the constituents who had elected you. Am I understanding that correctly?" He replied by noting, "My job, as I view it, is that I'm here to represent the people in my district. So, that played a part to it. But I also felt, personally, that a twelve-week was better than a twenty-week. And a twelve-week was something that both sides didn't love."

[160] Riepe, discussion.

[161] Albrecht, discussion.

[162] Albrecht, discussion.

NFA's Communications Specialist recounted.[163] "I was incredibly discouraged," explained Newland, who had stayed in Nebraska to work on LB 626 after her husband was stationed overseas. "I wondered if all our work had been wasted."[164]

Despite the setback and limited time remaining in the legislative session, committed pro-life senators decided to make a final attempt to pass a pro-life bill. Albrecht, working with the governor's office and NFA, identified LB 574 as a bill that could be friendly to an amendment. LB 574, known as the "Let Them Grow Act," was a bill aimed at protecting children from cross-sex hormones and experimental sex-change surgeries.

However, LB 574 had already proceeded to final reading. To add an amendment, the bill would need to be returned to select file. "It was extraordinarily risky to send the bill back," Sen. Kathleen Kauth, the bill's sponsor, recalled.[165] But Kauth, who holds deep pro-life convictions, knew an amendment to her bill was the best opportunity to pass pro-life protections in the current legislative session, and she agreed to add a twelve-week amendment to the bill.[166]

Notwithstanding the resolve of pro-life lawmakers, the fate of LB 574 was still far from certain. The day before final passage, Senator Albrecht needed surgery to treat breast cancer. Before surgery, Albrecht told her doctor, "No matter what happens today, I need to be at the capital tomorrow."[167]

On May 19, as final reading for LB 574 was set to proceed, another unforeseen development took place. Sen. Julie Slama, a twenty-seven-year-old conservative lawmaker who had been battling hyperemesis gravidarum

---

[163] Marilyn Newland (Communications Coordinator, Nebraska Family Alliance), in discussion with the author, July 7, 2023.

[164] Newland, discussion.

[165] Kathleen Kauth (Sen., District 31, Nebraska Legislature), in discussion with the author, July 11, 2023.

[166] "Sending LB 574 back to select file was a calculated risk," Bowling told me. "But everyone involved agreed it was worth the risk if we could protect just a few more babies in our state."

[167] Albrecht, discussion.

(a severe form of nausea) throughout her pregnancy, took a turn for the worse. Unable to keep water down for forty-eight hours, she had become severely dehydrated and was hospitalized.

Kauth, whose desk is next to Slama's, texted her colleague around 10:00 a.m., asking if she was feeling alright. "No, hospital in Omaha," came the response. "Baby first, bill second," Kauth replied.

With debate set to begin at 2:00 p.m. and a final vote scheduled for 4:00 p.m., conservatives quietly began to strategize. "Where's Julie?" some of their Democrat colleagues asked. "She's just resting," came the response. Not wanting to alert Democrats that Slama was an hour away, preparations were quietly made to bring the ailing senator back to Lincoln for the vote.

As debate started, protestors began chanting in the rotunda, their voices audible on the chamber floor. Knowing that Senator Slama was on her way, Republican senators stayed in the queue, ensuring that the entire time allotted for debate was used. Around 3:40 p.m., protestors in the balcony began shouting and throwing tampons at the lawmakers on the senate floor. The outburst prompted the Speaker to pause proceedings for the balcony to be cleared.

Unknowingly, the protestors had provided a crucial time extension. The seven minutes needed to clear the balcony provided enough time for Senator Slama to be wheeled into the chamber and find her seat. "Julie was still a few minutes out. The protestors bought us some extra time to get Julie onto the floor and in her chair," Kauth recalled.[168]

Escorted through back entrances, Slama, with vomit bag in hand, arrived in the chamber with minutes to spare. Within fifteen minutes of her arrival, the final series of votes on LB 574 was held. When the votes were tallied, LB 574 passed with thirty-three votes. The bill became law three days later with the governor's signature.

For pro-life leaders, passage of the bill capped an exhausting session. Although grateful that approximately 300 babies will be saved each year

---

[168] Kauth, discussion.

because of the law, Albrecht regrets they could not do more. "When you want protection at conception, and you've settled for heartbeat only to then have to settle again for twelve weeks . . . it wasn't a joyous occasion for me," explained Senator Albrecht. "We are still a destination state for abortions. That's why we need to do more. I'm hopeful that one day this body will do what they know is right and enact a bill that protects babies at conception."[169]

For Kauth, the experience was sobering. Like other pro-life lawmakers, Kauth was evacuated from the capitol building after the final vote. "There was so much hate directed against us for wanting to protect kids," Kauth explained.[170] "I'm grateful we saved some babies, but there is still so much we need to do to change hearts and minds," she continued.

"We witnessed a miracle that day," explained Bowling, who has worked in Nebraska politics since 2001.[171] "For me, 'Let Them Grow' is the most significant legislative victory I've seen."[172] Karen's colleague, Marilyn Newland, agreed, noting that the victory was surreal. Sitting on the front row as Governor Jim Pillen signed the bill into law, Newland reflected, "I was fourteen when the twenty-week law went into effect. I had never seen such a major pro-life victory; it was past due."[173]

## Progressive States and Abortion

In the years leading up to *Dobbs*, conservative lawmakers began more aggressively pursuing pro-life bills. Although many of these laws were voided by courts, some were not, such as Texas's heartbeat bill, which took

---

[169] Albrecht, discussion. For his part, Senator Riepe was thankful for the passage of LB 574 and the passage of a twelve-week amendment he had worked on. "Did I get everything I wanted? No, I didn't. Did I compromise? I thought I did," Riepe told me. "I was happy to move on. I was not in a mood to celebrate," Riepe explained after the vote.

[170] Kauth, discussion.

[171] Bowling, discussion.

[172] Bowling, discussion.

[173] Newland, discussion.

effect in 2021. In response to these new laws and anticipating the possibility of the Supreme Court overturning *Roe*, lawmakers in progressive states preemptively moved to liberalize their abortion laws. After *Dobbs*, many of these same states enacted further legislation to protect abortion access.

In this section, we will note how a few of the nation's most liberal states changed their abortion laws in the years before *Dobbs*. We will then look briefly at how liberal states responded to *Dobbs* with a focus on Minnesota, an example that illustrates the challenges facing pro-lifers when pro-abortion politicians control state government.

## *Progressive States before* Dobbs

In January 2019, Democrats in New York, empowered by their newly elected majority in the state Senate, passed the Reproductive Health Act, legislation that contained wide-ranging pro-abortion provisions.[174] The law allows for abortion up to twenty-four weeks of pregnancy but contains an exception clause for the mother's "health" that is intentionally not defined (some courts have interpreted "health" to refer to mental and emotional health with determination subject to the medical judgment of the abortion provider).[175] Additionally, the new law protects abortionists by moving abortion law from the state's criminal code to its health code.[176]

---

[174] Nick Niedzwiadek, "Cuomo Signs Reproductive Health Act in Front of Roe Lawyer," *Politico*, January 22, 2019, https://www.politico.com/states/new-york/albany/story/2019/01/22/cuomo-signs-reproductive-health-act-in-front-of-roe-lawyer-806169.

[175] Tom Strode, "N.Y. Abortion Bill: 'Alarming in Every Sense,'" *Baptist Press*, January 24, 2019, https://www.baptistpress.com/resource-library/news/n-y-abortion-bill-alarming-in-every-sense/.

[176] Incredibly, the New York law also removed the authority from coroners and medical examiners from investigating a death "caused by suspected criminal abortion." See New York State Assembly, Bill No S00240, 2019, https://nyassembly.gov/leg/?default_fld&leg_video&bn=S00240&term=2019&Summary=Y&Actions=Y&Committee%26nbspVotes=Y&Floor%26nbspVotes=Y&Memo=Y&Text=Y.

To celebrate passage, Gov. Andrew Cuomo ordered One World Trade Center's 408-foot spire and other landmarks to be lit pink.[177]

Also in 2019, legislators in Illinois passed the Reproductive Health Act that enshrined a "fundamental right" to abortion into state law.[178] The pro-abortion law repealed the state's Partial-Birth Abortion Act as well as provisions of a 1975 law that required spousal consent and waiting periods.[179] In unambiguous terms, the law states, "A fertilized egg, embryo, or fetus does not have independent rights under the laws of this State."[180]

In February 2021, New Mexico repealed a 1969 pro-life law.[181] Although unenforceable, the dormant law was seen as a threat after Justice Amy Coney Barrett joined the Supreme Court (the Court had not yet agreed to hear *Dobbs*).[182]

In New Jersey, lawmakers preemptively moved to codify abortion into state law. On January 13, 2022, Governor Phil Murphy signed the Freedom of Reproductive Choice Act, which states abortion is a "fundamental right

---

177 "Governor Cuomo Directs One World Trade Center and Other Landmarks to be Lit in Pink to Celebrate Signing of the Reproductive Health Act," Governor Andrew M. Cuomo, January 22, 2019, https://web.archive.org/web/20190124003845/https:/www.governor.ny.gov/news/governor-cuomo-directs-one-world-trade-center-and-other-landmarks-be-lit-pink-celebrate-signing.

178 Illinois Legislature, Reproductive Health Act, 2019, https://www.ilga.gov/legislation/ilcs/ilcs5.asp?DocName=&ActID=3987&ChapterID=0&SeqStart=&SeqEnd=&Print=True.

179 Gabriel Resto-Montero, "Illinois Affirms the "Fundamental Right" to Abortion by Passing a New Bill," *Vox*, June 1, 2019, https://www.vox.com/2019/6/1/18648506/illinois-abortion-bill-2019-fundamental-right-repeal-restrictions.

180 Illinois Legislature, Reproductive Health Act.

181 New Mexico Legislature, An Act, https://www.nmlegis.gov/Sessions/21%20Regular/final/SB0010.pdf?bcs-agent-scanner=d44cfb95-2865-ff45-8f8b-9f2e5ac42a74.

182 Susan Dunlap, "Governor Signs Bill Repealing Abortion Ban into Law: 'A Woman Has the Right to Make Decisions about Her Own Body,'" NM Political Report, February 26, 2021, https://nmpoliticalreport.com/2021/02/26/governor-signs-bill-repealing-abortion-ban-into-law-a-woman-has-the-right-to-make-decisions-about-her-own-body/.

enshrined in the State Constitution."[183] Appearing alongside the governor at the bill signing was Alexis McGill Johnson, president of Planned Parenthood Action Fund, who spoke about the need for states to pass aggressive pro-abortion laws.[184]

## *Progressive States Respond to* Dobbs

In places where pro-abortion lawmakers controlled the legislative and executive branches of government, the Supreme Court's decision in *Dobbs* provoked an immediate response. Even in states with permissive abortion laws, lawmakers moved quickly to enact protections for abortion providers and abortion seekers. In these states, a variety of new measures were passed within a year of *Dobbs*, including so-called interstate shield laws that provide legal protections for abortion providers who prescribe and mail abortion pills to women in other states. Additional new laws codified protections for chemical abortion, expanded the types of health care providers who can legally perform an abortion, and enshrined the right to abortion in state statute. In the years to come, these laws—and others like them—will be vigorously promoted in purple and red states, which is why awareness of them is crucial.

---

[183] New Jersey Legislature, Senate, Bill S49, Session 2020–2021, https://www.njleg.state.nj.us/bill-search/2020/S49. It is worth noting that the words "woman" and "women" do not appear in the New Jersey statute. The practice of omitting mentions of women in pro-abortion legislation has become more common as liberal states embrace the logic of transgenderism, which argues that transgender men (biological women who identify as men) can get pregnant. Though pro-abortion policies have historically been cast in the language of women's rights, the embrace of LGBTQ rights has forced those on the Left to adjust and sometimes erase references to women when discussing abortion. See legislation: New Jersey Legislature, Chapter 375, https://pub.njleg.state.nj.us/Bills/2020/PL21/375_.PDF.

[184] "Governor Murphy Signs Historic Legislation to Expand and Protect Reproductive Freedom in New Jersey," State of New Jersey Department of Health, January 13, 2022, https://www.nj.gov/health/news/2022/approved/20220113a.shtml.

In terms of post-*Dobbs* abortion legislation, the first state to adopt a new law was Delaware, where legislators passed House Bill 455, which increased access to abortion throughout the state.[185] A "shield" provision of the bill protects those who perform an abortion or recommend abortion services from other states' regulations and disciplinary actions. Governor John Carney signed the bill into law on June 29, 2022, only five days after *Dobbs.*[186]

Massachusetts also moved quickly to change state law after *Roe* was overturned. On July 29, 2022, Governor Charlie Baker signed legislation to protect abortion providers and abortion seekers from actions and investigations originating in other states.[187] The law notes that access to abortion is secured by the state's constitution.[188]

In September 2022, California Governor Gavin Newsom signed thirteen pro-abortion bills into law in response to the overturning of *Roe*. The laws were recommended by "California Future of Abortion Council," a group convened by Newsom in 2021. Of note, Assembly Bill 2223 prohibits investigations into fetal death after twenty weeks, even if a coroner sees evidence of foul play such as drugs in the baby's system.[189] Another

---

[185] Delaware General Assembly, House Bill 455, 151st General Assembly, 2022, https://legis.delaware.gov/BillDetail/109604. House Bill 455 was introduced on June 2, 2022. The Delaware House passed the bill on June 14. Four days after *Dobbs*, Delaware's Senate voted and passed the bill. The governor signed it into law the next day.

[186] Amy Simonson, "Delaware Governor Signs Bill Expanding Abortion Access and Provider Protection," CNN, June 29, 2022, https://www.cnn.com/2022/06/29/politics/delaware-governor-signs-abortion-access-law/index.html.

[187] Massachusetts Legislature, Bill H.5090, 192nd Legislature, https://malegislature.gov/Bills/192/H5090.

[188] Additionally, House Bill 5090 requires the state's Medicaid program to cover abortion procedures, allows contraception to be sold in vending machines, and requires public colleges and universities to create "medication abortion readiness" plans for students. See Steve Leblanc, "Massachusetts Governor Signs Bill Protecting Abortion Access," AP News, July 29, 2022, https://apnews.com/article/abortion-us-supreme-court-health-charlie-baker-massachusetts-67ae91877315527cb5f5166cf2b91d8a.

[189] California Legislature, Assembly Bill No. 2223, September 27, 2022, https://leginfo.legislature.ca.gov/faces/billTextClient.xhtml?bill_id=202120220AB2223.

bill, Assembly Bill 1242, prohibits California law enforcement from assisting or cooperating with other states' abortion-related investigations.[190] Additionally, Senate Bill 1142 creates a state-funded "abortion care services website" that connects women to abortion clinics and services.[191] Finally, Senate Bill 1375 allows nurse practitioners to perform abortions without the supervision of a physician or surgeon.[192]

Additionally, following *Dobbs*, Newsom sponsored seven billboards in conservative states, advertising how residents in those states can access abortion.[193] Notably, billboards in Mississippi and Oklahoma quoted Mark 12:31, which says, "Love your neighbor as yourself. There is no greater commandment than these."

In 2023, California legislators introduced further pro-abortion legislation, including bills seeking to launch a public information campaign against pro-life pregnancy resource centers (AB 710) and a bill that would require California's Medicaid funding to fully reimburse providers for chemical abortions up to seventy-seven days gestation, despite the FDA only approving the use of abortion pills up to seventy days gestation (AB 576).[194]

"Even before *Roe* was overturned, California was doing whatever it could to become the pro-abortion capital of the country," explained

---

[190] California Legislature, Assembly Bill No. 1242, September 27, 2022, https://leginfo.legislature.ca.gov/faces/billNavClient.xhtml?bill_id=202120220AB1242.

[191] California Legislature, Senate Bill No. 1142, September 27, 2022, https://leginfo.legislature.ca.gov/faces/billNavClient.xhtml?bill_id=202120220SB1142.

[192] California Legislature, Senate Bill No. 1375, September 27, 2022, https://leginfo.legislature.ca.gov/faces/billNavClient.xhtml?bill_id=202120220SB1375.

[193] "Newsom Launches Website and Billboards to Advertise Abortion across the Country," California Family Council, September 21, 2022, https://www.californiafamily.org/2022/09/newsom-launches-website-and-billboards-to-advertise-abortion-across-the-country/.

[194] California Legislature, AB-576 Medi-Cal: reimbursement for abortion, introduced February 8, 2023, https://leginfo.legislature.ca.gov/faces/billNavClient.xhtml?bill_id=202320240AB576; California Family Council, "AB 710 Hearing in the Assembly Health Committee," April 26, 2023, YouTube video, https://www.youtube.com/watch?v=oQ8wNmefTk0.

Sophia Lorey, who serves as the Outreach Coordinator at California Family Council.[195] "Since *Dobbs*, the legislature and governor have prioritized abortion over nearly every other issue facing the people of the state. Over a dozen new pro-abortion laws, additional executive orders, and other mandates make California the most dangerous state for the unborn, she added."[196]

In January 2023, Illinois enacted additional pro-abortion legislation designed to protect out-of-state abortion seekers from prosecution by authorities in other states.[197] The law requires insurance companies that provide pregnancy-related benefits to include "abortion care" such as abortion pills.[198]

In Hawaii, legislators passed an expansive pro-abortion bill on March 22, 2023.[199] The new law allows physician assistants to perform medical and surgical abortions during the first trimester (previously only doctors or surgeons could perform an abortion) and repeals the requirement that abortions be performed at a hospital or clinic.[200] The law also struck down

---

[195] Sophia Lorey (Outreach Coordinator, California Family Council), in discussion with the author. Lorey has testified multiple times before the California legislature on abortion-related bills. Most recently, she testified against AB 576 on June 29, 2023. To see her testimony, see https://www.youtube.com/watch?v=ElRo29Y-NLk.

[196] Lorey, discussion.

[197] Illinois General Assembly, HB4664, 102nd General Assembly, https://www.ilga.gov/legislation/BillStatus.asp?DocNum=4664&GAID=16&DocTypeID=HB&SessionID=110&GA=102.

[198] The new law states: "Regardless of whether the policy otherwise provides prescription drug benefits, abortion care coverage must include medications that are obtained through a prescription and used to terminate a pregnancy, regardless of whether there is proof of a pregnancy." See legislation: Illinois General Assembly, HB4664, https://www.ilga.gov/legislation/102/HB/PDF/10200HB4664lv.pdf?bcs-agent-scanner=88e4beb1-6bf3-7744-a47f-52e42b924860.

[199] Hawai'i State Legislature, SB1 SD2, https://www.capitol.hawaii.gov/session/archives/measure_indiv_Archives.aspx?billtype=SB&billnumber=1&year=2023.

[200] "New Hawaii Law Expands Abortion Access, Protects Providers," AP News, March 22, 2023, https://apnews.com/article/hawaii-abortion-access-expansion-protections-003082a83d189832869b8eae1c9bd6ee.

a provision that required minors to receive consent from a parent or guardian before getting an abortion. Finally, abortion providers are now shielded from abortion-related investigations conducted by other states.

Following *Dobbs*, two counties and three cities in New Mexico passed pro-life ordinances. One of them, passed in the city of Clovis, restricted the mailing of abortion pills and medical supplies used in abortion procedures.[201] In response to these ordinances, the New Mexico legislature passed and the governor signed into law a measure that overrode the local ordinances.[202] On April 5, 2023, Governor Michelle Lujan Grisham signed another bill into law aimed at protecting abortion providers from disciplinary action originating in other states.[203]

On April 27, 2023, Governor Jay Inslee signed legislation designed to protect out-of-state abortion seekers coming to Washington.[204] The law blocks the state's courts from cooperating with other states investigating unlawful abortions.

In May 2023, the Maryland legislature passed a series of pro-abortion bills, including measures that require colleges and universities to "develop and implement a reproductive health services plan." The new interstate shield law prevents judges in other states from requiring testimony in cases that involve a legally obtained abortion in Maryland and prohibits the disclosure of medical information to ensure abortion procedures remain

---

[201] Gabriel Chavez, "City of Clovis Introduces Ordinance to Ban Abortions," KRQE News, October 20, 2022, https://www.krqe.com/news/new-mexico/city-of-clovis-introduces-ordinance-to-ban-abortions/.

[202] Morgan Lee, "New Mexico Gov. Signs Bill Overriding Local Abortion Bans," AP News, March 16, 2023, https://apnews.com/article/abortion-transgender-rights-new-mexico-b0f945afe9cc2d8e4f90bb956e62694a.

[203] Morgan Lee, "New Mexico Governor Signs Bill to Shield Abortion Providers," AP News, April 5, 2023, https://apnews.com/article/abortion-transgender-rights-new-mexico-195c27ab1a60a8d7c07a71f157c07384.

[204] Washington Legislature, House Bill 1469, 68th Legislature, 2023, https://lawfilesext.leg.wa.gov/biennium/2023-24/Pdf/Bills/Session%20Laws/House/1469-S.SL.pdf?bcs-agent-scanner=034dd0de-f6c0-2149-bc16-c6660a71959f.

confidential.[205] Maryland leaders also approved a constitutional referendum that, if passed by voters in 2024, will enshrine a "right to reproductive freedom" into the state's constitution.[206]

Nevada passed a similar shield law in May 2023 when Governor Joe Lombardo signed Senate Bill 131 into law. The legislation protects abortionists in the state as well as abortion seekers from out-of-state. The law prohibits the governor from "issuing an arrest warrant" for a person charged in another state with a criminal violation related to "certain reproductive health care services."[207]

On May 18, 2023, Rhode Island Governor Daniel McKee signed legislation that provides insurance coverage for abortion to those on Medicaid as well as state employees.[208] Known as the "Equality in Abortion Coverage Act," the law applies to the one-quarter of Rhode Islanders covered by Medicaid.

In Oregon, lawmakers faced off over abortion throughout the spring and summer months of 2023. Democrats, who maintained majorities in the state legislature, introduced expansive pro-abortion bills that would have allowed, among other provisions, minor children of any age to procure an abortion without parental consent. In response to this bill and another

---

[205] General Assembly of Maryland, Senate, Senate Bill 786, Introduced February 6, 2023, https://mgaleg.maryland.gov/2023RS/bills/sb/sb0786T.pdf?bcs-agent-scanner=699d4210-5697-9845-a1c0-f07ad2044221; General Assembly of Maryland, Senate, Senate Bill 859, Introduced February 6, 2023, https://mgaleg.maryland.gov/2023RS/bills/sb/sb0859T.pdf?bcs-agent-scanner=acbd66d7-c780-1b49-8a6f-5f10c968f714; General Assembly of Maryland, Senate, Senate Bill 341, 2023, 1, https://mgaleg.maryland.gov/2023RS/bills/sb/sb0341E.pdf?bcs-agent-scanner=675c7fa9-9621-824f-bd8a-67e6bceac90c.

[206] General Assembly of Maryland, Senate, Senate Bill 798, Introduced February 6, 2023, 1, https://mgaleg.maryland.gov/2023RS/bills/sb/sb0798T.pdf?bcs-agent-scanner=31c3e3c9-8a6e-e445-80f8-b7e6649f6aaf.

[207] Nevada Legislature, Senate, SB131, 82nd Session, Introduced February 9, 2023, https://www.leg.state.nv.us/App/NELIS/REL/82nd2023/Bill/9800/Overview.

[208] "Equality in Abortion Coverage Act Enacted," press release, State of Rhode Island General Assembly, May 18, 2023, https://www.rilegislature.gov/pressrelease/_layouts/15/ril.pressrelease.inputform/DisplayForm.aspx?List=c8baae31-3c10-431c-8dcd-9dbbe21ce3e9&ID=373592.

one dealing with gender transition surgery, Republican lawmakers staged a six-week legislative walkout, grinding deliberations to a halt. After weeks of negotiations, progressive lawmakers agreed to keep parental consent rules in place for children under the age of fifteen who seek an abortion.[209] Democrats also dropped a provision that would have expanded abortion access on university campuses.[210] On July 13, 2023, Governor Tina Kotek signed House Bill 2002 into law.[211]

Finally, on February 21, 2023, the governors of twenty-one states announced the launch of the "Reproductive Freedom Alliance," a coalition of governors committed to working together to expand access to abortion.[212] Collectively, governors in the alliance represent 170 million Americans. According to the alliance, senior-level staff from governors' offices began meeting frequently in 2023 to "share best practices and respond quickly to the changing legal landscape."[213] In the first year, members of the coalition shared strategies for advancing legislative and executive action to protect

---

[209] Lauren Dake, "Oregon Reproductive Rights and Gender-Affirming Care Bill Heads to Governor's Desk," OPB News, June 21, 2023, https://www.opb.org/article/2023/06/21/oregon-legislature-republican-senate-walkout-reproductive-rights-bill-governor-tina-kotek-desk/.

[210] Like other laws passed around the country in 2023, the final version of the Oregon law retained provisions to protect abortionists from out-of-state investigations. See Oregon Legislative Assembly, House, House Bill 2002, 2003, https://olis.oregonlegislature.gov/liz/2023R1/Downloads/MeasureDocument/HB2002/Enrolled.

[211] "Kotek Signs Controversial Abortion, Gender Care, Ghost Gun Bills into Law," KPTV Fox 12 Oregon, July 13, 2023, https://www.kptv.com/2023/07/13/kotek-signs-controversial-abortion-ghost-gun-bills-into-law/.

[212] "Twenty-One States Announce Historic Governor-Led Reproductive Freedom Alliance," press release, Office of Governor Gavin Newsom, February 21, 2023, https://www.gov.ca.gov/2023/02/21/twenty-states-announce-historic-governor-led-reproductive-freedom-alliance/.

[213] "ICYMI: Governors Hold Inaugural Convening of the Reproductive Freedom Alliance, Vow to Continue to Strengthen and Expand Abortion Care," press release, Office of Governor Gavin Newsom, July 24, 2023, https://www.gov.ca.gov/2023/07/24/icymi-governors-hold-inaugural-convening-of-the-reproductive-freedom-alliance-vow-to-continue-to-strengthen-and-expand-abortion-care/.

abortion.[214] On July 2, 2023, governors in the alliance met in Los Angeles to reaffirm their commitment to work together to "build a firewall for reproductive freedom."[215] As part of the meeting, governors were briefed by abortion providers.

## *Minnesota*

Following the 2022 midterm elections, Democrats in Minnesota took control of the state legislature for the first time in eight years.[216] Although the state Supreme Court had decided in 1995 that abortion was protected by the state's constitution, access to abortion was not without guardrails, and the legislature had previously passed bipartisan laws to regulate the abortion industry. However, shortly after taking power, pro-abortion lawmakers in Minnesota rewrote the state's abortion laws, ensuring that the Land of 10,000 Lakes was an abortion destination by the end of the legislative session.

When the legislature convened on January 3, 2023, the first bill filed in both chambers was a pro-abortion bill known as the Protect Reproduction Options Act (referred to as the "PRO Act").[217] In short, the PRO Act enshrined a "fundamental right" to abortion into law. Although Republicans

---

[214] When it was announced on February 21, twenty states were part of the alliance, including California, Colorado, Connecticut, Delaware, Hawaii, Illinois, Maine, Maryland, Massachusetts, Michigan, Minnesota, New Jersey, New Mexico, New York, North Carolina, Oregon, Pennsylvania, Rhode Island, Washington, and Wisconsin. Arizona, under Governor Katie Hobbs, joined the alliance on February 23. On May 2, 2023, Guam joined the alliance. For Guam's announcement, see "Guam Joins Reproductive Freedom Alliance," press release, Office of the Governor, May 2, 2023, https://governor.guam.gov/press_release/guam-joins-reproductive-freedom-alliance/.

[215] "ICYMI."

[216] In Minnesota, the affiliate of the national Democratic Party is the Minnesota Democratic–Farmer–Labor Party (DFL).

[217] Minnesota Legislature, HF 1, 93rd Legislature, 2023, https://www.revisor.mn.gov/bills/text.php?number=HF1&type=bill&version=0&session=ls93&session_year=2023&session_number=0.

introduced amendments to limit its scope, the amendments were rejected, and the legislation was signed into law by Governor Tim Walz on January 31, 2023.[218]

"When Democrats took control, they wasted no time enshrining unfettered access to abortion into law," explained Rebecca Delahunt, director of public policy at Minnesota Family Policy Council. "It was unapologetically their number one priority."[219]

Although the PRO Act guaranteed access to abortion, activists in the state wanted to go further. To this end, pro-abortion lawmakers introduced the Reproductive Freedom Codification Act (HF91/SF70), legislation that would repeal nearly every state health and safety protection pertaining to abortion. Specifically, the legislation lifted prohibitions on taxpayer funded abortions, nullified parental notification requirements for minors seeking an abortion, removed provisions that required fetal remains to be treated with dignity, defunded pro-life pregnancy resource centers, and removed abortion-related reporting requirements.

Additionally, the legislation sought to amend the state's Born-Alive Infants Protection Act by removing language that mandated lifesaving care for infants who survive an abortion. Under the new language, references to lifesaving respiratory care were replaced by the undefined term

---

[218] Steve Karnowski, "Minnesota Governor Signs Broad Abortion Rights Bill into Law," AP News, January 31, 2023, https://apnews.com/article/abortion-politics-minnesota-state-government-timothy-walz-11c3b1d5269c929e442b979ff1bac73b. The rejected amendments include prohibiting abortion based on sex, prohibiting abortion based on a Down syndrome diagnosis, prohibiting abortion at thirty-six weeks, prohibiting partial-birth abortion, prohibiting abortion when a woman is in active labor, and requiring licensure of abortion facilities. See Alpha News (@AlphaNewsMN), "Here's a running list of every amendment that has been rejected by Democrats in the Minnesota Senate tonight:" Twitter, January 28, 2023, 12:04 a.m., https://twitter.com/AlphaNewsMN/status/1619214690705616897.

[219] Rebecca Delahunt (acting director of public policy, Minnesota Family Council), in discussion with the author, August 3, 2023.

"care," a change opponents claimed would undermine the original intent of the legislation.

Renee Carlson, general counsel for True North Legal, laid out the consequences of the Reproductive Freedom Codification Act. Testifying before the Committee on Health and Human Services, Carlson explained, "This means cattle and reptiles will have more legal protections in Minnesota than Minnesota's vulnerable preborn children. Legal penalties for animal cruelty in Minnesota range from misdemeanor up to a felony while there is no criminal penalty for leaving a preborn child to die on a cold metal table."[220]

As Minnesotans learned about the proposed legislation, pro-life advocates across the state were galvanized. On February 28, 2023, hundreds of pro-life supporters packed inside the state capitol for a "United for Life" rally. Carlson, who emceed the rally, explained the stakes of the pending legislation. "We have our work cut out for us," Carlson acknowledged. "[But] life is a human right, and we are right to implore our legislators to protect it," she encouraged.[221]

Not surprisingly, the scope of the legislation troubled even some progressive lawmakers. Likely due to the hesitancy of these lawmakers, neither

---

[220] Minnesota Senate Media Services, "Committee on Health and Human Services—01/18/23," January 18, 2023, YouTube video, https://www.youtube.com/watch?v=YnvEpuCs6Ms&t=2386s. Carlson testified against SF70 before the Senate's Committee on Health and Human Services on January 18, 2023. On February 3, 2023, the Committee on Judiciary and Public Safety held a hearing on the same bill. Although she had followed the regular protocol, Judiciary chairman Ron Latz claimed that Carlson could not testify because the testimonial slots had been filled. When Ranking Member Warren Limmer appealed, Latz allowed Carlson to proceed with her testimony. The rare, public exchange between lawmakers about whether Carlson could testify underscored the tension surrounding the bill. See Minnesota Senate Media Services, "Committee on Judiciary and Public Safety—PART 2—02/03/23," February 3, 2023, YouTube video, https://www.youtube.com/watch?v=UWVou26RKmU&t=6422s.

[221] Minnesota Family Council, "United for Life 2023," March 1, 2023, YouTube video, https://www.youtube.com/watch?v=ZBAQZpccySg.

the House nor Senate ended up taking a straight up or down vote on the Reproductive Freedom Codification Act. However, party leaders indicated they would merge provisions of the pro-abortion bill into the Democrats' nearly 900-page omnibus health bill, SF2995.[222]

The details of the omnibus bill remained under wraps for two months between April 1 and May 21. At some point, many of the pro-abortion provisions in HF91/SF70 were added to the bill, including the amended version of the Born-Alive Infants Protection Act. On May 21, at 11:54 p.m., the omnibus, with its pro-abortion provisions, was quietly published online, hours before a mandatory vote the next day.

Although legislators were given only a few hours to read it, the legislature narrowly passed the omnibus bill on May 22.[223] Several pro-abortion provisions were included in the final version of the bill, such as a measure that weakened the Born-Alive Infants Protection Act and another that repealed significant portions of the state's abortion reporting requirements. Additionally, the bill changed the requirements of the Positive Alternatives Grant Program—a program designed to encourage and support women who carry their pregnancy to term—by mandating providers refer for abortion, a decision that forced pregnancy resource centers to withdraw from the program.

"Democrats in the Minnesota legislature gave our state the most extreme abortion laws in the U.S. without putting any guardrails in place to protect the health and safety of women, girls, and babies," recounted Rep. Peggy Scott, who led the ultimately unsuccessful effort to moderate some of the strong pro-abortion provisions.[224] "Minnesota's abortion

---

[222] Minnesota Legislature, Senate, S.F. No. 2995, 93rd Session, Introduced March 20, 2023, https://www.revisor.mn.gov/bills/text.php?number=SF2995&version=4&session=ls93&session_year=2023&session_number=0&format=pdf.

[223] Journal of the Senate, State of Minnesota, May 22, 2023, https://www.senate.mn/journals/2023-2024/20230522077.pdf.

[224] Peggy Scott (Rep., District 31B, Minnesota Legislature), in discussion with the author, August 1, 2023. In my correspondence with her, Representative Smith

policies are now on par with tyrannical regimes like China and North Korea," she added.[225]

"It's a reminder of how important elections are," Delahunt explained at the conclusion of the 2023 legislative session. "Because of one election, Minnesota has become one of the most extreme abortion regimes in the country and is being called an 'abortion destination,'" she reflected.[226]

Significantly, Democrats controlled the Senate majority by one seat—a seat that had been decided by 186 votes—throughout the legislative session. Underscoring the adage about elections having consequences, Minnesota proved in 2023 just how rapidly, absent federal pro-life protections, pro-abortion lawmakers can transform the abortion laws of an entire state.

## Federal Response to *Dobbs*

At the federal level, Democrats in the House of Representatives reacted to *Dobbs* by scheduling another vote on the Women's Health Protection Act. Although the bill had previously passed the House in September 2021 (and subsequently failed to advance in the U.S. Senate), House Democrats passed the bill again on July 15, 2022.[227] If enacted into law, the Women's Health Protection Act would override nearly every state-level pro-life law in the country.[228] Additionally, the bill would weaken conscience protections

---

reiterated that despite the most pro-abortion legislative session in state history, she remains hopeful. "Despite the Democrats' extreme, activist agenda, the pro-life movement in Minnesota will continue standing up for commonsense guardrails to protect women, girls, and babies."

[225] Scott, discussion.

[226] Delahunt, discussion.

[227] U.S. Congress, House, Women's Health Protection Act of 2022, 117th Congress, 2021, https://www.congress.gov/bill/117th-congress/house-bill/8296. The Senate vote on the Women's Health Protection Act was on February 28, 2022. The measure failed 46–48. Joe Manchin was the only Democrat to vote against the bill.

[228] David Closson, "Unconscionable: New Bill Proves Democrats Are Okay with Abortion up until Birth," Family Research Council, September 28, 2021,

for medical professionals, jeopardize prohibitions on taxpayer funding for abortion, and enshrine late-term abortion into law.

The post-*Dobbs* abortion votes in Congress underscore the challenge of passing any abortion-related federal legislation. Although Democrats controlled both the Senate and House in the 117th Congress (January 3, 2021–January 3, 2023), lawmakers were unable to pass pro-abortion legislation due to the 60-vote threshold needed in the Senate to break the legislative filibuster. Likewise, given divided control of the legislative branch between Republicans and Democrats during the 118th Congress (January 3, 2023–January 3, 2025), legislators have been unable to pass meaningful pro-life protections.

Following the 2022 midterm elections, Republicans retook the majority in the House of Representatives. After members were officially sworn in on January 9, 2023, Republicans wasted little time in voting on pro-life legislation. On January 11, Republicans used their new majority to pass the Born-Alive Abortion Survivors Protection Act, legislation requiring medical care for babies who survive botched abortions.[229] They also passed a resolution condemning violence against pro-life facilities.[230] The votes were significant because they represented the first time the House had voted to provide legal protections for unborn children since 2018.[231]

The debate surrounding these pro-life measures once again illustrated the divide between the two political parties. Tragically, but not

---

https://www.frc.org/blog/2021/09/unconscionable-democrats-are-okay-killing-babies-day-birth.

[229] U.S. Congress, House, Judiciary Committee, Born-Alive Abortion Survivors Protection Act, 118th Congress, Introduced January 9, 2023, https://www.congress.gov/bill/118th-congress/house-bill/26.

[230] U.S. Congress, Judiciary Committee, H.Con.Res.3, 118th Congress, Introduced January 9, 2023, https://www.congress.gov/bill/118th-congress/house-concurrent-resolution/3.

[231] During her second tenure as Speaker of the House (January 3, 2019–January 3, 2023), Nancy Pelosi did not allow any pro-life bills to come to the House floor for a vote.

surprisingly, both measures passed on nearly partisan lines. Representative Henry Cuellar (D-TX) was the lone Democrat to vote for Born-Alive (Representative Vicente Gonzalez [D-TX] voted "present"), and only three Democrats (representatives Vicente Gonzalez, Chrissy Houlahan, and Marie Gluesenkamp Perez) voted in favor of the resolution condemning attacks against pro-life organizations and churches.[232] Republicans unanimously supported both.

The ever-widening chasm between the two parties on abortion presents major challenges to the pro-life movement. The reality is that the Democratic Party has become beholden to the abortion lobby to the degree that they refuse to publicly oppose violence directed at pregnancy resource centers or cast a vote for a bill that would provide legal protection for babies who survive botched abortions. Significantly, Born-Alive is not even about abortion. Representative Jim Jordan (R-OH) made this point repeatedly during debate on the bill, noting that although unborn children are "precious" and "sacred," "that's not what this legislation is about."[233] Jordan went on to explain, "This legislation is about those kids who are born alive . . . what should be undisputed is the care of a child who is born alive after an attempted abortion."[234]

Despite the clear scope of the legislative proposal, pro-abortion lawmakers spread lies and misinformation about the bill as it was debated on the House floor. One representative, Hillary Scholten (D-MI), went so far as to offer a biblical defense of abortion as she spoke against Born-Alive. Although it is not unusual for politicians to advance moral and even theological arguments when discussing of legislation, Representative Scholten

---

[232] See "Final Vote Results for Roll Call 29," House, January 11, 2023, https://clerk.house.gov/evs/2023/roll029.xml; "Roll Call 30," United States House of Representatives, January 11, 2023, https://clerk.house.gov/Votes/202330.

[233] Prolifeinformation, "Chairman Jordan Opening Statement on Protections for Born Alive Survivors," January 11, 2023, YouTube video, https://www.youtube.com/watch?v=ezF_Wpd0cxE.

[234] Prolifeinformation, "Chairman Jordan Opening."

outpaced even Senator Warnock when she offered a tortured theological argument in support of abortion. "As a pro-choice Christian who chose life," Scholten began, "this issue is personal to me." She went on to quote Scripture, noting, "When I read the Scripture, I turn to passages, and I'm guided by passages like Jeremiah 1:5 which states, 'I knew you before I formed you and I placed you in your mother's womb.'"[235] Scholten then argued that the reference to the "mother's womb" rather than the "government's womb" implied that the state should not regulate abortion.[236]

As we saw in chapter 2, Scholten's exegesis is off the mark. But it is nevertheless telling that pro-abortion lawmakers are publicly offering theological arguments in favor of abortion, even as they debate bills that are not even about abortion.

## 2024 Election

On April 25, 2023, President Joe Biden officially announced his campaign for reelection. Notably, abortion was featured prominently in his first official reelection video.[237] One of the video's first images—a woman standing outside the Supreme Court building holding a sign that says "Abortion is healthcare"—made it clear that the president intended to campaign on the issue.

---

[235] Greg Price (@greg_price11), "Rep. Hillary Scholten (D-MI): "As a pro-choice Christian who chose life, this issue is personal to me. . . . When I read scripture, I turn to Jeremiah 1:5 which states 'I knew you before I formed you and placed you in your mother's womb.' It doesn't say the government's womb," Twitter, January 11, 2023, 1:51 p.m., https://twitter.com/greg_price11/status/1613262392841871366.

[236] Greg Price (@greg_price11), "Rep. Hillary Scholten (D-MI)."

[237] Joe Biden (@JoeBiden), "Every generation has a moment where they have had to stand up for democracy. To stand up for their fundamental freedoms. I believe this is ours. That's why I'm running for reelection as President of the United States. Join us. Let's finish the job. JoeBiden.com," Twitter, April 25, 2023, 5:00 a.m., https://twitter.com/JoeBiden/status/1650801827728986112.

President Biden's support for abortion is well-documented.[238] Before his presidency, Biden voted on dozens of abortion-related bills as a U.S. senator. Although he started his political career as a centrist on the issue, Biden, like his party, shifted dramatically in a pro-abortion direction. For example, although Biden supported the Hyde Amendment throughout the '80s and '90s, and even voted in favor of a prohibition on partial-birth abortion from 1995 to 1999, as a presidential candidate in 2020, Biden endorsed the repeal of the Hyde Amendment.

Although President Biden's significant abortion-related decisions were reviewed in chapter 4, a few additional actions deserve mention. For example, two days after taking office in January 2021, President Biden observed the 48th anniversary of *Roe* by describing the decision as a "foundational precedent" to which all judicial nominees should commit.[239] Additionally, in 2021, the U.S. Justice Department filed suit against Texas over the state's Heartbeat Act, a pro-life law the courts had allowed to go into effect.[240] Also in 2021, the White House issued a statement supporting the Women's Health Protection Act.[241]

---

[238] David Closson, "The 2020 Election: A Clear Distinction on Abortion," *Public Discourse*, September 20, 2020, https://www.thepublicdiscourse.com/2020/09/71555/.

[239] "Statement from President Biden and Vice President Harris on the 48th Anniversary of Roe v. Wade," The White House, January 22, 2021, https://www.whitehouse.gov/briefing-room/statements-releases/2021/01/22/statement-from-president-biden-and-vice-president-harris-on-the-48th-anniversary-of-roe-v-wade/.

[240] See "Tracking the Biden Administration on Life, Family, and Religious Freedom," FRC Action, accessed May 17, 2024, https://www.frcaction.org/bidenactions; Ed Whelan, "DOJ Lawsuit against Texas Heartbeat Act—A Quick Overview," *National Review*, September 13, 2021, https://www.nationalreview.com/bench-memos/doj-lawsuit-against-texas-heartbeat-act/.

[241] Executive Office of the President, Office of Management and Budget, "Statement of Administration Policy," September 20, 2021, https://www.whitehouse.gov/wp-content/uploads/2021/09/SAP-HR-3755.pdf?bcs-agent-scanner=0503e12c-b3c2-204c-a124-b030f4e98aba.

Following the leak of the U.S. Supreme Court's decision in *Dobbs v. Jackson Women's Health Organization*, President Biden gave a speech supporting abortion.[242]A few days after the *Dobbs* ruling, the president called for an exception to the Senate filibuster rule in order to pass a law codifying a federal right to abortion.[243] In July 2022, the president issued an executive order that contained directives to convene volunteer lawyers to sue against pro-life legislation and an interagency task force to promote abortion.[244]

In addition to official administrative policy, President Biden wielded the bully pulpit of the presidency to champion abortion. Following the *Dobbs* decision, the president tweeted: "It's a sad day for the country. Nearly 50 years ago, Roe vs. Wade was decided. Today, the Supreme Court of the United States expressly took away a constitutional right from the American people. Personal freedoms are on the ballot this fall."[245] The president tweeted repeatedly in support of abortion; five weeks after *Dobbs*, he publicly celebrated the defeat of a pro-life constitutional amendment in Kansas.[246]

---

[242] "Statement by President Joe Biden," press release, The White House, May 3, 2022, https://www.whitehouse.gov/briefing-room/statements-releases/2022/05/03/statement-by-president-joe-biden-4/.

[243] "Remarks by President Biden in Press Conference," The White House, June 30, 2022, https://www.whitehouse.gov/briefing-room/speeches-remarks/2022/06/30/remarks-by-president-biden-in-press-conference-madrid-spain/.

[244] "Protecting Access to Reproductive Healthcare Services," Federal Register 87, no. 2022-151138: (July 8, 2022), https://www.federalregister.gov/documents/2022/07/13/2022-15138/protecting-access-to-reproductive-healthcare-services.

[245] Joe Biden (@JoeBiden), "It's a sad day for the country. Nearly 50 years ago, Roe vs. Wade was decided. Today, the Supreme Court of the United States expressly took away a constitutional right from the American people. Personal freedoms are on the ballot this fall," Twitter, June 24, 2022, 5:55 p.m., https://twitter.com/JoeBiden/status/1540468564402094080?s=20.

[246] Joe Biden (@JoeBiden), "Voters in Kansas rejected extreme efforts to amend the state constitution to take away a woman's right to choose. This vote makes clear what we know: The majority of Americans agree that women should have access to abortion and the right to make their own health care decisions," Twitter, August 4, 2022, 4:22 p.m., https://twitter.com/JoeBiden/status/1555303061186379776?s=20.

In the lead-up to the 2022 midterm elections, Biden repeatedly emphasized his commitment to abortion, promising, "If you give me two more Democratic senators, and Democrats keep the House, I promise you we will codify Roe v. Wade. We will once again make Roe the law of the land."[247] President Biden promised repeatedly that codifying *Roe* would be his first priority in the new Congress if Democrats retained the House and expanded their Senate majority.[248]

After the new, divided Congress took office in 2023, the president touted his support for abortion, issuing a strong denouncement of a federal judge's ruling that mifepristone (also known as the abortion pill) had been illegally approved by the FDA in 2000.[249] On April 26, 2023, lawyers for

[247] Joe Biden (@JoeBiden), "If you give me two more Democratic senators, and Democrats keep the House, I promise you we will codify Roe v. Wade. We will once again make Roe the law of the land. We will once again protect a woman's right to choose," Twitter, September 23, 2022, 12:18 p.m., https://twitter.com/JoeBiden/status/1573361187491921920?s=20.

[248] Joe Biden (@JoeBiden), "We must elect more Democrats to the Senate and keep control of the House. If we do that, here's the promise I make to you and the American people: The first bill I will send to Congress will be to codify Roe v. Wade. And when Congress passes it, I will sign it in January," Twitter, October 18, 2022, 12:07 p.m., https://twitter.com/JoeBiden/status/1582418009540292620?s=20; Joe Biden (@JoeBiden), "If we elect two more Democratic senators and keep control of the House, here is my promise to the American people: The first bill I will send to Congress will be to codify Roe v. Wade. When passed, I will sign it in January—50 years after Roe was decided the law of the land," Twitter, October 24, 2022, 9:45 a.m., https://twitter.com/JoeBiden/status/1584556593978408964?s=20; Joe Biden (@JoeBiden), "If we elect more Democrats to the Senate and keep the House, here is the promise I make to you and the American people: The first bill that I will send to Congress will be to codify Roe v. Wade," Twitter, October 29, 2022, 6:18 p.m., https://twitter.com/JoeBiden/status/1586497656251105282?s=20; Joe Biden (@JoeBiden), "Republicans in Congress have already introduced legislation to ban the right to choose nationwide, but if we elect more Senate Democrats and keep control of the House, we will codify Roe v. Wade as the law of the land," Twitter, November 6, 2022, 8:30 p.m., https://twitter.com/JoeBiden/status/1589445031307485186?s=20.

[249] President Biden (@POTUS), "Today, a federal district judge in Texas ruled that a prescription medication available for over 22 years, approved by

the Biden administration defended the approval of mifepristone in a court filing at the U.S. Court of Appeals for the Fifth Circuit.[250] On March 26, 2024, the government's lawyers, led by Solicitor General Elizabeth Prelogar, argued that restricting access to abortion drugs would "inflict grave harm on women across the nation."[251]

Finally, as the 2024 campaign narrowed between former President Trump and President Biden, the incumbent's campaign repeatedly highlighted the president's support for abortion. On January 23, 2024, President Biden held his first campaign rally of the year underneath a massive sign that read "Restore Roe." At the rally, the president described the *Dobbs* decision as "a nightmare" and called abortion a "fundamental right."[252]

---

the FDA, and used safely by millions of women should no longer be approved in the U.S. Here's why this matters. And how my Administration is going to fight it," Twitter, April 7, 2023, 10:11 p.m., https://twitter.com/POTUS/status/1644538493740171265?s=20; Joe Biden (@JoeBiden), "Let's be clear: Vice President Harris and I will continue to lead the fight to protect a woman's right to an abortion, and to make her own decisions about her own health. That is our commitment," Twitter, April 8, 2023, 12:08 p.m., https://twitter.com/JoeBiden/status/1644748942926643200?s=20.

[250] John Fritze, "Biden Officials Defend Mifepristone Approval as Abortion Pill Fight Returns to Appeals Court," *USA Today*, April 26, 2023, https://www.usatoday.com/story/news/politics/2023/04/26/abortion-pill-biden-mifepristone-fifth-circuit-appeals-court/11743893002/. On August 16, 2023, a unanimous panel for the U.S. Court of Appeals for the Fifth Circuit upheld significant portions of a district court's decision, finding that the FDA's changes to chemical abortion protocols in 2016 and 2021 were illegal. For more on this decision and chemical abortion, see chapter 6 in this book.

[251] Transcript of Oral Arguments at page 4, *FDA v. Alliance Hippocratic Medicine*, March 26, 2024, https://www.supremecourt.gov/oral_arguments/argument_transcripts/2023/22-235_q8l1.pdf?bcs-agent-scanner=b0c424fe-16a1-3e4c-8fdb-afcc97904a14https://www.supremecourt.gov/oral_arguments/argument_transcripts/2023/22-235_q8l1.pdf?bcs-agent-scanner=b0c424fe-16a1-3e4c-8fdb-afcc97904a14.

[252] "Remarks by President Biden at a Campaign Event | Manassas, VA," The White House, January 24, 2024, https://www.whitehouse.gov/briefing-room/speeches-remarks/2024/01/24/remarks-by-president-biden-at-a-campaign-event-manassas-va/.

For her part, Vice President Kamala Harris kicked off a national "Fight for Reproductive Freedoms" tour in January 2024, that included a visit to a Planned Parenthood clinic on March 14. Harris became the first sitting president or vice president to tour an abortion clinic. After touring the facility, Harris spoke to reporters and argued that restricting abortion is "just plain old immoral." She went on to argue that no one needed "to abandon their faith or deeply held beliefs" to support abortion.[253] Other stops on the vice president's national abortion tour included appearances in important swing states including Arizona, Georgia, Michigan, Minnesota, and Wisconsin.

Although more could be said, suffice it to say that the Biden-Harris administration has secured its place as the most energetic and forceful defender of abortion in the nation's history. Through executive orders, statements of administrative policy, personnel appointments, judicial appointments, and campaign rhetoric, President Biden has made it clear that expanding access to abortion is among his top priorities.[254]

## Conclusion

As I write this chapter, the 2024 presidential election is in full swing. Although there will undoubtedly be twists and turns leading up to November, one thing is sure: abortion will feature prominently in the campaign. In fact, regardless of the outcome of the 2024 campaign, abortion will remain a

[253] "Remarks by Vice President Harris and Doctor Sarah Traxler During the Nationwide 'Fight for Reproductive Freedoms' Tour | St. Paul, MN," The White House, March 14, 2024, https://www.whitehouse.gov/briefing-room/statements-releases/2024/03/14/remarks-by-vice-president-harris-and-doctor-sarah-traxler-during-the-nationwide-fight-for-reproductive-freedoms-tour-st-paul-mn/.

[254] "2022 Joseph R. Biden, Jr. Executive Orders," Federal Registrar, https://www.federalregister.gov/presidential-documents/executive-orders/joe-biden/2022; "Statements of Administration Policy," The White House, https://www.whitehouse.gov/omb/statements-of-administration-policy/; "Biden Personnel," FRC Action, https://www.frcaction.org/biden-personnel, all accessed July 16, 2024

perennial issue in American public life. Thus, pro-lifers, and especially pro-life Christians, must commit to thinking carefully about the issue.

In the aftermath of *Dobbs*, the pro-life movement faces an assortment of challenges—some old, some new. To engage effectively in a post-*Roe* world, pro-life Christians need to navigate a rapidly changing cultural, legal, and political landscape. In our final chapter, we will take a realistic assessment of the current pro-life movement, consider present obstacles to establishing a culture of life, and consult some of the movement's most influential leaders.

# 6

# The Next Chapter in the Pro-Life Movement: Ongoing Challenges in the Fight for Life

Eighteen years old and unexpectedly pregnant, Becky Currie was afraid and unsure of what to do next. A freshman in college, she had been raised in a Southern Baptist home and was convinced abortion was wrong. But the year was 1975, and Becky knew she could legally obtain an abortion and quietly end the ordeal. She was in a difficult position to raise a child, and family members encouraged her to consider abortion. But the more Becky thought about it, the more resolute she became. "I just knew I couldn't get an abortion," Becky explained.[1] So, Becky carried her pregnancy to term and gave birth to a little girl in 1976.

With her parents' help, Becky finished nursing school and went to work at a local hospital. She soon transferred to the Labor and Delivery unit,

[1] The following quotations are from Rep. Becky Currie (R-MS), interview with the author, July 28, 2023.

which needed additional help. Becky loved the work. Every time she delivered a baby, she would get a knot in her throat and quietly thank God that she had carried her own baby to term.

In 1983, Becky cared for a patient with a rare condition known as an incompetent cervix, a medical condition where the muscles in a woman's cervix are weak and sometimes open early in pregnancy without any symptoms of labor. In the early 1980s, there was little doctors could do to help women with this condition. The patient, who had previously lost multiple babies, was fifteen weeks pregnant. Tragically, shortly after she was admitted, the woman delivered a fifteen-week-old baby girl. Becky's job was to put the baby's body in a plastic container to send to the lab. However, as Becky took the baby into another room, she noticed the baby's heart was beating. Knowing there was nothing she could do to save her, Becky stayed with the baby. She talked to her and even sang "Jesus Loves Me" to the dying infant. Becky stayed until the baby's heart stopped beating, doing everything she could to keep her comfortable. "I will never forget her," Becky thought to herself.

After decades of practicing nursing, Becky decided to get involved in politics. "I always wanted to run for office but never thought I was good enough," Becky explained. But in 2007, with the help of gifted friends, Becky ran a successful campaign and won a seat in the Mississippi legislature.

After arriving in the legislature, Becky went to work on pro-life legislation. "When I got to the legislature, that baby was always on my mind. I wanted to do whatever I could to pass legislation to protect babies like the sweet girl whose life had intersected with mine so many years before." In 2016, Becky sponsored a nineteen-week protection bill that the governor signed into law. Citing *Roe*, the courts declared it unconstitutional. In 2017, Becky worked on another bill, this time a fifteen-week bill. Known as the Gestational Age Act, the legislation provided protections for babies at fifteen weeks' gestation and offered a direct challenge to *Roe*'s prohibition on all pre-viability restrictions on abortion.

"I know it may sound crazy, but I knew there was something special about this bill. It was a bill that I felt God had touched," Becky explained. At fifteen weeks' gestation, research shows that babies can feel pain, suck their thumb, and taste the food their mother eats. "It was a humane, commonsense bill," Becky argued. Throughout the legislative process and the law's subsequent journey through the courts, Becky regularly thought of the baby girl she had helped deliver in 1983 and prayed the legislation would stand. "These babies deserve to be protected by our nation's laws," Becky thought as she waited for the courts to decide the fate of Mississippi's law.

On June 24, 2022, Rep. Becky Currie stood in stunned silence as she read the news. The U.S. Supreme Court had just upheld the law she had authored and overturned *Roe v. Wade*. The single mother, who had struggled much of her life, had played a decisive role in reversing the most notorious abortion decision in the nation's history. "I was in disbelief," Currie recounted. "I think God picked me in 1976 and stayed with me the entire way," explained the nurse turned legislator.

Like Currie, most pro-lifers remember where they were the day *Roe* fell. For nearly half a century, reversing *Roe* had been a rallying cry for the pro-life movement. Under *Roe*, over 60 million babies were killed, countless women were emotionally and physically harmed, and the nation's morals were coarsened. Overturning this unjust decision will go down in history as a landmark achievement for the pro-life movement. For Christians, *Dobbs* is most fundamentally a God-given victory that ought to elicit gratitude for decades to come.

Although June 24 will remain etched in the hearts of pro-lifers, overturning *Roe* was never the final goal of the pro-life movement. The final goal has always been to make abortion illegal and unthinkable. But in the post-*Dobbs* era, pro-lifers face stiff headwinds. Tragically, in the years since *Dobbs*, approximately half of the states have pressed forward with laws that go well beyond *Roe* in allowing abortion on demand until the moment of birth. As we discussed in previous chapters, pro-abortion activists and politicians have successfully channeled rage over the *Dobbs* decision into numerous legislative and political victories.

Thus, by most honest accounts, the pro-life movement has been on its heels since *Dobbs*. In the lead-up to the 2024 presidential election, abortion has often been described as a "dilemma" for Republican candidates.[2] In 2023, public polling revealed that more Americans identified as pro-choice than at any moment in the previous quarter century.[3] In 2022, pro-life measures failed in conservative states, including Kansas, Kentucky, and Montana. Additionally, pro-abortion strategists have seized on the lack of unified messaging from pro-life candidates and have even convinced some ostensibly pro-life politicians that supporting pro-life legislation is a political liability.[4]

In this closing chapter, we will take stock of the pro-life movement in the aftermath of *Dobbs*. Specifically, we will look at the most urgent threats facing the movement, which include abortion drugs, lack of consensus on legislative strategy, strategic messaging, low thresholds for amending state constitutions, complacency and confusion within the church, and a secularizing culture. The chapter will also examine the post-*Dobbs* debate within pro-life circles about whether to pursue pro-life action through federal legislation or in individual states. Although the overturning of *Roe* gave elected officials at all levels of government the ability to protect life, there is currently little consensus on strategy or messaging among pro-life supporters.

---

[2] Aaron Blake, "What Do Antiabortion Groups Do about Trump?," *Washington Post*, September 18, 2023, https://www.washingtonpost.com/politics/2023/09/18/what-do-antiabortion-groups-do-about-trump/.

[3] Lydia Saad, "Abortion Remains a Potent Issue for Pro-Choice Voters," Gallup, June 21, 2023, https://news.gallup.com/poll/507527/abortion-remains-potent-issue-pro-choice-voters.aspx.

[4] This was demonstrated after the first Republican debate in the 2024 election cycle. Following the debate, the Biden reelection campaign released a $25 million television advertisement featuring Republican candidates talking about abortion. In the aftermath of *Dobbs*, Democrats have become convinced that supporting abortion is a political winner.

In this chapter I sketch the broad contours of a strategy that encourages simultaneous engagement on both the federal and state levels.

Life begins at conception, and all children, born and unborn, deserve equal protection under the law. Federal legislation or an amendment to the U.S. Constitution that explicitly protects life from the moment of conception should be the ultimate legislative goal of the pro-life movement. Scripture, reason, and science confirm that life begins at fertilization, and our laws should reflect this reality.

However, in a post-Christian culture that has been catechized for decades by pro-abortion messaging, the final goal of making abortion both illegal and unthinkable is a long way off. Thus, while working toward our final goal, the pro-life community should adopt a legislative and political strategy that educates and builds consensus in an incremental manner.

Once again, the goal of the pro-life movement should be to protect life from conception through natural death. With this goal in mind, pro-lifers should aggressively advocate for strong pro-life protections—such as laws that protect life at conception or at the point when a fetal heartbeat can be detected—in places where such laws have the possibility of success. Additionally, pro-lifers should advocate for federal legislation. At present, 72% of Americans indicate they support a minimum national threshold of fifteen weeks, the point when babies in the womb can feel pain.[5] Other studies suggest that a plurality of voters support laws that protect life when a heartbeat can be detected.[6] Although political realities change and can sometimes change quickly, national legislation protecting unborn children (whether at fifteen weeks or at the point when a heartbeat can be detected)

---

[5] Harvard Harris Poll, accessed November 13, 2023, https://harvardharrispoll.com/wp-content/uploads/2022/07/HHP_June2022_KeyResults.pdf?bcs-agent-scanner=47c0caa7-cd3a-c548-8253-855b5e71d5b2.

[6] For example, internal polling conducted by FRC Action in May 2022 showed that total support for a heartbeat bill outpaced total opposition by 14 points (47% to 33%; 20% of respondents were unsure). This survey data will be examined later in this chapter.

represents the convictions of tens of millions of Americans. Like efforts aimed at overturning *Roe*, federal legislation that aims to protect unborn babies at fifteen weeks or when a heartbeat is present should be seen as incremental steps toward the ultimate goal of making abortion illegal and morally unimaginable. Once a federal law is achieved (whether at fifteen weeks or heartbeat), the movement should proceed to whatever is most politically feasible (whether a heartbeat bill or a bill that protects life at conception).

Pro-lifers should not be naive. The current political environment in Washington, DC, and state capitals around the country is hostile to the pro-life message. Thus, educating the public, employing proper messaging, and building consensus will be crucial in reshaping our nation's warped conscience. Unfortunately, much of the cultural and political deck is stacked against those who want to extend legal protections to unborn children. However, as evident by *Dobbs*, the Lord is still working, and there are opportunities before us today that the founders of the modern pro-life movement could have scarcely imagined. Those of us alive today owe it to God, pro-life men and women who preceded us, and millions of unborn children to continue working toward the movement's ultimate goals of ending abortion and creating a culture that celebrates families and values children.

## On Its Heels: The Pro-Life Movement after *Dobbs*

On August 26, 2022, I published an article for *World Opinions* titled "Is Abortion an Election Game-Changer?"[7] I argued that despite the backlash following the reversal of *Roe v. Wade*, abortion would not play an outsized role in the 2022 midterm elections.

---

[7] David Closson, "Is Abortion an Election Game-Changer?," *World Opinions*, August 26, 2022, https://wng.org/opinions/is-abortion-an-election-game-changer-1661513297.

In retrospect, my analysis was off by a country mile. As we saw in chapter 4, the 2022 midterm elections delivered surprisingly strong results for pro-abortion candidates and referendums. In every state where abortion was on the ballot—either in the form of a referendum or constitutional amendment—the pro-abortion side won. Moreover, despite Republicans winning a narrow majority in the House of Representatives, the Republican majority was smaller than many had predicted. Republicans also failed to win back the U.S. Senate and key Rust Belt gubernatorial races. Clearly, *Dobbs* had not ended America's long-standing debate on abortion, and post-election analysis suggests that overturning *Roe*, at least in the short-term, energized the pro-abortion side.

To understand why pro-life referendums were trounced in the 2022 midterms, let's review my faulty preelection analysis. Writing just over two months before the election, I argued that the American electorate was paying attention to issues beyond abortion.[8] I also suggested that most people already knew where the major parties stood on abortion.

Here's how I explained this second point in August 2022:

> [A]lthough reaction to the Supreme Court's *Dobbs* decision has underscored the worldview divide between Republicans and

[8] This claim was supported by several leading polls, including one from Gallup that showed only 8% of respondents named abortion as their most important issue. Although 8% was the highest percentage since Gallup began tracking abortion in 1984, inflation (17%), concerns about dysfunctional government (17%), and the economy (12%) outpaced abortion as the most pressing issue for voters. Thus, from my perspective, although voters were thinking about abortion more than usual, other issues were more urgent. See Frank Newport, "Abortion Moves Up on 'Most Important Problem' List," Gallup, August 1, 2022, https://news.gallup.com/poll/395408/abortion-moves-important-problem-list.aspx. Also in favor of my analysis was the historical pattern that first-term presidents generally fare poorly in their first midterm. Presidents Bill Clinton, Barack Obama, and Donald Trump saw their party lose 54, 63, and 41 seats in the House of Representatives in their first midterm, respectively. Thus, history and the fact that Americans were focused on a litany of issues suggested the saliency of abortion would be muted.

> Democrats on abortion, most Americans have known for a long time where each party stands on the issue. Even before *Roe* was reversed, Democrats were working to expand abortion access. . . . Congressional Democrats have opposed every commonsense protection for the unborn for years now. Because of recent votes, every lawmaker is on record regarding abortion, and the fact that Democrats want to expand abortion is well known. The *Dobbs* decision may have motivated pro-abortion members of the Democratic base, but the reality is that Americans have long known where both parties stand.

Despite my confidence that abortion would not be a major factor in the 2022 midterms, some mainstream election prognosticators suggested that abortion could be decisive in the midterms. Writing for the *New York Times* on August 14, 2022, Shane Goldmacher and Katie Glueck wrote, "With national protections for abortion rights suddenly gone and bans going into effect in many states, senior White House officials and top Democratic strategists believe the issue has radically reshaped the 2022 landscape in their favor."[9] The writers continued, "In the fallout of the [*Dobbs*] ruling, Democrats see the potential to upend the typical dynamic of midterm elections in which voters punish the party in power."

[9] Shane Goldmacher and Katie Glueck, "Why Abortion Has Become a Centerpiece of Democratic TV Ads in 2022," *New York Times*, August 14, 2022, https://www.nytimes.com/2022/08/14/us/politics/abortion-midterms-2022-ads-democrats.html. Paul Waldman, writing for the *Washington Post*, also believed that abortion would play an outsized role in the midterms. According to Waldman, "The court's decision to overturn *Roe v. Wade* has not only angered Democrats, but also produced a wave of national news about state-level Republicans devising ever-more draconian abortion laws, and the horrific effects those laws are already having. Combined with other unpopular court decisions, this could move independent voters away from Republicans while motivating Democrats to turn out." See Paul Waldman, "5 Reasons Democrats Could Defy History in the Midterms," *Washington Post*, July 26, 2022, https://www.washingtonpost.com/opinions/2022/07/26/five-reasons-democrats-not-lose-midterm-elections/.

After the votes were counted, Goldmacher and Glueck's predictions proved prescient. Exit polls demonstrated that abortion and frustration about the Supreme Court's *Dobbs* decision had been a significant motivating factor for many voters. Articles published in the weeks following the election argued that abortion likely staved off a "red wave" election.[10]

The trend of progressive candidates running successfully on abortion continued in 2023 with Janet Protasiewicz's blowout win in an election for a seat on the Wisconsin Supreme Court. In what was technically a nonpartisan race, Protasiewicz broke long-standing judicial norms by publicly identifying with abortion supporters. "I can't tell you how I'll rule in any case, but . . . I value a woman's freedom to make her own reproductive health care decisions," Protasiewicz pledged on the campaign trail. As the race unfolded, political observers on both sides saw the Wisconsin judicial race as a proxy vote over abortion, and Protasiewicz's eleven-point win in an otherwise evenly divided state led to headlines, including one in *Politico* that stated, "Abortion was a 50/50 issue. Now, it's Republican quicksand."[11]

## Reviewing the 2022 Midterms

Is abortion "political quicksand" for Republicans? How long will the backlash to repealing *Roe* help pro-abortion candidates? Why do increasing numbers of Americans identify as "pro-choice" and claim abortion is "morally acceptable"?

Answers to these questions are multifaceted; no single rationale explains the attitudes and voting behavior of the American people. However, at least two factors can help explain the outcome of the post-*Dobbs* elections:

---

[10] Ally Mutnick et al., "'The Weirdest Election I've Ever Been a Part Of': How the GOP Almost Blew," *Politico*, November 15, 2022, https://www.politico.com/news/2022/11/15/gop-house-midterm-election-results-00066907.

[11] Steven Shepard, "Abortion Was a 50/50 Issue. Now, It's Republican Quicksand," *Politico*, April 8, 2023, https://www.politico.com/news/2023/04/08/republican-party-abortion-trap-00091088.

political will and shallow pro-life commitment. In the years to come, successfully navigating these challenges will be crucial for pro-lifers.

## *Political Will*

Following *Dobbs*, pro-abortion forces went on offense like never before. Unfortunately, their fervor was largely unmatched by pro-lifers. In terms of money, pro-abortion forces vastly outspent their opponents. Whereas Democrats had spent less than $6 million on abortion-related television advertising in the 2018 midterm elections, Democrats poured hundreds of millions into abortion advertising in 2022. By September 20, 2022, Democrats had invested more than $124 million in television advertising referencing abortion.[12] In the final month of the election, Democratic campaigns and aligned groups spent an additional $214 million on broadcast television ads on abortion, accounting for nearly half (45%) of their ad expenditures.[13]

---

[12] In House, Senate, and governor's races in 2018 and 2020, abortion was mentioned in only 2% of Democratic campaign ads. Elena Schneider and Holly Otterbein, "'THE Central Issue': How the Fall of Roe v. Wade Shook the 2022 Election," *Politico*, December 19, 2022, https://www.politico.com/news/2022/12/19/dobbs-2022-election-abortion-00074426; Steve Peoples and Aaron Kessler, "Ad Spending Shows Dems Hinging Midterm Hopes on Abortion," Associated Press, September 20, 2022, https://apnews.com/article/2022-midterm-elections-abortion-health-congress-4be6df000de67933fcdabcd6f7b56a3d.

[13] Chris Cillizza, "Did Democrats Place a Losing Bet on Abortion?," CNN, November 2, 2022, https://www.cnn.com/2022/11/02/politics/democrats-losing-bet-abortion/index.html. Outside groups, including Planned Parenthood, spent a record $50 million in the election to assist pro-abortion candidates. EMILYs List spent $102 million to elect pro-choice Democrat candidates. Brian Slodysko, "Planned Parenthood to Spend Record $50M in Midterm Elections," Associated Press, August 17, 2022, https://apnews.com/article/abortion-2022-midterm-elections-health-congress-71871318f3c725a7df0bbe183e6c84be; Press Release, "MEMO: Our Impact in the 2022 Midterms," EMILYs List, November 7, 2022, https://emilyslist.org/news/memo-our-impact-in-the-2022-midterms/#:~:text=This%20cycle%2C%20we%20raised%20%24100,we

In the crucial states of Arizona, Georgia, Michigan, Pennsylvania, and Wisconsin, Democrat candidates spent more than $41 million on abortion ads, which were played more than 69,000 times.[14] In one race, Gov. Gretchen Whitmer (D-MI) spent $605,462 on two abortion ads that aired 2,544 times in the general election. Her Republican challenger, Tudor Dixon, did not air any advertisements explaining her view on the issue. Dixon's approach was typical of other Republican candidates. In the closing months of the general election, Republican gubernatorial candidates in the five key swing states barely mentioned abortion. As an example, for the week of September 12, Democrat gubernatorial candidates aired 37,392 television ads referencing abortion.[15] In the same time span, Republicans aired 2,660, which was an uptick from their mere 843 ads three weeks earlier. Overall, 27% of Democratic ads in the 2022 midterm cycle (House, Senate, and gubernatorial) talked about abortion.[16] By comparison, only 5% of GOP ads highlighted the issue. In total, Democrats spent around $358 million in abortion-related ads in House, Senate, and gubernatorial races. Republicans spent about $37 million.

---

%20are%20proud%20to%20support.&text=There%20has%20never%20been%20a,pro%2Dchoice%20women%20to%20office; NARAL Pro-Choice America boasted that they knocked on over 330,000 doors, made over 391,000 calls, sent over 436,000 texts, filled over 4,100 volunteer shifts, and held 424 events in thirteen states. Press Release, "NARAL Pro-Choice America Runs Its Largest-Ever Midterm Program to Galvanize Voters after the Fall of Roe," Reproductive Freedom for All, November 7, 2022, https://reproductivefreedomforall.org/news/naral-pro-choice-america-runs-its-largest-ever-midterm-program-to-galvanize-voters-after-the-fall-of-roe/.

[14] Kimberly Kindy and Greg Morton, "Democrats Spend Heavily on Abortion Ads in Key Gubernatorial Races," *Washington Post*, November 2, 2022, https://www.washingtonpost.com/politics/2022/11/02/democratic-governor-candidates-abortion-ads/.

[15] Peoples and Kessler, "Ad Spending Shows Dems Hinging Midterm Hopes on Abortion."

[16] Schneider and Otterbein, "'THE Central Issue.'"

In short, many pro-life candidates were assured by political consultants that abortion was a losing issue and ignored it altogether. By ceding the topic to their opponents, many pro-life candidates were characterized as "extreme" on abortion even though pro-abortion candidates repeatedly declined to identify any limits to abortion.[17] By offering no competing narrative, the impression that Republicans were extreme on abortion stuck in the minds of voters. But even as Democrats drilled Republican candidates on abortion and poured millions into abortion-related advertising, the National Republican Congressional Committee urged candidates to focus on the economy. "We can't make emotional decisions," the Republican campaign arm's political director advised.[18]

---

[17] In my conversation with her, Marjorie Dannenfelser, who serves as the president of SBA Pro-Life America, drew attention to this dynamic. According to Dannenfelser, "The other side can't name a limit and won't name a limit because they don't want the American people to know that they don't have one. The abortion lobby doesn't have a limit. The worst thing pro-life candidates can do is throw away a clear advantage, which is failing to contrast the extremism of the abortion lobby with a very modest popular limit, which is a fifteen-week protection bill at the federal level." Marjorie Dannenfelser, interview with the author, August 21, 2023.

[18] Mutnick et al., "'The Weirdest Election I've Ever Been a Part Of.'" Of course, campaigns are complex, and the narrative that Democrats simply outspent Republicans or that Republicans ignored the issue to their peril does not explain the whole story. Although Republican candidates themselves did not spend much money on abortion-related advertising, one outside group, SBA Pro-Life America, poured over $78 million into the election. SBA's team of 1,300 canvassers reached over 8 million voters. Specifically, the group spent $2.5 million in Florida, where Ron DeSantis and Marco Rubio cruised to reelection. The group also spent $4 million in Georgia, where Gov. Brian Kemp was reelected, and $2.5 million in North Carolina, where pro-life candidate Ted Budd won a seat in the U.S. Senate. See "SBA Pro-Life America's Voter Mobilization Effort to Elect a Pro-Life Majority in the U.S. House and Senate and Elect Pro-Life Governors," SBA Pro-Life America, accessed November 3, 2023, https://sbaprolife.org/wp-content/uploads/2022/11/2022-Election-By-the-Numbers-1.pdf?bcs-agent-scanner=8489d066-22e7-7444-90d1-838ee93a456e.

## *Shallow Pro-Life Commitment Exposed*

The backlash triggered by the Supreme Court's overturning of *Roe* has exposed the reality that in some circles commitment to the pro-life cause was, all along, nominal at best. For example, after Janet Protasiewicz's victory in the Wisconsin Supreme Court race in April 2023, conservative pundit Ann Coulter wrote, "The demand for anti-abortion legislation just cost Republicans another crucial race. Pro-lifers: WE WON . . . Please stop pushing strict limits on abortion, or there will be no Republicans left."[19]

An uncomfortable but sober analysis of the outcome of recent elections reveals that many Americans who identified as pro-life before 2022 never adopted a deep-rooted, consistent pro-life conviction in the first place. As Albert Mohler has noted, "What we now seem to understand is that many Americans who actually turned to something of a pro-life position, didn't turn to anything like an authentic pro-life position. They were morally repulsed by abortion, but they don't yet see the issue clearly enough or they don't have sufficient pro-life conviction to move to any actual courage."[20] As it turns out, opposition to *Roe* did not equate with supporting a holistic pro-life position. Post-*Dobbs*, the pro-life movement has learned the hard lesson that some candidates who professed a pro-life position are not as committed to the cause as we had been led to believe.

The 2022 midterm results defy a simplistic explanation. However, there are a few lessons pro-lifers should note. First, many pro-life candidates who campaigned on a strong pro-life record won their elections—for example, governors Greg Abbott (Texas), Ron DeSantis (Florida), Brian Kemp (Georgia), and Mike DeWine (Ohio). Second, pro-life candidates who allowed their opponents to frame the conversation about abortion struggled and in many cases lost. This was especially true in states where abortion access is contested

---

[19] Ann Coulter (@AnnCoulter), Twitter, April 4, 2023, 10:57 p.m., https://twitter.com/AnnCoulter/status/1643462761626705920?s=20.

[20] Albert Mohler, The Briefing, April 10, 2023, https://albertmohler.com/2023/04/10/briefing-4-10-23/.

(e.g., Michigan, Pennsylvania, Wisconsin, etc.).[21] Third, in places like New York, where abortion was already enshrined into state law, abortion proved less galvanizing, and voters focused on other issues.

The 2022 midterms demonstrated that America remains deeply divided on abortion. Although the post-election punditry focused on how abortion helped Democrats thwart the expected "red wave," several high-profile GOP candidates—Abbott, DeSantis, Kemp, and DeWine—won by campaigning on their pro-life record. These results remind us of the difficulty of ascribing a single cause to any single election result. However, the success of pro-abortion candidates can be attributed, in part, to a calculated political strategy to paint pro-life candidates as extreme on abortion. Additionally, the Democrats' gamble to deploy vast resources on abortion messaging—that went mostly uncontested—paid off in many races. Nevertheless, the midterms underscored political realities that pro-lifers can learn from; namely, that political will, messaging, and sincere commitment to a cause matter. Learning these lessons will be crucial for success in future elections.

## Post-*Roe* Challenges to the Pro-Life Movement

Although overturning *Roe* was a major milestone in the pro-life movement, the work to restore a culture of life in America has just begun. At least six challenges face the pro-life movement after *Dobbs*: abortion drugs, lack of consensus on legislative strategy, the need for strategic messaging, low thresholds for amending state constitutions, complacency and confusion within the church, and a secularizing culture. For Christians, caring for our

---

[21] According to exit polls, voters in two of the nation's most hotly contested states (Michigan and Pennsylvania) ranked abortion as their most important issue. Before the election, abortion was illegal in both states due to pro-life laws that were triggered after *Dobbs*. "2022 Exit Polls," CNN, accessed November 3, 2023, https://www.cnn.com/election/2022/exit-polls/michigan/governor/0.

unborn neighbors requires an awareness of these challenges and a commitment to working for spiritual, practical, and political solutions that cultivate a pro-life ethic in our congregations and communities.

### *Abortion Drugs*

The first challenge to a culture of life is the availability of abortion drugs (also known as chemical abortion or abortion by pill). Although space does not permit a full discussion of the history of abortion drugs, recent litigation and increased usage necessitate a brief overview to appreciate the scope of this challenge.[22]

Many Americans are surprised to learn that although surgical abortions in the United States declined by 24% between 2009 and 2018, the use of abortion drugs has grown exponentially in the same time frame.[23] In fact, abortion drug usage is at an all-time high, increasing by 73% from 2008 to 2017 and accounting for 53% of all abortions in 2022.[24]

Chemical abortion is a two-drug regime that uses mifepristone (Mifeprex; also known as RU-486) and misoprostol (Cytotec). Mifepristone is a synthetic steroid that blocks the release of progesterone, a hormone that prepares the uterus for the implantation of the embryo and provides nutrition to the developing baby. By blocking progesterone, mifepristone chemically destroys the uterine lining and starves the baby to death. After ingesting mifepristone, women must wait one to two days before taking the

---

[22] For a detailed review of the politicized approval process of mifepristone, see Chris Gacek, *Politicized Science: The Manipulated Approval of RU-486 and Its Dangers to Women's Health* (Washington, DC: Family Research Council, 2007), https://downloads.frc.org/EF/EF07A29.pdf.

[23] Mary Szoch, "The Next Abortion Battleground: Chemical Abortion," FRC, accessed November 3, 2023, https://www.frc.org/chemicalabortion.

[24] Rachel Jones et al., "Medication Abortion Now Accounts for More Than Half of All US Abortions," Guttmacher, February 24, 2022, https://www.guttmacher.org/article/2022/02/medication-abortion-now-accounts-more-half-all-us-abortions.

second drug, misoprostol, which induces uterine contractions intended to expel the deceased fetus.[25]

After a controversial and expedited process, mifepristone was approved by the Food and Drug Administration (FDA) on September 28, 2000. Notably, the FDA approved mifepristone under its Subpart H regulations, which allow for expedited authorization for drugs that treat "serious or life-threatening illnesses" and provide a "meaningful therapeutic benefit."[26] The FDA required several post-approval safeguards for mifepristone, which later became known as REMS (Risk Evaluation and Mitigation Strategies). These include (1) limiting use of the drug by pregnant women through forty-nine days' gestation; (2) requiring three in-person visits to a health care provider; (3) mandating that only physicians can prescribe Mifeprex; and (4) requiring the reporting of all adverse events related to the drug.

In 2016, the FDA modified several of these safeguards, including (1) increasing the maximum gestational age at which women can use the drug from forty-nine to seventy days; (2) reducing the number of required in-person visits to a health care provider from three to one; (3) allowing non-doctors to prescribe and administer the drug; and (4) eliminating the requirement to report non-fatal adverse events related to the drug.

[25] Misoprostol was approved by the FDA to reduce the risk of gastric ulcers induced by nonsteroidal anti-inflammatory drugs (NSAIDs) in patients at high risk of complications from gastric ulcers and patients at high risk of developing gastric ulceration. Misoprostol's label warns that the drug "should not be taken by pregnant women to reduce the risk of ulcers." See www.accessdata.fda.gov/drugsatfda_docs/label/2002/19268slr037.pdf?bcs-agent-scanner=19daa281-03e3-a346-98d4-598ce7758e59. As Gacek notes, although the FDA does not allow pharmaceutical companies to promote drugs for purposes other than those approved by the agency, the FDA, in approving mifepristone, mandated an off-label use of misoprostol. See Gacek, *Politicized Science*, 16.

[26] In December 1992, the FDA promulgated "Subpart H" regulations to promote rapid approval for life-saving drugs during the HIV/AIDS epidemic. The authorization accelerates the approval of drugs "that have been studied for their safety and effectiveness in treating serious or life-threatening illnesses and that provide meaningful therapeutic benefit to patients over existing treatments." 21 C.F.R. § 314.500.

Additionally, in April 2019, the FDA approved a generic version of mifepristone. In April 2021, the FDA, citing the COVID-19 pandemic, allowed mifepristone to be dispensed through the mail; in December 2021, the FDA announced it would permanently remove the in-person dispensing requirement for the drug. In January 2023, the FDA announced that retail pharmacies could sell abortion pills with a prescription.[27]

Significantly, since its hasty approval, mifepristone has been responsible for a myriad of negative health outcomes for women. Between 2000 and 2021, 4,207 adverse events related to abortion drugs were voluntarily reported to the FDA, including 26 maternal deaths, 97 ectopic pregnancies, and 1,045 hospitalizations.[28] According to mifepristone's own medical label, between 2.9 and 4.6% of women who take the drug end up in the emergency room.[29] Many women experience serious complications, including hemorrhage (which can require a blood transfusion), failed or incomplete abortion, sepsis, infection, the inability to carry later pregnancies to term, and even death.[30]

In 2022, pro-life doctors filed a lawsuit against the FDA, arguing that the rushed approval of mifepristone was illegal because it required the FDA to classify pregnancy as a "serious illness" and claim that abortion pills offered a "meaningful therapeutic benefit."[31] The pro-life doctors also

---

[27] "Risk Evaluation and Mitigation Strategy (REMS) Single Shared System for Mifepristone 200 Mg," accessed November 30, 2023, https://perma.cc/MJT5-35LF.

[28] Szoch, "The Next Abortion Battleground."

[29] "Highlights of Prescribing Information," accessed November 3, 2023, https://www.accessdata.fda.gov/drugsatfda_docs/label/2019/020687s022lbl.pdf?bcs-agent-scanner=15f6498c-8728-944c-b66d-160e0943a3a6.

[30] Erin Hawley, "SCOTUS Pauses Abortion Pill Restrictions," *World Opinions*, April 24, 2023, https://wng.org/opinions/scotus-pauses-abortion-pill-restrictions-1682336191.

[31] Alliance for Hippocratic Medicine v. FDA, United States District Court, November 18, 2022; online at https://litigationtracker.law.georgetown.edu/wp-content/uploads/2024/02/Alliance-Hippocratic-Medicine_2022.11.18_PLAINTIFFS-BRIEF-in-Support-of-Preliminary-Injunction.pdf?bcs-agent-scanner=38a41209-b60a-fc4a-874f-aa2982e834d2.

cited mifepristone's record of negative health consequences and the FDA's removal of nearly every safeguard as reasons for bringing their lawsuit.

On April 7, 2023, Judge Matthew J. Kacsmaryk ruled that the FDA's approval of mifepristone violated federal law.[32] According to Kacsmaryk, the FDA's approval and subsequent deregulation of the drug was illegal. On August 16, 2023, a unanimous panel for the U.S. Court of Appeals for the Fifth Circuit upheld significant portions of Kacsmaryk's decision, finding that the FDA's changes in 2016 and 2021 were indeed illegal.[33] Additionally, the Fifth Circuit reinstated the original 2000 safeguards, including the seven weeks' gestational limitation, in-person doctor visits, non-fatal adverse event reporting, and physician dispensation. Abortion providers were also prohibited from sending abortion pills through the mail.[34] On June 13, 2024, the Supreme Court ruled that the pro-life doctors behind the lawsuit lacked standing to challenge the FDA's regulatory actions regarding mifepristone. The unanimous opinion declined to address the merits of the case. As a result, the FDA's removal of safeguards in 2016 and 2021 is allowed to stand.[35]

---

[32] Alliance for Hippocratic Medicine v. FDA, United States District Court, April 7, 2023.

[33] Alliance for Hippocratic Medicine v. FDA, United States Court of Appeals, August 16, 2023; online at https://litigationtracker.law.georgetown.edu/wp-content/uploads/2024/02/Alliance-Hippocratic-Medicine_2023.10.10_OPINION-5th-Circuit.pdf?bcs-agent-scanner=7911f8d0-d16c-804e-9fbf-2b3dd068b0d4.

[34] As of late 2023, the Fifth Circuit's ruling was not in effect because of a prior order from the Supreme Court. On April 21, 2023, the Supreme Court issued a stay in the case that blocks any lower court decisions from taking effect until the Supreme Court takes further action. In their August 16, 2023, decision, the Fifth Circuit referred to this order, noting, "But to repeat, all of this relief is subject to the Supreme Court's prior order, which stays the district court's order until the disposition of any petition for certiorari."

For the Supreme Court's order, see https://www.supremecourt.gov/opinions/22pdf/22a901_3d9g.pdf?bcs-agent-scanner=2c01164f-e9f7-4d44-9511-1fd0b1f36b89.

[35] FDA v. Alliance for Hippocratic Medicine 602 U.S. 367 (2024).

## Two Challenges Posed by Abortion Drugs

In post-*Roe* America, abortion drugs pose a twofold challenge. First, the deregulation of chemical abortion pills allows states to circumvent pro-life laws. In the year after *Dobbs*, several states, including California, Colorado, Connecticut, Delaware, Hawaii, Illinois, Massachusetts, Minnesota, New Mexico, New York, Oregon, Vermont, and Washington, passed so-called telemedicine shield laws that legally protect doctors who mail abortion pills into states that prohibit abortion.[36] In just one month (July 2023), seven U.S. doctors affiliated with Aid Access (a European-based abortion pill supplier) mailed 3,500 doses of abortion pills to women in states with pro-life laws.[37] It is expected that this number will grow exponentially as more doctors join programs like Aid Access.

Significantly, abortion drugs are rapidly becoming the preferred method of carrying out an abortion. Citing an "explosion of access to abortion pills through telehealth and underground networks," a *New York Times* report in September 2023 noted that "legal abortions most likely increased in the United States in the first six months" of 2023 compared with 2020.[38] In terms of specific numbers, 465,000 abortions were recorded across

---

[36] For an overview of which states have implemented shield laws, see Randi Seigel and Alice B. Leiter, "State Abortion Shield Laws: Key Findings and Infographic," Manatt, September 26, 2023, https://www.manatt.com/insights/white-papers/2023/state-abortion-shield-laws-key-findings-and-infogr. Also, the Center for Reproductive Rights maintains a website that tracks the status of abortion laws, including shield laws. See Center for Reproductive Rights, "After Roe Fell: Abortion Laws by State," accessed July 3, 2024, https://reproductiverights.org/maps/abortion-laws-by-state/.

[37] One New York abortionist profiled in the *Washington Post* quipped, "Texas might say I'm breaking their laws, but I don't live in Texas." See Caroline Kitchener, "Blue-State Doctors Launch Abortion Pill Pipeline into States with Bans," *Washington Post*, July 19, 2022, https://www.washingtonpost.com/politics/2023/07/19/doctors-northeast-launch-abortion-pill-pipeline-into-states-with-bans/.

[38] Amy Schoenfeld Walker and Allison McCann, *New York Times*, "Abortions Rose in Most States This Year, New Data Shows," September 7, 2023, https://www.nytimes.com/interactive/2023/09/07/us/abortion-data-bans-laws.html.

fifty states and Washington, DC, in the first six months of 2020. Around 511,000 abortions were estimated across thirty-six states and Washington, DC, in the first six months of 2023. In other words, since the overturning of *Roe*, there have been *more* abortions, not less, and a large percentage have come through abortion drugs.

From a policy perspective, lawmakers in blue states, with help from the Biden administration, have aided and abetted an essentially unregulated chemical abortion industry. This is why, according to Erin Hawley, an attorney with Alliance Defending Freedom (ADF) who litigated against the FDA's approval of mifepristone in 2023, chemical abortion has quickly become an "existential threat to pro-life laws."[39] As Hawley explained, state-level shield laws coupled with deregulation of abortion drugs at the federal level are part of a "coordinated strategy by pro-abortion advocates to evade lawfully enacted pro-life laws to get these drugs into the hands of women in states that prohibit abortion." In other words, abortion drugs have become the abortion industry's "work-around *Dobbs*" and have ensured that abortion in some form has continued in all fifty states.

Second, abortion drugs are a threat to the pro-life movement because they facilitate "self-managed," unsupervised abortions. When the FDA dropped the in-person dispensing requirement in 2021, women were no longer required to see doctors who could assess eligibility, diagnose ectopic pregnancies, and provide surgical intervention in the case of an incomplete abortion or severe bleeding. The result was an explosion of self-managed abortions not very different from the back-alley, "coat hanger abortions" activists decry. As Hawley explained, "Under the FDA's new rule, a woman doesn't need to see or even talk to a doctor. She can just go online and in about five minutes, fill out a form, and have chemical abortion pills mailed to her doorstep. This is entirely unlawful." Of course, do-it-yourself abortion has long been the abortion industry's goal despite the predictably negative effects for women's health that result when basic safeguards such as

[39] Erin Hawley, interview with the author, August 15, 2023.

in-person dispensing requirements are removed (e.g., infection, heavy and prolonged bleeding, etc.).[40]

**Responding to Abortion Drugs: Legislation and Education**

Abortion drugs present an urgent threat to women and their unborn children. Thus, while litigation related to these drugs continues to play out, there are two practical ways pro-life Christians can respond: legislation and education. First, although the FDA under the Biden administration has sought to liberalize policies governing the dispensing of abortion pills, states should follow the example of Wyoming, which passed a law in March 2023 that made it illegal for a person to "manufacture, distribute, prescribe, dispense, sell, transfer or use any chemical abortion drug in the state for the purpose of procuring or performing an abortion."[41] The law explicitly criminalized the dispensing of mifepristone and misoprostol for the purposes of causing an abortion. Although a state judge enjoined the law from taking effect while a lawsuit proceeds, Wyoming's legislation offers a helpful model for how states can enact meaningful legislation related to chemical abortion.

Second, education about the reality of abortion drugs is necessary because the abortion lobby has successfully convinced millions of Americans that abortion pills are as safe as Tylenol despite the FDA's own

[40] For example, one pro-abortion activist admitted, "Lifting the REMS [Risk Evaluation and Mitigation Strategies] could significantly expand access to medication abortion and increase the options available to people seeking abortion care. In theory, anyone could access medication abortion in the absence of the REMS just like most other prescription drugs: by receiving a prescription from a provider and purchasing the medication from a pharmacy. The potential significance of this change should not be overlooked." See Megan K. Donovan, "Self-Managed Medical Abortion: Expanding the Available Options for U.S. Abortion Care," Guttmacher Policy Review, October 17, 2018, https://www.guttmacher.org/gpr/2018/10/self-managed-medication-abortion-expanding-available-options-us-abortion-care.

[41] State of Wyoming, SF 0109, accessed November 3, 2023, https://wyoleg.gov/2023/Introduced/SF0109.pdf?bcs-agent-scanner=792a09f3-9c19-964e-8419-5bc3edc752ca.

"black box" warning that admits that roughly one in twenty-five of women who take mifepristone end up in the emergency room. Those committed to the pro-life cause need to aggressively counter the ubiquitous lies that abortion pills are safe and develop straightforward talking points that communicate the well-documented risks of these pills. As Senator James Lankford (R-OK) explained, "We need to be able to get the real-life stories out because it seems so simple to take a pill and the whole thing is over."[42] But, as Lankford made clear, "It's not that simple." As we have seen, abortion drugs often lead to serious complications that put women's lives at risk. Thus, pro-lifers must devote energy and resources to educating the public about the true nature of abortion drugs. Practically, our education efforts should include talking about medical consequences and telling the real-life stories of women who have suffered the awful side effects of these drugs.[43] Another aspect of educating our friends and neighbors about chemical abortion should include raising awareness about Abortion Pill Reversal, a

---

[42] Senator James Lankford, interview with the author, September 18, 2023.

[43] According to Senator Lankford, "The pro-abortion crowd is protecting the stories and not letting stories get out of women saying, 'I had all this bleeding, I went to the Emergency Room, I ended up being infertile in the days ahead because I got access to this drug, I didn't know I had the wrong blood type on it and now I am not able to have children in the future.' We have got to be able to have the real-life stories get out because it seems so simple to take a pill and the whole thing is over but it's not that simple." Lankford, interview.

Likewise, Carol Tobias, who serves as the president of the National Right to Life, has warned about the physical and psychological dangers of abortion drugs for years. In our conversation, Tobias warned, "We're being sold a bill of lies that chemical abortion is safe. We're told it's as safe as taking Tylenol, but that's a lie." Tobias regularly points to the psychological and emotional impact of abortion drugs, noting how the two-pill regimen results in severe cramping and bleeding as well as, for many women, seeing their dead baby fall out in a toilet or onto the shower floor. According to Tobias, "We're going to see more psychological problems from women who can't accept the fact that they are the ones now responsible for killing their baby because they took these pills." Carol Tobias, interview with the author, August 23, 2023.

process that uses the hormone progesterone to reverse the effects of mifepristone. Medical professionals have been able to save around 65% of unborn babies through abortion pill reversal.[44]

### *Lack of Consensus on Legislative Strategy*

A second challenge facing pro-lifers in the aftermath of *Dobbs* is a lack of consensus on legislative strategy. Currently, there is vigorous debate within the pro-life movement about the most effective legislative and political strategies for ending legal abortion. Although internal strategy discussions are nothing new, for decades, the mainstream pro-life movement favored an incremental strategy that chipped away at the foundation of *Roe* while working toward its overturning. With that goal achieved in *Dobbs*, where and how do pro-lifers engage now? If the final goal is to make abortion illegal and morally unimaginable, where should pro-lifers focus their energies? Should we engage at the federal level or the state level? Should we advocate for incremental steps or full protection at conception? These are important questions, and the current lack of consensus is diluting the movement's influence at the exact moment pro-abortion forces are more united and determined than ever.

#### Two Perspectives: Federal or State Approach

One popular perspective argues that the post-*Roe* pro-life movement should focus its energies on protecting life through action at the state level. According to this position, the states are laboratories of democracy, and efforts in the states have a higher likelihood of reaching consensus to protect life. A state-by-state approach also honors the principles of federalism and

---

[44] Abortion Pill Reversal, accessed November 3, 2023, https://www.abortionpillreversal.com/abortion-pill-reversal/overview.

respects the autonomy of the individual states. Additionally, some conservative legal scholars argue that the federal government lacks the constitutional authority to enforce a national abortion law.[45] Thus, to save more babies, we must focus on the states.

Following *Dobbs*, many national Republican lawmakers endorsed the state-by-state approach. In September 2022, Republican Senate Leader Mitch McConnell (R-KY) noted, "I think most of the members of my conference prefer that [abortion] be dealt with at the state level."[46] Likewise, when asked about Sen. Lindsay Graham's proposed federal fifteen-week protection bill, Sen. John Cornyn (R-TX) stated, "There's obviously a split of opinion in terms of whether abortion law should be decided by the states. . . . I would keep an open mind but my preference would be for those decisions to be made on a state-by-state basis."[47] In April 2024, former President Donald Trump endorsed a similar position, stating, "My view is now that we have abortion where everybody wanted it from a legal standpoint, that states will determine by vote or legislation or perhaps both. And whatever they decide must be the law of the land—in this case, the law of the state."[48]

---

[45] William Hodes, "A Federal Gestational Age Abortion Ban Is the Wrong (and Unconstitutional) Hill for the Pro-Life Movement to Die On," The Federalist Society, August 17, 2023, https://fedsoc.org/commentary/fedsoc-blog/a-federal-gestational-age-abortion-ban-is-the-wrong-and-unconstitutional-hill-for-the-pro-life-movement-to-die-on.

[46] Alexander Bolton, "McConnell Throws Shade on Graham's Proposed National Abortion Ban," The Hill, September 13, 2022, https://thehill.com/homenews/senate/3641225-mcconnell-throws-shade-on-grahams-proposed-national-abortion-ban/.

[47] Burgess Everett et al., "Graham's Abortion Ban Stuns Senate GOP," Politico, September 13, 2022, https://www.politico.com/news/2022/09/13/grahams-abortion-ban-senate-gop-00056423.

[48] See Donald J. Trump, Video Announcement, Truth Social, April 8, 2024, https://truthsocial.com/@realDonaldTrump/posts/112235238031827342. President Trump's comments on abortion in April 2024 were similar to a statement released by his campaign during the Republican primary a year earlier, which stated, "President Donald J. Trump believes that the Supreme Court, led by the three Justices which he supported, got it right when they ruled this is an issue that should be decided at the State level." See Josh Dawsey et al., "Abortion Divides 2024

Most proponents of a state-focused pro-life strategy believe federal policymakers still have some role to play in protecting life, such as ensuring federal Medicaid dollars do not fund abortion, prohibiting military hospitals from carrying out abortions, and preserving pro-life legislative riders such as the Hyde, Helms, and Weldon Amendments in federal lawmaking.[49] Nevertheless, the state strategy believes that the energy and resources of the pro-life movement should focus on incremental progress in the states.[50]

A second perspective argues that the pro-life movement should press for a federal strategy to restrict and eventually end abortion. Some proponents of this view believe the federal government can claim constitutional

---

Candidates and Confounds Many within the GOP," *Washington Post*, April 20, 2023, https://www.washingtonpost.com/politics/2023/04/20/republicans-abortion-dobbs-election/.

[49] The Hyde Amendment, included in the annual appropriations acts for the Departments of Labor, Health and Human Services, and Education, and related agencies, is a legislative provision that restricts the use of federal funding to pay for abortions. For more information, see "The Hyde Amendment: An Overview," Congressional Research Service, July 20, 2022, https://crsreports.congress.gov/product/pdf/IF/IF12167. The Helms Amendment, an amendment to the Foreign Assistance Act of 1961, prohibits the use of foreign assistance to pay for the performance of abortion as a method of family planning or to motivate or coerce any person to practice abortion. For more information, see "Abortion Funding Restrictions in Foreign Assistance Legislation," The Congressional Research Service, October 20, 2022, https://crsreports.congress.gov/product/pdf/IF/IF12235. The Weldon Amendment, which has passed in every federal Health and Human Services' appropriations bill since 2005, prohibits federal funds from going to states that discriminate against any health care entity that does not pay for or provide coverage for abortions. For more information, see "The History and Effect of Abortion Conscience Clause Laws," The Congressional Research Service, January 29, 2010, https://crsreports.congress.gov/product/pdf/RL/RL34703.

[50] For an argument advancing the state-by-state approach, see Daniel Suhr "COUNTERPOINT: Let's Make Incremental, Achievable, Constitutional Progress," *World Opinions*, April 27, 2023, https://wng.org/opinions/lets-make-incremental-achievable-constitutional-progress-1682555620.

authority to protect the unborn under the Fourteenth Amendment. This argument notes that the amendment, adopted in 1868, forbids states from denying "any person within [their] jurisdiction the equal protection of the laws."[51] From this perspective, the Fourteenth Amendment guarantees the equal protection of laws for everyone, irrespective of sex, age, ethnicity, stage of development, or condition of dependency. In other words, the Constitution already entitles unborn children to the equal protection of the nation's laws, and the federal government has a duty to prevent state and local authorities from denying such protection.

Those who argue for a federal law note that most abortions are happening in liberal states like California, Illinois, and New York, which together accounted for 34.2% of all abortions in 2020.[52] In other words, strong pro-life laws in Alabama or South Dakota do not cover the overwhelming number of babies in need of protection. Furthermore, abortion tourism and mail-order chemical abortion drugs make abortion possible in states where it is prohibited by state statute.[53] Thus, according to proponents of a federal strategy, without nationalizing the issue, abortion will remain, in some form, legal in all fifty states.

---

[51] Section 1 of the Fourteenth Amendment reads: "All persons born or naturalized in the United States, and subject to the jurisdiction thereof, are citizens of the United States and of the State wherein they reside. No State shall make or enforce any law which shall abridge the privileges or immunities of citizens of the United States; nor shall any State deprive any person of life, liberty, or property, without due process of law; nor deny to any person within its jurisdiction the equal protection of the laws." For a succinct summary of the pro-life argument concerning the Fourteenth Amendment, see Robert P. George and Josh Craddock, "Even If Roe Is Overturned, Congress Must Act to Protect the Unborn," *Washington Post*, June 2, 2022, https://www.washingtonpost.com/opinions/2022/06/02/roe-abortion-congress-fourteenth-amendment/.

[52] Guttmacher Data Center, accessed November 4, 2023, https://data.guttmacher.org/states/table?state=NY+US+CA+IL&topics=66&dataset=data.

[53] Katelyn Walls Shelton makes this argument in "POINT: 'A House Divided' Yet Again," *World Opinions*, April 27, 2023, https://wng.org/opinions/a-house-divided-yet-again-1682554986.

## A Multi-Pronged Strategy Is Needed

Given the merits of both federal and state-focused strategies, which approach is correct? What is the most effective strategy for ending abortion in America?

There are at least two reasons for why a state-only approach is unsatisfactory: the unevenness of the states and the certainty that pro-abortion policymakers will impose nation-wide abortion laws at the earliest opportunity.[54] Although American politics have always been divisive, the recent development of states that can be consistently categorized as either "red" or "blue" is indicative of deep shifts in ideology and worldview.[55] Increasingly, people with similar worldviews congregate together; those with a progressive worldview are likely to be found in cities or near college campuses, while those with a conservative worldview are more likely to live in a rural or suburban setting.[56] This is why the cultural norms in California now appear bizarre to those in Iowa and vice versa.[57] Stark differences in customs, laws, and values can make two states, even states that share a border like Oregon and Idaho, appear to inhabit different worlds.

---

[54] Albert Mohler points to these reasons for why a combined federal and state strategy is needed. See R. Albert Mohler Jr., "What Comes Now in the Great Battle for Life?," *World Opinions*, April 27, 2023, https://wng.org/opinions/what-comes-now-in-the-great-battle-for-life-1682593847.

[55] For example, a Republican candidate for president has not won California, Connecticut, Delaware, Illinois, Maine, Maryland, New Jersey, or Vermont since 1988 (George H. W. Bush). A Republican candidate winning any of these states in today's political climate seems almost eschatological.

[56] As Albert Mohler has repeatedly observed, "When it comes to worldview, geography matters. . . . The closer you get to a coast, the closer you get to a city, the closer you get to a campus, the closer you get to moral progressivism or liberalism." R. Albert Mohler Jr., The Briefing, April 11, 2023, https://albertmohler.com/2023/04/11/briefing-4-11-23.

[57] For a good example, consider a 2023 article in the *New York Times* that featured two families, one in Oregon and another in Missouri, that moved because of disagreements over their home state politics. Trip Gabril, "Two Families Got Fed Up with Their States' Politics. So They Moved Out," *New York Times*, October 7, 2023, https://www.nytimes.com/2023/10/07/us/politics/politics-states-moving.html.

The fact that most states now consistently vote in a predictably conservative or liberal direction must inform our pro-life strategy. The acute polarization of American politics renders a state-only strategy insufficient because efforts to limit abortion and protect life in conservative states will inevitably be undermined by progressive states through shield laws, abortion drugs, and abortion tourism.

Additionally, efforts to pass the Women's Health Protection Act make it clear that pro-abortion legislators in Washington, DC, are committed to liberalizing federal abortion law. In 2022, national abortion legislation likely would have passed had it not been for two senators—Joe Manchin (D-WV) and Kyrsten Sinema (I-AZ)—opposing the abolishment of the legislative filibuster.[58] In other words, progressives are actively working to pass federal pro-abortion legislation; their success threatens state laws, which is why pro-lifers must engage nationally as well.[59]

Our laws should reflect the reality—supported by Scripture, reason, and science—that life begins at conception. However, we must also be realistic; after decades of pro-abortion messaging, our culture has been catechized to see abortion as a moral good.[60] Regrettably, these cultural and political realities mean that the final goal of making abortion illegal and morally

---

[58] Notably, in 2024, both Manchin and Sinema announced they would not run for reelection.

[59] As a conservative, I share the conviction that federalism offers important safeguards against an overreaching, tyrannical federal government. For years, many pro-lifers rightly complained that *Roe* usurped the right of individual states to make abortion policy. *Roe*'s unconstitutional curtailment of state rights was egregious and received an appropriate rebuke from the Supreme Court in *Dobbs*. In retrospect, however, the emphasis on state rights may have unwittingly undermined or obscured the animating conviction of the pro-life movement, which is protecting unborn persons made in God's image. One's location should not determine rights, which is why a pro-life strategy that engages only conservative states is inadequate.

[60] A 2023 Gallup survey showed that 52% of Americans believe abortion is "morally acceptable" compared to 41% who said it was "morally wrong." See "Morality of Abortion Demographic Table," Gallup, May 2023, https://news.gallup.com/poll/244625/morality-abortion-2018-demographic-tables.aspx.

unthinkable is likely a long way off. Thus, a morally consistent, politically effective strategy to end abortion in all fifty states must engage on two fronts.

First, at the state-level, pro-lifers should adopt a legislative strategy that pursues ambitious, politically feasible goals. For the foreseeable future, abortion will remain one of the most contested issues in politics. Thus, lawmakers should expect strident opposition to even the most basic pro-life bills and be prepared to fight with conviction and courage. In places where pro-life lawmakers hold legislative majorities, legislators should aggressively advance and pass strong pro-life legislation. Thankfully, as we have seen, many states have successfully passed pro-life protections since *Roe* was overturned. In conservative and conservative-leaning states that either lack pro-life laws or have weak pro-life laws, legislators should push for strong pro-life protections, including heartbeat laws and laws that protect life at conception.

Likewise, although their efforts may have only a minimal effect on legislation, pro-life legislators in deep blue states can also fight for life. Even when vastly outnumbered, pro-life legislators should use the procedural tactics at their disposal to delay pro-abortion legislation and use every opportunity to address the consciences of their fellow legislators by speaking clearly about the morality of abortion.

Second, pro-lifers should press for federal legislation at the point where national consensus already exists. Although there is debate amongst pro-lifers on where the point of consensus is, polling consistently shows that most Americans favor a minimum national threshold of protecting life at fifteen weeks. For example, a 2022 Harvard-Harris poll taken days after *Dobbs* showed that 72% of voters favored limiting abortion by no later than fifteen weeks, including 75% of women, 70% of independent voters, and 60% of rank-and-file Democrats.[61]

---

[61] The Harris poll was conducted from June 28 to June 29, 2022, among 1,308 registered voters by The Harris Poll and HarrisX. The results can be found at https://harvardharrispoll.com/wp-content/uploads/2022/07/HHP_June2022_KeyResults.pdf?bcs-agent-scanner=40ba4195-881c-c94a-af03-2a7fb78c3886.

There is also polling that demonstrates that many Americans support laws to protect life when a fetal heartbeat can be detected. In May 2022, FRC Action commissioned a nationwide survey of registered voters. One question on the survey specifically asked, "Do you support or oppose protecting unborn children when a fetal heartbeat can be detected, which is usually around the sixth week of pregnancy?" The results were as follows: strong support (35%), somewhat support (13%), unsure (20%), somewhat oppose (13%), and strongly oppose (20%). Overall, total support (47%) outpaced total oppose (33%). The fact that 20% of respondents were unsure indicates that a fifth of the electorate could be persuaded to support heartbeat legislation.[62]

The headwinds facing the pro-life movement are stiff. Given current political realities, a natural starting point for a federal law is acting on the already-existing fifteen-week consensus. But federal legislation that focuses on protecting life after fifteen weeks cannot be the final goal; any law that limits abortion after a gestational age (whether fifteen weeks or six weeks) must be understood as an incremental step toward legal protection for all unborn children. Once a fifteen-week law is achieved, the movement should immediately proceed to whatever is most politically feasible, which would likely be a federal heartbeat law. However, the goal of protecting unborn children at conception must remain the goal, and as legislative battles play out, the work of education must continue in earnest.

## National Pro-Life Leaders Support a National and State Strategy

National pro-life leaders agree that the federal government possesses the legal and moral responsibility to protect unborn children. As Sen. Cindy Hyde-Smith (R-MS), the chair of the Senate Pro-Life Caucus, explained,

---

[62] Unpublished polling conducted by FRC Action. The polling was conducted by WPA Intelligence, a nationally recognized provider of survey research. The polling was conducted in late May 2022, three weeks after the *Dobbs* leak.

"The right to life is the first of our God-given rights enshrined in the Declaration of Independence. So, absolutely, we have a duty to protect life at every level of government, including in Congress."[63] According to Hyde-Smith, in the years before *Dobbs*, Congress passed commonsense pro-life laws, including banning partial-birth abortion, prohibiting the mailing of abortion drugs, and stopping taxpayer funding for abortion. With future pro-life majorities in the Senate, Hyde-Smith believes Congress can enact further protections.

For Kristan Hawkins, president of Students for Life, the basis for the federal government engaging abortion policy is rooted in the fact that geography should not determine human rights. Hawkins notes that the abortion industry understands that abortion is a federal and state issue, citing Planned Parenthood's efforts in Arkansas in 2024 to pass a referendum to undo the state's pro-life protections. "Why is the abortion lobby focusing on states where the abortion numbers are relatively low?" Hawkins asked. "They understand that you can't have a generation of people in America born in a nation where in half of your states you are free to be born and in half of your states you are free to kill. They understand that sooner or later one of the two ideologies is going to win out," she explained.[64]

Marjorie Dannenfelser, the president of SBA Pro-Life America, the largest pro-life grassroots organization in the country, also believes that "protecting life is a federal responsibility." According to Dannenfelser, "Justice Kavanaugh made it clear that abortion policy is now a matter of the legislators including Congress, so the door is open." At the federal level,

---

[63] Senator Cindy Hyde-Smith, interview with the author, September 15, 2023.

[64] In my interview with her, Hawkins made this point emphatically, noting, "The reality is that protecting life was never just a state issue. This is a federal issue. This is the primary function of government. In the hierarchy of rights there's a reason why life is first before liberty, before the pursuit of happiness. And if your government can't make sure you're alive, can't guarantee your right to life, what even is the purpose of government?" Kristan Hawkins, interview with the author, August 9, 2023.

Dannenfelser believes that Mississippi's fifteen-week protection law—the law that led to the *Dobbs* decision—provides a good model for an initial federal law. "On the federal level, being ambitious for life and maintaining our majorities and maximizing the possibility that we get something, means taking our cue from Mississippi. We should insist that fifteen weeks or better is the minimum standard."[65]

According to Dannenfelser, "There is already consensus," and pro-life leaders in office "should not wait for the rest of eternity" to act. At the earliest possible opportunity—which will occur whenever pro-life leaders control the White House, Senate, and House of Representatives—elected leaders should act upon the broad consensus that believes babies who can feel pain deserve legal protection. Although pro-abortion candidates have won some important elections since *Roe* was overturned, Dannenfelser believes that candidates who campaign on a national minimum threshold of fifteen weeks would reap political benefits. "It shouldn't be hard for any of our candidates to be standing with the crowd and it should be very difficult for Democrats to be standing alone when it comes to some sort of federal minimum standard," Dannenfelser argued.[66]

Other pro-life leaders, including Erin Hawley and Tony Perkins, agree that a fetal pain law at the national level would have broad public appeal. According to Hawley, "If you look at where the American people are on this, Gallup polls for a long time have consistently shown that Americans oppose abortion in the second trimester because they know the baby is fully

---

[65] When it comes to advocating for pro-life laws in the states, Dannenfelser notes, "Our position has been from the beginning that we have to be as ambitious as we can possibly be in every arena where we fight. And that means that Congress is not Alabama, Alabama is not California which is not Montana. Each state has its own personality, its own dynamic, and being ambitious in each one requires something slightly different." Marjorie Dannenfelser, interview with the author, August 21, 2023.

[66] Dannenfelser, interview.

formed—you can look at an ultrasound and see legs and arms and noses—it's also quite likely that babies are capable of feeling pain. I think that would be a first step." Similarly, Perkins noted, "I support life from the moment of conception, but I realize I've got to build consensus to successfully pass legislation. So, when we look at where we are nationally, we can take the temperature of the country, and again and again we see that around 70% of the population supports the idea that we should protect a child once they can feel pain in the womb."[67]

Recent polling confirms the statistics referenced by Hawley and Perkins. A 2023 Knights of Columbus-Marist Poll revealed that 69% of Americans support limiting abortion to, at most, the first three months of pregnancy (twelve weeks).[68] The same poll showed that 77% of Americans believe doctors, nurses, and other health care professionals with religious objections to abortion should not be legally required to perform them. Thus, despite the outcomes in some recent elections, most Americans support protecting life and limiting abortion.

---

[67] Perkins pushed back against the notion that supporting a fetal pain law would compromise his pro-life convictions. "I think we should protect life from the moment of conception but I'm going to start where I can get consensus. I don't think that's compromising my principles because without efforts like Mississippi's fifteen-week law we wouldn't have seen *Roe* overturned. The way we saw *Roe* overturned is that we chipped away at its foundation. We need to continue to talk, educate, and move toward a place where all human life is protected, and that will be an incremental process." On this final point, Perkins provided a football analogy: "Sometimes you throw a long pass and you succeed but more times than not you succeed by just simply gaining a little bit here and a little bit there and you steadily move your way down the field." Tony Perkins (president, Family Research Council), interview with the author, August 30, 2023.

[68] "New 2023 Knights of Columbus–Marist Poll: Post Roe, A Majority of Americans Continue to Support Legal Limits on Abortion," Knights of Columbus, January 18, 2023, https://www.kofc.org/en/resources/communications/polls/majority-americans-still-support-abortion-limits.pdf?bcs-agent-scanner=be1f5b55-8104-9a48-80d4-d8567e4e1dc6.

### *Strategic Messaging*

A third challenge for the pro-life movement relates to messaging. In the aftermath of *Dobbs*, pro-abortion forces have often used incendiary language to impugn the motives of theologically conservative Christians and pro-life lawmakers. Unfortunately, pro-lifers were not always effective at re-framing debates about abortion into conversations about loving and protecting mothers and their children. Far from wanting to take away people's rights, the pro-life movement believes in securing the most basic right—the right to life—for society's most vulnerable members. However, this message is often intentionally distorted. This is why thought must be given to the most strategic ways for communicating the hopefulness and joy of the pro-life ethic.

To a great extent, pro-abortion activists have successfully framed abortion as an issue of "women's rights." Relatedly, the abortion industry has argued that abortion is an integral part of "women's health care" and that overturning *Roe* has unleashed a torrent of Republican-led attacks on women's autonomy. In terms of specific messaging efforts, abortion groups like Planned Parenthood are now encouraging women to talk "loudly and proudly" about abortion.[69] After *Dobbs*, Planned Parenthood asked women to use the social media hashtag #WhateverTheReason to "emphasize that every decision, for whatever reason, deserves respect." In a culture where popular maxims include "live your truth" and "live authentically," the notion of respecting everyone's decision—irrespective of the moral content of that decision—resonates deeply.

In short, pro-lifers must recognize that since *Dobbs*, pro-abortion forces have flooded the public square with messaging that frames pro-life efforts as attacks on the rights of women.[70] Unfortunately, a handful of

---

[69] "Our Bodies. Our Stories," Planned Parenthood, accessed March 23, 2024, https://www.plannedparenthood.org/about-us/newsroom/campaigns/our-stories.

[70] Worth noting is that the terms "pregnant people" and "birthing person" are beginning to replace the terms "pregnant woman" and "mother" in much of the

candidates have unwittingly contributed to this narrative. For example, during the 2022 midterm elections, Herschel Walker, while running for the Senate, stated, "There's not a national ban on abortion right now and I think that's a problem."[71] Predictably, Walker's opponent used this statement, particularly the use of the word "ban," to paint Walker in an unsympathetic light.

Polling shows that framing the public conversation about abortion in terms of protecting unborn children is effective. In a 2022 survey, 1,000 registered voters were asked, "Do you support or oppose protecting unborn children when a fetal heartbeat can be detected, which is usually around the sixth week of pregnancy?" Some 47 percent said they supported protecting children, only 33% opposed. Significantly, when the wording was tweaked to say, "Do you support or oppose banning abortions after a fetal heartbeat can be detected, which is usually around the sixth week of pregnancy?" the numbers changed to 40% support with 42% opposing. Significantly, this is a swing from +14 to -2 simply based on how the question was framed.[72] Practically, pro-life advocates should consciously use the language of "protecting unborn children" rather than "banning abortion."

Likewise, it is more accurate to use the term "pro-abortion" rather than "pro-choice." This subtle shift in language draws attention to the act of abortion. Unlike pregnancy care centers, the profit-driven abortion business does not actually offer women a choice; they offer women abortion

---

pro-abortion literature. For example, on Planned Parenthood's website, there is a section that encourages women to "share" their abortion story. The first time the word "women" appears on the web page, it is accompanied with an asterisk that leads readers to a footnote that states "Not just women get abortions!" See "Our Bodies. Our Stories," Planned Parenthood.

[71] Bridget Bowman, "Warnock Becomes Latest to Launch TV Ad on Abortion Rights," NBC, September 8, 2022, https://www.nbcnews.com/meet-the-press/meetthepressblog/warnock-becomes-latest-launch-tv-ad-abortion-rights-rcna46858.

[72] This information comes from an internal FRC Action survey conducted in May 2022.

and rarely offer other services such as adoption referrals.[73] Additionally, in general, the term "pro-life legislation" should be preferred to terms like "abortion restrictions" or "anti-abortion legislation." Again, framing the conversation around "protecting life" rather than "banning abortion" is not only more accurate, but it also avoids playing into the anti-woman rhetoric used by groups like Planned Parenthood. As Marjorie Dannenfelser explained, "The abortion lobby offers women an abortion and the door. The pro-life side saves lives and serves women."[74] Thus, in terms of messaging, pro-lifers should make every effort to frame conversations about abortion around efforts and policies that support women and their unborn babies. In terms of a communication strategy, this approach has the advantage of being faithful to the pro-life movement's mission as well as being rhetorically and politically effective.

Finally, when it comes to messaging, pro-lifers should regularly draw attention to the extremism of those who support abortion. As we have seen, despite Americans being evenly divided on abortion—and overwhelmingly in favor of protecting fetal life after the first trimester—groups like NARAL, Planned Parenthood, and the national Democratic Party now support abortion until the moment of birth.

Not surprisingly, the claim that many on the left support abortion until birth is disputed by abortion activists. For example, in response

---

[73] On this point, I'll share a personal anecdote. In August 2023 my friend from Ecuador was in the United States on a work visa. After she became pregnant, she visited a Planned Parenthood in Minnesota. When she informed the clinic worker that she was there for an ultrasound but not interested in an abortion, the employee refused to give her an ultrasound and asked her to leave the clinic. An analysis of the 2020–2021 Planned Parenthood Annual Report found that "For every one adoption referral, Planned Parenthood performed 198 abortions." See "Here for a Reason: Planned Parenthood Performs Almost 200 Abortions for Every One Adoption Referral," Charlotte Lozier Institute, September 21, 2022, https://lozierinstitute.org/here-for-a-reason-planned-parenthood-performs-almost-200-abortions-for-every-one-adoption-referral/.

[74] Dannenfelser, interview with author.

to a Republican presidential debate in 2023, former White House Press Secretary Jen Psaki tweeted, "No one supports abortion up until birth."[75] After receiving pushback, Psaki took to her MSNBC cable news show to defend her statement. "This claim that Democrats support abortion, up until the moment of birth is entirely misleading," she insisted. According to Psaki, "Abortions past the point of fetal viability do not happen often. They are incredibly rare, and those that happen involve agonizing emotional and ethical decisions." To substantiate her claim, Psaki cited a CDC study that showed that less than 1% of abortions occur at twenty-one weeks or later. As further evidence, she pointed to a late-term abortionist in Colorado who said that in an average week, 25–50% of his patients are carrying a baby with a "serious, catastrophic fetal abnormality." Psaki concluded the segment by insisting that "no one is rooting for late-term abortions" and that "no one is running on a platform of aborting viable babies."[76]

Ironically, Psaki's segment undermined her initial contention that no one supports abortion until birth.[77] First, Psaki conceded that late-term abortions (abortions twenty-one weeks or later) occur by admitting they "do not happen often." Second, Psaki cited a study to emphasize that "less than one percent happen after 21 weeks of pregnancy." But to put that number in perspective, consider that there were 1,037,000 abortions in 2023.[78]

[75] Jen Psaki (@jrpsaki), Twitter, August 23, 2023, 8:40 p.m., https://twitter.com/jrpsaki/status/1694525055663747157.

[76] *Inside with Jen Psaki* (@InsidewithPsaki), Twitter, August 27, 2023, 11:59 a.m., https://x.com/InsideWithPsaki/status/1695843524334297488?s=20.

[77] Following Psaki's show, John McCormack wrote an article exposing Psaki's claims about late-term abortion. See John McCormack, "Jen Psaki Isn't Telling the Truth about Late-Term Abortion," *National Review*, August 28, 2023, nationalreview.com/2023/08/jen-psaki-isnt-telling-the-truth-about-late-term-abortion/.

[78] This number comes from the pro-abortion Guttmacher Institute. See Isaac Maddow-Zimet and Candace Gibson, "Despite Bans, Number of Abortions in the United States Increased in 2023," Guttmacher Institute, updated May 10, 2024, https://www.guttmacher.org/2024/03/despite-bans-number-abortions-united-states-increased-2023.

According to a CDC report published in 2023, 0.9% of abortions in recent years were performed at twenty-one weeks or later. Based on these numbers, approximately 9,333 late-term abortions are carried out each year. Third, another look at the Colorado abortionist cited by Psaki reveals that 50–75% of the abortions he performs in an average week are on physically healthy babies (recall that the abortionist said 25–50% of his patients are carrying babies with fetal abnormalities). Thus, in the span of five minutes, Psaki went from asserting that late-term abortion essentially does not happen, to conceding they happen (albeit rarely), to admitting that the thousands of late-term abortions that occur are justified by the presence of fetal abnormalities (even though the abortionist she cited confirmed himself that most of the late-term abortions he performs are on healthy babies).

In recent years, high-ranking Democratic politicians have been asked what limits on abortion, if any, they would support. The responses have been revealing. For example, in 2019, while running for president, Elizabeth Warren (D-MA) was asked, "Would you put any limits on abortion?"[79] She responded, "I would make certain that every woman has access to the full range of reproductive healthcare services and that includes birth control, it includes abortion." Likewise, Pete Buttigieg was asked in 2019 if "there should be any limit on a woman's right to have an abortion?"[80] Buttigieg responded, "I trust women to draw the line."[81] Senator Bernie Sanders (I-VT) also provided a similar answer in 2019 when asked if "a woman should be able to terminate a pregnancy up until

---

[79] "Full Transcript: Democratic Presidential Debates, Night 1," *New York Times*, June 26, 2019, https://www.nytimes.com/2019/06/26/us/politics/democratic-debate-transcript.html.

[80] "Iowa Town Hall with Pete Buttigieg: Part 1," Fox News, January 27, 2020, https://www.foxnews.com/video/6126871237001.

[81] Darragh Roche, "Pete Buttigieg's Abortion Comments to Chris Wallace Go Viral: 'I Trust Women to Draw the Line'," *Newsweek*, October 12, 2020, https://www.newsweek.com/pete-buttigiegs-abortion-comments-chris-wallace-go-viral-i-trust-women-draw-line-1538231.

the moment of birth."[82] After alleging that late-term abortions occur "very, very rarely," Sanders pivoted to a predictable response: the "decision over abortion belongs to a woman and her physician, not the federal government, not the state government."[83]

In summary, the fact that many politicians routinely refuse to identify a single limitation on abortion they could support demonstrates the duplicity in Jen Psaki's contention that "No one supports abortion up until birth." In practice, abortion-supporting politicians, including most elected Democrats who serve in Washington, DC, support abortion until the moment before birth. At the very least, this reality underscores the effectiveness of the abortion industry's lobbying and demonstrates the need for strategic pro-life messaging to shame and expose this extremism.

### *Low Threshold for Amending State Constitutions*

In many states, a fourth challenge facing pro-lifers is the ease by which pro-abortion amendments can be added to the state constitution. Although the

---

[82] John McCormack, "On Late-Term Abortion, 2020 Democrats Are to the Left Even of Obama in 2008," National Review, July 12, 2019, https://www.nationalreview.com/2019/07/on-late-term-abortion-2020-democrats-are-to-the-left-even-of-obama-in-2008/.

[83] Infamously, Delegate Kathy Tran (D-VA) was asked if her late-term abortion bill would allow for an abortion even after a woman showed "physical signs she is about to give birth." Tran responded, "My bill would allow that, yes." See Julie Carey, "Virginia Late-Term Abortion Debate Erupts over Viral Video," NBC Washington, January 30, 2019, https://www.nbcwashington.com/news/local/virginia-late-term-abortion-debate-erupts-over-viral-video/4919/. Responding to Tran's comments and the public outrage that ensued, then-Virginia Governor Ralph Northam (D) was asked what would happen to a baby who survived a late-term abortion under the proposed legislation. His response was shocking: "The infant would be delivered. The infant would be kept comfortable. The infant would be resuscitated, if that's what the mother and family desired. And then a discussion would ensue between the physician and the mother." See Devan Cole, "Virginia governor faces backlash over comments supporting late-term abortion bill," CNN, January 31, 2019, https://www.cnn.com/2019/01/31/politics/ralph-northam-third-trimester-abortion/index.html.

process differs in each state, most amendments to state constitutions (about 80%) originate in state legislatures. However, in eighteen states, citizens can initiate the process to amend their state's constitution. Typically, supporters of a constitutional amendment must gather a certain number of signatures for their proposed amendment to appear on the ballot. Once placed on the ballot, the amendment must receive a certain percentage of the vote for successful passage. Significantly, fourteen states—Arizona, Arkansas, California, Massachusetts, Michigan, Mississippi, Missouri, Montana, Nebraska, North Dakota, Ohio, Oklahoma, Oregon, and South Dakota—require only a majority vote (50% plus one) for passage.[84] Nevada requires a simple majority vote in two consecutive elections. Colorado requires 55% of the vote, and Florida and Illinois require 60% of the vote to pass a citizen-initiated constitutional amendment.

By comparison, the process to amend the United States Constitution is much more rigorous. To amend the Constitution, a bill must pass both the U.S. Senate and House of Representatives by a two-thirds vote and then subsequently be ratified by three-fourths of the states.[85]

Practically, the ease by which state constitutions can be amended puts pro-life laws at risk in states that allow citizen-initiated amendments. In

[84] In Massachusetts, the number of affirmative votes cast for the measure must be greater than 30% of the votes cast in the election. In Mississippi, it is a simple majority (50% +1) provided that the number of votes cast on the initiative is equal to at least 40% of total ballots cast. However, on May 14, 2021, the Mississippi Supreme Court issued a decision that stated that it is impossible for any petition to meet the state's distribution requirement and has been impossible since congressional reapportionment in 2001. In Nebraska, a majority vote must be at least 35% of the total vote at the election. For more information about states that provide for initiated constitutional amendments, see "Initiated constitutional amendment," *Ballotpedia*, accessed March 24, 2024, https://ballotpedia.org/Initiated_constitutional_amendment.

[85] The U.S. Constitution has been amended twenty-seven times. The fifty states' constitutions have been amended about 7,000 times. John Dinan, "Constitutional Amendment Processes in the 50 States," State Court Report, July 24, 2023, https://statecourtreport.org/our-work/analysis-opinion/constitutional-amendment-processes-50-states.

2022, voters in California, Michigan, and Vermont were the first to approve pro-abortion constitutional amendments. Although the amendments in California and Vermont originated in their respective state legislatures, the Michigan proposal was placed on the ballot after citizens gathered enough signatures to trigger a vote. Similarly, in 2023, voters in Ohio approved a citizen-initiated pro-abortion constitutional amendment.

The 2023 Ohio election demonstrates the ominous challenge posed by low thresholds for amending state constitutions (especially in states that allow citizens to initiate the process). In the lead-up to the 2023 election, conservative Ohio legislators recognized this vulnerability and sought to raise the threshold for amending their state's constitution to 60%. However, the effort, which required a statewide vote, failed 57–43%. Significantly, both sides understood that the vote to raise the threshold was a proxy vote on abortion.

Unfortunately, failure to fortify Ohio's constitution in the lead-up to the election prefigured the ultimate loss in November when Ohio voters, by a 56.8–43.2% margin, codified a right to abortion into the state's constitution.[86] Notably, if the previous attempt to raise the threshold to 60% had succeeded, the amendment would have failed.

"Ohio is a pro-life state," explained state representative Jena Powell, who opposed the pro-abortion amendment and campaigned to raise the threshold to amend Ohio's constitution. "Ohio voters overwhelmingly elected a pro-life governor and a Republican supermajority in successive elections," noted Powell. "Let's not pretend Ohio is pro-abortion. However, the pro-life side was outspent 5 to 1 when we tried to raise the threshold for amending the constitution." For Powell, Ohio's failure to protect their state constitution led to the adoption of a radical pro-abortion amendment and

[86] "Ohio Issue 1, Right to Make Reproductive Decisions Including Abortion Initiative (2023)," Ballotpedia, accessed March 24, 2024, https://ballotpedia.org/Ohio_Issue_1,_Right_to_Make_Reproductive_Decisions_Including_Abortion_Initiative_(2023).

should serve as a warning to legislators in other conservative states, "The aggressive campaign to enshrine a pro-abortion amendment in our state's constitution was fueled by outright lies. It's a shame, but what happened in Ohio will happen in other states if state legislators do not act to raise the threshold for amending their state's constitution. Constitutions should not be easy to amend, and legislators owe it to their constituents to protect their state's constitution from out-of-state billionaires who do not share the values of their voters."[87]

As of 2024, efforts are underway in multiple states to place pro-abortion constitutional amendments before voters. Pro-abortion activists in Arizona, Arkansas, Colorado, Florida, Missouri, Montana, Nebraska, Nevada, and South Dakota are actively gathering signatures for abortion initiatives to be included on the fall ballot. These measures, if passed, would amend state constitutions to include abortion and nullify pro-life laws in those states.[88]

After success at the ballot box in 2022 and 2023, the abortion lobby sees citizen-initiated constitutional amendments as a way to circumvent state legislatures by placing pro-abortion measures directly before voters. With vast sums of money at their disposal, abortion activists believe they can influence voters in conservative states to pass these amendments. Thus, in the coming years, the pro-life movement must counter, wherever possible, and safeguard state constitutions by requiring a higher number of signatures to qualify for the ballot, raise the threshold for amending state constitutions, and, in some states, introduce their own pro-life ballot initiatives.[89]

---

[87] Representative Jena Powell, interview with the author, August 11, 2023.

[88] For a summary of these initiatives, see Geoff Mulvihill and Kimberlee Kruesi, "Which States Could Have Abortion on the Ballot in 2024?," AP, March 19, 2024, https://apnews.com/article/abortion-ballot-amendment-ban-protection-states-2024-052ff9846f8416efb725240af22b92ec.

[89] For example, in Florida, a 60% vote is required to approve an amendment to the state constitution. This provision provides a safeguard against out-of-state money that, for example, flowed into Ohio in the 2023 election. For the Ohio election, Ballotpedia estimates that the pro-abortion side raised $41.7 million in contributions, much of it from outside the state. By comparison, pro-life supporters

### *Complacency and Confusion within the Church*

A fifth challenge to the pro-life movement is complacency and confusion within the church. After forty-nine years of abortion on demand imposed by the Supreme Court, overturning *Roe* and *Casey* was a generational moment and an answer to prayer. However, as we have seen, overturning *Roe* has generated enormous backlash that threatens to undo much of the progress of the pro-life movement. Thus, the pro-life movement cannot afford to become complacent. In fact, as pro-abortion forces notch successive legislative and political victories, there is a need for increased urgency among those who care for the dignity of human life.

Unfortunately, at a time when clarity is needed, many churchgoers are confused about what the Bible teaches regarding when life begins and whether abortion is morally permissible. As we noted in chapter 1, 65% of churchgoers believe the Bible indicates when life begins. Notably, among those who believe the Bible teaches on the topic, only 52% think Scripture demonstrates that life begins "upon fertilization of the female egg." Thus, only 34% of churchgoers believe the Bible teaches that life begins at fertilization. This finding demonstrates that most churchgoers have not embraced the Bible's teaching on when life begins. Additionally, 63% of churchgoers identify as "pro-life" compared to 22% who identify as "pro-choice." The reality that one out of five parishioners identifies as "pro-choice" also suggests confusion and a lack of discipleship on this topic in many churches.

Evangelical Christians were the most likely group in the survey to express pro-life convictions (76% identified as "pro-life" and 13% "pro-choice"). In terms of the Bible's teaching, 73% of evangelicals believe the

---

raised $26.4 million. Worth noting is that Democrat political operatives will assuredly attempt to use pro-abortion referendums to motivate their supporters to vote in forthcoming elections similarly to how Republicans benefited in 2004 from marriage amendments that appeared in eleven states. President George W. Bush's re-election success depended on crucial battleground states like Ohio, where many people were motivated to vote because of the marriage amendment.

Bible indicates when human life begins. However, among these evangelicals, only 49% identified fertilization as the point when Scripture teaches life begins (12% said they were unsure, 8% said "after fertilization, before birth," 4% said once the child has been delivered and begins breathing).

Significantly, in the year after *Roe* was overturned, only 41% of evangelical churchgoers heard a sermon or teaching about abortion in a weekend worship service.[90] Although it is probable that some, if not most, churches acknowledged the outcome of *Dobbs* in some way—in a pastoral prayer or in-service announcement—it is nevertheless noteworthy that most evangelicals who regularly attend church told pollsters they had not heard a sermon or teaching on abortion since *Roe* was overturned. As we previously noted, 70% of churchgoers in 2023 indicated a desire for their church to provide additional biblical worldview education related to abortion and the value of life. Additionally, about a third (31%) of churchgoers indicated a desire for their church to teach "more often" about abortion in the weekend worship service (13% said they wanted to hear about abortion "less often"). Among evangelicals, 30% said they wanted abortion teaching "more often" (only 6% of evangelicals indicated they wanted "less" teaching on abortion). Thus, many churchgoers desire to learn more about abortion at church, whether in a morning sermon or Sunday school class. This desire for more teaching offers pastors a strategic discipleship opportunity.

In the face of stiff cultural winds, many Christians appear to be unsure of their convictions on abortion. Although a lack of knowledge concerning the Bible's teaching on abortion is a major problem, an equally if not more pressing issue is the courage deficit that seems to keep some leaders from speaking clearly about the topic. In a post-*Roe* world, pastors and

---

[90] According to the 2023 Center for Biblical Worldview survey, 45% of Pentecostal churchgoers reported hearing a sermon on abortion followed by 41% of evangelicals and 32% of independent/nondenominational churches. A majority of Roman Catholics (54%) credited their church with teaching on abortion in the year after *Roe v. Wade* was overturned.

Bible teachers can play a leading role in modeling courage and repairing our nation's damaged conscience by speaking clearly about abortion and the value of human life. This conviction was held by Dr. Andrew Nebinger, a pro-life doctor who campaigned against abortion in the nineteenth century. His view on a pastor's responsibility to speak about abortion is instructive.

Writing to the Medical Society of Pennsylvania in 1876, Nebinger presented a report on criminal abortion to "excite and awaken" the "spirit of inquiry and reform" among doctors, pastors, and legislators. From his perspective, silent pulpits bore much of the responsibility for the lack of "moral instruction in relation to the moral turpitude" of abortion.[91] Although "ignorance of the true physiology of gestation" prevailed, Nebinger was convinced that "a wide-spread diffusion of the necessary information among women, by those in whom they have confidence as moral and religious instructors, will in a brief cycle very perceptibly diminish, and finally almost entirely prevent, the commission of the crime of abortion."[92]

In his report, Nebinger noted with frustration that Protestant women seek abortions at higher rates than women who belong to other religious traditions.[93] For Nebinger, this discrepancy was contrary to Protestant theology. As fellow pro-life doctor Horatio Storer explained, Protestantism in no

---

[91] Andrew Nebinger, *Criminal Abortion: Its Extent and Prevention*, extracted from the transactions of the Medical Society of the State of Pennsylvania for 1876 (Philadelphia: Collins, 1876), 3.

[92] Nebinger, *Criminal Abortion*, 15.

[93] On this point, Nebinger quoted another doctor who stated, "I have never treated a case in a Catholic or Hebrew which I believed to be wilful." The doctor went on to note, "I have naturally inferred that there must be some special instruction given by Romish and Jewish churches which has the effect of largely preventing the existence of the crime of abortion among their communicants." Another doctor quoted by Nebinger noted the same trend, remarking, "The work of preventing the practice of the crime of abortion is with ministers of the gospel. There are none I know who are so correctly instructed by their ministers upon this matter as Catholic women." See Nebinger, *Criminal Abortion*, 16–17.

way "permits the practice of inducing abortion" as "its tenets are uncompromisingly hostile to all crime." However, according to Storer, there remained "popular ignorance regarding this offence" among Protestant women so that "an abstract morality is here comparatively powerless."[94]

Dr. Nebinger concluded his report by urging his fellow doctors to "beg, nay, implore, all Christian ministers to organize and make systematic preparations for a well-concerted attack upon the front and flank of the abomination, and never, never to cease the employment of all their intellectual, moral, and religious instrumentalities until success shall have crowned their efforts, and woman shall stand in glorious grandeur disenthralled from the great vice of our day, the murder of unborn babes."[95] Tragically, Nebinger's advice was not heeded by nearly enough pastors in his day. But his admonition still rings true today.

Thus, practically speaking, pastors ought to do everything in their power to form the moral imagination of their people on the value and dignity of life. It is a mistake for pastors to assume there is a widespread pro-life ethic in their churches. Unfortunately, surveys consistently show that most Americans—including many in our churches—are unaware of the Bible's teaching on the personhood of the unborn. In fact, according to a 2020 study by the Cultural Research Center, 44% of evangelicals believe the Bible is ambiguous in its teaching on abortion.[96] More than ever, congregations

---

[94] Andrew Nebinger, *Criminal Abortion*, 18. According to Nebinger, "All Christian ministers . . . are quite as competent to give the required important information, relative to conception, pregnancy, the viability of the fœtus and the nature of the crime, of its premature dislodgement from the uterus, as are priests and Jewish Rabbis, and it is their duty to do so if such imparted information will even limitedly, much more extendedly, control the commission of the crime." For Nebinger, discipling Christians to think biblically about life was a task "worthy of the heads and hearts of the most zealous of the laborers in the vast vineyard of the Lord." See Nebinger, *Criminal Abortion*, 20–21.

[95] Nebinger, *Criminal Abortion*, 21.

[96] "American Worldview Inventory 2020—At a Glance," Arizona Christian University, accessed November 3, 2023, https://www.arizonachristian.edu/wp

would benefit from expositional sermons on key pro-life passages such as Psalm 139:13–16 and Luke 1:39–45.

As Americans continue to debate abortion, there is no better time for pastors and church leaders to equip their congregations to think biblically about the value of life. "Too often pastors speak in generalities, they speak at a 50,000-feet level. But there is a hunger and need to educate people on all areas of Scripture, including the intricacies of life," explains Mat Staver, founder and chairman of Liberty Counsel.[97] A steady dose of teaching on the sanctity of life would prove tremendously beneficial for church members navigating the ongoing conversation about abortion. As Senator Lankford, who served for decades in pastoral ministry, explained, "Pastors should not preach politics, but should preach the whole Scripture and make it clear what is a biblical worldview and equip the people in their congregation to get comfortable with speaking about the issues with a biblical worldview." According to Lankford, "If people don't get their thoughts about the value of life and the origins of life from Scripture or from conversations with their pastors, they will get it from social media and the news."[98]

---

-content/uploads/2020/10/CRC_AWVI2020_Release11_Digital_04_20201006 .pdf?bcs-agent-scanner=e205acfb-3973-6e42-a730-cee9868b9c84.

[97] Mathew Staver, interview with the author, September 11, 2023.

[98] Lankford, interview with author.

When I asked Erin Hawley what role the church should play in the pro-life movement, she explained: "The Left tries to pit women against their unborn child and nothing could be further from the truth. Those interests are aligned. So, I think that's where the church and pastors come in. We must have a culture, especially in the church, that affirms not only unborn life, but also mothers. We have to facilitate a culture that recognizes that these interests go together—that the flourishing of women means the flourishing of their children and vice versa." Erin Hawley, interview with the author, August 15, 2023. A great example of pastoral leadership is Archbishop Salvatore Cordileone, whom we discussed in chapter 3. After his decision to bar Nancy Pelosi from communion, Cordileone wrote a letter to the priests in the Archdiocese of San Francisco. In his letter, Cordileone cut straight to the heart of the issue, writing, "Let us not fool ourselves: this is, essentially, a spiritual battle. It is not poetic rhetoric to call the proliferation of abortion demonic." Notably,

### *A Secularizing Culture*

The sexual ethics of an increasingly secular culture represent a sixth challenge to the pro-life movement. Particularly in Western nations, the loosening of sexual mores over the last century has led to the acceptance of "hookup culture," where frequent casual sexual encounters are encouraged and even glamorized. As hookup culture has become the norm—especially on college campuses and in large, urban areas—the mere suggestion that sex ought to be confined within certain boundaries is mocked as prudish and dismissed as a harmful denial of one's autonomy and self-expression.

The ubiquity of hookup culture has massive implications for abortion because when sexual promiscuity is normalized, abortion follows. Although tens of millions of Americans admit that abortion is not morally good, many nevertheless vote for pro-abortion candidates and referendums because they are convinced that their sexual fulfillment and, consequently, their happiness are dependent on the availability of unlimited, consequence-free sex.[99] According to this thinking, because sex sometimes results in pregnancy, abortion is a necessary evil. Thus, the normalization of hookup culture is why efforts at instilling a culture of life without addressing society's sexual ethics are shortsighted; a culture

---

Cordileone urged his fellow priests to preach on abortion, writing, "[P]reach about it. This is no time to be intimidated into silence. Do not dodge addressing the grave evil of abortion, but do so, obviously, with great pastoral sensitivity, recognizing that many of your people in the pews listening to you have been personally affected by this terrible scourge." Cordileone concluded his letter with an apt quotation from 1 Kings 2:2: "Take courage and be a man." See Salvatore Cordileone Archbishop of San Francisco, "Letter to priests of the Archdiocese on the Notification sent to Speaker Nancy Pelosi," Archdiocese of San Francisco, May 20, 2022, https://sfarchdiocese.org/letter-to-priests-of-the-archdiocese-on-the-notification-sent-to-speaker-nancy-pelosi/.

[99] According to a 2023 Gallup study, 52% of Americans said they considered abortion "morally acceptable" compared to 41% who considered abortion "morally wrong." See "Where Do Americans Stand on Abortion?," Gallup, July 7, 2023, https://news.gallup.com/poll/321143/americans-stand-abortion.aspx.

that champions unrestrained libido will always see pregnancy and babies as unwelcome intrusions.

Two additional cultural developments are related to the sexual revolution and abortion. First, liberalizing attitudes toward sexual behavior were facilitated, in part, by the arrival of modern contraceptive technology in the middle of the twentieth century. From the 1960s onward, many people came to see sexual behavior and pregnancy as conceptually and practically separated. As Albert Mohler explains, "Once the Pill arrived, with all its promises of reproductive control, the biological check on sexual immorality that had shaped human existence from Adam and Eve forward was removed almost instantaneously."[100] Whereas potentially conceiving a child had long served as a natural deterrent when it came to engaging in illicit sex, the Pill and other contraceptive technologies led to an exponential increase in recreational and noncommittal sex. In short order, the resulting contraceptive mindset quickly eroded the institution of marriage and helped to mainstream hookup culture.

Second, according to Pew Research Center, 65% of American adults identified as Christian in 2019 (down from 77% in 2009).[101] In the same period, the percentage of American adults who identified with no religion rose to 26% (up from 17% in 2009). In 2024, 28% of U.S. adults were religiously unaffiliated.[102] The rise in religious "nones" is most pronounced in younger generations (Gen Z and Millennials). Predictably, as the populace has become more nonreligious, values rooted in Christian ethics have been replaced by those informed by expressive individualism and secularism.

---

[100] R. Albert Mohler Jr., *We Cannot Be Silent: Speaking Truth to a Culture Redefining Sex, Marriage, and the Very Meaning of Right and Wrong* (Nashville: Thomas Nelson, 2015), 11.

[101] "In U.S., Decline of Christianity Continues at Rapid Pace," Pew Research Center, October 17, 2019, https://www.pewresearch.org/religion/2019/10/17/in-u-s-decline-of-christianity-continues-at-rapid-pace/.

[102] "Religious 'Nones' in America: Who They Are and What They Believe," Pew Research Center, January 24, 2024, https://www.pewresearch.org/religion/2024/01/24/religious-nones-in-america-who-they-are-and-what-they-believe/.

As fewer people embrace the tenets of a biblical worldview, fewer people accept the premise that marriage is the only appropriate context for sexual relations.[103] Not surprisingly, as overall Christian identity has decreased, attitudes about sexual behavior have become more permissive. Although some evangelical Christians hold permissive attitudes toward casual sex, studies show that Christians are still much more likely to disapprove of sex outside of marriage. For example, a 2020 Pew Research study showed that 36% of evangelical Protestants approved of casual sex—defined as sex between consenting adults who are not in a committed romantic relationship—compared to 84% of those who are religiously unaffiliated (including 94% of atheists and 95% of agnostics).[104]

The simultaneous rise in those who identify as religiously unaffiliated and the loosening of society's sexual morals is not incidental; religious "nones" overwhelmingly hold a permissive sexual ethic. Thus, for pro-lifers, the changing religious landscape, hookup culture, and abortion present an interconnected and urgent challenge. Put simply, to build and sustain a pro-life culture, a spiritual solution is ultimately needed. Specifically, the tenets of a biblical worldview—particularly the Bible's teaching on anthropology and sexual ethics—need to be embraced before society can be expected to embrace a holistic pro-life ethic.

In summary, advances in contraceptive technology and Christianity's loss of cultural influence (alongside other factors such as changes in laws

---

[103] In 2021, the Family Research Council's Center for Biblical Worldview published a nationwide survey that showed 51% of Americans believe they have a biblical worldview. However, when beliefs and behaviors are measured, only 6% have a biblical worldview as measured by researcher George Barna. Additionally, although 81% of those who attend an evangelical church believe they have a biblical worldview, the number is only 21% (when beliefs and behaviors are measured). To read the study, see FRC.org/worldview.

[104] Jeff Diamant, "Half of U.S. Christians Say Casual Sex between Consenting Adults Is Sometimes or Always Acceptable," Pew Research Center, August 31, 2020, https://www.pewresearch.org/short-reads/2020/08/31/half-of-u-s-christians-say-casual-sex-between-consenting-adults-is-sometimes-or-always-acceptable/.

and even morally neutral developments such as the rise in urbanization) have contributed to a revolution in morality where gratifying personal sexual desire is seen by many as the goal of life. But elevating sexual expression to the level of unquestioned moral good has consequences. When the goods of marriage—such as pleasure and intimacy—are pursued outside the context of marriage and pursued as ends in themselves, children—another good of the marital union—will inevitably be seen by many as inconvenient and unwanted "products of conception" rather than gifts to be received with joy.[105]

## Pregnancy Resource Centers Provide Help and Hope

The abortion lobby has pushed the narrative for decades that motherhood sets women back in life. As Kristan Hawkins observes, "A whole generation of women like me were told that we could do whatever we wanted except be a

---

[105] The successful effort to redefine marriage in the United States (by the Supreme Court in 2015 with the *Obergefell* decision and legislatively in 2022 with the Respect for Marriage Act) is evidence that the perceived sexual needs of adults have been elevated as a dominant cultural value. From the dawn of human civilization, societies have rightly believed that a married man and woman are best suited to care for and raise their children. Even ancient societies indifferent to the morality of same-sex behavior recognized the truth that men and women bring different gifts to parenting and that children are best served when they are raised by their mother and father. This is why the state's primary interest in marriage has always centered on children and why marriage law has historically reflected the biological reality that every child has a mother and father and the moral reality that children have a right to a relationship with both parents. Yet despite the link between a strong marriage culture and stable societies, in many places, the welfare of children has largely been replaced by a preoccupation with meeting the perceived emotional and sexual desires of adults. According to Justice Samuel Alito, redefining marriage requires accepting the premise that "the fundamental purpose of marriage is to promote the well-being of those who choose to marry." This view of marriage prioritizes "emotional fulfillment" and "happiness" for adults and, as Alito notes, ignores the fact that for millennia "marriage was inextricably linked to the one thing that only an opposite-sex couple can do: procreate." See *Obergefell v. Hodges*, 576 U.S. 644 (2015).

mother and a student."[106] Similarly, president of National Right to Life Carol Tobias notes, "Generations of Americans have been raised, especially women, being told they can't succeed, they can't get a good education, and they can't have a good job if they have a baby, especially one that was unplanned."[107]

In response to the claim that motherhood sets women back, we should acknowledge that pregnancy and raising children often exact a disproportionate emotional, mental, and physical toll on women. Additionally, most women who choose abortion do so because they feel as if it is their only choice. A 2023 study revealed that 60% of women would have preferred to give birth if they had received either more emotional support or had more financial security.[108]

As pro-lifers rightly advocate for pro-life legislation around the country, it is equally if not more important to come alongside women in unplanned pregnancies and remind them they are not alone. Thankfully, thousands of pregnancy resource centers offer spiritual and tangible support to expectant mothers and their children.[109] In fact, the heroic, often

---

[106] Hawkins, interview with author.

[107] Tobias, interview with author.

[108] According to the peer-reviewed study, 67% of women described their abortion as "accepted but inconsistent with their values and preferences" (43%) or "unwanted or coerced" (24%). Only 33% of women surveyed said their abortions were wanted. See David C. Reardon, Katherine Rafferty, and Tessa Longbons, "Hidden Epidemic: Nearly 70% of Abortions Are Coerced, Unwanted or Inconsistent With Women's Preferences," Charlotte Lozier Institute, May 15, 2023, https://lozierinstitute.org/hidden-epidemic-nearly-70-of-abortions-are-coerced-unwanted-or-inconsistent-with-womens-preferences/.

[109] When I asked her what was necessary for creating a culture that cherishes life, Sen. Hyde-Smith pointed to the work of pregnancy resource centers, noting, "Creating a culture of life requires that we protect the unborn child as any other member of the human family and support their mothers. No woman wants to ever find herself facing an unplanned pregnancy, so we must do more to support these women. Pregnancy centers in particular do amazing work to empower pregnant women facing difficult circumstances by making important resources available to them to choose parenting or adoption." Senator Cindy Hyde-Smith, interview with the author, September 15, 2023.

unsung, work of these centers is perhaps the most compelling apologetic for the pro-life movement.

According to a 2023 study, 2,750 pro-life pregnancy resource centers provided over $358 million in material goods and services and engaged in over 16 million client visits (both in person and virtually) in 2022.[110] In a single year, 17,646 paid staff and 44,930 volunteers—including 10,175 licensed medical professionals (both staff and volunteers)—provided vital services and supplies at no cost, including pregnancy tests, ultrasounds, parenting programs, baby diapers, wipes, formula, clothing, and more.[111] Significantly, 89.2% of pregnancy resource centers offer material help, 87.7% offer parenting/prenatal education, and 81.9% offer ultrasounds. Additionally, a 2022 report showed that over the course of five years (2016–2020), pregnancy resource centers saved more than 800,000 lives.[112] Thus,

---

[110] To view the full report, along with related reports about the services provided by pregnancy resource centers, visit https://lozierinstitute.org/pcr/. For the 2022 report, see "Pregnancy Centers Offer Hope for a New Generation," Charlotte Lozier Institute, https://lozierinstitute.org/wp-content/uploads/2024/05/Pregnancy-Center-2024-Update-full-1.pdf.

[111] In terms of numbers, pregnancy resource centers provided 703,835 free pregnancy tests, performed 517,557 free ultrasounds, provided 19,383 clients with after-abortion support, hosted parenting education programs that were attended by 408,301 clients, and performed 203,171 STD/STI tests. In terms of material goods, the centers provided 3,590,911 packs of diapers (valued at $40,218,203), 1,216,438 packs of wipes (valued at $3,649,314), 4,256,274 baby clothing outfits (valued at $21,281,370), 300,008 containers of baby formula (valued at $6,000,160), 43,192 new car seats (valued at $3,455,360), 23,486 new cribs (valued at $3,522,900), and 30,188 strollers (valued at $452,820). See "Pregnancy Centers Offer Hope for a New Generation," Charlotte Lozier Institute.

[112] "Real-World Data: More Than 800,000 Lives Saved via Pro-Life Pregnancy Centers Since 2016," Charlotte Lozier Institute, June 23, 2022, https://lozierinstitute.org/real-world-data-more-than-800000-lives-saved-via-pro-life-pregnancy-centers-since-2016/; "Pro-life Pregnancy Centers Served 2 Million People with Essential Medical, Education and Support Services in 2019," Charlotte Lozier Institute, October 21, 2020, https://lozierinstitute.org/pro-life-pregnancy-centers-served-2-million-people-with-essential-medical-education-and-support-services-in-2019/.

although carrying a baby to term and raising children requires resources that may initially seem out of reach for an individual mother, the reality is that thousands of centers with scores of staff and volunteers stand ready to serve every mother and child in need of help.

Among leaders of national pro-life organizations, there is agreement that educating the public about pro-life resources is one of the best ways to counteract the lies of the abortion industry. As Hawkins concedes, "We have a damaged brand in the pro-life movement.[113] Our brand is synonymous with the GOP which is seen by younger generations as a bunch of angry white men." Supporting and investing in the work of pregnancy resource centers not only counteracts lies about pro-lifers, but, over time, can help change the public's perception of those in the pro-life movement.[114] As Hawkins explains, "We must tell people about who we are and what we do. Even if people still support abortion, we can soften their hearts to our message and our true intentions by first telling them what it is we do, and all that we do, and explaining all that Planned Parenthood doesn't do."[115]

## Conclusion

Writing in the late 1970s, theologian Francis Schaeffer argued that the threat to human dignity and the right to life was "the greatest moral test to

---

[113] Hawkins, interview with the author.

[114] An example of this comprehensive care for pregnant moms is Her PLAN (Her Pregnancy and Life Assistance Network). Started in 2020 by SBA Pro-Life America, Her PLAN connects life-affirming providers across seven categories of care that offer moms and babies a community of support and widely respected care and resources to empower them to thrive. Her PLAN's free, online directory includes over 3,700 vetted provider listings in twenty-five states. The Her PLAN Pathways to Life Guide inspires and equips churches, community leaders, and individuals with ideas of how to support vulnerable women and families in their community. See https://herplan.org.

[115] Hawkins, interview with the author.

be put before us in this century."[116] For Schaeffer, the credibility of Christian witness depended on the church's willingness to unequivocally affirm the Bible's teaching that every person is made in God's image and possesses inherent value. He predicted, "Future generations will look back, and many will either scoff or believe in Christ on the basis of whether we Christians of today took a sacrificial stand in our various walks of life on these overwhelmingly important issues." He added, "If we do not take a stand here and now, we certainly cannot lay any claim to being the salt of the earth in our generation."[117]

Nearly fifty years of nationwide abortion on demand and over 60 million aborted babies is a moral stain on our nation. The U.S. Supreme Court's acknowledgment in 2022 that *Roe* was "egregiously wrong" was a long-overdue step toward restoring a culture of life in America. But the Court's admission cannot erase decades of pain and trauma wrought by abortion, nor can it bring back the children who were aborted.

Nevertheless, the overturning of *Roe* is an answer to prayer and the result of tireless work. But the work is not over. Since the overturning of *Roe*, two trends have emerged. First, in states where pro-life laws have gone into effect, there have been massive declines in both surgical and chemical abortions. For example, in its full 2022 abortion report, Oklahoma reported that total abortions were down by 70.4% (chemical abortions were down 74.9%) compared to the previous year.[118] Among other states with 2022 numbers available, Arkansas, Ohio, North Dakota, Texas, South Dakota, and West Virginia reported significant declines in abortion numbers.[119]

---

[116] Francis A. Schaeffer and C. Everett Koop, *Whatever Happened to the Human Race?* (Old Tappan, NJ: Revell, 1979), 195.

[117] Schaeffer and Koop, *Whatever Happened to the Human Race?*, 195.

[118] According to the Charlotte Lozier Institute, there were 2,160 abortions in Oklahoma in 2022, down from 7,287 in 2021. See Tessa Longbons and Mia Steupert, "Abortion Reporting: Oklahoma (2022)," Charlotte Lozier Institute, July 13, 2023, https://lozierinstitute.org/abortion-reporting-oklahoma-2022/.

[119] According to the Charlotte Lozier Institute, Arkansas reported 1,621 total abortions in 2022 (down 48.3% from 2021; chemical abortion was down 68.2%),

Conversely, abortion rates have risen in states that either maintained the status quo or liberalized their abortion laws after *Dobbs*. For example, in its full 2022 abortion report, Kansas reported that total abortions were up 56.9% (chemical abortion was up 37.9%). In states that liberalized their abortion laws in 2022—such as Colorado (abortions up 22.2%) and Minnesota (abortions up 20.1%)—abortion rates spiked. Additionally, in the aftermath of *Dobbs*, abortion rates ticked up in Nebraska (abortions up 6.2%) and South Carolina (abortions up 15.9%) as legislators spent the second half of 2022 debating a legislative response to *Dobbs* (see chapter 5).

Overall, in the nine months following *Dobbs*, the number of abortions in pro-abortion states increased by 56,000. Notably, states with strong pro-life protections saw 81,000 fewer abortions.[120] However, as reported by

---

Ohio reported 18,488 abortions in 2022 (down 15.2% from 2021; chemical abortion was down 9.9%), North Dakota reported 754 abortions in 2022 (down 34.6% from 2021; chemical abortion was down 41.7%), South Dakota reported 137 abortions in 2022 (down 28.6% from 2021; chemical abortion was down 29.6%), and West Virginia reported 831 abortions in 2022 (down 39.5% from 2021; chemical abortion was down 46.8%). Additionally, the statistics, which come from multiple sources, reveal the effect of pro-life laws. In 2020, there were 55,132 abortions in Texas. This number dropped to 51,860 in 2021 (in September, Texas's heartbeat law went into effect). The number of abortions dropped to 17,514 in 2022. Through the first five months of 2023, Texas reported just 22 abortions. It should be noted that Texas reports all abortions occurring in the state and abortions performed in other states on Texas residents (although not all states share data with Texas, so this number is incomplete). Additionally, not all tables in the state's report differentiate between abortions occurring in Texas vs. all Texas abortions. However, to provide a better picture of the impact of Texas's law and allow for comparisons with other states, the aforementioned numbers are just abortions reported in Texas. It is also important to note that the 22 abortions previously cited are abortions performed in Texas on state residents (nonresidents are not included in this figure). These statistics were compiled by Tessa Longbons and Mia Steupert and published at lozierinstitute.org/state-abortion-reporting/.

[120] Data regarding abortion is regularly updated, and the numbers cited here represent the most accurate information available as of November 2023. These numbers were taken from a WeCount Report released on June 15, 2023: https://societyfp.org/wp-content/uploads/2023/06/WeCountReport_6.12.23.pdf.

the *New York Times* in September 2023, monthly totals from January to June 2023 indicate that more abortions occurred during these six months (511,000) than during the same six-month span in 2020 (465,000).[121] In short, laws matter, and the available data from 2023 indicates that state abortion laws—whether pro-abortion or pro-life—had a demonstrable effect on the abortion rate after *Roe* was overturned.

The law's ability to either curb or promote abortion underscores not only the importance of the law per se, but also the character and convictions of the lawmakers. An example from Virginia illustrates this point. Following the 2019 elections, Democrats in Virginia assumed control of the House of Delegates and Senate, giving them both houses and the governor's mansion for the first time since 1994. Shortly after taking power, pro-abortion lawmakers with one pro-abortion bill (Senate Bill 733) eliminated most of the state's pro-life laws, including a twenty-four-hour waiting period, an ultrasound requirement, and a provision that provided mothers with information about abortion alternatives. The bill also ended regulations meant to ensure abortion facilities met the same safety standards of facilities that perform outpatient surgery and erased the requirement that only physicians could perform abortions.

As Delegate Kathy Byron explained to me, "Effectively, Virginia now has one of the least restrictive abortion laws in the country."[122] Byron pointed to a statement made by her former colleague Jennifer McClellan, who authored Virginia's 2020 abortion law. After *Dobbs*, McClellan boasted, "Because of our strong state laws, abortion remains legal in Virginia. As other states face restrictions, Virginia will remain a safe haven for abortion care."[123]

---

[121] Amy Schoenfeld Walker and Allison McCann, "Abortions Rose in Most States This Year, New Data Shows," *New York Times*, September 7, 2023, https://www.nytimes.com/interactive/2023/09/07/us/abortion-data-bans-laws.html.

[122] Delegate Kathy Byron, interview with the author, September 1, 2023.

[123] Dean Mirshahi, "Gov. Youngkin Wants 15-Week Abortion Law in Virginia," WRIC, June 24, 2022, https://www.wric.com/news/politics/capitol-connection/gov-youngkin-wants-15-week-abortion-law-in-virginia/. When we spoke in 2023,

Although abortion is more than politics, it is not less than politics. Elections have consequences, and pro-life Christians must defend the unborn at the ballot box. But abortion transcends politics, and the string of statewide pro-life losses since *Dobbs* demonstrates the cruel and hellish ways *Roe* has warped the American conscience and culture. The elections are a sober reminder that absent a thorough moral education, acknowledgment of the rights and humanity of the unborn will remain suppressed.

The post-*Roe* world presents a larger challenge than most of us anticipated. The majority of our fellow citizens are not yet persuaded that a culture of life is a societal good that fulfills our nation's highest ideals. This reality is tragic news for unborn babies as well as their mothers, fathers, and families. Although a society that perfectly affirms the dignity and personhood of everyone will not be realized until Christ returns, those committed to the cause of life have no choice but to press forward.

Obedience to the Lord Jesus requires nothing less than active engagement in the greatest human rights issue of our day. The fight for life requires pastors preaching and applying what God's Word teaches about the sanctity of life. It requires Christian lawmakers advocating for just laws. It requires Christian citizens in every state bearing witness to the personhood of the unborn and the horrors of abortion. And it requires parents discipling their children in the truths of Scripture and the power of the gospel.

The task before us is great. But obedience requires, if nothing else, staying in the fight.

---

Sen. Cindy Hyde-Smith underscored the significance of elections, explaining, "The bottom line is that it's critical for voters to elect a pro-life Senate majority and President in 2024, both to advance pro-life legislation and to confirm judges who won't legislate a pro-abortion agenda from the bench." Senator Cindy Hyde-Smith, interview with the author, September 15, 2023.

# ACKNOWLEDGMENTS

Although writing is a solitary act, I've learned that publishing a book takes the encouragement and efforts of a team. I am grateful to God for the team he surrounded me with for this project.

Many individuals read portions of the manuscript and provided valuable feedback: George Barna, Tessa Cox, Laura Grossberndt, Lainey Greer, and Mary Szoch.

Three young women—Alaina Cothran, Sara Smith, and Natalie Spaulding—read the manuscript in its entirety and provided thoughtful suggestions. Alaina, Sara, and Natalie are sharp thinkers for their age, and that is only complemented by their kindness and eagerness to serve.

My experience of working with B&H Academic has been terrific. From the onset, Michael McEwen believed in the project and his suggestions sharpened my argument and overall writing. Logan Pyron and the creative team at B&H have done a marvelous job with the cover and layout. Additionally, Renée Chavez and the editing team were a joy to work with.

I am grateful to the many state legislators who shared with me their personal experiences with passing pro-life legislation in the aftermath of *Dobbs*. These legislators include Joni Albrecht, Jim Burgin, Kathy Byron, Becky Currie, Erin Grall, Larry Grooms, Kathleen Kauth, John McCravy, Jena Powell, Merv Riepe, Peggy Scott, and Amy Sinclair. Many of these legislators have devoted their careers to fighting for the unborn, and I admire their convictional leadership and courage.

I'm also appreciative of U.S. Senators James Lankford, Tommy Tuberville, and Cindy Hyde-Smith, who took time out of their busy schedules to talk with me about their work to protect life at the federal level. Their leadership and advocacy for pro-life, pro-family policies makes our nation more compassionate and virtuous.

My work in the pro-life space has introduced me to colleagues who are working tirelessly to serve families: Karen Bowling, Renee Carlson, Rebecca Delahunt, Brittany Jones, Jonathan Keller, Sophia Lorey, Lauren McAfee, Marilyn Newland, Mitch Prosser, John Rustin, Anna Slayton, John Stemberger, Joy Stockbauer, Nicole Theis, and many others. These men and women fight daily for women and unborn babies in state capitals across the country, and their insights were useful as I wrote portions of this book. I'm grateful for their friendship as well.

Additionally, national leaders, including Marjorie Dannenfelser, Kristan Hawkins, Erin Hawley, Jonathan Mitchell, Tony Perkins, Mathew Staver, and Carol Tobias, were generous to me with their time. Under their leadership, the pro-life movement is in good hands.

I count myself incredibly blessed to work alongside the joyful warriors at the Family Research Council. Special thanks to Tony Perkins, Harold Harper, and Travis Weber for believing in this project.

My family encouraged me throughout the process of writing this book. I'm grateful for the support of my parents, Rodney and Nancy Closson, and my in-laws, Dave and Diana Ross. I'm also grateful for the encouragement of my brother-in-law and sister, Brad and Michelle Klimkowski, and my sisters-in-law, Emilie, Melia, and Annika. I'm especially thankful for my wife, Abby, whom this book is dedicated to, for selflessly supporting me as I wrote this book during the first year of our marriage. Abby, thank you for believing in me and the message of this book. You are an endless source of joy to me.

Finally, thanks are due to my readers. Abortion is a contentious topic with unavoidable theological and political dimensions. The fact that you picked up this book suggests a desire to critically engage with this pressing moral concern. My prayer is that this book encourages, informs, and equips you to fight for life today.

# APPENDIX 1

# Glossary of Key Terms

## Legal Cases

***Roe v. Wade*** (1973): a landmark decision in which the Supreme Court ruled that the U.S. Constitution protects a woman's liberty to choose to have an abortion. In its ruling, the Court recognized for the first time that the constitutional right to privacy is broad enough to encompass a woman's decision whether or not to terminate her pregnancy. *Roe* has come to be known as the case that legalized abortion nationwide.

It also ruled that this right must be balanced against governments' interests in protecting women's health and prenatal life. The Court resolved this balancing test by tying state regulation of abortion to the three trimesters of pregnancy:

- First trimester: governments cannot prohibit abortions at all.
- Second trimester: governments can require reasonable health regulations.
- Third trimester: abortions may be prohibited with exceptions for cases when they are necessary to save the life or health of the mother.

***Doe v. Bolton*** (1973): a decision of the Supreme Court that overturned the abortion law of Georgia that permitted abortion only in cases of rape, severe fetal deformity, or the possibility of severe or fatal injury to the mother. The decision was released on January 22, 1973, the same day as the decision in *Roe v. Wade*. In its ruling, the Court declared abortion could not be restricted when sought for a woman's health, which is defined very broadly to include all factors, including physical, emotional, and psychological. This new legal definition of health meant the *Roe v. Wade* "health" exception effectively nullified any government actions in the second and third trimester, securing the right to abortion throughout the nine months of pregnancy (until *Casey* in 1992).

***Planned Parenthood v. Casey*** (1992): a U.S. Supreme Court case that established that restrictions on abortion are unconstitutional if they place an undue burden on a woman seeking an abortion before the fetus is viable.

***Dobbs v. Jackson Women's Health Organization*** (2022): a landmark U.S. Supreme Court case that overturned *Roe v. Wade* and *Planned Parenthood v. Casey*. According to the Court, the Constitution does not confer a right to an abortion. The decision returned the authority to determine abortion law to the American people and their elected representatives.

## Legal Terms

**Safe Haven Law:** legislation that permits individuals to safely and anonymously relinquish newborn infants at designated locations (Safe Havens) to prevent abandonment and ensure the well-being of the child.

**Shield Law:** In the context of abortion, these laws provide legal protection for abortionists and those who undergo an abortion from potential legal action from prosecutors in other states.

**Trigger Laws:** a law that takes effect upon the occurrence of an event (such as a court decision). These laws are unenforceable until they are "triggered" and become enforceable.

## Pro-Life Medical Terms

**Abortion Pill Reversal:** The Abortion Pill Reversal protocol is an antidote to abortion drugs. The protocol must be started within seventy-two hours after taking the first abortion drug, mifepristone, and before the second drug, misoprostol, is taken. "The medical provider will prescribe bioidentical progesterone to outnumber and outcompete the mifepristone in order to reverse the effects of the mifepristone. An ultrasound is performed as soon as possible to confirm heart rate, placement, and dating of the pregnancy. The progesterone treatment will usually continue through the first trimester of pregnancy in an attempt to reverse the effects of mifepristone." (Source: Charlotte Lozier Institute, "Abortion Pill Reversal: A Record of Safety and Efficacy," September 24, 2021, https://lozierinstitute.org/abortion-pill-reversal-a-record-of-safety-and-efficacy/.)

**crisis pregnancy center:** a traditional term familiar to those in the Christian community that is often used to describe both medical and nonmedical pregnancy help centers that offer support for women experiencing unexpected pregnancies.

**ectopic pregnancy:** a pregnancy in which a fertilized egg implants outside the uterus, where it cannot survive. If left to grow, it can damage nearby organs and prove life-threatening to the mother.

**fetal viability:** the ability of a fetus to survive outside the uterus. Fetal viability is generally considered to begin at twenty-four weeks gestational age.

**implantation versus fertilization:** Fertilization is when the sperm joins the egg and fertilizes it, conception takes place, and a whole, unique, separate, living human being is created. Implantation is when a fertilized egg (human being) has attached to the lining of the uterus.

**pregnancy help center:** the modern term used to describe a service provider, whether medical or nonmedical, offering life-affirming services and support for women experiencing unintended pregnancies at risk for abortion. The centers serve women who are planning to abort, undecided, or planning to carry.

**pregnancy resource center:** a subcategory of pregnancy help center; the pregnancy help movement often uses this term to describe a nonmedical organization that offers life-affirming services for women experiencing unexpected pregnancies.

The three trimesters and stages of life development (according to AAPLOG guidelines):

- First trimester (Week 0–13): the fertilized egg will change from a small grouping of cells to a fetus. The neural tube, facial features, fingers, toes, and eyes form.
- Second trimester (Week 14–26): the baby will start to develop facial features and the mother will feel movement. The nervous system is starting to function, and the baby's gender might be detectable at a midpregnancy ultrasound.
- Third trimester (Week 27–40): the baby continues to mature and develop, including most internal organ systems. The baby has coordinated reflexes and can blink, close the eyes, turn the head, grasp firmly, and respond to sounds, light, and touch.

**pro-life:** *See under* "Abortion-Specific Terms," *below.*

## Abortion-Specific Terms

**abortion:** the intentional taking of an unborn child's life in the termination of a pregnancy.

**abortion travel/tourism:** a term used in the abortion industry; the process where women travel across state lines to avoid abortion regulations and to find abortion services. Use "abortion trafficking" to refer to situations where women are pressured to cross state lines to procure an abortion to avoid complying with state laws.

**chemical abortion:** another term used for the abortion pill or medication abortion. Pregnancy termination protocol that involves taking two different drugs, mifepristone and misoprostol, that the FDA claims can be safely used up to the first seventy days (ten weeks) of pregnancy.

**induced abortion:** a process that involves a medical procedure to end a pregnancy.

**late-term abortion** (or **partial-birth abortion):** terminating a pregnancy in the second or third trimester. Also known as intact dilation and evacuation, partial-birth abortion is a surgical procedure that removes an intact fetus from the uterus. Partial-birth abortion is not an accepted medical term and is not used by abortion practitioners or the medical community at large.

**medical/medication abortion** (*see* **chemical abortion):** a process that uses medication or medical drugs to end a pregnancy.

**mifepristone** (or, **Mifeprex; RU-486):** This drug is a synthetic steroid that blocks the release of progesterone. By blocking progesterone, mifepristone chemically destroys the uterine lining and starves the baby to death. It is FDA approved up to week ten of pregnancy (up to seventy days after the first day of the last menstrual period). Mifepristone is usually used together with another medicine called misoprostol. Mifepristone must not be used if the pregnancy is outside the womb (ectopic pregnancy). It will not end the pregnancy in this case.

**misoprostol:** This drug is used in combination with mifepristone to end pregnancy. It causes contractions to occur, which results in the expelling of the embryo from the uterus. It is taken by mouth and must be taken exactly as directed by a doctor. This medication also protects the lining of your stomach and is also prescribed to prevent stomach ulcers.

**partial-birth abortion.** ***See*** **late-term abortion**

**Plan B:** Known as the "morning-after" pill, this drug is used as an emergency contraceptive designed to prevent pregnancy after contraceptive failure. It is not the same as the abortion pill or medication abortion. It contains a high dose of levonorgestrel, a synthetic hormone that controls the release of an egg from the ovary or slows it long enough to prevent fertilization. If fertilization has already occurred, it may prevent the fertilized egg from implanting in the uterus, ending the pregnancy post-conception.

**pro-life:** the belief that all human life has inherent value and is worthy to be affirmed and protected from conception to natural death. A pro-life ethic maintains every person's life should be respected and protected at every stage.

**surgical abortion:** an operation that uses surgical means to end a pregnancy by removing the fetus and placenta (afterbirth) from the uterus. The most common of these are vacuum aspiration (also known as dilation and curettage, or D&C, or in later pregnancies, dilation and evacuation, or D&E).

## APPENDIX 2

# Effective Pro-Life Messaging

| Not Recommended | Prefer | Reasoning |
|---|---|---|
| Abortion | The intentional killing of an unborn child/ intentionally ending the life of an unborn child | When possible, remind people what the cultural term "abortion" means. The term has become so commonplace that its actual meaning—the intentional killing of an unborn child—has become obscured. Also, by using specific language such as "the intentional killing of an unborn child," you will be removing ambiguity since, in medical terminology, "spontaneous abortion" refers to a miscarriage. |

| | | |
|---|---|---|
| Anti-abortion | Pro-life | Although the pro-life movement does indeed oppose abortion, the phrase "anti-abortion" does not effectively capture the movement's dedication to preserving the lives of unborn children and their mothers. |
| Anti-choice | Pro-life | Pro-life advocates support freedom of choice in regard to many things. However, deliberately killing an unborn child is not something anyone should ever legally have the power to choose. |
| Pro-choice | Pro-abortion | No one should legally have the power to choose to kill an innocent, unborn child. To support people having the option of abortion is to condone the intentional killing of an innocent, unborn child. |
| Abortion ban | Pro-life protection | The goal of this legislation is to protect the lives of unborn children. |
| Total abortion ban | Protect unborn children from the moment of fertilization | The goal of this legislation is to protect unborn children from the moment of fertilization. (The use of "fertilization" is preferred over "conception" because conception now refers to implantation, whereas fertilization refers to the union of the sperm and egg.) Also, using this language avoids confusion since, in medical terminology, "spontaneous abortion" refers to a miscarriage. |

| Pain ban | Protect unborn children once they can feel pain | The goal of this legislation is to protect unborn children once they can feel pain. |
|---|---|---|
| Fetal heartbeat ban | Protect an unborn child once their heart begins beating | The goal of this legislation is to protect unborn children once their hearts begin beating. Calling it a fetal heartbeat ban is confusing, as it implies the exact opposite. |
| Telemedicine abortion ban | Guarantee in-person examination | The goal of this legislation is to prioritize women's health by ensuring they receive necessary, in-person examinations that could save their lives. |
| Allow abortion in cases when it is necessary to save the life of the mother. Abortion laws have exceptions to save the life of the mother. | Medical procedures to save the life of the mother are not abortions because the goal is not to intentionally kill the unborn child, and the action taken does not directly kill the unborn child. | The goal of a lifesaving medical procedure is to save the mother, not to intentionally kill the unborn child. Also, the action taken does not directly kill an unborn child. In some instances, it is simply the unfortunate case that we do not have the technology to save the child's life as well (e.g., the goal of removing an ectopic pregnancy is not to kill the child, but to save the mother's life; it is currently impossible for the child to survive the procedure).<br>For more information on responding specifically to "exceptions," see FRC.org/DifficultConversations. |

| | | |
|---|---|---|
| Fetuses can be aborted. | Abortionists kill unborn children. | It is clearer to state that an abortionist kills an unborn child, as the term "abort" can also refer to a spontaneous abortion (miscarriage). |
| Pro-abortion movement | Abortion industry | Abortion is ultimately about making money and exploiting women, not protecting rights or providing health care. Individuals supporting "abortion access" and "reproductive freedom" are, regardless of their personal motives, contributing to the abortion industry. |
| Abortion clinic | Abortion facility | The term "clinic" gives the impression that health services are being provided. Abortion is not health care. |
| Restrict access to abortion | Direct funding toward true health care for mothers and their unborn children | The term "restrict access" carries a negative connotation and fails to communicate the positive fact that funds are being directed away from abortion and towards true health care. |
| Women/Men | Mothers/Fathers | Every woman whose egg is fertilized becomes a mother immediately, and the man whose sperm fertilized her egg becomes a father immediately. Certainly, there are other ways a person can become a mother or father, but if a person is biologically a parent, regardless of what happens next, that person will forever be a mother or father. |

| | | |
|---|---|---|
| Advocate for abortion | Pressure to abort/support the killing of unborn children | The term "advocate" carries a positive connotation and fails to communicate the harmfulness of abortion. |
| We want the people/states to decide. | We will work until each life is protected in America. | No child's right to life ought to be a matter for public debate. The right to life should be guaranteed for all human beings. |
| Abortion provider | Abortion business | Abortion is not health care, so people or entities carrying out abortions are not health care providers. |
| Perform abortions | Carry out abortions | Abortion is not a health care procedure. It is the killing of an unborn child. |
| Abortion doctor | Abortionist | We want to avoid using any language that makes abortion sound like health care. Also, abortionists are most often *not* OB/GYNs. |
| Receive an abortion | Undergo an abortion | Using the word "receive" makes it sound like the person is obtaining medical treatment, and abortion is not health care. |
| Crisis pregnancy center | Pregnancy care center or pregnancy resource center | The crisis is not the pregnancy. |
| Crisis pregnancy | Unplanned pregnancy/ unexpected pregnancy | The crisis is not the pregnancy. |

| | | |
|---|---|---|
| Chemical abortion | Mifepristone/ abortion drug | This is more accurate/easily understood. Also, using the singular "drug" as opposed to "drugs" removes any confusion about whether one is referring to mifepristone only or both it and misoprostol. Mifepristone is the only drug approved by the FDA solely for the purpose of killing an unborn child. Although misoprostol is sometimes used (extremely dangerously) to kill an unborn child, it has other, actually helpful, uses, such as helping a woman complete the miscarriage of a baby who has already died. |
| The right to life for the unborn is not in the Constitution. | The pro-life movement will work until every life in America is protected. | Many legal scholars argue that the Fourteenth Amendment does protect unborn children. Regardless of the outcome of this debate, we will work for a future where no one's right to life is up for discussion at the ballot box. |

Adapted from a resource originally published by the Family Research Council's *Washington Stand*. Authored by Mary Szoch and used with permission.

# APPENDIX 3

# An Incrementalist's Response to Abortion Abolitionists

## Context and Definitions

In a post-*Roe* world, there are more opportunities to protect life than ever before.[1] However, those who oppose the intentional killing of unborn children do not always agree on the best means of achieving their shared goal of ending abortion. Within pro-life circles, there are two primary schools of thought: incrementalism and abolitionism. Unfortunately, the disagreement over which approach is best is currently dividing churches, pro-life organizations, and the broader pro-life movement.

### *Incrementalism*

The mainstream pro-life movement has long followed an incrementalist approach. Incrementalists support legislative measures that gradually chip

[1] Coauthored with Natalie Spaulding.

away at the prevalence of abortion with the hope of saving the greatest number of unborn children en route to completely outlawing abortion. Any law that makes it more difficult to end the life of an unborn child is an incrementalist law (e.g., heartbeat protections, fetal pain laws, ultrasound requirements, and parental consent provisions), and limited but significant gains against the abortion industry are viewed as strategic advances toward the final objective.

Given the serious cultural and political challenges, incrementalists understand that changing the law and public opinion about abortion is likely to be a lengthy process. Although they would like to bring abortion to an immediate end, they also believe it is morally right to save as many lives as is feasible in the current climate.

### *Abolitionism*

Abortion abolitionists only advocate for laws that eliminate legal abortion immediately and completely. Christians who hold this view argue that attempts to limit or regulate abortion in an incremental fashion amount to a sinful capitulation to pragmatism. Animated by the convictions that abortion is wicked and that Christians cannot compromise with unrighteousness, abolitionists demand that lawmakers outlaw abortion immediately. As one prominent abolitionist group has explained, "The abolitionist calls for the total and immediate criminalization of abortion as murder and never attempts to simply regulate or reduce abortion by treating it as healthcare."[2]

[2] See "We Are Abolitionists," Free the States, accessed April 29, 2024, https://freethestates.org/abolitionist-not-pro-life/. Likewise, abolitionist James Silberman argued in 2019, "We've got to demand it be wholly outlawed. That demand will rally the people of God. That demand will spread the Kingdom and bring an end to abortion the world over. Anything less undermines those objectives by . . . tacitly affirming abortion's status as health care, compromising God's commands, not communicating what actually makes abortion wrong, and lulling the church to sleep." James Silberman, "Immediate, Not Gradual Abolition of Abortion," Free

A Christian holding abolitionist views will likely point out that God hates partiality (Rom. 2:11) and argue that many pro-life laws passed to date are equivalent to the unequal weights and measures denounced in the Bible (e.g., Prov. 20:10) because they permit abortion in certain situations and under specific circumstances.

According to this reasoning, heartbeat laws or prohibitions on late-term abortion are sinful because they codify partiality. For example, when Texas successfully passed a heartbeat law in 2021, an abolitionist group criticized the law, saying, "This law is ungodly and Christians should not support it."[3] Likewise, a 2021 resolution passed by the Southern Baptist Convention said, "Traditional Pro-life laws, though well intended . . . appallingly have established incremental, regulatory guidelines for when, where, why, and how to obtain legal abortion of innocent preborn children, thereby legally sanctioning abortion."[4] The resolution went on to call for "the immediate abolition of abortion without exception or compromise."

## The Incrementalist Response to Abolitionism's Critique

The implications of the abolitionist critique of incrementalism are serious. Does the incrementalist approach amount to a sinful compromise? Is support for incremental measures a challenge to "God's Lordship over the heart and conscience,"[5] as some abolitionists have argued?

In response to the claims of abolitionists, here are some important points to consider:

---

the States, February 28, 2019, https://freethestates.org/2019/02/immediate-not-gradual-abolition-of-abortion/.

[3] James Silberman, "Abolitionist Perspective on the Texas Heartbeat Bill: Three Quick Observations," Free the States, September 2, 2021, https://freethestates.org/2021/09/abolitionist-perspective-on-the-texas-heartbeat-bill-three-quick-observations/.

[4] "On Abolishing Abortion," Southern Baptist Convention, June 21, 2021, https://www.sbc.net/resource-library/resolutions/on-abolishing-abortion/.

[5] This language appeared in the 2021 SBC Resolution.

### *1. Incrementalists and abolitionists share the same goal but differ on the best means of achieving it.*

Both camps agree that abortion wrongfully takes innocent life; both agree that abortion is sinful and that any morally upright society ought to outlaw it. Abolitionists rightly convey a sense of moral urgency and are right for wanting to apply biblical principles to the topic of abortion. Their frustration with the gradual pace of pro-life progress and refusal to become complacent in the fight for life is understandable and even commendable; abortion is one of the most pressing moral issues of our time, and too many politicians who profess pro-life convictions have proven ineffective or susceptible to changing political winds.

Although both sides agree that abortion is sinful and ought to be outlawed, incrementalists and abolitionists disagree on what to do when that objective cannot be immediately achieved. While the abolitionist refuses to accept anything less than complete, immediate abolition, incrementalists view the fight for life as a war of attrition: every pro-life measure chips away at the abortion industry's power and makes it harder to kill unborn children. For incrementalists, a perfect law—a law that protects all unborn life—cannot become the enemy of good, albeit imperfect, legislation that saves lives.

### *2. Contrary to abolitionist claims, incrementalism is not a compromise.*

One of the abolitionists' most oft-repeated critiques of incrementalism is that incrementalists are compromising biblical principles by supporting legislative measures that do not protect all unborn children. However, this critique confuses the situation. By supporting a heartbeat law in a jurisdiction where it can be passed and, thereby, save some lives, the incrementalist has limited evil, inasmuch as it was possible, given the social and political realities. In the United States and much of the world, committed pro-lifers are a minority and operate, regrettably, from a position of political weakness.

Thus, although supporting pro-life laws that do not protect all unborn children is not ideal, in many situations, wisdom compels us to secure the best possible result among a host of imperfect options.

Incrementalists are working toward a political atmosphere where every child can be saved from abortion. This culture currently does not exist, and it is fallacious to blame the death of some children not protected by current pro-life laws on incrementalists; it is the abortion industry, not pro-lifers pursuing an incrementalist strategy, who are morally accountable for the lives they take.

### *3. The abolitionist approach ignores political reality.*

All pro-lifers want to protect every unborn child and would do so immediately if they could. But the reality is that pro-lifers do not currently have—nor have they ever had—the political power to abolish abortion in all fifty states. Between 1973 and 2022, federal courts struck down most pro-life laws as unconstitutional, and since the overturning of *Roe v. Wade* in 2022, there have been few states with the political will to enact full legal protections for the unborn.

In my view, abolitionists have adopted a naive political strategy. Although Christians can and should play a prophetic role in calling for the complete outlawing of abortion, politics is the art of the possible. In most jurisdictions it is simply impossible to pass pro-life legislation without any exceptions.[6]

When abolitionists lack the votes for an abolition bill—which they have lacked in every instance that they have introduced a bill—they refuse, on

---

[6] Furthermore, although abolitionists claim that "any statute, court opinion, or regulation that allows for unequal protection of the law is null and void by nature," as Scott Klusendorf has explained, "To abolish abortion in a constitutional republic like ours, pro-lifers need legal authority. . . . Declaring that abortion-permitting laws are null and void doesn't make them null and void." See "Abortion Bill FAQ," Free the States, accessed April 29, 2024, https://freethestates.org/abortion-bill-faq/; and Scott Klusendorf, *The Case for Life: Equipping Christians to Engage the Culture*, 2nd ed. (Wheaton: Crossway, 2023), 336.

principle, to support anything else. To date, this strategy has not resulted in the successful passage of a single law. Significantly, pro-lifers pursuing an incrementalist strategy have secured the overturning of *Roe v. Wade* and passed a variety of legislative protections for the unborn. By taking what they can get while continuing to work for complete victory, pro-life incrementalists have moved the ball forward and, as a result, have saved lives.

## Conclusion

The differences between abolitionists and incrementalists constitute an important dialogue between those who share the same goal: the complete outlawing of abortion. In my view, abolitionists have made many morally consistent arguments about the value of every single unborn child and are well-intentioned. However, they are pursuing a strategy that has yielded zero results and is characterized by messaging that has been noticeably contentious toward fellow pro-lifers.[7]

The post-*Roe* cultural and political climate has proven more challenging than many pro-lifers expected. The abortion industry and its allies in the media and politics are working overtime to push pro-abortion narratives that paint pro-lifers as anti-woman. In the years to come, pro-lifers will need to work harder than ever to change the hearts and minds of their friends and neighbors while simultaneously pushing back against the lies of the pro-abortion lobby. In the arena of public policy, wisdom requires us to work to save as many lives as possible; moral consistency demands we resolve not to be content until everyone is safe from the scourge of abortion.

---

[7] For a more detailed response to the slander of abortion abolitionists, see Bart Barber, "Working toward the End of Abortion: A Pro-Life Response to Abolitionism's Critiques," *Light* magazine 8, no. 2, Winter 2022, https://erlc.com/resource-library/commentary-articles/working-toward-the-end-of-abortion/. Also see Denny Burk, "Abolitionism vs. Incrementalism: Why Can't We All Just Get Along?," Dennyburk.com, September 6, 2021, https://www.dennyburk.com/abolitionism-vs-incrementalism/.

# AFTERWORD

On November 5, 2024, Donald J. Trump won the 2024 US presidential election, defeating Kamala Harris and becoming only the second president to be elected for nonconsecutive terms, the first being Grover Cleveland in 1892. For beleaguered pro-lifers, Trump's victory offers hope and an opportunity.

Although "unprecedented" is a word overused in modern politics, the 2024 election featured a series of events truly without precedent in American history. For example, in the June 27 debate between Trump and incumbent President Joe Biden, Biden's halting and uneven delivery shocked most observers and resulted in many prominent Democrats calling for him to withdraw from the race.

On July 13, just two days before the start of the Republican National Convention (RNC), Trump survived an assassination attempt at an outdoor campaign rally in Butler, Pennsylvania. After an assassin's bullet grazed his ear, Trump, with blood streaming down his face, clenched his fist and exhorted the crowd, "Fight!" (Trump would survive an intended second attempt on his life on September 15 outside his golf club in West Palm Beach, Florida.)

Fewer than forty-eight hours after the first assassination attempt, Republicans formally named Trump as their presidential nominee. Notably, delegates approved a scaled-back party platform that omitted the robust pro-life language of previous platforms. Although the platform condemned late-term abortion, it noticeably lacked specificity on the subject, a change reportedly directed by Trump himself.

Following the RNC, calls for Biden to withdraw from the race intensified. On July 21, Biden became the first incumbent to withdraw from a presidential campaign after winning his party's primary, immediately endorsing his vice president, Kamala Harris. The Democratic Party quickly coalesced behind Harris.

On August 6, Harris announced Minnesota Governor Tim Walz as her running mate. Only a year before, Walz had signed into law an abortion expansion bill that, among other provisions, removed protections for babies who are born alive following an abortion.

At the Democratic National Convention (DNC), Democrats unveiled a platform that included a lengthy section on abortion. The abortion messaging at the convention previewed the priorities of the Harris–Walz campaign, which, along with allied groups, poured $570 million into pro-abortion advertisements during the general election.[1]

On September 10, during their lone presidential debate, Harris attempted to tie Trump to the *Dobbs v. Jackson Women's Health Organization* decision, claiming, "Donald Trump hand-selected three members of the United States Supreme Court with the intention that they would undo the protections of *Roe v. Wade*."[2] For his part, Trump drew attention to his opponent's support for late-term abortion. Despite protestations from Harris (and the ABC moderators), Trump doubled down, stating, "The

---

[1] Ad Impact post-election report; information provided by Susan B. Anthony Pro-Life America, forwarded by Anna Callahan, email message to author, November 8, 2024. If primaries are included in the data, Democrats spent $846,554,796 on abortion-related advertising during the 2024 election cycle.

[2] Kamala Harris, quoted in Riley Hoffman, "READ: Harris-Trump Presidential Debate Transcript," ABC News, September 10, 2024, https://abcnews.go.com/Politics/harris-trump-presidential-debate-transcript/story?id=113560542.

Democrats are radical. . . . [Harris's] vice presidential pick says abortion in the ninth month is absolutely fine. He also says execution after birth, it's execution, no longer abortion, because the baby is born, is okay. And that's not okay with me."[3]

In the final stretch of the campaign, Harris emphasized her support for abortion in interviews, rallies, and campaign statements. On September 19, she told television host Oprah Winfrey that state pro-life laws constituted a "health care crisis."[4] Additionally, on October 22, Harris stated that she would not support any "concessions" to pro-lifers, including religious exemptions.[5] Likewise, during an October 25 rally with singer Beyoncé Knowles, Harris promised to sign into law a bill that would "restore reproductive freedom."[6] Campaigning the next day in Michigan, Harris again blamed the *Dobbs* decision for triggering "a health care crisis."[7]

Although the Trump campaign deliberately focused on issues besides abortion, the issue still came up. Notably, on the campaign trail, Trump

---

[3] Donald Trump, quoted in Hoffman, "READ: Harris-Trump Presidential Debate Transcript."

[4] "Remarks by Vice President Harris in a Moderated Conversation with Oprah Winfrey at a Unite for America 2024 Event," The White House, September 19, 2024, https://www.whitehouse.gov/briefing-room/speeches-remarks/2024/09/19/remarks-by-vice-president-harris-in-a-moderated-conversation-with-oprah-winfrey-at-a-unite-for-america-2024-event/.

[5] NBC News, "Full transcript: Vice President Kamala Harris interviewed by NBC News' Hallie Jackson," NBC News, October 22, 2024, https://www.nbcnews.com/politics/2024-election/transcript-president-kamala-harris-interview-nbc-news-hallie-jackson-rcna176330.

[6] "Remarks by Vice President Harris at a Campaign Event | Houston, TX," The White House, October 5, 2024, https://www.whitehouse.gov/briefing-room/speeches-remarks/2024/10/25/remarks-by-vice-president-harris-at-a-campaign-event-houston-tx/.

[7] See "Remarks: Kamala Harris Meets with Health Care Workers in Portage, Michigan," *Roll Call*, October 26, 2024, https://rollcall.com/factbase/harris/transcript/kamala-harris-remarks-health-care-workers-portage-michigan-october-26-2024/.

promised to veto a national abortion ban.[8] On October 8, Melania Trump published a memoir in which she expressed strong pro-abortion views, specifically, "A woman's fundamental right of individual liberty, to her own life, grants her the authority to terminate her pregnancy if she wishes." Elsewhere, she argued that the "cultural stigma associated with abortion must be lifted."[9]

In a disappointing result for pro-lifers, voters in seven states approved pro-abortion ballot measures. Arizona, Colorado, Maryland, Missouri, Montana, and New York added permissive pro-abortion amendments to their respective state constitutions that essentially allow abortion through all stages of pregnancy. Nevada also passed a pro-abortion measure that must be passed again in the 2026 general election in order to take effect. In a positive development, voters in Florida, Nebraska, and South Dakota rejected similar pro-abortion referendums. In Nebraska, voters not only approved a pro-life measure that codified the state's twelve-week protection law into the state's constitution but rejected a competing pro-abortion measure. The victories in these three states are significant, as they represent the first statewide pro-life victories since *Dobbs*. However, the outcome of these ballot measures proves that statewide referendums will remain a challenge for the pro-life cause in the years to come.

In short, in the first presidential election since the overturning of *Roe*, abortion played an outsized role. Although the candidate ostensibly committed to protecting life won, Trump's relative reluctance to speak on the issue, coupled with the Republican Party's truncated platform, indicates that pro-life policies were considered a political liability by Trump and many Republican operatives.

---

[8] See Laura Kusisto, "Trump Commits to Vetoing National Abortion Ban," *Wall Street Journal*, updated October 2, 2024, https://www.wsj.com/livecoverage/vance-walz-vice-presidential-debate-election-2024/card/trump-commits-to-vetoing-national-abortion-ban-u9gIefKceH3sBSKrry4V.

[9] Melania Trump, *Melania* (New York: Skyhorse, 2024), 172, 173.

Overall, pro-lifers have many reasons to be grateful for the outcome of the 2024 election. Kamala Harris campaigned on the most aggressive pro-abortion platform in American history; her commitment to expanding abortion animated her quest for the White House, and many pro-life Christians interpreted her defeat as undeserved mercy. With a Republican-controlled House and Senate to start Trump's second term, pro-lifers should expect to see a reprieve from the aggressive pro-abortion advocacy of the Biden–Harris administration. However, as the recent campaign demonstrated, there are those within the Republican Party who are not committed to the pro-life cause, and pro-lifers who supported the president's campaign need to use their political capital to hold pro-life officials accountable.

In the years since *Roe* was overturned, Christians have learned that the nation is more pro-abortion than we would have liked to imagine. However, the results of the 2024 election demonstrate that pro-life candidates can still win office and that the pro-life movement is still a significant force in electoral politics. Moving forward, the work of winning hearts and minds must continue in earnest, as it is evident that five decades of *Roe* coarsened the nation's conscience more than we realized. Clearly, much work remains to convince our fellow Americans that every unborn child is a gift from God.

In closing, the fight for life continues. Though daunting, the fight must be engaged; the lives of untold millions hang in the balance. Motivated by love for our neighbors, may we Christians be faithful in our work as we advocate for babies, their mothers, and their families.

# GENERAL INDEX

## B

## D

## S

## T



## U

## V



## W



## Z

# SCRIPTURE INDEX